THE GREATEST FIGHT OF OUR GENERATION

The Greatest Fight of Our Generation

Louis vs. Schmeling

LEWIS A. ERENBERG

OXFORD

UNIVERSITY PRESS

2006

OXFORD
UNIVERSITY PRESS

Oxford University Press, Inc., publishes works that
further Oxford University's objective of excellence
in research, scholarship, and education.

Oxford   New York
Auckland   Cape Town   Dar es Salaam   Hong Kong   Karachi
Kuala Lumpur   Madrid   Melbourne   Mexico City   Nairobi
New Delhi   Shanghai   Taipei   Toronto

With offices in
Argentina   Austria   Brazil   Chile   Czech Republic   France   Greece
Guatemala   Hungary   Italy   Japan   Poland   Portugal   Singapore
South Korea   Switzerland   Thailand   Turkey   Ukraine   Vietnam

Published by Oxford University Press, Inc.
198 Madison Avenue, New York, NY 10016
www.oup.com

Oxford is a registered trademark of Oxford University Press

Library of Congress Cataloging-in-Publication Data
Erenberg, Lewis A., 1944–
The greatest fight of our generation : Louis vs. Schmeling /
Lewis A. Erenberg.
p. cm.
Includes bibliographical references and index.
ISBN-13: 978-0-19-517774-9
ISBN-10: 0-19-517774-6
1. Boxing—Social aspects—History.
2. Nationalism and sports—History.
3. Louis, Joe, 1914–
4. Schmeling, Max, 1905–
5. Sports rivalries—History.
I. Title.
GV1136.8.E74 2005
796.83'09043—dc22   2002048981

Excerpts from *Joe Louis: My Life*, copyright © 1978 by Jeffrey Hoffman,
reprinted by permission of Harcourt, Inc.

Excerpts from *Max Schmeling: An Autobiography*,
by permission of Bonus Books.

1 3 5 7 9 8 6 4 2
Printed in the United States of America
on acid-free paper

This book is dedicated to Berndt Ostendorf

ACKNOWLEDGMENTS

A s this project has developed over several years, I have drawn on the help and support of many different friends, colleagues, and scholars as well as several important institutions. The staff of the Museum of American History at the Smithsonian Institution, Washington, D.C., made my research in the Julian Black Collection of Joe Louis Scrapbooks both efficient and enjoyable. The Interlibrary Loan Librarians at Loyola University made my task so much easier with their fast work in filling my orders for the *Chicago Defender*, the *Pittsburgh Courier*, and numerous other books and periodicals. In Germany, the Amerika-Institüt, at the University of Munich, under the direction of my old friend Berndt Ostendorf, was gracious enough to provide me with research assistants who helped me comb through the newspaper collections at the Bayerische Staatsbibliothek. One of those research assistants, Miriam Held, deserves special thanks for assisting me in gathering essential material from the Nazi press. I also want to thank the staff at the Institute for Newspaper Research in Dortmund for allowing me to use their vast collection of German newspapers. Equally important, the staff of the library at the Sporthochschule in Cologne was most helpful in assisting me in locating the invaluable German boxing magazine, *Box-Sport* and various clipping files on Max Schmeling. Unfortunately, the only year missing in the library's run of *Box-Sport* was the crucial year 1938. Similarly, the staff at the Bundesfilmarchiv in Berlin helped me locate the film *Max Schmeling's Sieg—ein Deutscher Sieg*.

At critical stages, various leaves and fellowships have made the arduous task of research and writing much easier. When I was first beginning the project, Loyola University provided me with a Research Stimulation Grant, which enabled me to travel to the Museum of American History. At another crucial phase, I was awarded a Fulbright Distinguished Fellowship to the University of Salzburg, Austria, where I had the opportunity to pore over my sources and improve my German language skills. I want to thank the Fulbright Commission of the United States and Austria for this wonderful opportunity. Loyola was helpful here too, awarding me a Faculty Research leave that allowed me to stay on in Europe after my Fulbright was over so that I could complete a huge chunk of my German research and continue to improve my facility—such as it is—in the German language. My colleagues and students at the University of Salzburg, especially Dorothea Steiner and Reinhold Wagnleitner and his wife Elisabeth, made my stay in that beautiful city an absolute delight.

This project would have taken much longer had I not received a Fellowship to the National Humanities Center, Research Triangle Park, in North Carolina for the academic year 2003–2004. The opportunity to devote full attention to my research and writing without the distractions of everyday academic life was truly a blessing. I want to thank the director Geoffrey Harpham and the assistant director Kent Mullikin for inviting me to the Center. In addition, I want to thank the entire staff of the Center for making my stay so productive and rewarding. Librarians Betsy Dain, Jean Houston, and Eliza Robertson did a marvelous job of retrieving all types of source materials related to boxing. Marie Brubaker also went beyond the call of duty by volunteering to do microfilm research for me. Karen Carroll also deserves thanks for her fine job of copyediting the entire first draft of the manuscript with a fine-tooth comb. In addition, the Center provides excellent computer support for novices like me. I want to thank Joel Elliott and Philip Barron for their superior help and for treating me as if I knew what I was doing. Corbett Capps, Bernice Patterson, Pat Schreiber, Lois Whittington, and Marianne Wason, among too many to mention, made my stay at the Center a real pleasure. My landlords, Don and Marilyn Hartman, welcomed me with open arms and offered me a residence amidst the natural wonders of Chapel Hill and its "magic creek."

My work also benefited from participation in two seminars at the Center, the Seminar on Gender and Sexuality, and the Seminar on Race, Nation, and Diaspora. Being surrounded by so many bright people was particularly stimulating. While I have fond memories of all the fellows at the Center, I want to thank several (and their spouses and/or partners) in particular for their friendship and support: Wendy Allanbrook, Lee Baker, Daniel and Jane Bornstein, John Carson, Chris Celenza, Tom and Carol Cogswell, Esther Cohen, Francis Ferguson, Sam Floyd, Brian and Jennifer Kelly, Jeffrey Kerr-Richtie, Elizabeth Kennedy and Bobbi Prebis, Stephen Murray, Theda Perdue and Michael Green, David and Kathy Ringrose, Carol Summers, and Barbara Will and Michael Ermath. While at the Center, I also had the opportunity to present my work in lectures for the Friends of the Center, the Duke University Americanist Seminar, and the Jewish Study group.

A number of other people deserve special mention. While I was in Munich I began the lengthy process of translating German materials into English. When I was at my wit's end, Kristiane Deska, the secretary of the Amerika-Institüt cheerfully came to my rescue on more than one occasion. Back in the United States I relied on various translators to help speed the project along. Without the dedication of Michael Andre, Josh Davis, and Eric Schroeder this book could not have been completed. Numerous colleagues helped in other ways, some by alerting me to special sources and others by sharing their work. I thank a number of these people in the footnotes, but Michael Ermath deserves special mention for sharing with me his work on German history. Jeff Schutts was very generous in sharing source materials and the findings of his own research. My colleague at Loyola, David Dennis, answered my questions about German history, provided me with material from the German press, and taught me how to make an umlaut on the computer. Tom Knapp was equally forthcoming when I appealed to him for basic facts of German history. The comments on research leave proposals by members of Loyola University's History Department Advisory Committee, especially those by Barbara Rosenwein and Ted Karamanski, were very helpful. Elliot Gorn, Steve Riess, and Patrick Miller invited me to present an overview of my project at the Newberry Library Sports History Seminar in Chicago, as did Michael Ebner who asked me to the Urban History Seminar at the Chicago Historical Society. J. Fred MacDonald of Macdonald and Associates in Chicago came through with films of Joe Louis's fights. My research assistant at Loyola, Elizabeth Myers, has done a tremendous job of securing photographs, permissions, and library material at a moment's notice. Lillian Hardison's help was invaluable. I also want to thank Athena Angelos for doing photo research at the Library of Congress, and Frank Driggs for supplying me with photographic material. Margot Conk and Steve Meyer were wonderful hosts when I did my research in *Ring* magazine at the Milwaukee Public Library, as were Bonnie and Randy Beers in Washington, D.C.

There are more usual suspects. My good friend Lary May, fight fan extraordinaire, read through several drafts of an article that served as the basis of this book, as well as several chapters of the book itself. His insightful suggestions have made this work much stronger. Susan Hirsch helped immensely by suggesting an organizing framework for the first two chapters of the book and by offering her firm editorial eye on the last revision. Susan Ferber of Oxford University Press made critical editorial suggestions on the first draft that much improved the organization and narrative flow of the book. Doug Mitchell of the University of Chicago Press deserves special thanks for his encouragement and support at a critical stage of this project. The late John Higham served as a model historian until the end of his life. Of course, the errors are my own. I also want to thank other people for their enduring friendship:

Malcolm Bush, Bucky and Toni Halker, Lary and Elaine May, Mary O'Connell, Harold Platt, Carol Woodworth. Above all, there are Susan Hirsch and our son and daughter, Jesse and Joanna. They know how I feel.

This book is dedicated to Berndt Ostendorf, director of the Amerika-Institüt at the University of Munich. There would not be a book of this sort had he not invited me to Munich as a Fulbright Fellow in 1990–91. He and his wife Jutta welcomed my family and me to many delightful dinners and engaged us in insightful conversations about the differences between German and American society, politics, and culture. I have especially fond memories of team teaching a course with Berndt on the 1960s. Also enjoyable were our forays to delightful restaurants in Munich and the United States, and our many discussions of jazz while listening to his formidable record collection. Ten years later in Spring–Summer 2001, he and Jutta hosted us again, this time when Susan held the Fulbright at the Amerika-Institüt. They made our stay thoroughly enjoyable. Having the opportunity to live and work in Germany and Austria opened my eyes to the long-standing relationship between Germany and the United States, and fostered in me an awareness of the possibilities of transatlantic scholarship. Through his friendship and scholarship, Berndt has served as a model of a transatlantic scholar.

CONTENTS

INTRODUCTION
"MORE THAN A PRIZEFIGHT"   1

1

DOWN BUT NOT OUT:
BOXING IN THE GREAT DEPRESSION   7

2

COMING OFF THE CANVAS:
THE RENAISSANCE OF BOXING IN THE GREAT
DEPRESSION   37

3

MAX SCHMELING'S SIEG—EIN DEUTSCHER SIEG
(MAX SCHMELING'S VICTORY—A GERMAN VICTORY)   71

4

THE BRADDOCK AFFAIR AND THE COLOR LINE   103

5

THE GREATEST FIGHT OF OUR GENERATION   134

6

THIS IS THE ARMY   166

7

LAST ROUNDS   199

EPILOGUE
WINNERS AND LOSERS   223

NOTES   233

INDEX   267

THE GREATEST FIGHT OF OUR GENERATION

INTRODUCTION

"MORE THAN A PRIZEFIGHT"

O n the evening of Wednesday, June 22, 1938, German boxer Max
Schmeling, a former heavyweight champion, clashed with the sensational young American titleholder Joe Louis for the Heavyweight
Championship of the World. This second Louis-Schmeling fight proved to
be one of the most dramatic boxing matches on record. As a rematch, the
bout brought together two foes who had fought to a thrilling climax two years
before in the same stadium. In 1936 Schmeling handed Louis his only defeat,
but now the African American fighter was champion, having won the title
from James J. Braddock in an eight-round slugfest in 1937. With the title at
stake, could Schmeling repeat his victory and achieve what no heavyweight
champion in history had managed to do: come back and retake the title? Could
Louis erase the one blot on his record? For both boxers, their careers and
their reputations were on the line. The ensuing battle would prove to be the
most memorable fight of their lives and a fight that boxing fans across the
globe have never forgotten.

There was intense international interest surrounding the event because,
as liberal journalist Heywood Broun observed, this was "more than a prizefight." Louis was only the second African American heavyweight champion
in United States history, and Schmeling, Germany's most successful boxer,
"came into the ring as a symbol of a political philosophy" and "was expected
to dramatize the new German anthropological theories and demonstrate
Nordic superiority." The fact that his opponent was a Negro "emphasized
this phase of the contest." For months German and American sportswriters

and cultural commentators had speculated about the political, racial, and social implications of the big fight. While many Germans fervently hoped that a victory by "unser (our) Max" would vindicate their nation in the eyes of the world, black Americans eagerly put their faith in "our Joe" to knock out this hero of Aryan Supremacy. Many other Americans, terrified by the rise of Nazism, also rooted for the black boxer as an all-American hero vying against a symbol of aggressive military conquest.[1]

Filled with anticipation, 70,000 spectators jammed Yankee Stadium almost to capacity. Record numbers of newspaper and radio reporters from across the country and around the globe applied for press passes to cover a bout that seemed the sporting equivalent of a war. The rich, the powerful, and the celebrated assembled in the ringside seats, while in the upper reaches of the grandstand, a large group of African Americans, many from as far away as Los Angeles, Chicago, and Detroit, anxiously waited to root for their hero. Seventy million other fans gathered about their radios to listen to the match at home and in taverns, restaurants, and nightclubs. In Germany sports fans, ordinary citizens, and the elite of the National Socialist regime stayed up until 3:30 A.M. to hear the transatlantic broadcast, while a select contingent of hard-core German fans took advantage of special excursion fares to support their man in person.[2]

In many ways, the protagonists in this fight were central figures in a form of international political theater. Contemporary black historian, sports commentator, and avid Joe Louis fan C. L. R. James noted that "the state of the . . . nation or the world can invest a sporting event with dramatic intensity such as is reached in few theatres. When the democrat Joe Louis fought the Nazi Schmeling the bout became a focus of approaching world conflict." By their very nature, boxing matches are dramatic. As unscripted events, the battles in the ring encapsulate the struggle between life and death, good and evil, craft and power, brain and brawn, youth and age that many fans experience in their own lives. The Louis-Schmeling bout, however, went beyond the drama of two individual sportsmen.[3]

The elevation of the fight to nationalist drama on the international stage is a powerful indication of the politicization of international sport during the 1930s and 1940s. Historians usually think that the rise of globalism occurred after World War II, but even before that conflagration, American sports and entertainment had an enormous influence on the rest of the world. In Weimar Germany, many prizefight analysts acknowledged that boxing had an Americanizing effect on German sporting culture. But the internationalization of sport was not a one-way street. In fact, during the 1930s America's relationship with the world also influenced events at home. The struggle against Nazi Germany began in the boxing ring and at the Berlin Olympics of 1936. The German National Socialist regime was determined to increase its national prestige and international respect through victories in the realm of sport.

Because the Louis-Schmeling fights raised issues of political values and racial ideologies and beliefs, they had a fundamental impact on the nature of liberty and freedom in the United States. By posing a white "Nazi" against a black American, this international battle outlined the Nazis' master race philosophy in the starkest terms and began the challenge to an American national identity firmly rooted in a racial hierarchy of whiteness. As an arena of white male power, boxing in the United States had displayed deep hostility toward prizefighters of color. Under the influence of international events, however, this picture began to change.[4]

The international politicization of boxing has had a long history. The heavyweight title match between American titleholder John C. Heenan and the British champion Tom Sayers in England in 1860 attracted more transatlantic public attention than any other sporting event from 1830 to 1870. Fought on the eve of the Civil War, the bout turned into a major nationalist event, with championship boxers standing in for national virility. The penny press in the United States published special editions to keep up with local interest, and even Currier and Ives, a bastion of Victorian virtues, chipped in with cheap lithographs of both heroes. As domestic conflict threatened to split the nation, this international event was filled with intense patriotic fervor. In the twentieth century, with the shift to the United States as the capital of the sport, and the invention of the fast ocean liner, international matches became a regular part of the sport. During the 1920s, Jack Dempsey fought Georges Carpentier from France and Luis Firpo from Argentina for the heavyweight title, while Dempsey's successor, Gene Tunney, held his last title defense in 1928 against the New Zealander Tom Heeney. With the rise of the million-dollar gate in the 1920s, boxers from around the world, among them a young Max Schmeling, traveled to New York City, the epicenter of prize fighting, for big paydays and international respect. While all of these bouts excited a measure of nationalist fervor, it was in the 1930s that rising international tensions transformed boxing into a central arena for competing nationalisms on an unprecedented scale.[5]

As male sporting heroes, boxers imparted a gendered dimension to nationalism on both sides of the Atlantic. Louis and Schmeling framed male power as essential to national identity. The Great Depression threw millions of men out of work in two of the most industrialized countries of the world. Outlets for breadwinning were few, and images of impotence abounded. In this atmosphere, boxers with knockout power like Schmeling and Louis served as powerful male heroes. Louis became a superman at first for African Americans and eventually for whites in America in a period when superheroes and tough guys multiplied across the American cultural landscape. Schmeling, meanwhile, was transformed into an Aryan superman by the National Socialist regime, bent on remilitarization and German expansion to offset a persistent German culture of defeat. Overcoming the experience of weakness and humiliation, Americans and Germans transformed "unser Max" and "our Joe" into heroic masculine national symbols in a time of Depression and war.[6]

While Schmeling became a German national hero, Louis first symbolized an African American political and cultural awakening that followed the Great Migration of blacks from rural oppression and southern segregation to what they hoped would be the promised land of northern freedom and opportunity. After he won the championship and thereby broke the color line in boxing that had reserved the greatest symbol of male strength for the "white" race, Louis became the biggest popular hero African Americans had ever had. As the Germans attempted to restore national strength after a period of national humiliation, African Americans were in a process of de-colonization, which consisted of rethinking the racial hierarchy that placed them at the bottom and whites at the top of the American social order by virtue of race alone. A successful and powerful black superhero offered a new myth of masculine fighting strength to wipe out memories of slavery, lynching, and dependence on whites. As black athletes began to dominate track and field and the boxing ring in the 1930s, they contributed to a dream of the future that included strong black men on the public stage fighting back against white supremacy in athletics and everyday life. But Louis also became a hero to a growing number of white Americans who were wrestling with a new civic nationalism, one that was far more inclusive than previous American self-definitions rooted in Anglo-Saxon white supremacy. Indeed, the racial nationalism that remained, especially but not exclusively in the South, deepened awareness that American racial ideas bore a striking similarity to those of the Nazis. The Louis-Schmeling bouts serve as windows showing the effects that international tensions had on the views of race and nationalism held by white Americans as they were forced to choose between rooting for a black American or a white German.[7] In an atmosphere of growing global conflict, Louis became one of the first black heroes that many white Americans saw as a standard-bearer for American national values. Spurred by international conflict, this development proved a power stimulus to the fight for African American rights even before World War II.[8]

In writing about the role of Joe Louis and Max Schmeling in the politicization of international sport, my goal is to give each boxer comparable weight. Rather than aiming at a full-scale dual biography, my intention is to demonstrate how global affairs and national developments transformed their interactions inside and outside the ring. In the many American books and articles about Louis, Schmeling assumes a secondary role. Few Americans understand the iconic importance that "unser Max" played in German society from the 1920s to the present or the stature of boxing in German life. Their epic ring battles transformed each man into the symbolic representative of his nation's values and aspirations. To provide some measure of comparable treatment, each chapter develops the relationship of the two fighters to each other, to the political and cultural tensions of their respective nations, and to their symbolic importance in world affairs.

This book opens with the Great Depression, the most powerful factor in the careers of both combatants and in the political and cultural history of Germany and the United States. As the older of the two, Max Schmeling had taken German boxing to its heights when he became World Heavyweight Champion in 1930, and then saw his career and the sport of boxing decline in Germany and the United States under the impact of the economic disaster. For his part, the young Joe Louis faced dim prospects as he began his amateur and professional career during the nadir of the Depression. The obstacles he faced on the way to the title appeared daunting: the economic depression, the overwhelming poverty of African Americans, and the racism in prizefighting. Yet in the middle of the Depression boxing experienced a renaissance in both the United States and Germany. My focus is on the factors that made it possible for Louis to contend for the heavyweight title despite the intense racism that surrounded American prizefighting. Similarly, I explore how Schmeling's career took another of its many unexpected turns as the leaders of the new Nazi regime transformed boxing to make it accord with their political philosophy of Aryan supremacy.

By the time of their first spectacular bout in June 1936, Schmeling and Louis had both become cultural and political symbols. His career seemingly over, Schmeling was taken up by the National Socialist regime and transformed by the propaganda ministry into a Nazi hero after his dramatic upset of his young opponent. Despite his loss to Schmeling, by the mid-1930s Joe Louis already had become an African American folk hero as blacks wrote about his victories, celebrated his wins, and lionized him in music and folklore. The continuing battles in America and Germany over who was the rightful champion, the role of Jewish Americans in boxing, and the influence of the radical left also helped make Louis an anti-fascist hero.

When Louis beat Schmeling in their climactic rematch in 1938, he was no longer just a black hero; he stood atop the American world. In contrast, just as quickly as they had built him into a national and international symbol of Nordic supremacy, the Nazis attempted to undermine Schmeling's role as a public figure because of his defeat. At the same time, many whites were forced by global events to choose between nationalism and racism. By aligning themselves with Louis, they opened the door to a wider, more cosmopolitan sense of American national identity. The 1938 fight took on even greater importance after the match, becoming an American metaphor for the goals of the United States in World War II, a conflict in which Louis cemented his role as all-American hero. While the Nazis initially sought to utilize Schmeling's army service to promote the German war effort, his experience led to an irreparable break with the National Socialists and left him charged with treason. Ironically, the fighters experienced a last reversal of fortune after the war. Initially an American hero, Louis was increasingly tortured by a life badly out of control. Schmeling, on the other hand, went from being a suspected Nazi sympathizer to a wealthy Coca-Cola executive in the new Germany. By the time he and Louis renewed their relationship in the 1950s, racial and economic realities had overtaken the Brown Bomber, and the new economic miracle and Cold War alliances had made Schmeling a hero again in Germany and the United States. Inside the ring and out, international events and domestic realities continued to have a profound effect on the relationship of the two men.

1

DOWN BUT NOT OUT:

BOXING IN THE GREAT DEPRESSION

"Is boxing dying?"
Vorwärts, 1931

In July 1935, a year before the first bout between Joe Louis and Max Schmeling, and three years before the battle that defined their careers, sports cartoonist Burris Jenkins, Jr., caricatured the two future combatants in the *New York Evening Journal.* Entitled "Carrying the 'Males,'" the cartoon depicted "The Brown Bomber" facing off against "The Black Uhlan." These two strong, well-proportioned specimens, their muscles rippling and their eyes intent on each other, appear in the sky like two ascending gods above a speeding locomotive labeled "20th Century S.C"—the Twentieth Century Sporting Club, the corporation that would promote the bout. Their naked torsos in fighting poses and their sense of fierce determination make Louis and Schmeling outsized heroes coming together in a battle to determine the future. The streamlined engine conveys the role of a new, more powerful promotion company to replace the old antiquated Madison Square Garden Corporation situated murkily in the background. The powerful locomotive, situated between the two fighters, also conveys the importance of male phallic power during this Depression decade when masculinity itself was imperiled by the economic catastrophe. That there was a national and racial angle any sports fan could see. The designation for Schmeling, "Black Uhlan of the Rhine," was a made-up name to link him to a heroic German past,

Carrying the "Males," *New York Evening Journal*, July 15, 1935, by Burris Jenkins, Jr., predicted the eventual clash between Joe Louis and Max Schmeling a year before they first fought. (Harry Ransom Humanities Research Center)

while Louis's nickname, the "Brown Bomber," referred not only to the dynamite in both fists but also to the color of his skin.[1]

"Carrying the 'Males'" turned out to be accurate in its predictive power. In June 1936, Louis and Schmeling fought round one of their two famous international battles in front of a large audience. Two years later, on June 22, 1938, the hottest ticket in the sports world was their rematch. In the United States and Germany, the homelands of the two combatants, fan interest was intense for a battle that brought together the national champions of Democracy and Nazism, African American self-assertion and German pride, American Pluralism and Aryan Supremacy. The match assumed the aura of a major international event as boxing fans around the globe awaited the results of the biggest fight since the late 1920s. In the annals of boxing, the two Louis-Schmeling bouts are considered among the most exciting and intense sporting dramas of the Great Depression era, and of the entire twentieth century.

These matches defined the careers of the two combatants and transformed them from individual athletes into national icons.

Just a few short years earlier, in the dark days of the early 1930s, however, no sports cartoonist as prominent as Burris Jenkins would have predicted that these two improbable athletes would have represented their respective nations in such widely anticipated international battles. Nor would most sports fans have assumed that boxing itself would be able to generate enough excitement to fill huge outdoor stadiums the size of New York's Yankee Stadium and Chicago's Soldier Field, or substantial indoor arenas such as Berlin's Sportpalast and Manhattan's Madison Square Garden. From 1930 to 1934, most observers assumed that the Great Depression had wreaked profound havoc on boxing, just as it had on the automobile, steel, rubber, housing, and motion picture industries. In the early 1930s, boxing, according to one sportswriter, was suffering "its own private depression." Attendance at matches fell off drastically and even heavyweight championship bouts, traditionally the biggest moneymakers in sports, drew only lackluster interest. Dreams of million-dollar fights, so common during the 1920s, seemed preposterous. In the pit of such a dire economic catastrophe, the veteran German heavyweight slugger Max Schmeling and Joe Louis Barrow, the shy African American youngster just entering the amateur ranks, were battling in a sport that offered few opportunities for rewarding careers. At the moment, their prospects could not have been worse.[2]

As the two most industrialized countries in the world, Germany and the United States were hit hardest by the economic collapse of the 1930s. In the United States the stock market crash of 1929 set off a destructive ripple effect through the economy. By the winter of 1932–1933, the *nadir* of the Great Depression, 25 percent of non-farmworkers officially, and perhaps 33 percent unofficially, were unemployed, another huge number of workers labored fewer hours, and new workers had few opportunities to enter the economy at all. Among those industrial and agricultural workers who lost their jobs because of the lay-offs and slow-downs, African Americans were hit the hardest. More than 50 percent of urban African Americans were unemployed, and they made up the highest percentage of applicants for relief. While all young people suffered in the Depression, black youth were the least likely to find a job. With his family on relief, food hard to come by, and economic prospects nil, young Joe Louis Barrow, like other young African Americans, seemed destined for a life of poverty, crime, or dissolution.

The Depression's effects on Germany were even more devastating. While the economic catastrophe led to a profound change in political direction for the United States, in Germany, by contrast, it caused the abandonment of any semblance of a democratic system and the triumph of fascism. As workers lost their jobs at rates equal to or greater than those of the United States and the lower-middle classes faced the loss of their savings, their homes, and what little property they had managed to accumulate, the future appeared bleak. The disillusion of the vast majority of the German population, moreover, was compounded by a series of prior political and economic disasters. For most Germans, the Depression recalled horrible memories of the great hunger during World War I, and the inflation that rocked Germany after the nation's defeat. With the nation devastated by war and its economy in ruins, German currency had proved worthless. Heavy reparation payments demanded by the allies drove prices up dramatically, and savings and national confidence were wiped out. Germans connected the inflation to the humiliating defeat on the battlefield and the Treaty of Versailles that blamed them for starting the war. In 1924, the Dawes Plan, initiated by the United States, spread out the reparation payments and helped reorganize the currency. Five short years of prosperity followed, a period when Max Schmeling and German boxing flourished as never before. The Great Depression, however, wiped out these years of prosperity and made them seem merely a short interval between periods of economic chaos and national crisis. The Depression resurrected old fears of starvation, national humiliation, and a crushing sense of loss that historians have called a Culture of Defeat. It was in that period that Max Schmeling found himself at the lowest stage of his career, mirroring for a nation the shock and despair of constant defeat as he lost his heavyweight title and suffered through a series of ignominious losses from 1932 through most of 1934. He was faced with the possibility that his long career had ended.[3]

If ever there was a boxer who experienced constant reversals of fortune it was Max Schmeling, whose career rose and fell along with the sport in Germany and the United States. With Schmeling as its leading proponent, German boxing should have stood at its acme. When he was born on September 28, 1905, in the small town of Klein-Luckow in the eastern part of Germany, boxing had virtually no place in German sports. Prizefighting developed under international influences in the wake of World War I, as German prisoners of war brought the sport home from their British guards. *Ring* magazine's Wilbur Wood declared it doubtful "if one out of a thousand Germans ever even saw a boxing glove until the Great War." Although no nationwide law prohibited boxing in Imperial Germany, police banned public fights and raided them continuously. As a result, the sport remained confined to small circles and had a reputation as a disreputable endeavor. Because Max and his family moved to Hamburg shortly after his birth, he was in a perfect spot to be influenced by this and other foreign imports. International shipping and travel dominated the life of the city, where Max's father worked as a merchant seaman and navigator for the Hamburg-America Line. Influenced at an early age by his father's constant journeys and the large number of emigrants to America who flocked to Hamburg's docks, young Max hoped to follow in his father's footsteps as a seaman and live a life of adventure and international travel. He started school in 1912, but proved a poor student. His interests lay in sports. Big and strong, he preferred playing goalie for the St. Georger Fussball-Club von 1895.[4]

World War I and its aftermath hit the family hard. His father served in the navy and in his absence the family experienced periods of hunger common to other Germans during the conflict. For a time, Max was sent off to live with his grandparents in Brandenburg. For young Schmeling, as for all Germans, the end of the war ushered in a period of political chaos and economic uncertainty. Immediately after the cessation of hostilities, the youngster found himself on the streets of Hamburg, as revolutionary leftists battled fiercely but unsuccessfully with police and the army for control of the city. Eager for money in a time of economic distress, Max acceded to his parents' wish that he find a respectable job. In 1920 he began a three-year period of training as a salesman. This was not a propitious time to start such a career, nor did he much like office work. More to the point, Max longed for a job that would relieve him of the burdens of lower-middle-class existence.[5]

Much to the dismay of his increasingly religious parents, boxing came to his rescue as he entered adolescence. After the lifting of the police bans on prizefighting in 1918 and the return of the POWs, the sport spread quickly. Young Max was alerted to the sport by another international influence— American fight films. In July 1921 he watched the movies of the championship match between the American Jack Dempsey and the Frenchman Georges Carpentier, which convinced him that boxing was a way to make something of himself far beyond his origins. In pursuit of his goal of becoming a professional fighter, he took a construction job and moved from the Lutheranism of Hamburg, which frowned on boxing as a wasteful and brutal "Anglo-American" activity, to several Rhineland towns, where Catholic culture proved more open to all forms of sport. In addition, the continued occupation of the Rhineland by British troops made the area a hotbed of boxing, with numerous clubs and the opportunity to train and fight regularly. After learning his craft in the amateur ranks during 1923 and 1924, he decided to turn professional at the age of nineteen in 1924, ten years before Joe Louis would do the same, because times remained hard and his family needed the money. The discovery that United States champions such as Jack Dempsey earned millions had a profound effect on both men. As a result, Max quit his construction job and moved to Cologne, where he undertook serious training for his professional debut. In his first professional bout on August 2, 1924, Schmeling knocked out Johann Czapp in Düsseldorf in front of 5,000 fans. Fighting as a light heavyweight, he made 80 deutsche marks (DM) and was on his way. By the end of the year, he had had ten professional bouts, winning seven by knockout and two on points; one was a disqualification. Although he still had much to learn, it became clear that the German slugger had a powerful right hand that potentially could earn him a good deal of money.[6]

Professional boxing offered more than money. As Schmeling recalled in his autobiography, boxing offered "dreams of epic battles." Similar to other German and American men, young Max dreamed of a more exciting alternative to the factory and office routines that were commonly the only jobs for working- and lower-middle-class men during the early 1920s. Max found the sport exciting because it put "one's own existence on the line." In a mass society, moreover, it provided "a means to break away from the crowd to climb into the world spotlight." As a craft, meanwhile, the sport was a way to take "my life into my own hands and make something of it." The young man also saw a similarity between boxing and circus work. In the summer of 1925, after an injury, a disappointing loss, and a lack of matches, Schmeling spent a month with a circus teaching the owner's son to box. There he realized that risk "made the lifestyle of the boxer, like that of the [circus] *artiste* so uncertain; but in the risk lay . . . a great attraction." Unlike most work in the modern world, boxing required the "commitment of his entire self," which meant "mental and spiritual commitment too." To succeed, he willingly gave up tobacco and alcohol and followed a strict diet. It was "a matter of attitude and will." Already inclined by his upbringing toward rigid self-discipline, the young man found that boxing required exacting standards of behavior and self-control. It became a matter of pride that he was never out of shape.[7]

On June 15, 1926, Schmeling's desire for an adventurous professional career brought him to Berlin, a cosmopolitan city that was then emerging as the capital of German, and some would say European, boxing, Max was completely broke and looking for a new manager who knew something about the sport. Without a place to stay or a job, the twenty-year-old Schmeling headed for the offices of *Box-Sport*, Germany's premier weekly prizefight trade journal, which had taken notice of his power in the ring and had begun to refer to him as "Dempsey II." There he took up with two influential men who directly shaped his career. Arthur Bülow, the publisher of *Box-Sport*, was a war hero, an important manager and referee, and a tireless promoter of amateur and professional boxing in Berlin and across northern Europe. Having refereed several of Schmeling's bouts, Bülow recognized Max's potential and consented to manage him and promote his career. Equally important, he agreed to pay for the young slugger's costs at a camp in the woods run by Max Machon, who became Schmeling's trainer and friend and remained with him for the rest of his career. For the first time, the fighter was able to focus completely on his sport, and under Machon's guidance, he engaged in a highly disciplined exercise regimen. Starting at 6:30 A.M. he rose for his roadwork, after breakfast he engaged in discussions about ring tactics and strategy, and in the afternoon he exercised and sparred. In this Spartan environment Schmeling soon rounded into top shape.[8]

With a knowledgeable and active manager, improved boxing skills, and a better left to go with his powerful right, Schmeling rapidly ascended the ranks of the German and European prizefighting world. On August 24, 1926, he won the German Light Heavyweight Championship in Berlin, by knocking out the titleholder Max Diekmann in thirty seconds of the first round, the shortest German title match to date. A year later in June 1927 in Dortmund he took the European title at the same weight against the Belgian Fernand Delarge on a thirteenth round technical knockout (TKO), making Schmeling the first German to become a European champion. His spectacular knockout of the Italian titleholder, Michele Bonaglia, at Berlin's Sportpalast in early 1928 made him a national hero. Since Benito Mussolini had personally supported Bonaglia as an example of Italian fascism, a number of leftists hailed Schmeling's knockout as a victory of democracy over fascism. Even more, German fans sang the national anthem after the bout, thereby turning the event, according to *Box-Sport*, into "a national affair." At the age of twenty-two Schmeling had become a national hero and a mass celebrity. Soon after, he moved up to the heavyweight division and won the German title on points against the champion, Fritz Diener, in the sporting event of the year.[9]

In a direct parallel to his American namesake, the "German Dempsey" played a critical role in the rise of German boxing from an illegal, lower-class, disreputable activity to the pinnacle of mass spectator sports in the Weimar Republic. The urban masses and the highest social classes attended boxing matches, celebrated the sport's champions, and followed their ring exploits in the nation's newspapers, motion pictures, music, and literature. In fact, the sport resonated in popular culture far beyond any other, as it mixed both athletics and show business into a modern, hybrid form of popular entertainment. Under the influence of American primacy in the sport, a slew of American sporting terms such as "KO," "training," and "form" now entered the German language. A poem of 1925 captured boxing's mass appeal: "A big fight beckons today . . . whether you ride or whether you sail . . . whether you flicker or foxtrot—you have to go there: there will be boxing!"[10]

The sport's new social cachet reversed its earlier reputation as an illegal activity associated with brutal bloodlust and the disreputable working classes. In fact, during his career Schmeling went from fighting in amusement parks and beer gardens located in industrial suburbs, "where the price of admission was perhaps ten cents," to Berlin's grandiose Sportpalast, the city's equivalent to Madison Square Garden, in front of crowds attired in tuxedos and evening gowns. The sport was so popular in 1926, according to Nat Fleischer, editor of *Ring* magazine, that "in the elementary high schools and colleges, in the gymnasiums and in the police and military schools, boxing is the one sport which everyone must follow. . . . It is compulsory for the police of every city in Germany to take boxing lessons." Many women, upper-class swells, working-class fans, and artists and theater folk felt compelled to attend the matches, and radio broadcasts extended the sport's diverse audience into the countryside. In fact, Schmeling rode the remarkable boom in German boxing after

World War I to the pinnacle of international accomplishment and national renown in 1930 when he won the heavyweight title against Jack Sharkey in Yankee Stadium, the first European to accomplish this momentous feat. When Schmeling defended his world title in New York in 1932, listeners across Germany stayed up late to catch the broadcast. According to one observer, in a small Berlin villa on the top floor, "an entire family in pajamas and bathrobes sits around the shrieking loudspeaker, while at the same time burglars downstairs are packing up 5,000 marks in silver and carpets unnoticed."[11]

The acclaim that Schmeling and other German boxers received throughout his career arose from the vital role that the sport played in Weimar culture. To some extent, its rise in popularity can be seen as a diversion after the war, part of the search for pleasure and experience long denied by the conflict. German sportswriter Willy Meisl noted: "The war was over and peace had broken out. . . . Many people had learned how transitory life is; they felt that life was there to be lived. Subconscious drives ruled them; they had returned from the land of the dead and sought life; they were open to adventure, for the old way offered them no chance. . . . The body was in . . . sport and all its ramifications were the future." Boxing also served as a metaphor for the turbulent nature of postwar German society, but in a safe, ordered environment. In this sense, boxing counteracted the irrational violence of the war and the early 1920s in Germany by allowing fans to express their aggressive impulses in a rational and ritualized form. Schmeling seemed to agree. He maintained that boxing expressed more than physical violence. Rather, boxing was a trade, and a boxer was "in a sense a craftsman." In order to advance his trade, the athlete had to "develop his tools—the hands, legs, and eyes—and keep them in top working order" just liked an artisan. Moreover, it was not just the body that led to success. He maintained that boxing was like a chess match. He used the first few rounds to study his opponent in order to fight him correctly, claiming that "only the intelligent boxer can make major adjustments in the course of the fight." In the ring as elsewhere, "it's intelligence that is the decisive factor. With tactics and strategy, even a less physically gifted boxer can outmaneuver a giant."[12]

Boxing also appealed to the powerful individualistic feelings unleashed by the war and the collapse of the legitimacy of the Wilhelmine order that had produced the devastating conflict and in the 1920s stood for stuffiness, hypocrisy, and class rigidity. In the past, respectable Germans had disdained boxing because they feared its power to foster working-class violence and rebellion against the established order. The various city bans against the sport did not target upper-class dueling and swordplay, suggesting a deep class bias against this much simpler and less expensive form of self defense. In the Weimar years, boxing provided the individual with the means to survive and succeed in a less hierarchical world. Perhaps this explains why Schmeling and other boxers were treated as American-style success stories. They were young men who had fought their way from the bottom of the social order to riches and fame, and they were admired and rewarded for their achievements. In a society still worried about the transformations in postwar Germany—the criticism of the class order, the emergence of a more assertive Modern Woman who attended the fights—boxing had the advantage of having well-defined rules and regulations for individual conduct.[13]

In Germany's big cities, prizefighting became a dramatic arena in which new possibilities and dangers were acted out for a mass public. In his memoir, Schmeling recalled that artists and intellectuals often saw boxing as a theater of deadly individualism. The actor Fritz Kortner, one of the sport's many avid fans in the theater world, told him, "What happens in the ring reflects life. So unmerciful, so angry the way you go at each other, that is how we all struggle for our own existence." Actors, he told Max, could present such a scene on the stage, "but for us it's only theater. . . . But for you the matter is really one of life and death. . . . That's what's so exciting about boxing: nowhere else is the lust for fame and success so palpable, so deadly earnest! Boxing is really not a sport. It's a battle for life compressed into twelve rounds." Schmeling and other German boxers symbolized the individual who fought his way in the battle of life.[14]

Having successfully fought the battle of life in a realm outside modern corporations and factories, Schmeling was entitled to the rewards of the new consumer society just as he was becoming a hero of this world. The chief reward was money, which was a much more fluid medium of status than the older markers of class identity. By the end of the decade, Max had become a wealthy man, and his purses were recorded in the daily press. He first earned big money as a boxer when he received 20,000 marks for a bout against Hein Domgörgen in 1927. When he fought Johnny Risko in New York in early 1929, he took home $25,000 or about 70,000 marks. In his championship match against Jack Sharkey in 1930 he made close to a million marks. By the end of the 1920s, Schmeling lived the life of a rich man. While he was far from ostentatious, the press showed photos of his expensive new sports car and his thoroughbred racehorse. He also was pictured in front of his rural mansion just outside Berlin, which featured idyllic grounds and a private swimming pool. The successful boxer, in other words, had an opportunity to live the life of a movie star. To top it off, on July 6, 1933, he actually married a movie actress, the Czech ingénue Anny Ondra, then at the acme of her career, an event that received considerable coverage in the German press. Like his American counterpart, Jack Dempsey, Schmeling also had the opportunity to star in movies himself. In 1929 he appeared in *Lieben im Ring* ("Love in the Ring") and actually sang "The Heart of the Boxer," which became a popular

Max Schmeling and fiancée Anny Ondra, the movie actress, 1933. During the 1920s and early 1930s, boxers and other athletes achieved new status as popular celebrities equivalent to movie stars in both Germany and the United States. (International News Photos, Library of Congress)

song on German radio. As historian Siegfried Gehrmann has noted, Schmeling's career "touched a chord in the collective psyche; this is what in the United States came to be called the 'American Dream.'"[15]

German fight fans identified with their favorites, and the personality and charisma of top boxers attracted large crowds. In fact, the public idolized boxers more than other types of celebrities. In a poll taken of fourteen-year-olds in 1930, world champion Schmeling proved better known than statesman Gustav Streseman, popular writer Karl May, or industrialist Henry Ford. As the socialist newspaper the *Vorwärts* sniffed in distaste, "Germany, once the land of thinkers and poets, is on the fastest road to becoming the land of football players and boxers." The display of the boxer's body added to his charisma, drawing women fans and causing some dismay among boxing experts. Appearing half-clad, boxers had erotic appeal, which led various social observers and boxing commentators to warn that fighters unleashed the passions of women, who were drawn not only to bloodlust but also to the sexual possibilities of the male body.[16]

As the most prominent German prizefighter, Schmeling's success catapulted him into the cosmopolitan Weimar world of writers, artists, and show people for whom boxing was a modernist symbol. Berlin was the metropolis that drew ambitious young people—actors, directors, artists, musicians, and fighters from the provinces. This quality gave Berlin, much like New York City, the sense of being "a huge cultural train station," a "city of gold for anyone who wanted to make it to the top." The influx of outsiders into the capital helps explain the excitement of its urban life and the explosion of the Weimar cultural world. As he accumulated his titles, Schmeling became part of Berlin society, which, he recalled, "did not consist of the important or influential people; nor the rich or the powerful. Rather it was the people about whom everyone was talking: artists and showgirls, actors, journalists and authors, bicycle riders and intellectuals." There were no outsiders in this world, "since all in their own way were themselves outsiders. They were *the* society; and this society was now clamoring for me." Emil Jennings and Ernst Deutsch, the great actors, opera singer Michael Bohnen, the sculptor Josef Thorak, film stars Hans Albers, Willy Fritsch, and Olga Tschechowa, along with director Josef von Sternberg all became his friends and companions. He also became a favorite of artists and sculptors like Georg Grosz, Ernesto de Fiori, Renee Sintenis, and Rudolf Belling. All of these outsiders, many sympathetic to leftist politics and artistic modernism, and a large number of them of Jewish descent, contributed to making Berlin the capital of a new, more cosmopolitan cultural life in which boxing and the body played central roles.[17]

In revolt against the high idealism of the grand German intellectual and cultural tradition that was exploded by the pointless mechanized horror of World War I, artists, writers, and performers turned to the cult of the body and the boxer as the irreducible element of human existence. As a fighter, Schmeling noted, "I symbolized sports." From the moment that conventional behavior lost its power, he recalled, "the natural reigned triumphant," and a cult of the physical emerged in Germany: "a glorification of the body and a cult of nakedness, which stretched from vaudeville to nudist culture." For the first time since antiquity, artists made the body in sport the subject of their art. Ernesto de Fiori, Renee Sintenis, and Rudolf Belling sculpted him, the latter in the nude. George Grosz, with whom he became friendly, painted him as "The Fighter." Outside the restrictions of social class and social custom, the boxer was a symbol of freedom, a man who dealt with the harsh realities of life without recourse to obfuscating ideas or ideals.[18]

Unlike later Nazi art that glorified the Greek ideal of gladiatorial power and Aryan racial perfection, Weimar artists especially valued the American boxer's body for its playfulness and natural spontaneity, its "swaying and whirling," its toughness and lack of inhibition, its ability to forget tradition and live in the present. As a student of the game, Schmeling early on modeled his bobbing and weaving on American models, and it was the links among boxing, modernity, and America that made him a cosmopolitan hero to the German intellectual and cultural avant-garde. The sport's standing with the German cultural rebels of Weimar Berlin gave the German fascination with boxing its unique place in the Western world and helps explain the mutual friendships that developed between Schmeling and various artists. Weimar's left avant-garde viewed the American connection as giving sports the power to subvert nineteenth-century Wilhelmine authoritarian and militaristic culture. American sports, many intellectuals hoped, would cause a "renewal of Life feeling," buried under the vestiges of a decaying cultural order. "Americanism is the materialization of vitality." The athlete, especially the boxer, demystified art and culture, and took society out of "the realm of sensitivity into the realm of action; out of a tender and clinging world into one—if you will that is brutal and ruthless . . . real." Schmeling agreed. In a contribution to a Berlin symposium on Americanism, he hailed American sports. In his view, they offered a means to energize an older, stiffer German culture. "Americanism in sport does not take away from fairness. It does not necessarily mean the injection of the business spirit," he declared. Rather, sports were an American "national virtue," that "saves them from laziness and lethargy, gives them daily new impulses and makes them young, fresh and enterprising."[19]

Not all agreed, however. The popularity and success of a sport so closely associated with the United States led to criticism of prizefighting as too commercial and "Americanized." Some commentators criticized the mass audience for seeking sensation and showmanship rather than pursuing real knowledge of and appreciation for the finer points of boxing technique. It was the commercialization of sport that Socialists and National Socialists found most disturbing. They contrasted the promotion of star athletes, the creation of spectacle, and the stoking of the audience's demands for violence and sensation with the participatory nature of the worker sports movement in Germany or the older Turner tradition of gymnastic group exercise. Money and fame were the result of capitalist corruption of sport and hence were part of the new economic order that Socialists found deeply disturbing in Weimar Germany. To the Nazis, commercialization was the product of the sport's many Jewish promoters and managers. Instead of national greatness, sporting figures were being lured toward the love of money and individual accomplishment.[20]

Yet as Germany's most successful fighter during the 1920s and early 1930s, Schmeling was, according to *Box-Sport*, "the embodiment of a modern national hero." His victories in the ring over opponents from former enemy countries "functioned as some kind of collective psychic compensation for the national humiliation of Versailles," asserted historian Siegfried Gehrmann. When he won the European Light Heavyweight title from the Belgian Fernand Delarge in 1927, for example, a German newspaper charted the tremendous shouts of joy by the fans at the match in Dortmund. "Schmeling! Schmeling! The Champion of Europe . . . Schmeling the first German European Champion embodies from now on Germany's dominant position in boxing." And as the band played, the crowd proudly sang the national anthem, "Deutschland, Deutschland Über Alles!"[21]

During the 1920s and early 1930s, however, Schmeling's nationalist image was mitigated by his overarching cosmopolitan identity. When he traveled to New York City in May 1928 to contend for the world championship in the capital of world boxing, he continued to break boundaries as he had in Berlin. One of the first truly transatlantic athletes, he became an international figure who lived between worlds and made a name for himself in "America, my second home." From the time he first arrived in New York, the entire direction of Schmeling's career was shaped by his contacts with the United States, often to the disappointment of his many German fans who missed seeing him fight on German soil. When he discovered that success in the United States required an American manager who knew the ropes and had the right contacts in New York, he parted with Arthur Bülow, his German manager. In his place, Schmeling hired the Yiddish-speaking Hungarian-born Jew, Joe "Yussel the Muscle" Jacobs. While Jacobs knew little about boxing, he did know how to negotiate a good deal. The two got along well and Jacobs worked hard to get him fights and build up his name in New York, where now Schmeling was not just a figure in society but a hero on the street. Closely tied to his Jewish American manager, Schmeling also developed associations with many German Jewish friends in New York. The German boxer also found a positive reception in the United States as a result of another Jew, *Ring* editor Nat Fleischer, who had alerted

Max Schmeling, Heavyweight Champion of the World 1930. (Library of Congress)

Madison Square Garden to Max's talent in 1926. In order to fight in New York, moreover, Schmeling made frequent transatlantic crossings. As a result, he was one of the best-traveled figures of the day. These factors contributed to a cosmopolitan identity that moderated his nationalist associations.[22]

His willingness to gamble on his chances in the international arena quickly turned Schmeling into a serious contender for the heavyweight crown. Despite discrimination against African American boxers, New York's boxing world proved welcoming when it came to white European fighters. In part, this goes back to the long history of transatlantic openness in the sporting world of the United States. British and Irish boxers had brought the sport to the United States in the early nineteenth century, and over the years European, Australian, Canadian, and South American prizefighters had made their way to America to take advantage of the lucrative rewards and worldwide acclaim possible only in the United States. When champion Gene Tunney retired in 1928 after taking the title from and defending against Jack Dempsey in two of the million-dollar matches of the era, American boxing was desperate for a box office draw. In this atmosphere, Nat Fleischer noted, "the German Menace's" resemblance to Dempsey in and out of the ring, has "almost overnight," gained him "world-wide acclaim." To work himself into contention, Schmeling fought his way through a series of fighters in the United States, including Joe Sekyra, Pietro Corri, Johnny Risko, and Paolino Uzcudun, the latter a well-known Basque campaigner during the late 1920s and early 1930s.[23]

Having earned his shot by beating Risko and Uzcudun, on June 12, 1930, he faced off against Boston's Jack Sharkey, the son of Lithuanian immigrants, in Yankee Stadium for the heavyweight championship. The promoters were thrilled as 80,000 fans filled the stadium, among them 30,000 German Americans. The match started slowly, which often happened when Schmeling fought, because he preferred to take his time to figure out his opponent before unleashing his deadly arsenal. In fact, both fighters seemed hesitant. Only in the third round did things pick up. Sharkey began rushing in and pummeling his opponent with a flurry of punches. Schmeling remained cool, but in the fourth he began to unload too. Suddenly Sharkey floored the German, who lay writhing on the canvas. His seconds dragged him to his corner where he sat in a crumpled state while the referee tolled the count. Schmeling's manager, however, still had his wits about him. Joe Jacobs started yelling at the referee and the judges that the blow was low. After minutes of indecision and uncertainty while fight officials conferred, and with the crowd growing restless, the judges declared Schmeling the winner on a foul. As a result, Schmeling became the first heavyweight champion to win the crown while sitting on the canvas. Only half-conscious, he was carried out of the ring. Although he became the first European to win the heavyweight championship, his reputation was damaged and the sport of boxing tarnished.[24]

The Sharkey-Schmeling fight sold out Yankee Stadium, but boxing's reputation and profitability went downhill from then on. As the first heavyweight champion to win the title on a foul, Schmeling found that both Germans and Americans were suspicious of his right to hold the championship. As he noted, "My crown was without glory." In fact, the New York State Athletic Commission initially refused to recognize his crown or award him his purse, and they made him promise to defend his title within a year, preferably against Sharkey. Former champion Jack Dempsey did not rank Schmeling as the number one heavyweight boxer in Ring's annual rankings for 1930 because he considered that Schmeling had not won the title through his boxing skills. The situation, Dempsey wrote, "has cast the world's heavyweight title back into the doubt from which it suffered before the Jeffries-Johnson fight." One of the judges concurred. "I was one of the judges, and I did not see a low blow struck," declared Charles F. Mathison. "Hundreds of others failed to see the low blow." All in all, he considered Schmeling's behavior "unmanly."[25]

This lack of respect was bad enough in the United States, but German boxing authorities also suggested that Schmeling consider returning the title. German fans, disappointed in their first world champion, derided him in the press as the "Low Blow Champion" and described his "grave damage to the testicles." Cabaret artists, many of whom he knew from his rounds of the Berlin cafes, now chided him for being "Beaten Into a World Champion . . .

The Low Blow Champion. Max wins the heavyweight crown against Jack Sharkey on a foul in 1930, tarnishing his championship and presaging the decline of boxing in the United States and Germany. (Associated Press, Library of Congress)

Our Future Lies with the Shot Below the Belt!" As the Socialist daily *Vorwärts* reported, a new saying emerged: "I am Schmeling humiliated." When he was introduced as world champion at the Berlin Sportpalast on October 31, 1930, the crowd booed him unmercifully. The fact that his fiancée Anny Ondra had accompanied him to a boxing event for the first time only deepened his humiliation. Despite the greatest international success a German boxer had ever known, Schmeling suffered a blow to "German honor," and he bore the shame of a nation still suffering from defeat in World War I and in crisis over masculinity in a deepening depression. When he avoided a return match with Sharkey, despite contract obligations, and waited a year to defend his title for the first time against a lesser opponent, Young Stribling, he did not help his reputation or that of the prizefight game. While he regained some respect by defending his title successfully in 1931 against Stribling in Cleveland, the fight proved a "financial fiasco," lost half a million dollars, and drew the fewest fans in heavyweight championship history.[26]

As the Stribling fight indicates, the Depression had begun to affect boxing. Audience attendance fell drastically, and for the next several years Schmeling and boxing on both sides of the Atlantic continued their downward slide. On June 21, 1932, at the Madison Square Bowl on Long Island, he finally defended his title against Jack Sharkey, only to lose the rematch on a disputed fifteen-round decision that raised doubts about the honesty and fairness of the New York boxing world. When the announcement came after a fairly balanced fight, Jacobs shouted, "We wuz robbed." In a poll of twenty-four newsmen who attended the bout, fourteen voted for Schmeling, eight for Sharkey, and two did not respond. The loyal Jacobs accused the New York State Athletic Commission of rigging the match; he was suspended. Still, the commission got what they wanted—an American champion who they hoped would fight on a regular and more lucrative basis and bring back fan interest and bigger gates.[27]

A year later, in 1933, Schmeling was completely outclassed by Max Baer, losing on a TKO in the tenth round in what the German called the "worst defeat of my career." This defeat, to a heavyweight who wore the Star of David on his trunks and identified himself as Jewish, hurt Schmeling badly since it occurred shortly after the Nazis had taken power. Baer's victory over an Aryan boxer did not go down well with the new regime. "Schmeling's defeat," noted *Box-Sport*, "is the end of a fortunate career." When he then lost to a relative novice, *Der Angriff*, the Nazi press outlet for Dr. Joseph Goebbels, wrote, "For Schmeling . . . we have no more interest at all." His career seemingly over, he fell "into a deep depression." In fact, Schmeling's fate prompted the *Vorwärts* to ask "Is Boxing Dying?" As the daily noted, "The prospects are very somber" for heavyweights. Boxing clubs were on the "verge of expiration." The press blamed promoters for overcharging in a depression and for not finding a "knock-out artist." While Socialists analyzed the situation, the Nazis were readying to take action to rid the sport of its Jewish influences and redefine boxing as preparation for war. As for Schmeling, it appeared that the old boxing adage had proven true: they never come back after losing the title.[28]

While Schmeling's career reached its lowest point in the early 1930s, Joe Louis's was just getting started. Yet his prospects did not look good either. He and his family were mired in the Depression that struck African Americans with special ferocity. In the absence of other opportunities during the 1930s about 8,000 poor black and ethnic working-class young men took up the sport of boxing. Eager to make a name for themselves while seeking economic sustenance, they also searched for an outlet for the anger and frustration associated with trying to make their way during the economic crisis. Louis was one of these young men. Like so many others, his family was part of the Great Migration from southern slavery, segregation, and sharecropping to the urban industrial world of Detroit. For blacks whose unemployment figures and rates of poverty belied their dreams of a better life in the North, Louis embodied their experience and their aspirations.

Born on May 13, 1914, in a sharecropper shack in rural Alabama about six miles from the nearest hamlet, Louis was the seventh son in a family of eight children headed by Munrow and Lillie Reese Barrow. Descended from African slaves, white plantation owners, and Blackfoot and Cherokee Indians, his family rented and sharecropped cotton in the Buckalew Mountains of Alabama. Broken under the strain of supporting a large family on the stingy red clay soil of the area, his father deserted when Joe was two years old and was later committed to an insane asylum. Believed dead, he was never seen by his family again. Joe's mother Lillie worked the land and raised her large family in an unpainted windowless shack that backed onto a cotton patch. A strict Baptist and a stern disciplinarian, she made sure, Louis recalled, that the Barrow children were not "wild or bad." Eventually Lillie married Patrick Brooks, the first of several surrogate father figures in Louis's life, who had five children of his own. Together, Pat and Lillie had even more children. Struggling to survive, the family moved farther into the mountains, near Mt. Sinai, where they lived in an unheated cabin, the children went without shoes, and Louis shared a bed with two of his older brothers. As was common in poor sharecropping families, the children were expected to work in the fields when they were old enough, and young Joe was no exception. School consisted of one room for fifteen to sixteen youngsters, with an outhouse out back. Joe attended only intermittently and found school discouraging. He had a speech impediment that made it hard for him to speak clearly. "When I went to school the teacher made me say my words over and over, and by-and-by I got stubborn . . . and wouldn't say them at all." Because the other children made fun of his stammer, he often skipped school. Big and strong like his parents Louis seemed destined for life as an uneducated sharecropper living in a segregated world of limited opportunities and aspirations.[29]

With food hard to come by during the 1920s, the family listened to tales of "cars, factories, jobs, and money" available in Detroit. Relatives who migrated before them relayed the fact that "the Ford factory didn't mind hiring Negroes, and for once we'd have hard solid money we wouldn't have to share with the landowner." After the Ku Klux Klan threatened his mother and stepfather one night, Louis's family decided to migrate to Detroit in 1926, where they settled in the growing black neighborhood on the city's east side. On his northward journey, which like so many other southern blacks he made by train, Joe witnessed out the window a scene emblematic of the life he was leaving behind: black prisoners on an Alabama chain gang. He vowed that "I ain't never doing nothing to be chained up like some penned animal." With the economy booming, Louis's stepfather got a city job and his brothers were hired at the Ford Motor Company, giving the family a measure of prosperity over and above anything they had experienced in Alabama. After living with relatives, the family moved to a frame tenement on Catherine Street that had indoor plumbing and electric lights. For a youngster, the city offered endless excitement. "You can't imagine the impact that city had. I never saw so many people in one place, so many cars at one time. I had never seen a trolley car before." He had also never seen parks, libraries, brick schoolhouses, and movie theaters. As he put it, "Detroit looked awfully good to me."[30]

The Brooks-Barrow family soon learned that the North, while it offered greater personal freedom from the watchful and dangerous eye of such white terrorist groups as the Ku Klux Klan, was no Promised Land. While not all white ethnics had left their neighborhood or fled the schools, downtown Detroit was segregated. Movie theaters, restaurants, and places of public accommodation were off limits to African Americans. The Depression, moreover, delivered a major blow to their fortunes. Last hired and first fired, blacks in Detroit experienced the hard realities of the Depression before other groups. When automobile sales fell badly in the late 1920s, the economic boom turned to bust. The City of Detroit laid off Pat Brooks from his job as a street cleaner at the same time that the Ford Motor Company, the city's major private employer of blacks, let his brothers go. By the end of the decade his large family was forced to turn to relief, his mother had to wait on soup lines for the family's food, and for the first time Joe and his siblings went hungry.[31]

Like most impoverished African Americans coming of age in the Great Depression, young Louis had few choices for an interesting or lucrative career. Moreover, he had left Duffield elementary school after the fourth grade. A dreamy child who liked to be by himself, Joe still suffered from the speech impediment that made him reluctant to speak up in class, especially in Detroit as there were better educated and better dressed white and black students in his classroom. It was easy for teachers and fellow students to conclude that the shy youngster, who mumbled when called upon, was slow and probably mentally deficient. Already bigger and older than everyone else in his class, Joe would have had to repeat the fourth grade. As it was, he could hardly write his name, and he could barely read. On the advice of a teacher, Joe transferred to Bronson Trade School, to educate his hands rather than his head. At Bronson, he learned to make cabinets and tables, which came in handy because his family could afford little furniture on their own. When he left school at seventeen in 1931, however, there was little call for cabinetmakers or for anything else. Crime was always an option for a poor urban boy, and he might have continued to run with the street gang that dominated his neighborhood, the Catherine Street gang, where his street fighting skills were prized. This would have landed him in the illegal world of violence and gambling that flourished in black ghettoes during the Depression. With his family on relief, he needed money quick, and he was raised to work hard. However, he longed for an outlet for his power, a sense of developing a craft, as well as a way to earn money quickly. Boxing offered all of those opportunities. His mother's hopes for him lay elsewhere. Aware that music offered a potential career for black men, she painfully put aside small amounts of money so that Joe could take violin lessons.[32]

A number of institutions attempted to provide safe channels for Depression-era young men like Louis who might go astray. Northern cities, according to the Chicago Recreation survey, supported amateur boxing as an outlet in "those areas and among those groups where survival of the fittest was long dependent upon one's ability to defend his rights with fists rather than words."

In contrast to disorganization and crime, boxing offered young men the chance to discipline themselves through hard and rigorous training. In general, amateur boxing in the North was relatively open to black and ethnic working-class young men, and Louis used the money that his mother had set aside for him to study violin for boxing lessons. In 1928 the *Chicago Tribune* and the New York *Daily News* had created the Golden Gloves, a series of amateur boxing competitions in Chicago and New York. Soon after, the Amateur Athletic Union set up boxing tournaments throughout the nation's major cities, including Chicago and Detroit, where Louis took part. In addition, Bishop Bernard Sheil of Chicago inaugurated the Catholic Youth Organization (CYO) in 1930. The CYO stressed a Catholic Americanization that was less concerned with imposing a Protestant model of assimilation and more open to boys regardless of religion, race, or ethnic background. Boxing proved a key part of its mission. "We'll knock the hoodlum off his pedestal and we'll put another neighborhood boy in his place," declared Sheil. "He'll be dressed in CYO boxing shorts and a pair of leather mitts, and he'll make a new hero. Those kids love to fight. We'll let them fight. We'll find champions right in the neighborhood." While professional prizefighting declined in the early 1930s, the Golden Gloves did "more than any other organization to keep boxing alive during the depression" noted *Ring*, by "creating public interest in amateur tourneys in all parts of the country." Many stars of the professional boxing scene of 1935, including Louis, came up through the amateur ranks.[33]

Many African American and working-class ethnic young men took to the sport in the hopes of finding direction, masculine identity, and a start on earning a living. In the Depression, fighting for what one got seemed a realistic metaphor for daily life. Similar to Max Schmeling who found the sport a means to a more exciting life, Louis from the start took to amateur boxing as a calling. The first time he entered the Brewster Recreation Center when he accompanied his pal Thurston McKinney, a fellow student at Bronson and a Detroit Golden Gloves champion at 147 pounds, "It was love at first sight," Louis recalled. He said of nearly knocking McKinney out, "It was like power pumping through me. Maybe it's like people getting religion." Moreover, regulation bouts proved vastly different from street fights. "This was not like fighting because you mad at somebody or because you were defending somebody." Rather, "there was something professional about it." As he fought his way through the Golden Gloves, Louis realized he had a lot to learn, especially after he was knocked down seven times in his first amateur bout. For a man who would spend the next eighteen years in constant training, to the detriment of family and personal life, Louis resented the common notion that he was a "natural" fighter battling only on instinct. "There's no such thing as a 'natural.' A 'natural' dancer has to practice hard. A 'natural' painter has to paint all the time, even a 'natural' fool has to work at it. I had the God-given equipment to be a professional fighter, but I had to train at it, and train damn hard." Boxing earned him respect in his neighborhood, kept him away from a life of crime, and gave him a sense of identity to be able to say, "'I'm going to be a fighter. I'm going to be somebody.' It gave me a sense of pride and dignity to at last want to be something. Got to admit I strutted a little." Once he put on the gloves, the boy who seemed slow and clumsy began to see himself as quick and powerful.[34]

Boxing also offered poor boys a chance to escape lack of work or the monotonous jobs that awaited them. Athletes had the opportunity to travel beyond the narrow constraints of family and neighborhood, and to express themselves in action. For working class and black youth, sports and music offered a means to assert themselves in the world, to become active agents rather than merely being controlled by others. In boxing, Louis strove to test himself against others and to discipline himself in order to achieve a measure of perfection in one of the few areas of life open to him. While it entailed a great deal of hard work, athletics allowed him to work at something that was under his own control compared to the ordinary man who was out of work or stuck in a dead-end job. Louis, for instance, took jobs in the auto industry several times. Just after leaving Bronson in 1931, he heard that the Briggs automobile factory was hiring. After he and his brother Alonzo waited on line half the day, Louis was hired at $25 a week. The work was monotonous, however, and even more important, it cut into his training. He was too tired to work out seriously. After getting demolished in his first amateur bout, he used his boxing connections to get a job at Ford's Rouge River factory. However, pushing truck bodies to a conveyer belt was no fun. "Eventually, I couldn't stand it anymore. I figured, if I'm going to hurt that much for twenty-five dollars a week, I might as well go back to try fighting again." He left the factory in January 1933 and "I never returned."[35]

With his stepfather and brothers unemployed, Louis became the family breadwinner with earnings from amateur and then professional bouts. Amateur boxers received payments in checks for merchandise worth $7 to $25 dollars that could be redeemed at participating stores. This proved to be the factor that decided Louis against the violin and in favor of boxing. His friend McKinney convinced him that the violin required years of education before Joe could get in a band and make any money. His stepfather would have preferred that he stay with steady factory work, but when he began bringing in money regularly, Pat Brooks accepted the legitimacy of his stepson's athletic endeavors. Louis certainly could not have done this had he pursued his first love, baseball, a sport more segregated than boxing. His friend and fellow boxer at the Brewster Recreation Center, Holman Williams, discouraged him. "You don't want to do that. A colored ball player has the cards stacked against him and he can't even get merchandise checks. At least at fighting you might make a few bucks." It was not just a matter of survival in the short run. The possibility for big money proved a large part of boxing's appeal. Coming up through the amateurs Louis learned of the money made by previous champions. McKinney talked up how much top fighters like Kid Chocolate, Jack Johnson, and Jack Dempsey made in one fight. "That really triggered me—the idea of big money almost busted up my head." After his first big payday as a professional, Joe proudly repaid the relief money his family had received and thereafter sent money home on a regular basis. "They looked fine in new clothes. No more welfare, no more worrying about simple things like food." When his bouts began to produce real earnings, he bought his mother a home and set aside money for his sister's college education too. Perhaps Louis took this male role of family mainstay from the movie westerns he loved. "I guess I wanted to be the big, strong, good guy and help those poor defenseless folks who needed it."[36]

Still, it took the support of his mother and his friends, McKinney and Williams, to convince him to go on after his disastrous first amateur bout. At the end of 1932 or the beginning of 1933, he fought Johnny Miler at a stag event at the Edison Athletic Club in Detroit. Miler, a white boy, had boxed for a number of years, held several amateur titles, and the previous summer had fought in the Olympic Games in Los Angeles. The novice Louis, weighing 168 pounds, was clearly overmatched. "I never got in a solid punch against him," Louis remembered. "He knocked me down seven times in two rounds, more than any one ever did after that." Going home that night, he was "sore all over, and low." For his pains, he received a $7 merchandise check, which he turned over to his mother. Although discouraged, he listened to his mother and his friends and kept trying to master his craft at the gym. He began to improve more quickly, and he got his first knockout against an opponent at Detroit's Forest Athletic Club with two punches in the first round. Soon he was knocking out other amateur light heavyweights with abandon and making a name for himself around Detroit.[37]

Louis managed to achieve this while fighting with secondhand equipment. As he put it, "I used my hand bandage over and over, in different fights, because I didn't have money to buy new bandages every time." Initially he did not have proper boxing shoes, so he used old tennis sneakers. Nor could he afford to eat right. He knew very little about proper nutrition, and "even if I did the Barrows couldn't count on steaks and chops." They cost far too much, so he mostly lived on hot dogs. This pattern must have been a common experience for boxers who came from impoverished backgrounds. Henry Armstrong, a black champion who held three world titles during the late 1930s, often had to fight on bread and beans until he hooked up with decent management. Many boxers had to rely on dedication and toughness to carry them through, while most quit to take any jobs they could to contribute to their families' support.[38]

There were other factors, however, that could end a black youth's amateur career. When Louis was nineteen, he traveled to the Windy City for the International Golden Gloves tournament at Chicago Stadium. He had trained hard and was looking forward to the event. As Joe waited in the segregated dressing room, Arch Ward, head of the city's Golden Gloves program and a sports columnist at the *Chicago Tribune*, came in and told the young boxer that the police were looking for him. A Gary, Indiana, man had seen his Golden Gloves picture and charged that Louis had killed his wife back in 1926. When he got to Gary, the authorities realized Louis was much too young to have committed the crime and that it was all a mistake. Still, he missed the tournament, and in a society in which whites had a hard time distinguishing individual African Americans, he might have ended up as just one more jailed black boy similar to the black convicts he had seen on his way north.[39]

Unlike many other amateurs, though, Louis had the benefit of a dedicated manager who looked out for him, provided expert guidance and counseling, and was able to help him manage the difficult transition from the amateur to the professional ranks. John Roxborough first saw Joe during the Detroit Inter-City Golden Gloves tryouts in 1932, where he won two bouts that night, both by knockout. Properly impressed, Roxborough began a long relationship with the shy young man. A classy light-skinned African American, of Scots, Jamaican, Spanish, and Creole background, Roxborough had come to Detroit as a boy of seven in 1899. His father, a lawyer from New Orleans, settled in an all-white neighborhood. The family was solidly middle class, and his older brother Charles, also a lawyer and a Republican, became the first black member of the Michigan state legislature and a prominent figure in the Urban League and the Young Negroes Professional Association. John Roxborough, however, soon learned about the color line in the North. After one year of college at the University of Detroit, he realized the limited job opportunities for black college graduates as Detroit increasingly underwent segregation in response to the influx of masses of black migrants. He decided to take another path. "You'd ask for a job, tell them you were a college graduate, and they'd say, 'Oh yes, we have a porter's job for you.'" According to Louis's biographer, Gerald Astor, Roxborough's reaction was, "To hell with education. What good would it do me?" He made up his mind that "when I got a chance to make money, no matter how, I'd take it. I would avoid embarrassing situations, like asking for a job when I was qualified." He also promised he would help himself first and then help other blacks.[40]

At first, Roxborough made his money as a bail bondsman because the field required no special education and skin color did not matter. People in jail would take money from anyone who could get them out. Through this line of work, the ambitious go-getter found the key to his fortune when he was called to bail out a black man who ran the policy, or numbers gambling operation, in Kansas City. The latter invited him to his hometown, instructed him on the workings of the policy racket and advised him that a similar operation in Detroit would be lucrative since the Ford Company was hiring so many blacks. Roxborough was a quick study. He created his own policy bank, the Big Four, and his territory was the growing black slum called Paradise Valley. His operations soon spread throughout Wayne County and included the publication of guidebooks to winning numbers—dream books that interpreted dreams and omens as a source of winning numbers. To protect his business, he also began contributing to political campaigns and forming alliances with prominent local politicians. Although he presented himself as a businessman who had graduated from the University of Michigan, Roxborough was in fact a college dropout and the kingpin of Detroit's policy gambling world.[41]

Despite the illegal nature of his business, Roxborough's generosity toward blacks hard hit by the Depression and his dignified self-image earned him respect in the community. Like many other black numbers men, he assumed the role of a "race man" by using his wealth and position to help advance the African American community. He contributed to the Urban League and the Young Negroes Progressive Association, for example, invested in black businesses, and acted as a patron of the race. On a personal level, he handed out money for rent, food, and coal, and he supported a number of promising young black men through the University of Michigan. Equally important, during the Depression he promoted sports for black youngsters, and in this capacity played an enormously important role in the life of Joe Louis. Sensing something extraordinary about Joe's abilities, Roxborough unofficially adopted him, brought him to live in his home, paid for his supplies and clothing, and gave him pocket money to tide him over through his training. As he put it, "Joe became a kind of son to me." Indeed, Roxborough became a model for the impressionable young man. Louis loved the gracious living. "I never saw black people living that way, and I was envious and watched everything he did."[42]

Convinced that Louis had the physical and mental ability to become a professional champion one day, Roxborough brought Louis along slowly and helped him rack up an amateur record of forty-nine wins, two losses, and two draws, with most of the wins coming by quick and decisive knockouts. It was clear that there was "something extraordinary about Joe's makeup. He seemed to have the most perfect nervous system I'd ever seen in an athlete and was magnificently built. He took his boxing very seriously and trained like a beaver." More than that, "I was awed by the terrific power he packed in his right hand . . . The raw material of a champion was there." After Louis won the AAU light heavyweight title in 1934, he was determined to turn professional and finally make some real money from all of his hard work and athletic ability. At first, Roxborough resisted. He believed that Louis was still too young and inexperienced and wanted the twenty-year-old Joe to wait until after he won the Golden Gloves heavyweight title. Louis replied, "Mr. Roxborough, I want the money." That was something the numbers king could understand.[43]

Roxorough introduced Joe to Julian Black, a Chicago numbers operator, nightclub owner, and sportsman who as partner and co-manager agreed to put up the initial $2,000 to finance Louis for the first months of a professional career. A native of Wisconsin, Black was another enterprising African American who viewed the illegal world as more lucrative and accepting than the realm of respectable business. Black proved crucial for operating in the gangster-controlled world of American boxing. He had been close enough to the top of the Chicago syndicate run by Al Capone to expect protection against other parties who might want to muscle in on their young prospect. Together, their criminal backgrounds and business skill gave him and Roxborough the confidence that they could navigate through the murky world of shark-like promoters and greedy gangsters who traditionally had treated black fighters as mere cannon fodder for promising young white boxers.[44]

With the help of his two managers, Louis moved to Chicago in June 1934, where he rented a room on 46th Street and South Parkway from Bill

The Joe Louis Brain Trust. "Poker-face" Joe always had a serious and determined look on his face, leading some sportswriters to depict him as sullen. The press emphasized the smart African American businessmen who guided the young man from a successful amateur career to the heavyweight title. From left to right: Julian Black; Jack Blackburn; Joe; John Roxborough; Russell Cowans. (Associated Press, Library of Congress)

Bottoms, a chef and the former operator of the famed Café Dreamland. Most important, Louis needed a trainer, and here Black's experience in the nightlife and sporting worlds proved invaluable. His Apex nightclub served as the watering hole for local black sportsmen, and from among the wealth of talent Black tapped the former boxer and veteran trainer Jack Blackburn. A knowledgeable trainer and a strict disciplinarian, Blackburn took over Louis's tutelage, advised him on the finer points of the game, oversaw his workouts, and in many ways became another of Louis's several surrogate fathers. After several weeks of intense training, Blackburn announced that Louis was ready. In his first professional bout, he scored a one-round knockout over Jack Kracken on July 4, 1934. He made $59.[45]

Louis's entrance into the ranks of professional boxing occurred at precisely the time when the sport had reached its lowest ebb and seemed an unlikely field for a poor African American heavyweight desperate for recognition and wealth. If he took any notice of Max Schmeling's career, he would have observed that the German ex-champion's string of losses from 1932 to 1934 signaled the decline of boxing in the United States as well as in Germany. In the pit of the Depression, fans turned away from boxing. As boxing writer Wilbur Wood declared in *Ring*, "the customer cannot eat a boxing glove. . . . As long as a man has only enough to keep him alive by watching his pennies, he is not going to give much thought to watching two lads knock each other around in the ring." Constantly looking backward to the era of Dempsey and his spectacular record of five "Million-Dollar" gates, promoters worried that boxing was on the way out. While Germans bemoaned the fate of their top heavyweight prospect, American fight fans increasingly saw the dismal heavyweight picture that Schmeling symbolized as symptomatic of a deeply flawed sport and society.[46]

While ordinary men had difficulty fulfilling their role as breadwinners, the heavyweight division, which supposedly decided the strongest man in the world, proved unable to put up a powerful male hero for very long. Boxing champions of only modest ability and limited stature turned over with depressing rapidity, and in fights whose outcomes, boxing experts and fans agreed, were fixed in advance. The first disputed outcome was Schmeling's title victory in 1930, followed thereafter by his loss to Sharkey in 1932. It seemed to many boxing fans and observers that American boxing officials made sure that Sharkey won in order to dethrone an unpopular and inactive champion. Charges of fraud in subsequent championships abounded. After Sharkey lost the title to Primo Carnera, observers again charged that the fight was fixed. The Italian giant was then beaten by Max Baer, who quickly lost the crown to James J. Braddock, a beloved champion in the Depression but one who did not defend the title for two years. During this period, historian Jeffrey

Sammons notes, wrestling, with all its fakery, surpassed boxing because it had what boxing now lacked: "drama, action, and glamorous heroes and villains."[47]

The six-foot six-inch, 260-pound Primo Carnera epitomized the problem. A carnival strongman of average skills, the Italian boxer was discovered in 1928 by an American boxing establishment desperate for heavyweight gate attractions. From the start, fans wondered, "Is Carnera really a fighter, or is he a freak?" His only quality opponent was Young Stribling, and their two fights ended on fouls, with each fighter winning one of the matches. It was his size, not his boxing skill, that desperate boxing managers and promoters hoped would turn him into a popular draw. When he came to the United States in 1930, Carnera's career was overseen by William Duffy and Walter Friedman, front men for mobsters Owney Madden, the owner of the Cotton Club, and Dutch Schultz, the beer baron of the Bronx. With the mob behind him, Carnera went through a series of setups and fixed fights. Most of his knockouts, noted a reporter, "have been of a very suspicious character and it is understood . . . that the result of many of his bouts was prearranged." The California and New York state boxing commissions had suspended him, but when prospects for a big box office title match arose against Jack Sharkey, the New York State Athletic Commission reversed itself, making a mockery of government regulation of the sport.[48]

The Carnera-Sharkey title match was set for June 1933. Because of the suspicion of fraud and criminal influence, only 10,000 fans turned out for the bout, which Carnera won with a dubious punch. Carnera defended the title twice, the first match drawing only 8,624 fans and grossing a disappointing $44,598. In his second defense he was knocked down eleven times by Max Baer in 1934. Many fans believed that the sport could not sink much lower. Carnera's many "suspicious" fights led fans to conclude that boxing, like American business, was rigged, and only money mattered to the ruthless gangsters and greedy promoters who ran the fight game. Max Baer, Carnera's successor, proved only a slightly better draw at the box office because he embodied the failed consumer values of the twenties. "He made wisecracks and went to parties," noted one observer, and he could not stay out of nightclubs or away from showgirls. Boxing's low point paralleled the cultural and political malaise of the early 1930s. Crooked managers and fixed fights subverted fair play and honest sportsmanship. Champions seemed hollow.[49]

While the poor reputation of the sport and lack of fan interest might have discouraged Louis from pursuing a professional career and Schmeling from launching a comeback, there was a much bigger obstacle that young Louis would have to overcome if he were to seriously contend for the heavyweight championship. This was the blatant racial segregation of the heavyweight division and the extensive discrimination against all black fighters in American boxing. When Roxborough and Black first approached him about training

Louis, Jack Blackburn was skeptical about any black heavyweight's chances. "You know boy," he told Joe, "the heavyweight division for a Negro is hardly likely. The white man ain't too keen on it. You have to really be something to get anywhere." The key to the problem, as Blackburn explained it, was the legacy of Jack Johnson, the only African American to hold the heavyweight title. "White man hasn't forgotten that fool nigger with his white women, acting like he owned the world." According to Blackburn's vast experience, the deck was stacked against all black fighters since white men ran the boxing world in the United States. In his own career Blackburn had seen black fighters get a shot with a real contender only "to make the white fighters look good. They let you put up a good fight, but you dare not better [sic] look better than some of the worst white boxers you were supposed to be fighting." Often, in fact, white promoters and managers would allow a black fighter a good fight, but he had to promise to throw the match. This was the only way for a black fighter to make a buck. As a result of these practices, black boxers usually found it difficult to get title bouts, and their reputations did not stand very high. They ended up having to fight each other in an unofficial Negro boxing circuit.[50]

Blackburn's experience was accurate. When most whites in Louis's day thought of black heavyweights, Jack Johnson, the first black heavyweight to win the title, came immediately to mind as the "Black Menace" who defied the segregation of sports in American life. When he wrested the title from Tommy Burns in Australia in 1908, his success precipitated a crisis that revealed the white supremacist nature of the sport. Never as fully segregated as professional team sports, boxing nevertheless was an arena where white manhood dominated unfairly. From John L. Sullivan in 1882, white heavyweight champions refused to allow black contenders to battle for the crown, signaling the onset of segregation in all areas of American sports. This represented a change from the early period of boxing. The first real, though unacknowledged, American heavyweight champion was Tom Molineaux, who was born in slavery in Virginia. He went to England, claiming the American championship, where he fought two losing battles with the British champion Tom Crib in 1810 and 1811. In this era when Americans frowned on boxing as a brutal, aristocratic, and un-American sport, Molineaux's fellow citizens paid his matches no heed and being designated champion meant very little. When black Australian Peter Jackson challenged Sullivan to put his title on the line in 1891, the racial situation in the United States had changed. During the 1880s and 1890s, slavery was gone, Reconstruction was over, and whites now feared that black people did not know their proper place. In sports as diverse as baseball, horse racing, and prizefighting, where black athletes had participated on an equal basis, whites drew the color line to reinforce the inferior position of African Americans. Jackson had managed to fight white contenders. In his most notable match, he fought a sixty-one-round draw with Jim

Corbett, despite an injured leg. But fearing defeat at Jackson's hands, and concerned that few fans would pay to see a racially mixed match anyway, Sullivan drew the color line. After Corbett beat Sullivan for the championship, he too refused a return match with Jackson. While blacks in the lesser weights still managed to contend for titles, the heavyweight crown was now reserved for white men.[51]

The heavyweight division remained segregated until 1908, when Canadian heavyweight Tommy Burns, having been chased all the way to Australia, agreed to meet Jack Johnson for the crown. For an audience dominated by the white working class, boxing elevated poor white men to full manhood while excluding blacks whom they considered less than full men, morally weak, and physically and sexually indulgent. Moreover, the white public would not pay to see black men fight, so white champions, as in Sullivan's case, were reluctant to risk their crowns when so little money was at stake. Fans believed that prizefighting embodied the Anglo-Saxon virtues of individual will, aggression, and conquest, and they had contempt for the humiliation of submission. With physical superiority considered a sign of racial supremacy, most whites saw Johnson's crown as a threat to Caucasian racial and national prestige, and demanded that a "White Hope" defend the honor of the race. In an era of Social Darwinism, it was assumed that the strongest male individual represented the best race. If a black man won, then the white race had lost.[52]

The desperate cries for a savior of the white race spurred former champion Jim Jeffries to come out of retirement to meet Jack Johnson on July 4, 1910, in Reno, Nevada. As a band played "All Coons Look Alike to Me," the two fighters entered the ring. In a bout promoted as a racial test, Johnson completely outclassed the over-the-hill Jeffries. The champion talked, jeered, and smiled for fourteen rounds before knocking out the ex-champion in the fifteenth round. Not only did the press publish the astonishing news that a black fighter had completely dominated a standard bearer of the white race, they highlighted stories of race riots that broke out all over the country. In Uvalda, Georgia, for example, a white gang shot at blacks celebrating at a construction camp outside town. Three African Americans died and five were wounded. In Houston, Texas, a white man slashed the throat of a man who cheered Johnson's victory too loudly. Meanwhile, thirty people were hurt in a race riot in Pueblo, Colorado, a black man was beaten to death in New York City, and in Washington, D. C., blacks fatally stabbed two whites. Local and federal officials quickly blamed films of the bout for provoking the race riots, leading Congress to ban fight films to prevent subsequent violence and future depictions of black triumph over white manliness that might undermine the myth of white superiority. In attempting to enjoy the fruits of victory, moreover, Johnson continued to challenge other racial and sexual taboos. Not a retiring man, the champion married several white women, had affairs with many others, and owned a celebrated black and tan cabaret in Chicago, the

Café de Champion, where whites and blacks mingled freely. He was also known for driving luxurious cars at great rates of speed, paying no heed to speed limits or the admonitions of the police. With male honor, white women, and "civilization" at stake, he was indicted under the Mann Act, designed to punish individuals who took women across the state line for immoral purposes, forced into exile, and swindled out of his title.[53]

All black heavyweights, as Louis found out, labored under the color line that was re-imposed after Johnson's defeat by Jess Willard in 1915 under the blazing Havana sun. More important, the color line shaped the entire world of Anglo-American boxing. To avoid stimulating black unrest in the Empire, for example, Great Britain's Home Office responded to Johnson's desire to fight in London by banning all interracial bouts. In the United States, the new champion Jess Willard vowed not to allow any black boxer to fight for the title. Tex Rickard, promoter of the "White Hope" fight, was deeply disturbed by his contribution to the post-fight racial violence and worried about renewed efforts by moralists and reformers at the state and federal level to ban prizefighting. In charge of Madison Square Garden events throughout the 1920s, he used his monopoly over heavyweight boxing to enforce the color bar. This policy ensured that black contenders would not meet white champions in contests that implied racial equality.[54]

With the removal of the "Black Menace," boxing officials were in a position to make American boxing a mass spectator sport that enjoyed huge box offices during the 1920s. Even more than in Germany, American boxing rose from its semi-legal status to popular culture legitimacy after World War I. By racially cleansing the heavyweight title, Rickard and Madison Square Garden were in a better position to tap the drawing power of champion Jack Dempsey, one of the sport's most ferocious punchers. With the racial menace gone, Rickard made it safe for women to attend matches, which in turn elevated the tone of the largely male audience and made the sport more acceptable to a mass audience. Among other things, Rickard created a P. T. Barnum-like ballyhoo to publicize matches in the press and bring the sport to the heights of commercialization. In an era that glorified the revolt against "the feminization of American culture," the primitive Manassa Mauler drew crowds with his wild rushes and ferocious knockout power. Like Schmeling, Dempsey fought several international title matches. His bout with the Frenchman Georges Carpentier in 1921 produced the first million-dollar gate, while his battle against the Argentine Luis Firpo in 1923 also drew more than a million dollars at the box-office. Dempsey's fights with Gene Tunney in 1926 and 1927, in which he lost his title and then failed to regain it, set the all-time mark for gate receipts at close to $2,658,660. In another parallel to Schmeling, Dempsey became a celebrity, married a movie star, opened a famous Broadway restaurant, and was exalted in circles high and low. The heyday of American boxing, however, was based on the exclusion of black heavyweight contenders. In the United States, the "strongest man in the world" had to be white.[55]

As a case in point, Rickard barred Dempsey from defending his title against his main challenger, the African American Harry Wills. Although *Ring* called Wills "a clean athlete, a splendid sportsman, a boxer of high ideals who has proved himself a credit to the game and to his race," whenever his name came up race-conscious white promoters worried that he would turn into another Jack Johnson. When the African fighter Battling Siki defeated Georges Carpentier in 1923 for the light heavyweight title, he too brought to mind the danger of the Black Menace. Siki attracted tremendous attention in the United States because he socialized with French women, went everywhere with a pet lion, and was celebrated by the French public. He thus earned a reputation as both a savage and an international playboy. American promoters worried that he, like Carpentier, might move up in weight to challenge Dempsey for the title. Fearful of a global racial crisis, white Americans warned France that Siki's victories might cause their colonial subjects to lose respect for white men. In this atmosphere, white foreigners like Max Schmeling, Primo Carnera, and Paolino Uzcudun proved more acceptable candidates for the heavyweight title after Gene Tunney retired in 1928 than African American George Godfrey, whom *Ring* ironically called "the current black menace." As the bible of boxing declared, "Godfrey may be the best heavyweight in the world, but it is unlikely that he will be given an opportunity to prove it. He will have to struggle along as did Sam Langford and some others in the past, contenting himself with crumbs from the heavyweight table." In American boxing, race trumped nation.[56]

As Joe Louis turned professional and Max Schmeling attempted to come back from defeat, humiliation, and depression in 1934, they faced a sport that appeared down for the count. Despite its problems, however, boxing may have been down, but it was not out. By the mid-1930s a hunger arose for populist male heroes capable of challenging the corruption of the sport. As fans soon learned, changes were under way that would spark a revival on both sides of the Atlantic.

2

COMING OFF THE CANVAS:
THE RENAISSANCE OF BOXING
IN THE GREAT DEPRESSION

> In the midst of national Depression, in the thick
> of problems of national and international im-
> port and vexation, boxing just HAD to bring
> out a man like Louis, or go into hibernation.
> Louis was produced and today boxing interest
> is at a fever pitch.
>
> *Ring*, November 1941

On the evening of June 25, 1935, less than a year after his professional debut, Joe Louis fought ex-champion Primo Carnera in Yankee Stadium in a non-title bout that African American journalist Roi Ottley declared "had the competitive glamour and romance of a David-and-Goliath sort." Fifty-seven thousand boxing fans paid $340,000 to watch the match, puny totals when compared to the million-dollar gates of the Dempsey-Tunney years, but much higher even than recent title bouts. As Ottley put it, the fight "brought forth a youngster who looks like a real champion" and raised Joe Louis to national attention. The night proved memorable in other ways: the match transformed Louis into a black hero and heralded the revival of big-time boxing in the United States.[1]

Just as Louis's match with the giant Italian heralded a rebirth of American boxing, across the Atlantic German boxing was enjoying its own renaissance. As Joe Louis tore up local arenas in his first year of professional fighting, a seemingly washed-up Max Schmeling began to show his old form.

Knocking out opponents once again, he fought himself back into heavyweight title contention in 1934 and 1935 just as the Nazi Party took over Germany and turned its attention to boxing as an arena where Germany could shine in international competition. Eager to showcase a purified and revitalized nation under their leadership, the National Socialists emphasized that boxing held a special place in creating a new German man and a new Nazi culture. While German sports fans began paying attention, the question began to occur to Americans too: could the veteran German slugger and former champion prove the world wrong and successfully come back and regain his crown? As early as summer 1935 sportswriters speculated that the two heavyweights would have to fight each other.

One thing was sure: the success of American boxing rode on the shoulders of a black youngster who had come out of nowhere to contend for the crown. In just one year of professional boxing, the unbeaten Louis fought twenty-three times, winning twenty-one by knockout. His sensational rise and deadly power set the fistic firmament ablaze and established him at the remarkable age of twenty-one as a serious contender for the heavyweight throne. For the first of many times, *Ring* magazine declared Louis the Fighter of the Year, rating his achievements more important than those of the current heavyweight champion, James J. Braddock. As a black sports columnist noted, "The imposing figure of Fistiana's new superman, Joe Louis, stands out in bold relief in the shadows of the sinking sun of the gratifying sports renaissance of 1935." In fact, "Louis came as a modern Moses to lead the manly art out of the depression to a new 'high.'" Not only did he bring "a new era of interracial goodwill," he also brought "boxing back on a big time basis and the million-dollar gate." That a black fighter carried the future of boxing in his gloves suggests that major changes were afoot in American life. That his fate lay intertwined with Schmeling's suggests how important international factors were in the sporting world of the 1930s.[2]

Louis's string of victories in less than one year astounded boxing circles. "Just consider what this extraordinary colored youth has achieved in a professional career of less than nine months!" *Ring* magazine exclaimed. Writing in May 1935 just before the Carnera fight, Nat Fleischer recounted his achievements. Only four of his seventeen victims managed to last ten rounds with him, while the others went "out like snuffed candles under a two-handed bombardment that shattered their defenses beyond repair." Moreover, there were no set-ups or soft fights, which was astonishing, "for whoever heard of a colored boxer fighting his way upward being handed any 'soft' gifts between the ropes by philanthropic promoters?" Like Bob Fitzsimmons and Sam Langford, "the new colored sensation can shock an opponent into oblivion with either left or right." Indeed, Louis knocked out contenders such as Charlie Massara, Lee Ramage, Patsy Perroni, and Hans Berkie to rank as "the fistic sensation of the day!" These were no pushovers, either. Ramage had fought fifty-two times since 1929 and had once defeated former light heavyweight champion Maxie Rosenbloom, yet Louis easily beat him twice. Knocked out by the African American boxer's dynamite right hand in the first bout, Ramage attempted to stay away from Louis's right in the rematch, but "it was a dynamite-laden left that crashed" on his chin and "outed him cold in the second round." Fleischer was so impressed that he declared Louis a shoo-in for the title. "That is, provided he manages to hurdle the obstacles of hostility which history shows us have ever blocked the paths of Negro fighters aiming for a championship goal."[3]

After a year of constant fighting in arenas from Chicago to Los Angeles, Louis earned his first appearance in New York City. The fight against Primo Carnera, according to Roi Ottley, "marked a dramatic highlight in the race's march along the glory road." A "Negro born of poverty-stricken parents in the cotton patches of Alabama and a few short months away from the assembly line of Ford's Detroit factory" fought Carnera, the "massive Italian gladiator standing six feet five inches." This was Louis's first fight in New York City, his "acid test as a pugilist," and it propelled him to national attention. His opponent, a seasoned former champion, "looked very much like a grizzled gangster capable of handily beating anyone." Initially, blacks gave the bout little attention. Discouraged and rendered cynical and apathetic by the Depression, few African Americans saw the young Detroiter as anything more than a "run-of-the mill fighter despite the publicity lavished on him." Even Jack Johnson questioned his ability.[4]

As the fight neared, however, blacks began to pay attention. Some rooted for Louis because he was fighting an Italian, and the match took place as fascist Italy prepared to invade independent Ethiopia, the only African nation not colonized by a European power. For the many black Americans who had begun organizing in opposition to Mussolini's designs, Carnera symbolized white European imperialism and racial supremacy. Other African Americans, however, focused on the fact that Louis's opponent was a giant white man. Whatever their views, all blacks according to Ottley "joined in his corner because he was a *Negro!*" Indeed, the combination of domestic and international racial symbolism gave the bout a political dimension that boxing rarely attained. By stressing the theme of David and Goliath, the black press turned Louis into a battler against colonial oppression abroad and white supremacy at home. "Lots of black groups came up to camp telling me that I represented Ethiopia," Louis noted. "They talked to me about Marcus Garvey, who I hadn't even heard of. . . . They put a heavy weight on my twenty-year-old shoulders. Now, not only did I have to beat the man, but I had to beat him for a cause." In response to the bout's symbolic nature, black communities everywhere seethed with excitement, Ottley noted, but Harlem was on edge. Just months before, a riot had broken out in New York's black community, ravaged by the

Depression and angered over the alleged beating of a black boy by white police. As a result, despite hot and sultry weather, the black community adjacent to Yankee Stadium remained indoors glued to its radios. "From every apartment and tavern window, from every candy store and barber shop, shadows of Negroes could be seen in various anxious poses, many rigidly hunched over the instruments that would bring the news," recalled Ottley. The streets were deserted. "The atmosphere was tense, expectant, thrilling!"[5]

The atmosphere was tense for the boxing world too. This was also the first big money mixed-race fight since Harry Wills fought Luis Firpo in 1924, and the fight's publicists missed no opportunity to trumpet the themes of international and racial conflict. Concerned that these issues would cause renewed racial violence between blacks and Italian Americans, several white columnists demanded the cancellation of the racially mixed bout. Arthur Brisbane, Hearst's highest paid columnist, predicted that violence could erupt because the fight between "an American colored man and an Italian comes at a time when the Abyssinian question creates feeling between Italians and Negroes in New York." To allay these concerns, extra police stood guard around and outside the stadium. Mindful of possible trouble, ring announcer

The Harlem crowd celebrates after Louis annihilated former champion and Italian giant Primo Carnera on June 25, 1935, in Yankee Stadium. In a match that had racial and international implications, Louis became an African American folk hero. (Acme, Library of Congress)

Harry Balogh asked the crowd "in the name of American sportsmanship . . . that the thought in your mind and the feeling in your heart be that, regardless of race, creed, or color, let us all say, may the better man emerge victorious."[6]

Once the fight started, Louis, standing 6' 1-1/2" and weighing 200 pounds, quickly proved he was the dominant force in the heavyweight division. For five rounds the young David cut and slashed the Italian Goliath, who stood almost four inches taller and sixty pounds heavier, working on the taller man as if he were chopping down a tree. When the "Man Mountain" tried to man-handle his smaller opponent, Louis amazed the crowd with his strength by throwing the larger man off of him. In the sixth and fatal round, he smashed Carnera to the canvas three times. "Each blow was delivered with the flash of a cobra's strike; each time the two-hundred-and-sixty-pound mammoth crashed to the floor, his battered face smeared with streaming blood; and each time he gamely rose." After the third time Carnera was groggy and help-less and the referee stopped the fight. At that Harlem let go with a terrific roar. Unable to contain themselves, men, women, and children streamed into the streets. "They seemed to come from every doorway and basement, shout-ing with joy . . . 'Yeah, man!' . . . 'What a man!' . . . 'He's a killer-diller!'" Thousands of black people marched through the streets, slapping backs, shak-ing hands, and congratulating each other, while youngsters pounded dish-pans and yelled for their new hero: "We want Joe! We want Joe!" To the music of jukeboxes blaring from every bar and café, young couples broke into furious Lindy Hops and Susy Q's. The celebrating lasted all night. With this fight, a national race hero was born. Black communities that had teetered on the edge of despair now found someone to root for. Equally important, box-ing in the United States seemed reborn.[7]

While the fight held special meaning for African Americans, white fans paid attention too. "As has not always been the case where great colored fighters were concerned," declared *Ring*, "a multitude of white fistic followers sing the praises of the new star," and they came out in numbers that had not been seen during the previous five years. Three months later, after a summer of con-vincing victories—especially over a frightened Kingfish Levinsky in Chicago—Louis trounced Max Baer, another ex-champion, in a manner that propelled him to the top of the list of contenders for the heavyweight crown. In van-quishing both Carnera and then Baer in quick succession, Louis also blasted away some of the criminality and money-lust that had undermined the image of boxing. His victories raised widespread hopes for the revitalization of the sport. He was "not a monstrosity like the Italian he defeated, nor a play-actor like the dancing Baer, nor a colorless plodder like the champion of the mo-ment," sportswriters declared. Louis was different. He fought "with a serious and primitive thoroughness which awed the crowd." In many ways, he swept away the boxing doldrums. "Here was a heavyweight fighter who fought as champions used to fight when champions were worthy of the title," declared white sportswriter Richards Vidmer. Others called him "the Perfect Fistic Machine." While Carnera's bouts were phony and he defied all training rules, "Louis has never been out of training." He did not "smoke, drink, or chew," and "no athlete has come nearer living the ideal athletic life." Clean living and manly, declared white sports columnist George Clarens, Louis "intends to be a credit to his race and to his new profession." Given his punching power and box office draw, Clarens noted, "the color line has not been drawn."[8]

Louis's dramatic arrival on the national scene with his devastating knockouts over Primo Carnera and Max Baer, however, raised fears that a new "Black Menace" threatened the white supremacy that lay like a sodden blanket over the heavyweight division. Beating white men in the ring connoted more than a sporting victory. Rather, it placed black men on equal footing with white men and gave them the opportunity to assert their superiority in one of the few areas of American life open to them. Few whites looked forward to the return of Jack Johnson who had challenged white supremacy in and out of the ring with his taunting smile and penchant for white women and the fast life. Before the Carnera match, Grantland Rice, dean of American sportswriters, declared if Louis won, "there will again be the nation-wide argument that Jack Johnson and later Harry Wills stirred up." Afterward, noted Richards Vidmer, alarmists recalled Jack Johnson and "how the crown fell into disrepute through his activities outside the ring." They noted "what a bad example he set the Negro race while he sat upon the throne, and the criticism that was heaped upon him." In recalling the white hope hysteria, some whites in and out of the boxing world warned against giving another Negro a chance at the crown. While many white Americans saw the issue as moral and racial, boxing insiders feared that if another black champion appeared, moralists and reformers would have all the ammunition they needed to outlaw the sport, especially if mixed-race fights led to racial violence or racial rebellion. In this atmosphere, the common assumption remained that the heavyweight championship should be reserved for white men.[9]

The fact that Louis made his way by beating white fighters to their knees touched on deep-seated white American fears. Describing how Louis destroyed Max Baer in "a public pole-axing," for example, white columnist Paul Gallico noted that when his victim could no longer stand, "he bent his neck to his destroyer, bowed his knee and there remained." Louis's power was so deadly that white reporters feared he represented the rise of a strange black force, rooted in the primitive jungle, that threatened white civilization. In his nationally syndicated column, Davis J. Walsh declared that "something sly and sinister and perhaps not quite-human came out of the African Jungle," to obliterate Carnera. The jungle imagery was common. Grantland Rice described Louis as "the bush-master of the North American continent," stalking his prey "as the Black Panther of the jungle." Louis was not a rational creature equal to white men, but instead owed his success to "the instinctive speed of the wild." Davis recognized the stakes: "Africa, the dark continent, was ready to revel at the slightest notice over this amazing person who has arisen overnight to challenge and defy the white man's innate sense of superiority."[10]

Even admiring sportswriters noted that one of Louis's greatest strengths was "the savage streak in him that makes him a fearsome, even a disturbing figure in the ring." To offset his fearsome power and the rebellious potential it signified, white columnists and cartoonists also depicted Louis as a "darkie" figure out of blackface minstrelsy: he loved to sleep, devoured fried chicken, spoke in dialect, and had a "kinky head." They might be attracted to the power of Louis and even the efficient and at times poetic way he moved in the ring, but they found it difficult to accept Louis as the equal of white boxers. Their portraits of him emphasized that he was a creature of the body and an animal of the jungle, although it would have been hard to find many intellectual giants among the white heavyweights either. In addition, most white sportswriters could not mention Louis without reference to his race: "colored clouter," "tan tornado," "Dark Destroyer," and of course, "Brown Bomber." Most white cartoonists depicted him as a simple, slow, colored boy suitable for the cotton fields rather than the ring.[11]

Yet even as a contender, a large portion of the black and white press found much to admire in Louis, portraying him as the complete fighter, a smart and accomplished boxer as well as a stereotypical natural killer. This moved Louis beyond the traditional categories for American fighters. As boxing scholar Gerald Early asserts, white boxers usually assumed the republican image of the honest hard-worker, while black fighters were considered slick tricksters, good at defense and speed, able to hit and run but never standing toe to toe and mixing it up like real men. But Louis could box as well as punch, which caught Nat Fleischer's eye. "There is nothing of the flashily colorful style of boxer about him, nothing of the swift stab and get away, dazzling feinting, dancing footwork with which an agile mitt-handler sometimes draws admiring tributes to his cleverness." Yet, he "is clever in a far more deadly fashion." In Fleischer's estimate, Louis "belongs to the fighter-boxer type that wastes no time in desultory sparring or skipping around a ring with acrobatic activity, but makes every shot tell."[12]

In addition, Louis seemed the hard-working hick from the West and challenged representations of black boxers as bodies without minds. To be a good boxer one had to train hard and study one's craft in a serious way. Fleischer argued that "in the contest between Primo and Louis, we had on view everything that could be expected in good boxing, brainy headwork, unexcelled feinting, snappy short jolts, long, overhand, looping jolts and a defense that was beautiful." Louis won through "a masterly presentation of scientific boxing and clouting such as has not been seen in an American ring since Dempsey was in his prime." Louis fought with a plan, waiting to unleash his "cave-man

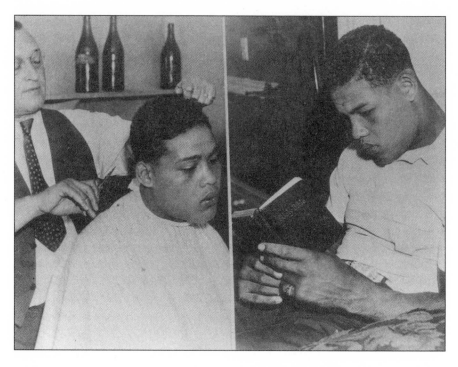

Joe Louis reading the Bible and getting cleaned up as part of the campaign to make him a model Negro athlete in direct opposition to Jack Johnson. (Associated Press, Library of Congress)

instinct until he saw his opening." Spectators watched "a cold, calculating young man who had just reached his majority" cutting down a giant in front of him. For every derogatory image of Louis in the white press, there emerged a portrait of him as a black producer hero, a figure of common decency and fair play.[13]

Many observers also noted that Louis was a hybrid hero, similar to many other such icons during the Great Depression. Not only did he combine boxing and punching, brain and brawn; his racial identity was also open to debate. Over the years, a number of boxing commentators described him as black, white, and Cherokee, a light-skinned "Brown Bomber," not a "Black Menace." Raising questions about racial definitions, Louis's silent and stony face, his "dead pan," while disturbing to white reporters, made it clear that he was absolutely calm in the ring as he laid claim to a key element of democratic citizenship and equality—self-possession and self-control. Newspaper photos and cartoons showed Louis in a common pose. Standing in a neutral corner after a knockdown, his arms stretched across the top strand of the ropes, he appeared calm, cool, and collected, wearing his "poker face," as he waited to go back into the fray. His modest, hard-working image allowed many white men to identify with him inside the ring. Louis could express some of their fury and the desire to destroy a corrupt civilization that had no use for their manhood.[14]

To offset white fears and break the color line required a good deal of ingenuity and skill. This was not something that Louis could achieve alone. In fact, his all-black managerial team played a critical role in carefully guiding him to the top, while also crafting a public mask for him to wear. Having all-black handlers, designated as Louis's Brain Trust by the press, proved critical to his success. For one thing, the activities of John Roxborough, Julian Black, and Jack Blackburn received a good deal of attention in the white sporting world. Just as Louis stood out as an anomaly, so did they. Calling them a Brain Trust acknowledged the intellectual and strategic abilities of some black people, at least. Even if many whites had doubts about Louis's intelligence, they could not miss the cleverness of his handlers. For another thing, having a black management team proved a source of pride in the black community. As a letter to the *Pittsburgh Courier* put it, "To my mind the finest thing about Joe Louis is the fact that he has a colored manager, and his whole working staff is made up of colored men." The team, the author of the letter emphasized, shows that "the colored man has the same ability as the white man." Together, Louis's management maneuvered the young sensation into position to contend for the championship and to overcome the color barrier that stood in his way. They also became part of his enduring image as a representative of racial progress.[15]

Louis's managers stood out in a world where whites controlled boxing. Except for their color, Roxborough and Black might have been successful mainstream business or professional men instead of numbers kingpins. Louis represented their opportunity to make a lot of money and put a black man atop the sporting hierarchy. The Brown Bomber's trainer, Jack Blackburn, had seen his alcoholism and violence lead to a manslaughter conviction that ended his lightweight boxing career at its peak. This was his chance to steer a surrogate son of his own color to the title he never had, and to that end he poured all of his ring knowledge into Joe. To convince Louis that he would be better off with an African American team, Roxborough reminded him that black boxers who signed with white managers found that these managers were only interested in the money and not their fighters' proper development. As Louis later recalled, "Mr. Roxborough was talking about Black Power before it became popular." Never before had black managers guided a black fighter into such prominence in the sport. Traditionally black managers had to beg for lucrative bouts, were in no position to hold out if the offered fee was below par, and usually had to hire white managers to advance in the rankings. Many of the matches were fixed; black managers and fighters had few choices because they needed to eat. This meant that African American fighters might start to rise but then had to fall. Louis's managers, however, demonstrated that they were able to compete equally with boxing's white businessmen.[16]

Because of their business skill and underworld connections, Roxborough and Black could fend off the rapacious demands of white promoters and managers, hold out for a percentage of the gate higher than challengers usually received, and refuse to fight in preliminary bouts. As kingpins of the numbers rackets in Detroit and Chicago, as well as investors in many black businesses, Black and Roxborough knew how to maneuver in a world of sharks. To fight in Detroit, for example, Roxborough encountered pressure by the head of the Michigan State Boxing Commission and several white fight managers tied to the Purple Gang to take on white co-managers or risk the possibility that Joe would never get another fight in Michigan. Roxborough refused and the group backed down. Similarly, Roxborough and Black used their ties with Chicago's mob to prevent attempts by New York's powerful Owney Madden mob to cut in on their control over their fighter. As Louis wrote angrily years later, "Those white people couldn't stand to see a black on the rise, and if you were moving up, they wanted a piece of you for free." Yet his Brain Trust made sure to ally themselves with white men like promoter Mike Jacobs, who would further their own designs. "Good business knows no race."[17]

Piloting a racial outsider to the world heavyweight title was a tricky operation "that took all of our combined experience and skill," Roxborough later recalled. "We knew we had a coming champion in Joe but we also realized that big barriers had to be overcome before he could get his chance." To successfully transcend white hostility toward black heavyweights, Louis's handlers consciously molded him into a black boxer acceptable to whites and the black middle class. Because there were so few black public figures, Louis's individual flaws would reflect badly on the entire race. "A colored fighter's got to be lots better than the other man if he's gonna go places," Blackburn told him. "But you gotta have more than just two good hands. You gotta do the right thing. And never leave yourself open so people can talk about you." His handlers instructed Louis on how to live his life to avoid becoming a second Jack Johnson, and they refused to hire Johnson as Louis's trainer because they wanted to develop Joe into "a clean-living champion, the exact opposite of what you've been." Committed to rigorous training, Louis enhanced his image by not smoking or drinking. There were no written rules, but wary of any hint of miscegenation, his managers advised Louis never to go out with a white woman or be photographed alone with one, or go to nightclubs alone. Yet white women were attracted to him. Once after a victory in Chicago, for example, long lines of white women, many with husbands, boyfriends, or fathers nearby, tried to embrace, stroke, and rub up against the virile young fighter. To avoid racial trouble, Roxborough and Black had to watch Joe like hawks. As part of Louis's idealized image, moreover, his press agents stressed that he read the Bible every day and that he followed his mother's stern principles of behavior. Roxborough and Black also hired Russell Cowans, a black sportswriter and college graduate, to tutor the uneducated

Louis in grammar, geography, history, and mathematics. In order to make his way in a white man's game Louis was careful not to openly challenge the racial status quo outside the ring.[18]

In order to channel Louis's powerful sex drive, Roxborough and Black may have urged him to marry Marva Trotter, a respectable young Chicago stenographer, at the age of twenty-one in September 1935. Married to an attractive black woman and seemingly on his best behavior, Louis was able to remove the fears of sexual danger and miscegenation that had destroyed Johnson. By marrying a black woman, the Brown Bomber also demonstrated his racial loyalty to legions of black fans who might otherwise have disapproved of his actions. Despite his image as a devoted husband and family man, however, Louis's idea of marriage was rooted in a double standard. He expected Marva to stay at home, attend to social events, provide a measure of class, and not bother with the important work of men who slugged it out in an all-male environment. To an extent, the demands of constant training and fighting kept the young couple apart. In Louis's day boxers still believed that sex and boxing did not mix. Before a fight a boxer was not supposed to have sexual relations, even with his wife, because it could soften him up before a fight. Since Louis was always in training, there was little room for Marva or family. Jack Blackburn might allow a one-night fling to release tension, but having a wife around on a constant basis was not tolerated.[19]

Inside the ring, his managers also crafted an image at odds with the public perceptions of Johnson. Roxborough and Black urged their fighter not to speak ill of opponents, nor gloat over fallen foes, and certainly not to taunt them as Johnson had done. Instead, he was to conduct himself as a sportsman who obeyed the rules of fair play. His managers taught him to compliment his opponents and never to brag about his victories. "And for God's sake," Roxborough told him, "after you beat a white opponent, don't *smile*." When Blackburn reluctantly agreed to train Louis, he made his young charge agree not to take any easy or fixed fights, and most of all not to rely on a decision of the referees. Aware of the odds stacked against good black prospects, Blackburn told him to always aim for the kill: "Let your fists be the referee." As Blackburn recognized, the only way for a black heavyweight to gain a shot at the title was to fight tough opponents and beat them decisively. From the start, according to *Ring*, "they sent Joe against fighters of far more experience, boxers whom the average managers would have shunted aside for fear that such a bout would have halted Joe's climb." And Louis fought an average of twice a month. Always in training, he was usually safe from trouble. Blackburn had him run five or six miles in the morning, do exercises every afternoon, and spar four times a week. "When in training Joe insisted that all camp rules should be observed by everybody," noted Roxborough. "If he arose at 4 a.m. for roadwork so did the rest of the camp staff. If he went to bed at 10 p.m. he saw that all others did likewise by personally turning out the lights." Unlike Carnera or Baer,

Louis rarely broke training, and he had "nothing but contempt for fixed fights and contempt for those who arranged them." Gamblers knew better than to approach him. The word got around fast that Louis could not be bought and would not "do business" with the underworld. In Louis, sportswriters thus found a man of purpose, decorum, and drive. In an era when white male heroes had fallen off their pedestal, black and white fans and reporters had good reasons to see him as a fitting hero and a credit to his race.[20]

In many ways, though, Louis's image went beyond humility and modesty to include dignity and self-possession. Whether their goals were as exalted as the press saw them, the Brain Trust understood that once he was allowed to fight for and win the championship, whatever the compromises, the precedent of breaking the color line would extend to other areas of life. Roxborough and Black sought to use Louis constructively. He could do "a lot of good" if he became champion and conducted himself so as not to "be a discredit to Negroes." While Louis was supposed to be clean living, his managers had no interest in turning him into an Uncle Tom. As men of power and dignity, they worked assiduously to avoid any hint of the minstrel public image under which most blacks labored. As Louis recalled, "One time we were talking about these little black toy dolls they used to make of fighters. These dolls always had the wide grin with thick red lips. They looked foolish. I got the message—don't look like a fool nigger doll. Look like a black man with dignity." Despite a lack of education and embarrassed silence around white reporters, Louis had a deep sense of pride and self-respect. Just before the Carnera fight, in fact, a white photographer tried to pose Louis with a watermelon. "Louis wouldn't do it. Now nobody told him not to, but instinctively he knew that this was a racist kind of a thing and he wouldn't do it." When they asked him why not, Louis said, "I don't like watermelon," despite the fact that he did. He also refused to pose for a photo that had him taking part in a fake crap game before the World Series of 1935.[21]

Louis's sense of self-esteem did not go unnoticed. The *Philadelphia Tribune* praised his decorum. "He refuses to be a buffoon or a clown," noted an editorial, "to satisfy the elite who believe that all colored people must of necessity be comedians of the lower variety." As a reporter for the *New Republic* put it, "Joe Louis Never Smiles." Indeed, white and black fans and reporters constantly referred to Louis as "dead-pan Joe," or "poker-faced Joe," a man who did not play the clown around whites. "He seems to be all serious side of life, all business," noted *Ring* magazine. In the past, "your Negro battler felt that he had to cater to the white customers, and that the white customers looked for a clown complex in every brown scrapper." But Louis did not clown. He was all business in the ring. His poker face often scared opponents half to death, while the public assumed he was either serious or sullen with a hint of menace and danger.[22]

In the privacy of his training camp, where he worked and lived primarily among other African Americans away from the eyes of the white world, Louis often displayed a sense of humor. He and his sparring partners often joked about sex and race, for example, and to break the monotony of training camp, Joe would indulge in practical jokes. Sometimes he electrically wired up a chair, or faked telephone messages from women. One night Louis and Carl Nelson provoked a loud quarrel with Freddie Wilson, another member of the entourage, in which Nelson pulled his pistol and started shooting, while Wilson ducked for cover. Louis hooted for joy. He and Nelson had contrived the argument and loaded the bodyguard's weapon with blanks. His sense of humor around other blacks suggests that Louis carefully crafted his public presentation of self.[23]

Much of the clean-living image that his managers helped fashion was not a difficult burden for Louis. As his son points out, Louis's upbringing and personality made the new regimen easy to follow. Mrs. Lillie Barrow Brooks reared her son as a strict Baptist, first in Alabama and then in Detroit. The family went to church three times on Sundays. Until Joe was sixteen and a half years old, she did not permit him to play cards, drink, or date. As a result, Joe did not smoke or drink while in his prime, nor did he endorse cigarettes and alcohol products. He was also a quiet and docile child who liked to be alone. His reserved nature around strangers derived from the speech impediment that he never overcame. Later in life, noted his son Joe, Jr., he read the paper every night, thought about things before making a decision, and had an excellent memory. The public may have thought him slow-witted, but noted his son, he was quick and had a dry sense of humor. The speech disability, however, made him ill at ease with strangers, especially white newsmen, and he earned a reputation for sullenness. The ring adage, "I'll let my fists do the talking," carried more weight in Louis's case. Despite those early white portraits of him as lazy, a speaker of dialect, and a man who indulged his love of food, Louis and white reporters gradually grew more at ease with each other and his pithy remarks took on the wisdom of the common man.[24]

The public rarely got to see Louis's lapses, however, because he practiced discretion if not asceticism, and his handlers watched him carefully. These lapses usually involved money and women. As part of his image, Louis was portrayed as a man who saved his money so that he would not die broke as so many other fighters had. Underneath this polished surface, though, Louis was a spender. Having grown up dirt poor, he was an easy touch with his family, his boyhood pals, black congregations and civic organizations, and anyone who asked him for help. In fact, he delighted in helping black people who came to him out of need. When he ran out of money, he asked his promoter for a loan until the next fight, which was granted interest free. While he was winning easily and making money this proved to be no problem, but in his later years, his borrowing and spending would get him into big trouble.

Joe and new wife Marva Trotter greet well wishers the day after their wedding and
the Max Baer fight on September 24, 1935. Married to the respectable and
beautiful Chicago stenographer, Louis enhanced his image as a domesticated family
man. (Library of Congress)

More problematic, Louis was drawn to women and they were drawn to
him. Despite his marriage and his discipline in training, he was on the road so
much of his career that it was easy to find accommodating partners. When he
first fought in New York in 1935, he became acquainted with Harlem entertainment columnist and sportsman Billy Rowe, who introduced him to the
area's hotspots, and from then on whenever Louis was in Harlem, he and
Rowe would make the rounds trolling for women. Throughout his life, in
fact, Louis pursued a host of young smartly dressed, light-skinned women
who worked as singers, showgirls, and chorus girls in cabarets and nightclubs.
Unbeknownst to the public, after a bout, Joe would celebrate by disappearing
for days on end into the black community where he would hole up with his
young lady of choice. As a wealthy, famous, and virile young man, he had his
pick of black women. Like other athletes, he followed a well-worn pattern:
the winner had the choice of women as his prize. Louis, then, not only established the power of black masculinity in the ring but he also demonstrated it
in his constant philandering. The more he made, the more he spent on women,
sometimes setting them up in their own apartments. In Hollywood, he had
affairs with Lena Horne as well as with white actresses Sonja Henie and Lana
Turner. The black press never let on, however, and Louis kept his affairs out

of the public eye. Although he maintained an admirable discretion, eventually these women would cost Louis dearly.[25]

In 1935, however, the future was a long way off, and the public knew little of the Brown Bomber's lapses. Despite white prejudice and condescension, Louis transformed himself into a New Deal-era working class hero, the first black athlete to achieve Galahad status. His handlers had him fight constantly, take on all comers regardless of ethnic background, and advance within the rules of the ring. In this, Louis adopted the hallmark of American sports that many white champions had ignored—one achieved by following the democratic rules of fair play. This led to admiration for his fighting ability and moral character by even those white sportswriters who disparaged him. "As far as I am concerned," declared Davis Walsh, "it seems possible that he's the greatest fighter that ever lived." Many whites supported Louis, noted the *Chicago Defender*, and demands for drawing the color line or finding white hopes to oppose him were muted. Ring experts, the paper found, "don't speak of Joe in the same breath with Jack Johnson," and they emphasized his gentlemanly character "to keep him from running into the race hatred and prejudice that had engulfed the bulk of Race battlers." Jimmy Jones of the *Richmond Times-Dispatch*, for instance, argued that there was no point in drawing the color line. In fact, he "would be far less objectionable . . . than some of our white champions." Admiring white sportswriters argued that character was the key. "Louis was as different from Johnson as Lou Gehrig is from Al Capone." He was "an ambassador of his race," taught by his managers that "the world will judge his brothers through him, and he conducts himself with immaculate care." Given boxing's sordid state, fans welcomed Louis as an idealistic hero who promised to breathe fresh air into the sport. *New Republic* columnist Jonathon Mitchell noted that his character, punching ability, and drawing power might force Madison Square Garden to "yield to a clamor for a 'mixed' fight."[26]

By adopting a respectable image, Louis made it possible for whites and blacks to view his sensational rise as a Horatio Alger success story, but with a Depression and racial twist. Stories about Louis repeatedly traced his spectacular rise from the cotton fields to the top of the boxing profession as an amazing and improbable event. As the *Philadelphia Record* put it, "Mammy Barrow, widowed, in debt, kept her brood together as only mothers of the poor the world over can perform the miracle," until hopeless, "she tore herself away from the homeland and set out sadly for new fields." The family settled in "the humblest section of Detroit." Joe picked cotton as a youth in the South and then carried ice in the Motor City at twelve, dropped out of school, and then worked as a laborer at Ford. The lack of childhood play perhaps "accounts for the seriousness of purpose beyond his 21 years." Now of course, the family was in "green pastures." The devoted son bought his mother a house and paid for his sisters' educations. To quote *Ring*, "a grand piano for the girls. A radio. . . . Carpets on the floor, easy chairs in which to sit, good pictures on the wall." As a former cotton picker and factory laborer, Louis was somebody with whom working people could identify as an under-dog. He had escaped from economic slavery and hit the big time through his physical abilities. At the same time, he fought fairly against opponents from every ethnic group America had to offer. Anyone who thought he could beat Joe was welcome to step up and take a chance.[27]

While Louis could be seen as a working-class hero, his race made his rags-to-riches story unique since whites had recognized few black success sto-ries heretofore. In the middle of the Depression, Louis represented the most forgotten of the forgotten Americans. The rise to riches and fame might tes-tify to the beneficence of American society, but it was clear to many people that he had to overcome tremendous obstacles and a racially stacked deck. It was his fighting power, the "dynamite" in his fists, that carried the day and helped him beat his enemies in the ring and in society. Most important, he did not rise alone. As historian Robert McElvaine argues, Depression-era popular culture valorized those who embodied cooperative rather than ac-quisitive individualism. Everyone in boxing understood that Louis was not a lone hero but part of a team along with the "Brain Trust" that oversaw his development and created the plan for his fights. Money was involved, but so too was the idea of creating a black champion. As *Ring* noted, "Louis seems to be a Negro fighter with a race mission—the winning of the heavyweight title." On this point, the publicity of "the Louis bloc" was clear. Louis represented more than his own success. As Louis told the *Philadelphia Tribune*, he had "a mission to perform"—to win the title "in a manner that will be a credit to my race." He was an ambassador of his race, designed to convey the best impres-sion of his people in order to better their chances in the United States. That he served his people meant he was a "people's champion." Finally, as the Alger tale made clear, "Louis is a Negro fighter with a family mission—the winning of a sufficient sum of money to make the Barrow clan" independent of "vicissitudes of fortune and time." Hence, his seriousness of purpose, his dedication to his task, and his drive to succeed were part of a larger quest beyond himself.[28]

Both blacks and whites appreciated him as an "ambassador" of his race. In 1935 the NAACP's *Crisis* printed a picture of Joe and Jesse Owens on its cover entitled, "Owens and Louis, Our Ambassadors." Although Roy Wilkins, the journal's editor, would have preferred black intellectuals, artists, scien-tists, and political activists as role models, he was aware that the success of Louis and Owens "aided materially in altering the usual appraisal of Negroes by the rank and file of the American public." Athletes held "the solution of the race problem in their hands." In the black community, the success of one individual did not belong "only to him," noted Roi Ottley, "but to the whole race." African Americans believed that "achievement by a Negro breaks down

Joe Louis and Jesse Owens, model athletes and ambassadors of the race. Many middle-class African Americans hoped that athletes such as Joe and Jesse would overcome white hostility toward the race and create greater interracial harmony. (Acme, Library of Congress)

the prevailing opinions of the Negro's inferiority." Ruby Berkley Goodwin, a contributor to the black newspaper the *Los Angeles Sentinel*, agreed. She wrote Louis that her four sons, like "every Negro lad in America," were "bragging" about him. "Don't fail them. Keep both your life and your fighting clean. Now, Joe, don't let us down. It's really pathetic the way we've been humiliated and sold out as a race." She expressed her confidence in him, but warned

him to avoid temptation, "whether wrapped up in a bottle or a skirt," by "thinking of the million little brown and black boys who want to be just like Joe
Louis." Others in the black press commended his humility and modesty despite his success. The *Pittsburgh Courier*'s Chez Washington, for example,
noted that Louis "has won the respect of both races and he intends to maintain that respect by clean fighting and clean living." White writers often treated
Louis fairly. As *Ring* noted, should Louis take the crown, "he will carry his
laurels in a manner befitting a respected citizen." Initially, Louis paid at least
lip service to the idea of serving as a racial ambassador. In doing so, he "reflects the acute social consciousness of the generation to which he belongs,"
noted black historian C. L. R. James. He was not just a boxer but also "a social
figure, someone whose actions can harm the struggle of Negroes for their
fully democratic rights. In that sense he feels he is a genuine 'representative'
of the Negro people."[29]

By 1935, thus, the professional fight game was "having a revival of sorts,"
despite the continued presence of the gamblers who had infested the sport
with the "odor of wrestling." Writing in the *Wichita Beacon*, syndicated columnist Jack Copeland declared, "Fans were getting pretty well fed up on the
activities of the gamblers in maneuvering the short-priced boys into victories." Improbable as it might seem, black fighters were instrumental in transforming boxing's image from a gangster-run enterprise to a sport that carried
a measure of purpose and idealism. In an era when white heavyweight champions had discredited the power of white masculine supremacy, Joe Louis,
Henry Armstrong, and John Henry Lewis roused fans from their apathy and
compelled admiration for their talents and their courage. As black boxers in
all major divisions contended for titles, they helped revive a dying sport and
bring boxing back to central stage in the arena of professional athletics. At the
center of the revival of boxing and the new-found assertiveness of black boxers stood Louis.[30]

While Joe Louis spearheaded the revival of boxing in the United States, Max
Schmeling was leading a remarkable resurgence of the sport in Nazi Germany. After his heartbreaking loss to Max Baer in 1933, he had suffered a
humiliating defeat at the hands of a relative novice, the American Steve Hamas.
In the tenth round of their February 1934 match-up, the former college athlete opened a deep cut over Schmeling's left eye and went on to take the
twelve-round decision. Deeply disappointed, German fans considered
Schmeling finished as a fighter. However, he did not give up. Later in 1934,
he began a successful comeback that placed him at the apex of German—and
later international—sport just as the Nazis were turning to international athletics as an integral part of their political revolution.[31]

Schmeling began his ascent by fighting the veteran Basque warhorse,
Paolino Uzcudun, to a draw in Barcelona on May 13, 1934. Although he was

dissatisfied with the outcome and the attendance, the fight boosted his self-confidence because he discovered that he had control over his reflexes again. Schmeling believed that he had won the fight and only a hometown decision deprived him of the victory. His breakthrough bout occurred against fellow German Walter Neusel, one of the younger crop of German heavyweights with a chance at a world title. This was the first match Schmeling had fought in Germany since 1928. Held at a dirt track in Hamburg on August 26, 1934, the bout drew 90,000 fans and was the biggest boxing event ever staged in Germany. Many fans picked "the blonde tiger," as Neusel was called, the perfect picture of an Aryan hero, to knock off the aging ex-champion. For Schmeling, this was make or break. If he lost, he would truly be finished, replaced by the younger man as the main German fighter in the United States. In a hard-fought bout, though, the older man outclassed his younger opponent. Neusel attacked repeatedly at the beginning, but Schmeling waited him out. By the seventh round the tiger had run out of gas and Schmeling began to unload his heavier punches. Exhausted and soundly beaten, Neusel proved unable to answer the bell for the ninth round. Schmeling was back.[32]

Throughout Germany, boxing fans and government officials were overjoyed with the results of the bout and the attention that the country's foremost boxers received throughout the world. The German boxing magazine *Box-Sport* declared, "It is Germany's greatest day of fighting . . . in terms of sporting and publicity value, the *high point* of German boxing history." American newspapers covered the event, and for Adolf Hitler the bout was a positive example of the new German regime. As the boxing journal noted, "The evening might have brought about a different image abroad of the new Germany and its leader." Indeed, the hall assumed the features of a Nazi Party rally and spectacle, with members of the audience starting the event by shouting out three booming "Sieg Heil" salutes. Party boxing authorities spoke to the crowd, and the paramilitary Brown Shirts (SA) marched about the arena with swastika flags aloft. At the fight's conclusion, the entire crowd stood for the German national anthem. Newspapers, moreover, stressed the role of the National Socialist leadership in helping to make arrangements for the bout. It was clear that the Nazis had a particular interest in the sport and were doing all they could to help its visibility. Schmeling proved that the Neusel bout was no fluke in his rematch with Steve Hamas, in Hamburg on March 10, 1935. Emerging from his corner carefully at the bell as he usually did, Max controlled the fight as he waited for an opening. In the sixth round he knocked Hamas down with a hard right, and the American took an eight count. The bell saved him, and he kept coming back for more despite a battering until the referee stopped the fight in the ninth. Hamas was so badly beaten that he never fought again. Schmeling, meanwhile, had slugged his way back into title contention.[33]

Max Schmeling leads a boxing revival in Germany under Adolf Hitler and the National Socialist regime. Schmeling was taken up by the new regime and transformed into a national hero, and boxing matches could turn into party rallies. After his victory over Steve Hamas on March 10, 1935, in Hamburg, the arena erupted in marches, speeches, the national anthem, and Heil Hitler salutes. Ironically, at the far right is Joe Jacobs, Max's Jewish manager, who created a stir when the Nazis saw him saluting with a cigar in his hand. (Associated Press, Library of Congress)

Just as significant as Schmeling's victory was the Nazi regime's demonstration that it was willing to promote boxing as an important German sport. Indeed, Nazi officials helped finance a new Hamburg arena, the Hanseatenhalle, where the Hamas fight was held, and helped guarantee that the purse of the foreign boxer would not be held up as a result of new currency exchange controls. Hitler and his Minister of Enlightenment and Propaganda, Dr. Josef Goebbels, cabled their congratulations and invited the German boxer to the Chancellery for a visit with der Führer. The large crowd, German victory, and world attention, moreover, signaled Germany's desire to compete with the United States as the capital of world boxing. To that end, Schmeling's reappearance on the German boxing scene represented an opportunity the Nazis would not miss. Madison Square Garden's Jimmy Johnston, aware that the Germans had captured two important matches, complained bitterly that "the German government wants to establish its prestige in the field of sports." They had already won the rights to hold the Berlin Olympics of 1936, and "now they are trying to take the world boxing championship back to Germany." However, all of the American press attention led *Der Angriff* to declare Schmeling "a true flag-bearer for his country."[34]

Schmeling's comeback was part of a German pugilistic, cultural, and political regeneration that fed on the Nazi rise to power. His reemergence at the top of the heavyweight picture occurred just as the Nazis sought to restore Germany's national strength and prestige. Faced with a massive depression, the regime spent lavishly on public works and relief, created new recreational programs, and began military rearmament. Having previously scorned international sports and mass culture—especially their American incarnations—for their weakening effects on German national character, once in power the new regime reversed itself and attempted to use the arena of international sports for nationalistic ends. The Nazis cultivated athletes, artists, and theater and movie stars to legitimize their power at home and abroad. In fact, as a famous boxer with international exposure, Schmeling was one of the first athletes that Hitler courted.[35]

Shortly after Hitler was appointed Chancellor in January 1933 he summoned the recently deposed champion to the Chancellery for dinner. Dining at the same table as Field Marshall Göring, Josef Goebbels, and other cabinet ministers, the German boxer realized that Hitler wanted him to provide favorable press for Germany. Profoundly aware of the importance of propaganda, the new Chancellor saw the athlete's many interviews in the United States abroad as a way to sell the regime. "Now you can tell the pessimists out there how peaceful everything is here and assure them that we are making progress," and that Hitler and the Nazis were not as bad as the world feared. In 1935 Hitler also asked him to help dissuade the American Olympic Committee from boycotting the Berlin games. As a believer in the independence of sport, Schmeling took the initiative to promise Avery Brundage that there would be no discrimination against Jewish or African American athletes; the United States narrowly agreed to compete.[36]

In later years, the former champion admitted to being flattered by the attention of the Nazis. "On the ride home I couldn't help but feel a little flattered; let's face it, one can also be bribed by small favors." Despite having been the German, European, and World Heavyweight Champion for years, no politician before Hitler had ever paid him the slightest attention. He had wanted to meet Hindenburg, the Reich's president, after he won the title in 1930, but one "had to be from the nobility" for this. Whereas officials of the old regime remained mired in hierarchies of status and caste with little room for common athletes, under Hitler the government went out of its way to honor popular heroes and recognize and expand popular culture as a means of legitimating the regime. As a national hero, Schmeling received full national accolades and honors under the Nazis. It would have been hard for a man who had just lost his title to ignore such attention.[37]

The issues go deeper, however. At first Schmeling, like so many other Germans, was drawn to a man who proposed to end unemployment and stop the deadly street rioting that was tearing Germany apart. On the surface, the Nazis brought a peaceful revolution, preaching personal sacrifice, national unity, and national honor. Schmeling was deeply dismayed by the stark economic and political conditions he found after 1930, and he was disturbed that politicians did nothing to alleviate the suffering and violence rife in German society. Having lived through the famine of World War I, the absence of his father serving in the Navy, and the inflation, unemployment, and street violence that accompanied the end of the war, Schmeling, like many Germans, probably felt that the country had returned to postwar chaos, class warfare, and political impotence. A man of action, he appreciated Hitler's promise of action. Schmeling's disillusionment would set in quickly, especially over Hitler's anti-Semitic plans for the Jews, but he and the regime proved useful to each other. Although he never joined the Nazi Party, he moved closer to the regime than was wise.[38]

Hitler and his top lieutenants were highly solicitous toward Schmeling in a variety of other ways. When he and Anny Ondra married in July 1933, for example, der Führer sent the couple a Japanese maple as a wedding gift and thereafter greeted Ondra very kindly whenever she accompanied Max to the Chancellery. As one of the few remaining celebrities left in Berlin after 1933, Ondra found herself courted by Dr. Goebbels. She spent a good deal of time at the soirees organized by the Propaganda Minister and his wife Magda. For an actress such as Ondra, it was essential to stay on the good side of the minister, who controlled the film industry, if she wished to continue working in the movies. Schmeling's acquaintance with Hitler paid off too. The boxer had to take large sums of German money with him on his frequent travels to fight abroad. When he was caught transporting amounts in excess of German currency regulations, he faced a potential sentence of six months in prison and a 10,000 mark fine. A word to Hitler and the matter disappeared. In addition, the regime proved generous when it came to favorable tax regulations that allowed Schmeling to write off travel abroad, essential for his career, as a business expense. At critical points, German officials guaranteed the purses of foreign fighters in the hope of luring them to Germany as Schmeling's opponents, and they underwrote the construction of new stadiums for boxing events. As a result, the fighter proved willing to spread the good news about the regime.[39]

The attempt to use Schmeling was not accidental; the Nazis believed that sports were a valuable propaganda and educational tool in the service of a Germany rescued from defeat and demoralization. As Dr. Goebbels declared, "German sport has only one task: to strengthen the character of the German people, imbuing it with the fighting spirit and steadfast camaraderie necessary in the struggle for existence." In *Mein Kampf*, Hitler argued that boxing and hockey would transform German youth into proper Aryans and future soldiers. Eager to avenge the defeat of German manhood in the war and rescue the nation from what they considered Weimar degeneracy, the Nazis abandoned their preference for the German tradition of Turner gymnastics and glorified both fighting sports and exercise. The regime required mandatory physical education in schools and universities and promoted mass sports festivals. As Hitler declared, education should not aim at "pumping in mere knowledge, but at training bodies" to protect the nation as soldiers. As the overseer of education, the state could not leave physical training to the individual. "Not a day should go by," Hitler argued, "in which the young man does not receive one hour's physical training in the morning and one in the afternoon, combining every type of sport and gymnastics." One Nazi sports ideologue noted that sport was "outward testimony of a nation capable of athletic achievement and an inward maintenance of the health of the *Volk* and a promoter of the community of the *Volk*." Sport would produce the healthy racial body and the new fascist man. As an ally of politics, athletics became increasingly essential to the state. Although personally indifferent to all forms of athletics, Hitler bankrolled the Olympics of 1936 to validate the new Germany and the physical supremacy of the Aryan race.[40]

Eager to avenge the defeat of its manhood in World War I and rescue the nation from racial and sexual degeneracy, the Nazis promoted boxing to toughen young men and prepare them for battle against foreign enemies and their own weak impulses. As Hitler declared, "There is no sport that promotes the offensive spirit, demands lightning quick power of decision, and prepares the body to take punches" as does boxing. While the regime distanced itself from most professional sports because of their degrading "Jewish" commercial values, it viewed professional boxers as invaluable to the state because they were heroes to the masses and role models for young men. As the era's best-known idol, Schmeling was very important to the regime. Only athletes linked to the state could achieve greatness, while athletic success validated the state by symbolizing a renewed national culture. Sports victories, Schmeling noted in his autobiography, "were being converted into political currency."[41]

To rebuild the body politic, the Nazis first sought to rebuild the male body. This required purifying athletics of degenerate racial influences, especially "the alien and weakening presence of the Jew." In his desire for a new virile fascist man, Hitler argued that had the German elite been trained in boxing rather than in etiquette or the professions, the left-wing revolutions and social democratic regimes that followed World War I would have been impossible. Instead of bourgeois values, Jewish pacifism, and physical weakness that was infecting all of the German people, boxing would teach will power and reverse the collapse of Germany, the humiliation experienced in World War I, and their enslavement to other world powers. Boxing, the

Nazis believed, would produce the strong young men who would be different from the old "Jewish" representatives of the failed democratic order: paunchy, and shortsighted, more like old ladies or effeminate homosexuals than the vigorous men required by the new Germany. Hitler's support of boxing found expression in an appeal in *Box-Sport* in March 1936 to boxers and boxing fans alike to again vote for the Führer, whose powerful advocacy "of our German sport of boxing" gave "our sport that place in the sun for which we had so long striven." German boxers could "be proud that it was the Führer who took us to himself."[42]

As in all other areas of cultural life, athletics underwent a forced reorganization to make it serve the purposes of the racial state. Hitler appointed Reichssportführer Hans von Tschammer und Osten, a brutal regional leader of the Brown Shirts (SA) and an elected Nazi member of Parliament, to oversee all of German sports, and tapped Brown Shirt Sturmbannführer Dr. Hans Joachim Heyl as president of the German Boxing Association. Under their leadership, the Turners and other independent Marxist, Catholic, and Protestant sport organizations were dissolved and incorporated under state control. Of supreme importance, the regime embarked on the policy of expelling Jews, Gypsies, and Afro-Germans from boxing and all other sports. All Jews were dropped from the membership rolls of the professional boxing association, and all new members were required to be of "Aryan origin." Convinced that Jewish money and management had corrupted German sport and German manhood, the Nazis released Aryan boxers from managerial contracts with Jews and banned Jewish capital and personnel from organizing boxing events or entering the ring in any way. Even Jewish doctors, dentists, and lawyers were banned. These rules attempted to remove what they saw as the source of the depression in boxing and the degeneracy in the body politic—Jewish financial machinations. As so many of the managers were of Jewish origin, the ban had a profound effect on the "racial" makeup of the sport. Because it was the official organ of the state boxing associations, the formerly independent *Box-Sport* was also incorporated under party control and had to promote Nazi sports philosophy. This explains the marked increase of criticism of Jews and "colored" peoples where none had existed before.[43]

The imposition of these new rules and the emergence of the new ideology were intended to draw clear lines between those of superior and inferior racial status. As a result, German athletics began to follow practices of segregation long established in the United States for the demarcation of African American athletes as separate and unequal. German boxers were forced to fire their Jewish managers, while a number of world-class boxers of Jewish descent were banned from boxing and either had to give up the sport or emigrate abroad. Manager and promoter Paul Damski, who worked with the up-and-coming heavyweight Walter Neusel, went into exile in France and was prevented from returning to Germany for any of his fighter's bouts, includ-

Joe Jacobs greets Max Schmeling as the latter disembarks after another of his many transatlantic voyages from Germany to New York. Jacobs proved invaluable to Schmeling's fortunes in New York, but his religion caused Schmeling continual problems with the Nazi regime. (Associated Press, Library of Congress)

ing the important one he lost to Schmeling in 1934. Similarly, Erich Seelig, the German middle- and light-heavyweight champion, was stripped of his titles and eventually left for the United States. Also banned were top tennis player Daniel Press, and world-class high jumper Gretel Bergman. The regime's sports authorities expelled Gypsies too, such as boxer Johann "Rukelie" Trollmann, who had his light-heavyweight crown voided. In 1938 he was arrested and, upon his release, sterilized. In 1943 he was shot to death in a concentration camp. While some Afro-Germans managed to participate at the local level of athletics, protected by friends and local networks, they were excluded from taking part in national competitions. Such was the case with Hans Massaquoi, an Afro-German who boxed as an amateur for several years in Hamburg. When his coach entered him in the national finals, he was prevented from participating on racial grounds.[44]

While the revival of boxing in Germany was predicated on the politically motivated banning of non-Aryans from the sport, the renewal of prizefighting in the United States was based on the awareness that commercial box office attractions were more important than the athlete's racial status. As a result of these competing dynamics, boxing in Germany and the United States began to move in different directions. Although deep-seated racism continued to follow Joe Louis in everything he did, he could draw people to boxing arenas in the middle of the Great Depression, and this might provide him with a title shot. At the same time, Max Schmeling's road back to the crown increasingly forced him to campaign under the banner of racial purity whether he wanted to or not. Germany classified whole hosts of its citizens as outsiders to their racial definition of the nation, whereas in the United States, racial and religious outsiders were moving from the margins to the center of boxing as they were slowly beginning to do in the definition of who was an American. In fact, American boxing circles as early as 1933 condemned the racial bans in Germany as an affront to Catholics and Jews. By implication, they saw American boxing as part of a more open and tolerant definition of American nationalism. Certainly Louis was proof of that.[45]

For all his good qualities, Louis's rise would have stood no chance had the economic circumstances of boxing not changed dramatically during the Great Depression. Faced with heavyweight champions who failed to excite public interest, boxing promoters saw Louis as an economic force that could no longer be denied because he attracted more fight fans than any of the current or recent titleholders. In mid-June 1935, for instance, when Max Baer lost his title to the plodding James J. Braddock in a spectacular upset, only 29,366 fans paid $205,355.37 to see the fight in Long Island City. Baer earned only $88,805, a paltry sum for a champion in a title match. By contrast, the Louis-Carnera non-title bout drew 57,000 spectators who paid $328,655.44. Carnera received the lion's share of the gate, $86,792.54 for his efforts, or nearly as much as the champion Baer had received. As the only fighter capable of generating big money, Louis now found white heavyweights and their managers eager to fight him. By the end of 1935, according to the *Saturday Evening Post*, "the coffee-colored boy of twenty-one who started life in an Alabama cabin as Joseph Louis Barrow was to act as the major factor in the creation of $1,650,808.86 worth of business at a profit to himself of

$363,714.97." Radio and movie rights in his fight against Max Baer pushed the total gross over a million.[46]

It was not just the box office that experienced increased revenues. The whole boxing game was making a comeback, according to Nat Fleischer, because of this "Moses of the Manly Art." In a feverish editorial, Fleischer responded to readers who complained that he was prejudiced against white boxers and in favor of Louis. As far as Fleischer was concerned, Louis had saved boxing, which "gives me my livelihood. It has enabled me to reach the station in life that I have attained." After the Depression nearly killed off the sport, "when I come across a man who is aiding the sport that is so dear to my heart, there is nothing too good for such a man." Moreover, Fleischer's *Ring* magazine had lost circulation during the Depression, and he spent a fortune keeping the magazine and the sport alive. He was more than happy to get behind the man who brought boxing back, regardless of his color. As he surveyed the sport, *Ring's* editor discovered that gyms were seething with activity, boxing paraphernalia was being purchased, and newspaper circulation was up based on the demand for boxing news. Even the sportswriters who had deserted the ring were once again covering the sport. What had happened? "Nothing more nor less than the rise of one fighter has so stirred the interest in pugilism, that fans who had been hibernating . . . are coming out again in droves." As a result, not only boxers, managers, and promoters but also manufacturers of shoes, trunks, shirts, gloves, bandages, leather goods for head guards, nose guards and protectors, punching bags, and other ring paraphernalia "are all benefiting by the new life set into motion by one fighter—Joe Louis." In addition, Louis had put back to work men who made athletic appliances, ushers, ticket takers, ticket sellers, special policemen, vendors, printers of programs, books, and tickets, engravers, and newsboys.[47]

The Depression also affected how the white southern press treated Louis. In a word, an exciting heavyweight boxer increased interest in the sports pages and helped sell newspapers. As historian Jeffrey Sammons notes, Louis came along at a period of relative superficial racial stability in the South. The furor over the Scottsboro Boys case had settled down, and the *Brown vs. Board of Education* decision was still twenty years off. In the interim, southern newspaper opinion makers were trying to rehabilitate the image of their region in the eyes of the rest of the nation. At the same time, the southern press, similar to its northern counterpart, had watched circulation plummet with the economic decline and the absence of exciting boxing champions. With Louis, excitement and circulation rose. As in the North, the Brown Bomber's image went a long way in convincing white opinion makers that Louis would not challenge southern racial mores. Moreover, his matches occurred in the North and posed little challenge to the South's ban on mixed-race bouts. Aware of the blatant racism in the region, however, white newspapers worked hard not to inflame public opinion. They relied on northern wire services to report

Louis's bouts, rarely mentioned the racially explosive elements of a black man beating white men, and referred to Louis as an Alabaman of whom all southerners could be proud. Of course the white news services carried plenty of racially demeaning language and images to satisfy local racists. The decision to use boxing to increase revenues also meant that the southern press rarely opposed Louis with the same viciousness they had used toward Jack Johnson. Still, the white southern press was decidedly more moderate than many white southerners, and the latter's opposition to Louis would pour forth at critical moments in the Brown Bomber's career.[48]

In many ways, though, the "political" atmosphere in the boxing world had also changed in the United States, though not as dramatically as it had in Nazi Germany. *Ring* magazine, the most prominent boxing journal in the world, championed an end to the color barrier. The editor and founder, Nat Fleischer, was part of the Jewish wave of interest in boxing that predated World War I. Growing up on city streets, Fleischer, like many other American Jewish males, was attracted to boxing as a means of self-defense in a tough urban environment that pitted street gangs of one ethnic group against another. While Jewish parents hated boxing and other sports as a rejection of traditional customs and folkways, their American-born sons found boxing a way to prove their manhood and the courage of their people. Numerous Jews held championships in the lighter weight classifications from the 1910s through the 1930s. In the 1930s, moreover, Max Baer became the first boxer of Jewish descent to capture the heavyweight crown, and Barney Ross for several years held the lightweight, junior welter, and welterweight crowns until he lost the welterweight title to the great black champion Henry Armstrong in 1938. Those who went into boxing became champions of the Jewish people much as Joe Louis did for African Americans. When Hitler rose to power, moreover, champions like Ross and Baer dedicated their victories to proving that the Jews could not be defeated by Hitler's Aryan theories.[49]

As the editor and publisher of *Ring* magazine, which he founded in 1922, Fleischer was one of the world's acknowledged boxing experts. In his view, boxing expressed the essence of American culture, for it allowed the nation's many ethnic and racial groups to settle their differences in the organized world of the ring and according to widely accepted rules of fair play. When the Nazis barred Jews from participation in German boxing, closed Catholic sports clubs, and banned the sale of his magazine in Germany, *Ring* became one of the earliest American journals to publicize and condemn this virulent form of prejudice and anti-Semitism. As someone who had encountered anti-Semitism, Fleischer was able to understand that while blacks were part of boxing, the deck was horribly stacked against them. What he saw occurring in Nazi Germany he had also seen in the United States against African Americans.[50]

As far back as the earliest days of his magazine, Fleischer had campaigned for African American Harry Wills as a fitting challenger for the heavyweight crown, in opposition to the intransigence of Tex Rickard and Madison Square Garden. In the 1930s, Fleischer used his magazine to promote Joe Louis and to discuss the myriad problems of discrimination encountered by black boxers. Along with histories of Jews, the Irish, and foreigners in the sport, the magazine explored the fate of prominent black boxers and the special obstacles placed in their way. Various authors noted that the Garden's management maintained the color bar, while Fleischer, a friend of Jack Johnson, looked back on the difficulties that his favorite heavyweight had encountered in his career. In numerous articles, the staff referred sarcastically to attempts to create "white hopes." The editor and his writers recognized the rise of black fighters as following the same pattern, but with greater obstacles, as that of the representatives of various immigrant groups and thus foreshadowed a hopeful development in American culture. In 1938 Fleischer wrote the first history of black fighters, *Black Dynamite: The Story of the Negro in Boxing*, which he offered at a discount to his readers. The multivolume work offered the wider sporting public for the first time a counter narrative of heroic African Americans in the sport Fleischer loved at precisely a time when black boxers were translating that counter narrative into action in the ring. Although he was continually attacked for his stance, the editor of *Ring* insisted that he did not promote one race over another. Instead he argued that he believed in the principles of the boxing ring: fair play and let the best man win. In Fleischer's world, boxing could be the basis for a real democracy. It was only in the 1930s, however, that *Ring*'s voice on race was taken seriously, and this was because a larger transformation of the boxing business was under way.[51]

At the same time that Louis was fighting his way from outsider status into the heart of New York's boxing world, changes in that world in the early thirties enabled Louis to transcend the color line and contend for the heavyweight crown. The Madison Square Garden Corporation, the keeper of the flame of segregation in boxing during the 1920s, found its monopoly over the sport weakened by the Depression. Jewish promoter Mike Jacobs (unrelated to Joe Jacobs, Schmeling's manager), another outsider and a friend of Nat Fleischer, led the challenge. As Louis described him, Mike Jacobs, or "Uncle Mike" as everyone called him, was "a true hustler, but a damn good man—and he changed history." A street-smart promoter and ticket scalper, Jacobs had come to the United States from Eastern Europe via Dublin and had grown up in an Irish slum in New York. During the 1920s, he became an assistant to Tex Rickard at Madison Square Garden, and, some would say, the brains behind the great boxing promotions of the decade. When Rickard died in 1929, Jacobs expected to be named his successor as the promoter of the Garden. Instead, the arena's executives tapped diminutive and dapper former fight manager, Jimmy Johnston, who presided over boxing's decline. In the early 1930s, the Garden suffered the effects of the Depression along with the rest of the sporting and entertainment worlds. Needing to economize, the Garden's

Mike Jacobs, Louis's promoter examines the fists of dynamite that made Joe Louis a popular boxer. A major figure in the Louis camp, Jacobs and his 20th Century Sporting Club took the unprecedented step of guiding an African American contender to the title in an era of rampant discrimination in the heavyweight division. (Associated Press, Library of Congress)

management squeezed out Jacobs. At the same time they raised the rents they charged for their biggest charity event, the annual boxing matches staged to help poor city children, sponsored by the Hearst Milk Fund, a favored project of Mrs. William Randolph Hearst, the wife of the owner of the powerful newspaper chain. Even in the economic crisis, the Garden proved hesitant to change its policy toward black fighters. Johnston considered signing Louis but in a manner that convinced Roxborough that Joe would encounter the very exploitation he had worked so hard to avoid. "You got a colored fighter and you're a colored manager," Louis reports Johnston as saying, "You'll have to take less than other fighters, and your man will have to lose a fight, now and then."[52]

The canny and ruthless Jacobs did not take being squeezed out lightly. Instead, he formed his own promotion company, the 20th Century Sporting Club, in 1934 and outbid the Garden by offering to charge the Hearst Fund less money to hold its events at Yankee Stadium and other arenas. Initially three Hearst sportswriters—Ed Frayne, Bill Farnsworth, and Damon Runyon—formed part of his company, which meant that the national Hearst newspaper chain threw its weight behind the 20th Century Sporting Club's bouts. South and north, Hearst sports writers provided a barrage of press coverage for Jacobs's events, and when he signed Louis, the one attraction that could gain him control over boxing in New York and hence the nation, the Hearst sports department gave the young heavyweight invaluable free publicity.[53]

Unlike the Garden's management, moreover, Jacobs lacked Tex Rickard's deep-seated racism. According to boxing writer Barney Nagler, Rickard's successor, Johnston, was also "a bigot." Tipped to Louis by Nat Fleischer, Jacobs eagerly pursued the Brown Bomber and allegedly told Roxborough, "John, you and Joe are colored. I'm a Jew. It's going to be hard for us to do anything. But if you stick with me, I think I can do it." Louis recalled that Jacobs "had no prejudice about a man's color so long as he could earn a green buck for him." Jacobs proposed that he promote Louis's fights and that Roxborough and Black continue as Louis's managers at very favorable percentages. By gambling that Louis would turn into a major box office attraction, Jacobs successfully challenged the Garden's monopoly over boxing promotions. As a former ticket broker, he was more attuned to what the public would pay for and less interested in telling them what they should or should not support. Even more, he recognized what a lot of promoters ignored—that black fans turned out in record numbers for Louis's fight, at times totaling a fifth to a quarter of the crowd. This new audience could help make boxing extremely profitable again. As the *Saturday Evening Post* declared, Louis and Jacobs were the two outsiders who had revived boxing, "the Jewish boy from an Irish neighborhood who learned how to sell tickets to people, and the Negro boy born in an Alabama cabin on May 13, 1914. . . . They have brought back, together, the million-dollar gate."[54]

The first million-dollar gate after five long years returned in the match between Louis and former champion Max Baer on September 24, 1935, at Yankee Stadium. Billed as a fight between the two best heavyweights in the world, the bout placed the representatives of the old and new orders in boxing in stark contrast. Baer, known as "the Livermore Larruper," had knocked out Max Schmeling to seemingly end the latter's career and had demolished Primo Carnera in 1934 to take the title in what was as much a wrestling as a boxing match. Once champion, however, he had proven to be another of the lackluster titleholders of the early 1930s who seemed more interested in showgirls, wisecracks, and Hollywood appearances than in fighting. Two weeks before Louis defeated Carnera, Baer finally defended his title and was upset by the likeable but plodding James Braddock, who had come off the relief rolls to win the championship. Boxing writers and ordinary fans were convinced that Baer had fought listlessly, a result of his preference for a life of luxuriant play and self-indulgence rather than hard training. Louis, on the other hand, was all business once again, a fighter of serious purpose matched against a "dancing Baer." As the Baer-Louis match neared, black and white sportswriters picked the Brown Bomber to win because he did not drink, smoke, or go to nightclubs, the very opposite of the playboy activities in which Baer indulged. Apropos of the tie-in between the Hearst newspaper chain and Mike Jacobs's promotion company, the fight produced the greatest prefight publicity since the Dempsey-Tunney bout in 1927.[55]

With their fight billed as a battle between two devastating punchers, Baer and Louis seemed evenly matched. At the weigh-in on the morning of the fight, Max Baer came in at 6' 2" and 210½ pounds, while Louis, about a half-inch smaller, weighed 199½ pounds. But in an example of supreme self-confidence, earlier that evening Louis had put on a gray suit and walked downstairs to the apartment of a friend at 381 Edgecombe Avenue, on Harlem's Sugar Hill, where he married Marva Trotter. The wedding started at 7:45 and at 8:00 the Brown Bomber left for the fight. Mrs. Louis had a ringside seat when announcer Joe Humphreys introduced Baer as the "sensational . . . Californian and former world's . . . heavyweight champion," and Louis as "the new . . . sensational . . . pugilistic product," and "the idol of his people."[56]

Louis often referred to this fight as the best of his career. It may have been an exaggeration because he always complimented his opponents, but he certainly made fast work of another former champion, dispatching him in less time than it took to chop down Carnera. By the second round, Louis had Baer bleeding, confused, and hitting after the bell. While Baer tried to throw his

Joe Louis demolishes ex-champ Max Baer on September 24, 1935, in the first million-dollar fight since 1930. The image of Louis standing over a fallen white man excited fears among many white fans and sportswriters that white civilization was at stake. His ability to destroy former champions such as Baer and Carnera and attract huge audiences led boxing insiders to see Louis as the savior of boxing. (Library of Congress)

looping overhand right, Louis jabbed and hooked him to death, feinting, weaving, but always in front of the ex-champion. While neither man was fast afoot, Louis's hand speed was dazzling as he jabbed his left like a powerful piston and worked his man over. He was poetry in motion. Using efficient punches that did not stop, Louis put Baer down in the third round for a nine count. At the end of the round, Louis knocked him down again, but the bell saved him. In the fourth round, Louis threw left after left, jabs and hooks, with nearly every one landing, often to the chin or the face. After a series of five stiff lefts, Louis threw a fast right cross that got Max high on the jaw, and Max went into a clinch. Then Louis hit him with another powerful right and a left to the jaw, and Baer went to his knees. Radio announcer Clem McCarthy, who broadcast the fight to 130 stations over the NBC-WEAF-WJZ network, called the finish. "He's down, and the count is four . . . five . . . six. Baer's on one knee, seven, eight, nine. Baer is not up [boo!], and Baer is on his knee at the count of ten. Your fight is all over; your fight is all over." Many fans figured that true to form, Baer had quit in the ring just as he had quit in his training over the course of his career. When asked about taking the final count on one knee, Baer told a reporter, "I could have struggled up once more, but when I get executed, people are going to have to pay more than twenty-five dollars a seat to watch it."[57]

After the bout, it was clear to the American sporting world that Louis was the best heavyweight fighter in the world and that no white boxer was likely to beat him. As a result, there were the frequent descriptions of Louis as an animalistic jungle beast who fought on instinct and bloodlust, someone barely a man. Just as predictably, calls went out for another white hope to knock Louis off as the leading contender for the crown. Yet, as Shirley Povich of the *Washington Post* noted, "in the case of Joe Louis . . . it is obvious that the reaction has softened. There has been no great umbrage, no severely ruffled pride among the great body of whites. Never did the public as a whole show greater tolerance for the black man." If they did not care to see a white man lose to a black man on the way to the championship, they did not see the worth of making a fuss about it. In fact, "the cheers that greeted Louis almost shamed in volume the applause that greeted Baer's introduction." In the past, asserted Povich, "it would not have been a question of skill or conduct, but color." Baer's reputation as a braggart, a playboy, and a clown made him few fans, and being white made little difference. By contrast, Ed Frayne of the Hearst press declared that "boxing at last has found the faultless performer." In only Louis's second major New York fight, he noted, sportswriters were already calling him "in all probability the greatest heavyweight of all time. He makes no mistakes."[58]

Just as with the victory over Carnera, blacks were overjoyed. It seemed as though Louis served as a harbinger of better days to come for all African Americans. In a letter to the editor of the *Amsterdam News* entitled "Winner for His Race," B. Weldon Hayes from Lynchburg, Virginia, acknowledged that Louis's achievements surpassed boxing. "His life is a gift to the Negro race," noted Hayes, for "in him we find character saturated with love for his race, morality and fistic ability to bring his opponents to submission." More than in boxing, "we need a political Joe Louis to fight for our interests in every community; one who is as stern in the fight as the boxing king who brought the daring Max Baer to his knees." Black columnist Theophilus Lewis declared that Louis's place in the limelight made him the "world's most conspicuous Negro," one capable of changing white society's conception of blacks as minstrel stereotypes. White people were too intelligent, Lewis argued, to deal "with a race of yeomen as they would deal with a race of clowns. Yeomen are worthy of better terms." The average black youth might not be able to knock out a Max Baer, but "he does want to k. o. the color bar that stands between him and the realization of his dream of success." These sentiments would only grow stronger as Louis made his way to the championship.[59]

Louis also presaged better days for boxing and the larger American society. By decisively beating the titleholders of the worst years of the Great Depression, Louis established himself as a boxer who had blasted away the values of the past: the ruthless individualism, political chicanery, criminal activity, and hollow masculinity that had corrupted boxing and nearly destroyed the sport. As a serious, purposeful, ambassador of his race, he stood for cooperative individualism, higher principle, and the advancement of his group. In many ways acceptable to whites, he also embodied the forgotten man of the New Deal, one engaged in combat for higher ends. For many whites, it seemed he was a modest, humble young man who obeyed the official script of white supremacy. He would be allowed to fight in the ring in exchange for saying nothing outside it. Yet he and his managers knew what the British colonial authorities had learned: that a victory by a colonial subject over a representative of the colonial power had wide-ranging repercussions outside the ring. By gaining entrance to the ring through a variety of conscious compromises, Louis had a chance to blow open long-standing notions of white supremacy.[60]

With no serious domestic contenders left after Baer, it was assumed that Louis was only steps away from becoming the next champion. Only Max Schmeling, in the midst of a furious comeback, stood in his way.

3

MAX SCHMELING'S SIEG—
EIN DEUTSCHER SIEG
(MAX SCHMELING'S VICTORY—
A GERMAN VICTORY)

> With an amazing spirited strength, which he
> alone created out of his own belief in himself
> and out of his own knowledge of the task, he
> went into his toughest fight, which may be his
> greatest. One must believe that a man who can
> accomplish such unmistakable results fights not
> for himself alone—he fought for his nation,
> which he felt himself called upon to do.
>
> *Hamburger Anzeiger*, June 20–21, 1936

On June 18, 1936, young heavyweight sensation Joe Louis and veteran former champion Max Schmeling prepared to square off for the first time in open-air Yankee Stadium in a fight expected to attract a million dollars at the box office. The New York State Athletic Commission and boxing promoter Mike Jacobs agreed that the fight would serve as a qualifying match to decide the next opponent for the current heavyweight titleholder, James J. Braddock. Both contenders not only believed they could defeat each other but they also had every confidence that they could defeat the champion and claim the title for themselves.

For the former titleholder Schmeling, this bout was a crucial part of his campaign to do what no other former heavyweight champion had done—come back and retake the crown. As far as he was concerned, his convincing victories over fellow German Walter Neusel and the American Steve Hamas,

Louis and Schmeling weigh in for their June 1936 battle. (Associated Press, Library of Congress)

and his win on points against his old nemesis Paolino Uzcudun, had catapulted him back into the title picture. Although he fervently desired to meet Braddock for the title, he acceded to the New York State Athletic Commission's demand that he first defeat Joe Louis, the number one contender. For his part, Louis had beaten everyone in his path, including ex-champions Primo Carnera and Max Baer. Except for the retired Jack Sharkey, Max Schmeling remained the only former champion that Louis had yet to defeat. Among knowledgeable boxing experts, the Brown Bomber was the uncrowned champion on an inevitable march to the title, while Schmeling was merely an obstacle in the way. Very few American experts thought Schmeling had a chance. The German, however, had different ideas.

As a heroic example of German masculinity, Schmeling represented German national ideals. Yet as much as the regime wanted to use the international arena to show off its heroes and its racial values, the decision to participate in international sport led to inner conflicts in the regime. If they had had their way, for instance, German boxing officials would have insisted that Schmeling fight in Germany and only against opponents from proper racial backgrounds. When New York boxing officials decreed that Schmeling must meet Louis before he could fight Braddock for the title, National Socialist officials were disturbed, but there was little they could do to prevent the bout. Because Schmeling's decision to box Louis would place him on a level of equality with a member of an "inferior race," Nazi leaders greeted the bout with little outward enthusiasm. Equally important, German sports officials feared that the heavily favored African American would handily defeat their man and put the lie to their claims of racial superiority.

As the fight with Louis approached, German officials were wary. Hitler appeared disturbed and angry, according to Schmeling, that "I would put German honor on the line against a black man, especially one against whom I appeared to have so little chance of winning." *Box-Sport* worried about a loss to "not even a pure Negro, but some kind of *mixed breed* between black and white," an example of the horror of American miscegenation. The German position did not go unnoticed in the United States. The *New York Times* observed that Julius Streicher, a "prominent anti-Semite and ultra Aryan," had recently expelled a Negro wrestler from a tournament in Nuremburg on the grounds that Aryans should not be allowed to suffer defeat at the hands of non-Aryans. "A Schmeling victory would entail no race problem, but if he should be knocked out by the Brown Bomber he might find himself no longer popular." According to Roi Ottley, Nazi authorities were so concerned about the possibility of Schmeling losing that Dr. Goebbels forbade the German press to print further articles by Arthur Bülow, German boxing expert and Max's former manager, because he had predicted a win for Louis. Fearing a loss to a Negro and worried about the possibility of negative publicity as the Berlin Olympics were approaching, moreover, Dr. Goebbels ordered the German press to play down the racial angle. If Schmeling were to win, decreed the press office, "Fundamental racial issues are not to be brought up at all. One can say that Schmeling has earned the right to fight Braddock. This must then take place in Germany." If Schmeling were to lose, "then naturally racial issues would also not be mentioned." The *Völkischer Beobachter*, controlled by one of the Propaganda Minister's chief rivals, was more vocal on the fight's racial aspects. The Nazi newspaper claimed that white Americans heavily supported Schmeling as "the representative of the white race" in the hope that he would halt "the unusual rise of the Negro." The paper argued that "our patriotic ambitions" were at stake and predicted a victory since Max's strength "sprang from German character" and "this special race feeling."[1]

Nazi ambivalence accompanied Schmeling when he left for the United States on April 15. The *New York Times* reported that he "received a shabby send-off from his Fatherland when he left today aboard the *Bremen* to train in America." Few people turned out to see him off, and the German press ignored his departure. "Race conscious Germany cannot forgive Max for fighting a Negro and letting himself be paid therefore." The sports authorities dodged criticizing Schmeling on the grounds that Louis was a Negro, but their official journal, the *Reich Sportblatt*, carried plans for boycotting a special German excursion to the fight. The *Times* detected that Schmeling was bored with the Nazi attitude that "all German sport is political." In interviews with American reporters, he argued that he was a professional sportsman and pro boxers were not that popular in Germany. As the *Times* observed, "The semi-religious attitude toward sport adopted by the Nazi youth, heightened by the propaganda which endows the coming Olympics with an almost sacred character, has made the path of the professional athlete even more rocky than before."[2]

Nazi ambivalence toward Schmeling was matched by the former champion's ambivalence toward them. The German boxer's relationship with the regime was highly problematic, but it reflected his primary belief that sport was beyond politics, in a realm by itself. As a boxer who had made his way in the international arena throughout his professional career, he had a cosmopolitan view of athletic endeavor, one that he tried never to relinquish. He considered himself a sportsman, not a politician, whose major goal remained recapturing the title. Still, Schmeling had agreed to speak positively about the new regime when he went abroad, and he also helped bring the Olympic Games to Germany. His willingness to cooperate with the regime in his capacity as a sports star, moreover, rested on an unpleasant reality. To box in Germany or elsewhere in the world, a German fighter needed the assistance of the National Socialist authorities. More than others Schmeling enjoyed a good deal of leeway in his actions, but he still required the help of the authorities in tax and foreign currency matters if he were to pursue the championship in the United States. On the other hand, the regime acted pragmatically toward their star boxer, not insisting that he join the party because they recognized the enormous propaganda value that a German heavyweight champion would have. Yet, while Schmeling outwardly conformed to the dictates of the Nazis, privately his dissatisfaction with National Socialism began to mount.[3]

Disillusionment with the anti-Semitic racism of the regime set in quickly. He and his wife soon realized that the attacks on the Jews had a debilitating effect on their social and business circles. A popular movie star from Czecho-slovakia in the early 1930s, Anny Ondra had a production company with six partners, four of them Jews and two Czechs. Along with other film artists from the major German studios, they were prevented from working and had to emigrate as the Nazis consolidated their hold over all cultural institutions. As Schmeling noted, the formerly vibrant international nature of Berlin's movie business diminished when the National Socialists took over. Ondra consid-ered moving the company to the United States, but decided instead to liqui-date Ondra-Lamac. Moreover, many of Schmeling's friends from Berlin's cafés emigrated once Hitler assumed power; others ended up in concentration camps. As he admitted in his autobiography, his circle knew about the camps. Worse, "each of us had at least one person we were close to who had been forced to leave the country; others had been forced out of a profession or simply made to live in fear. And we all knew—or knew of—persons who had already been arrested." His New York friends were almost all Jews, and they kidded him when he fought Max Baer. Was not fighting a Jew a race crime, they asked him jokingly? Schmeling also regularly flouted the central prin-ciple of National Socialism at home. Even after the enactment of the Nuremburg Laws of 1935, which stripped Jews of German citizenship, im-posed American-style forms of public segregation, and attempted to prevent racial miscegenation, Schmeling and his wife continued to associate with Jews. Among them were his dentist, Dr. Kurt Schindler, who accompanied him to New York for the first fight against Louis in 1936. Upon his return to Ger-many, Schindler was placed in a concentration camp, but he eventually es-caped to South Africa. Another close Jewish friend was manager and boxing promoter Paul Damski, who first introduced Anny and Max, and who was forced into exile in the mid-1930s. The regime was not pleased with these continuing friendships. During a chance meeting, Dr. Gobbels chided him for his actions. "What do you really think, Herr Schmeling? You do what you wish. You don't bother about the law. You come to the Führer, you come to me and still you constantly associate with Jews."[4]

Even when Schmeling performed work for the regime, his attitude to-ward Jews and the sanctity of sport got him into trouble. As the best-known German athlete in international circles, he was asked by the assistant to the Reichssportsführer to intervene with American Olympic officials regarding the proposed boycott of the games when he traveled to New York to attend the Louis-Uzcudun bout in December 1935. "You know America well. Could you go over there and exert a positive influence on the right people?" Schmeling remembered being asked. After he agreed to cooperate, he received a note from the president of the German Olympic Committee, Dr. Theodor von Lewald, who asked him to deliver a letter personally to his American friend and colleague, Avery Brundage. At their meeting Brundage expressed his worry that news articles describing disturbances in Germany, arrests of communists, harassment of Jews, and reports of Jews being prohibited from using public swimming pools, would convince American Olympic officials to vote against participating in the Berlin games. When Brundage asked who would guarantee the safety and honor of the black and Jewish athletes on the American team, Schmeling replied that German athletes would not allow any discrimination for whatever reason. The German boxer's guarantee helped sway the American committee's vote not to boycott. When he visited with Hitler at the latter's home in Munich, the Chancellor inquired as to where the American Olympic Committee stood. Schmeling replied that the vote had been very close because of the American concern about the safety of black and Jewish athletes and visitors to Germany. Hitler became visibly annoyed. At one point he declared, "It's no wonder that there's so much uproar, where the press is so completely controlled by Jews." Then Hitler brusquely thanked him and left the room. Someone else advised, "You really shouldn't have said that, Herr Schmeling. He just can't tolerate that sort of thing." To every one's surprise, the Chancellor returned shortly with a signed picture of himself, and the day went on as if nothing had happened.[5]

The new rules banning Jewish participation in boxing gave Schmeling even more serious problems with the Nazis because the demands of international competition conflicted with Germany's new racial culture. When he sought a rematch with Max Baer for the title in 1935, for example, German officials refused to sanction the bout or help arrange the financing against someone identified as Jewish and also a boxer who had previously beaten an Aryan athlete. Furthermore, as long as New York remained the capital of international boxing, Schmeling would need his American manager to handle business arrangements on the other side of the Atlantic. Committed to Joe Jacobs, who was of Jewish descent, Schmeling turned to Reichssportsführer Hans von Tschammer und Osten for assistance. Von Tschammer voiced his protests against a Jew serving as a manager for a German boxer, but he reluctantly had to accept that the restrictions on Jacobs applied only in Germany, where he hoped Schmeling would do most of his future work.[6]

This was not the end of the problem. In March 1935, the irrepressible "Yussel the Muscle" Jacobs came to Berlin for the return match with Steve Hamas, and Schmeling had to fight with a Berlin hotel which initially refused to honor Jacobs's reservation because he was a Jew. After the victory, moreover, 25,000 sports fans stood and sang the "Deutschlandlied," Germany's national anthem, with their arms raised in the Hitler salute. Jacobs ironically raised his cigar, a gesture that was captured on film and in news photos. The authorities were outraged, and they called Schmeling onto the carpet. In a letter written immediately after the meeting, the sports minister said that they were upset about "shameful and scandalous pictures of a Jew in Germany and of Schmeling's being the only German athlete to work with a Jew."

Von Tschammer demanded that Jacobs be fired, which Max refused to do. He reiterated that he needed an American manager to box successfully in the United States, and he owed Jacobs a good deal for helping him advance to the championship in 1930. Disturbed by the prospect of having to fire the man most responsible for his American career, the German boxer went to Hitler about the problem. The Chancellor refused to discuss the matter, but boxing officials once again acted pragmatically. They came to accept that as long as Schmeling continued to fight in the United States, he would need Jacobs. They backed down.[7]

Moreover, the authorities were upset with Schmeling for preferring to box in the United States rather than in Germany. Eager to bolster the regime's prestige by staging international matches in the Third Reich, and desirous of an influx of foreign currency, the Nazi sports establishment continually pressured Schmeling to hold his bouts in his homeland. Equally important, von Tschammer insisted that by boxing primarily in America, the boxer was depriving German youth of a role model that they needed to emulate. "It's athletes like yourself that are needed in our new Germany," the head of German sports declared. Schmeling stood his ground. "When I box in America," he retorted, "I represent Germany!" Then the sports minister began yelling, "You shouldn't be so short-sighted Herr Schmeling—think of your age! You're going to want to be a trainer here some day. Over there no one's going to care about you when you're washed up. Force yourself to listen! It's dumb to burn all your bridges behind you!" Schmeling replied calmly that he hoped to "live off my savings and investments when I'm old." Von Tschammer was astounded when he learned that the boxer had earned more than a million marks in the United States for his second title match with Jack Sharkey in 1932. Continuous run-ins throughout the 1930s forced Schmeling to walk a fine line if he were to maintain his professional connections and pursue an active boxing career.[8]

While these persistent and nagging skirmishes occurred in private, in public Schmeling prepared for the toughest battle of his life. As the fight neared, the American press installed Joe Louis as an 8:1 favorite. Although the German boxer had many friends in the United States, among them Nat Fleischer of *Ring* magazine, they were convinced that he was no match for Louis, who had amply demonstrated that he could knock out any opponent at will. Among Louis's army of black supporters, moreover, it was inconceivable that he could lose—let alone to a boxer whose glory days had seemingly passed him by. Schmeling had been badly beaten by Max Baer, who in turn had been annihilated by Louis in four rounds. As recently as December 1935, moreover, the Brown Bomber had stopped Paolino Uzcudun for the first time in the latter's career, whereas Schmeling had managed only to earn a draw against the tough Basque heavyweight and a victory on points in their two recent matches. The next stop in the minds of African Americans was not Schmeling; it was the champion, James J. Braddock. Plagued with arthritic hands, Braddock had not defended his title in a year, and his mediocre record made him a likely victim of the Brown Bomber. As early as September 1935, on the eve of the Louis-Baer fight, *Ring* magazine maintained that while Schmeling may hit harder, "when it comes to general ring ability, Louis has it on all his rivals. That's why the Detroit Bomber at this writing, looms as the next world's heavyweight champion." Expert after expert picked Louis to knock out his opponent. On the eve of the fight Louis himself predicted that the German would not last past the second round.[9]

While Louis stood as the clear favorite, skepticism remained in certain quarters. Former champion Jack Dempsey, for one, remained unconvinced that Louis ranked among the greats of the heavyweight division. He, like veteran boxing writer Hype Igoe, believed that the Brown Bomber had not shown he could take punishment because to date no one had delivered any to him. According to *Ring*, some of this skepticism owed to racial thinking. "Let us be quite frank about all this. There is a certain school of white fighters which holds that, when hurt, a Negro will not carry the fight back to his opponent." As the boxing journal put it, however, "this fable has been exploded time after time. Courage is not racial." Former champion and fellow African American Jack Johnson was another skeptic. Braving charges of jealousy and race betrayal, Johnson insisted to all in his hearing that Louis could be hit with a right and knocked out because his fighting stance was not properly balanced. "When he gets someone to crash a real blow against his chin and he shows me that he can take it as we could," Johnson declared, "then I'll admit he deserves a rating with the greatest, but until then, I want to be shown."[10]

Most white American fight fans expected a Louis victory, but they continued to depict the Brown Bomber in stereotypical racial terms. Because the fight lacked much nationalist fervor on the American side and was consciously downplayed by the Germans, race rather than nation determined the white American view of Louis. A week before the fight, Meyer Berger summarized some of the racist writings about Louis in *The New York Times Magazine*. The language bore a striking similarity to views held by the Nazis. In both countries, the prospect of a member of an "inferior" race winning against representatives of a "superior" race produced an emphasis on the inferior mental status of the black boxer. "A physician who has observed the Louis routine compares the bomber to a primordial organism; says in temperament, he is like a one-celled beastie of the mire-and-steaming-ooze period. . . . Fighting, he displays boxing intelligence tantamount to the stalking instinct of the panther. . . . He becomes sheer animal." Whether North or South, much of the white press continued to depict Louis as either a savage animal or a sleepy-eyed southern darkie. A *New York Evening Journal* cartoonist had Joe trying to use the word "defeat " in a sentence. A woolly-headed cartoon Louis responds, "Sho. I pops 'em on de chin and dey drags 'em out by de feet." Other cartoonists made fun of him by portraying him with huge lips and a big smile. Many emphasized his fondness for food. The Associated Press quoted Monk Harris, one of Louis's sparring partners: "Joe is the eatingest and sleepingest man Ah ever saw. An' what's stranger, the more food he eats, the stronger and better he seems to get. Why it's nothing—nothing at all—for him to sit right down an' eat five chickens for one meal. How that man loves his chicken." In all of these depictions, the white press continued to portray Louis as someone who might beat a white man, but through natural animal physical superiority, not equal mental ability.[11]

Still, very little hostility toward the idea of a black champion surfaced, a testament to the successful job that Louis and his managers had accomplished in crafting his image as one of modesty, good behavior, and sportsmanship in the ring. Harry Stillwell Edwards of the *Atlanta Journal* remarked on the absence of animosity toward Louis in the white South. Surprisingly, Edwards declared, "He has the sympathy of the South. Not a loudly expressed sympathy, and none of it declared in the southern press. But just start a discussion of the chance for Schmeling in the bout next week, and note the reaction. You will hear the Louis saga in detail." That story included being born in Alabama, the grandson of slaves, his fine habits, and his debt to white southern ways. "The significant point is that all 'white hope' sentiment, which once went with any kind of white man who fought a black champion in the ring, is, at this time, altogether missing." In Edwards's view, white southern men, "especially readers of the sports pages of our press, [are] quietly pulling for the Alabama Twister." On the eve of the fight, Ed Van Every, a columnist for the *New York Sun*, published a breezy biography of young Louis which went farther. In *Joe Louis: Man and Super-Fighter*, Van Every declared that Louis had a holy mission to increase racial tolerance in the United States. "It is, and not extravagant to set down, as though the finger of God had singled this youth out for purposes of His own." Louis was "a Black Moses" to help lead his people "to a broader racial tolerance on the part of his white brother."[12]

Despite Louis's role as a race symbol, most of the white press ignored the political implications of the bout. By 1936, the white public was aware of Nazi racism and militarism, and this surfaced as an undertone in the United States as reporters referred to Schmeling as a German or a Nazi, just as they referred to Louis as a Negro. But this was usually as far as they went. In part, this reflected the American sporting press's fondness for Schmeling, which for many reporters went back to 1928 and predated the rise of National Socialism in Germany. Schmeling's cosmopolitanism still carried the day. As one reporter noted, "Almost every sports writer in this country likes Max, who is good natured, gentlemanly, sportsman-like, polite, thoughtful and almost every good thing imaginable." They also admired his courage. While other Louis opponents appeared frightened even before they climbed into the ring, notably King Levinsky and Max Baer, Schmeling showed no fear and confidently maintained that he possessed the tools to beat the Brown Bomber. Having declared his fondness for the United States on innumerable occasions, Schmeling had earned a measure of respect and affection from his second country.[13]

Although respect existed for Schmeling in the black community, few there expected him to win. With a few middle-class exceptions, the community stood solidly behind Louis, from the black elite to the man on the street. The *Amsterdam News*, for example, published a "Fight Prophecy" cartoon, which showed a fourth-round knockout by Joe. As a sign of Louis's extensive support, a panel of five other cartoons depicted, "When and if Joe Louis Loses." Aware of the heavy betting on the Brown Bomber, the cartoonist portrays black people wearing barrels because they have lost their shirts, or diving into the Harlem River to drown their sorrows. Others showed people standing at the back of a long line at the pawnshop, and "streams of moving vans coming down from Sugar Hill!" As L. E. Harrington, the *Pittsburgh Courier*'s fight critic, put it, it was not a question of the German's chances, "but the round the execution will take place."[14]

As the first black heavyweight to contend for the title since Jack Johnson, Louis succeeded in galvanizing black pride and placing the race issue squarely at the center of sports. Louis's preeminent role as a black hero reflected the growing self-confidence and assertiveness exhibited by black communities across the nation. The early 1930s had been a time of despair as the Depression hit African Americans hard, unemployment increased, and lynching rose astronomically across the South, including Louis's birthplace of Alabama. By the second half of the 1930s, however, several factors contributed to a renewed expression of self-confidence. The increase in poverty and bigotry in the context of international fascism forced black leaders to organize politically— against the invasion of Ethiopia and for an anti-lynching bill. At the same time Louis was battling his way up the ranks of contenders, the Brotherhood of Sleeping Car Porters was engaged in bitter but ultimately successful battles against the Pullman Company. On the left, black intellectuals, entertainers, and political officials flirted with the Communist Party as a means to challenge poverty and racial oppression. Louis's rise also accompanied the New Deal. Eleanor Roosevelt stood out as a champion of minorities, while new economic measures, inclusion in welfare and relief programs, and the institution of a Black Cabinet increased the sense among many African Americans that the Roosevelt administration recognized, if only haltingly, some of the problems of black America.[15]

It was at the vernacular level, however, that a new self-assertiveness emerged most strongly. In the fields of track and field, Jesse Owens, Eulace Peacock, Eddie Tolan, Ralph Metcalfe, and a host of others were dashing to new records and leaping over previous hurdles. Black dancers jumped high into the air in the elaborate patterns and gyrations of the Lindy Hop as they accompanied the powerful and elegant swing bands of Duke Ellington, Count Basie, Jimmie Lunceford, and Chick Webb. At the same time, black basketball players created the jump shot that brought them into the air, added a heavy dose of improvisation to the court, and changed the previously fixed pattern of the game. It was in boxing, however, that arena of masculine honor and combat, where black fighters such as Henry Armstrong, John Henry Lewis, and Joe Louis embodied the hopes and aspirations of the black masses.[16]

Although Louis never openly flouted society's moral code of sexual conduct and personal behavior, he still represented the hard man hero of black folklore. Operating within the tenets of the society's legal and social system, Louis defeated white society on its own terms and by its own rules. Heroes like Louis triumphed, not by breaking the laws of the larger society, as had Jack Johnson, but according to historian Lawrence Levine, "by smashing its expectations and stereotypes, by insisting that their lives transcended the traditional models and roles established for them and their people by the white majority." In that sense, his life was moral, for he provided models of "action and emulation for other black people." Nor was Louis a trickster like Br'er Rabbit, who won through guile. Rather, he was more like John Henry as he faced his oppressors directly and defeated them publicly. Blacks as well as whites hailed Louis as an exemplar of fair play, for not hitting after the bell, and for his willingness to fight anyone according to the rules of the ring, making him "a genuine sportsman." Like secular versions of the biblical Moses, to whom he was often compared, African Americans accorded Louis extraordinary powers and he was forced as well to undergo a superman test. This made him a cultural hero. A bad man's contests tended to be individual ones, which detached him from ordinary black folk who worried that he could turn on them too. Louis's battles, on the other hand, were never purely individual. He was a representative hero, whose life symbolized the lowly versus the powerful, black versus white, and thus allowed the black folk to share his victories and mourn his demise. It is this representative quality that gave his struggles epic proportions and made Louis the most important black folk hero until Muhammad Ali ascended the heavyweight throne.[17]

By knocking out white opponents on a wholesale basis, Louis became the superhero who was helping to liberate the black masses from memories of dependence and oppression. By triumphing as a powerful black man in the racial drama of boxing, he became a representative symbol for black men and women because he did what they wanted to do in real life—smash the faces of their tormentors. His migration from Alabama to Detroit, Chicago, and Harlem, where he fought many of his biggest fights, mirrored the black experience and strengthened communal identification with him, suggesting that Louis was a black everyman. Having fought his way from southern sharecropping and urban industrial poverty to the heights of wealth and national recognition, Louis stood as a new kind of fighting champion for black America. He showed the black community what it could achieve if it was willing to fight. The sports pages of the black press rang with pride over the feats of all African American athletes, but no one surpassed the coverage that Louis received. In 1935 the *Pittsburgh Courier* assigned special reporters to follow the Brown Bomber's every move to satisfy the black public's intense interest in the personal and professional life of their hero. Two years before he fought for the championship against James Braddock, black parents were already naming babies after him. Other black fans wrote poems to the black press, and sang songs about him. One verse portrayed Louis as a modern hero. "Louis can't be compared with men of old/ He's not to be classed that way/ He'll fight six men and whip all of them/ For he's trucking in a great big way." Irene Thompson penned a personal note to the *Courier* that accompanied the poem, "Fistic Idol": "I worship Joe Louis more than Father Divine's Followers Worship Him." Black fans also bought souvenir ashtrays, labeled "An Investment in Self-Respect," and they wrote in for autographed photographs of their idol. From 1935 to 1936, Louis's managers spent over $25,000 "to keep faith with his admiring public" by hiring secretaries to keep up with the mail and to dispatch requested autographed photos.[18]

The intense identification with Louis brought black fans into boxing arenas in unprecedented numbers. For his fights in Chicago and New York, African Americans constituted anywhere from one-fourth to one-third of the audience. While many of these came from the black entertainment and sporting worlds, average black fans filled many of the cheaper seats. The black press estimated that 20,000 African Americans attended the Carnera match and 25,000 put down their hard-earned dollars to see Louis whip Baer. It took a black hope to bring them out. For those in other cities or unable to afford tickets, radio brought Louis's fights directly into their homes. Black communities would go deathly quiet when the time of a Louis fight approached because so many people were at home listening to the broadcasts. Entertainment in bars and nightclubs, moreover, would halt as enterprising managers broadcast the bouts. For those without radios, black newspapers such as the *Chicago Defender* had special reporters who relayed the bout's events back to the office, which then broadcast the round-by-round happenings to crowds waiting outside the newspaper's building.[19]

The black press, moreover, served as the media link between Louis and his many African American fans. From the start of his career, black newspapers enjoyed special access to the Brown Bomber. The *Pittsburgh Courier*, for instance, had a special reporter cover Louis and his training camps exclusively, and billed itself as "the Joe Louis Newspaper." Like the *Chicago Defender* and other black papers, the *Courier* covered his every move, making him the newspaper's favorite black hero, bigger than any contemporary figure in black life. From biographical installments to wedding coverage, stories detailed his personal and professional life. The microscopic focus included coverage of his appearances at business openings, race uplift events, Baptist Church conventions, and benefits for a variety of charities. When in 1935 he met with President Roosevelt, it was big news too, especially given how politicians had shunned and persecuted Jack Johnson. Gossip items, pictures, cartoons, interviews, family life, rumors of divorce, and vacation plans were all grist for the mill. Joe Louis sold black newspapers just as he sold white ones.

For major bouts, moreover, papers ran special editions with extra pages and features. When Louis fought Baer, for example, the *Defender* not only promised special radio coverage, it also offered eight extra pages of stories "on and about Joe Louis, the finest souvenir you'll every buy." Inside features discussed Louis the Bible reader, wife Marva's social activities, and a biography of the boxer. In addition the special feature presented "Bronze Greats of the Ring," which provided black readers with a counter narrative of successful black boxers often ignored by the white press. Louis's positive relationship with the black press also led to improvements in the treatments of black sports reporters. When he first went to New York for the Carnera bout, Billy Rowe, the entertainment and sports reporter of the *Courier* and the *Amsterdam News*, complained that black newsmen were not allowed into the press row of sporting events. Louis reported the situation to Mike Jacobs, and at least in New York, black sportswriters were thereafter permitted in the press section on an equal basis with white reporters and international newsmen.[20]

It was the black press, moreover, aimed at a segregated audience, that printed advertisements and product endorsements that showed up nowhere in white newspapers. In contrast to so many of the depictions in white-owned media, Louis's advertisements in black newspapers showed him as a handsome, well-built, and determined young man. He consistently endorsed Murray's Superior Hair Pomade, which portrayed Louis as perfectly groomed. The advertisement conveyed Louis's image as a cool customer who never let his battles in the ring ruffle his feathers. Portrayed as "one of the best dressed men in America," the contender declares, "I always try to be well-groomed and the last thing I do before I go into the ring before any fight is to see that MURRAY'S POMADE has made my hair smooth and perfectly in place." Esso Gasoline also featured Louis as a spokesman: "The gasoline I choose has got to be smooth and full of punch." Another prominent product, the laxative Castoria claimed that Louis's mother, though "not rich," used it on him until his teens. Most major companies ignored the black market and severely limited Louis's endorsement opportunities compared with those of white athletes. Still, unlike other celebrities Louis refused to endorse products that he did not use or of which he disapproved. As a result, he never appeared in lucrative advertisements for tobacco or liquor.[21]

The newspaper coverage and advertisements succeeded in making Louis a household name in black communities, but it was the letters from ordinary

African Americans that demonstrate the deep connection between black fans and "our Joe," their race hero. As a handsome, powerful, and wealthy black celebrity, Louis was the type of person many black men admired and many black women adored. As a result, he received letters from young women professing their feelings for him. One Detroit woman, for example, wrote, "You really is my kind of a man. I don't like no weakling and a man like you should have a woman like me. . . . I always wanted a big strong man, and you are him." Another young woman from New Haven wrote, "I talk so much about you until I dream about you such lovely dreams. I wish they would come true." Other people asked for financial help, "to make a touch from the pile of gold Joe has accumulated in the past thirteen months." Mired in the Depression, blacks penned letters to Louis for assistance probably as much as the rest of the population communicated with President and Mrs. Roosevelt. From Texas came a letter asking Joe for a loan for $500 to purchase a two-ton truck to be used for the author's business. A woman in Virginia asked Joe to help her pay her mortgage, while a Texas minister wanted a $250 loan to save his church from foreclosure. Others asked for money for cars, suits, and dental work. Down on their luck, many black people in the Depression turned to the one seemingly invincible black superman who could provide a solution to their problems. But not everyone asked for something. The mother of three young boys, for example, told Louis how much of a role model he was for her sons, and urged him not to fail them. "Just that you keep both your life, and your fighting clean." If he lost, or was corrupted by nightlife, she wrote, "it would be a racial calamity" for black youth. "You won't let them down, will you Joe?" When Louis received her letter, he supposedly declared, "I'm going to try and keep faith with the kiddies."[22]

As someone who fought against the same obstacles imposed by the white world, Louis also became a hero to black entertainers and musicians. As black royalty, Louis's ties to the elite of show business were strong. He was identified as a "great patron of swing music," and he spoke of his admiration for bandleaders Duke Ellington and Jimmie Lunceford. Musicians, entertainers, and boxers all bolstered African American pride and accomplishment. As trumpeter and future bebop jazz innovator Dizzy Gillespie noted, "To be a 'hero' in the black community, all you have to do is make the white folks look up to you and recognize the fact that you've contributed something worthwhile." When Joe knocked out an opponent, Dizzy "felt like I'd scored a knockout. Just because he's black like me." As a result, from his first forays in New York, Louis had befriended Duke Ellington, who often visited his training camps. Bill "Bojangles" Robinson was another fixture at Louis's camps and matches. In fact, Robinson often appeared in the ring after a victory and spoke to the press of how much money Joe had made for him. Other entertainers, such as Jimmy Cross (Stump of the comedy duo Stump and Stumpy), also idolized Louis—and bet on him heavily. In fact, Cross claimed that he did not bet on

African American royalty and race heroes, Duke Ellington and Joe Louis. Black fans were convinced that Louis could not lose and would soon be king of the heavyweights. (Photo by Lauren, Frank Driggs Collection)

whether Louis would win, but rather on what round he would knock out his opponent."[23]

Solidly in his corner, black musicians poured the black community's feelings for the Brown Bomber into music. Folklorist William H. Wiggins notes that no other fighter or athlete of any kind has inspired the same number of songs as those recorded in Louis's honor. In 1935 Memphis Minnie recorded "He's in the Ring (Doin' the Same Old Thing)," and that summer, Carl Martin waxed "Joe Louis Blues" just before the bout with Max Baer. Lil Johnson's "Winner Joe (The Knockout King)," gloried in his power over white opponents such as Carnera and Baer: "Joe walked up to the man mountain and kindly shook his hand," she sang, "Then Joe backed up a step or two and knocked him in the Promised Land." Betting on Louis was also a prominent theme in songs written in honor of "our Joe." His victories in the ring translated into a better material and spiritual condition for his many black fans. Memphis Minnie declared that she "would chance my money with him" and made it clear that gambling on Joe improved her life. "I wouldn't pay my house rent/ I wouldn't buy nothing to eat/," she sang, "Joe Louis said take a chance on me/ I'm gonna put you on your feet."[24]

For the most part, blues dominated the music genres devoted to Louis, but whatever the genre, the songs glorified his exploits in and out of the ring while exaggerating his power and his prowess. His ability to unleash masculine power in ways that were frowned upon by white society—beating white men—made him a powerful symbol of black masculinity with which the majority of black people could identify. In "Joe Louis is the Man," (August 1935), Joe Pullum noted, "He's got a real good left/ And a real good right/ But when he jab with either one/ That stops the fight." In another verse, he declares, "He throws his fist/ Like a 45 throwing lead." Memphis Minnie McCoy topped this image of a two-fisted western hero, by singing that if he hits you with either his "mean" left or right, "Then it's a jolt of dynamite." Perhaps Carl Martin's "Joe Louis Blues" (September 1935), put it best. Charging into his opponents from the opening gong, "He battles them into submission/ And they all sing along."[25]

As a powerful and successful black man who whipped white men with ease, Louis became the most celebrated black hero of the mid-twentieth century. Standing up to the white world's expectations, Louis not only beat them at their own game but he actually demanded, implicitly, that white America live up to its own rules of fair play and manly competition. Many black commentators found Louis a symbol of what black manhood could accomplish if given the training and opportunity to compete with whites in all arenas of society. In fact, George Schuyler, a *Courier* columnist, called Joe a "master surgeon conducting a clinic," and emphasized the Brown Bomber's great skills, intelligence, and craft that had produced his victories. Analyzing the way he took Uzcudun apart, the columnist stressed that Louis moved coolly, scientifically—jabbing, feinting, and appraising his opponent. By calling him a master, Schuyler consciously contrasted him with the white image of Louis as acting solely on animal instinct. While his black forefathers had flinched "from the slaver's whip," Louis coolly showed with his "Poker-face" that he had the ability and strength to stand up to his racial oppressor. Rarely flustered inside the ring, outside of it he appeared little taken with his elevated celebrity. In both cases, he was a master of himself and of the world around him. No wonder he became a model of black masculinity.[26]

As a sign of how important Louis was to the black community, his victories produced great communal celebrations of a collective race victory. These impromptu mass outpourings in nearly every black community started with his victory over Carnera and continued after every major triumph of his career. Disparate black communities heard the same event over the radio at the same time and then took to the streets to share their joy, overturning the boundaries of life in a carnival mood. These spontaneous celebrations engendered analysis by African American intellectuals eager to plumb their meaning. Discussing baseball as an example of the segregation of sports in American life in his then unpublished novel *Lawd Today*, Richard Wright has a character say, but "we got old Joe Louis and there ain't nobody like him." Another replies, "It sure made me feel good all the way down in my guts when old Joe socked Baer. . . . Let them white folks *chew* that." When the radio announced Louis's victory, the second character declares, "I jumped up and flew into the street."[27]

Wright's many articles on the subject described blacks pouring from taverns, barbershops, and ghetto flats into Chicago's streets after the victory over Baer. Yelling his name at the top of their lungs, they formed long snake lines and "wove in and out of traffic." It seemed like "a revival. . . . It was a feeling of unity, of oneness." Watching this disruption of the routines of the everyday world, Wright saw a racial awakening as blacks recalled "four centuries of oppression, of frustrated hopes, of black bitterness." They "imputed to the brawny image of Joe Louis, all the balked dreams of revenge, all the secretly visualized moments of retaliation, AND HE HAD WON!" As Wright saw it, "Joe was the consciously-felt symbol. Joe was the concentrated essence of black triumph over white." They now felt free. "Invincible! A merciless victor over a fallen foe!" This "pent-up folk consciousness" that "beats and suffers and hopes—for freedom. . . . Here's the real dynamite that Joe Louis has uncovered!" As African Americans discovered, though, the ultimate victory would not be easy nor would it come as fast as they hoped.[28]

Despite the discouraging predictions against him and the grandiose expectations of the black community, Schmeling repeatedly declared that he would win. In an interview with the *Pittsburgh Courier*, he spoke confidently of the upcoming bout. He was unable to avoid politics completely, but he focused primarily on the fight as a sporting event. About his match with "the pride of the Negro race," Max exuded confidence. "I am absolutely sure that I can stop Louis," he asserted quietly. "Louis is not by any means a superman which the American press seems to imply. In spite of his spectacular ring career, he is just a human being like myself." He promised that he would hit Louis and

Louis would go down. And "he will stay down." Trained so that his legs were strong and his punching accurate, he pointed to the fight as a turning point in his career. "My last word," he told the *Courier*, "is that I would not have come to America for the money alone, though I profess to be a business man. If I did not think I would defeat Louis I would have stayed at home." If he beat Louis and then defeated Braddock, he declared he would retire as champion.[29]

After studying films of Louis's fights against Carnera and Baer, and attending the Uzcudun match on December 13, 1935, in person, Schmeling claimed to have found faults in the Bomber's fighting armor, which he now planned to exploit. "I saw something," Schmeling announced, a saying that would go down in boxing lore. As he explained to readers of the *Saturday Evening Post*, he formulated a plan to beat Louis. "Everybody laughs when Jack Johnson says Louis has a weakness, and says that he is jealous," but Schmeling saw the flaws for himself. When he made a special trip to watch Louis fight Paolino Uzcudun at Madison Square Garden, he recognized that everyone saw Louis's great knockout of the Basque stalwart, but "to me the knockout was the least important thing that I saw." After Louis jabbed with his left hand, "once, twice, he drops his left arm. The side of his face is wide open for a straight right cross." Schmeling realized that he was a faster and shorter counterpuncher, which meant that his own right would land quickly. He also noted that Louis had a dangerous left hook, but not a dangerous left jab. He planned to use his speed to get inside the hook, and counter with his right hand. "It is almost impossible to miss from that distance, but also it is more dangerous." If he mistimed the hook, he would be knocked out himself. "But my plan is not so much to counter his hook, but to discourage it simply by moving inside it." If he did that often enough, he believed he could "discourage that hook and he will go back to the punch he knows I cannot avoid, the left jab. And when he does that, I have him." As Schmeling concluded, his own right cross would be the decisive blow because Louis dropped his left when he threw the jab. To find the opening to deliver his right, however, Schmeling was prepared to take punishment for fifteen rounds from Louis's left.[30]

While Schmeling worked on his strategy at his camp in Speculator, New York, Louis trained indifferently in Lakewood, New Jersey. Flush with victory over every opponent, the young tyro took several months off, with his trainer's approval, after he knocked out Charley Retzlaff on January 17, 1936, in the first round. Named the number one boxer of 1935 by the Associated Press, the young man seemingly had it all—he was the most popular sports figure in the land, had a beautiful wife, lots of money, and offers to appear in movies. Out in Hollywood to star in a film loosely based on his life, *The Spirit of Youth*, designed for the African American market, Louis found time for discreet affairs with movie stars. During his training, moreover, Marva was in residence until a week before the match, thus affording opportunities to break one of boxing's cardinal rules: "Thou shalt not make Love before a fight." When she was sent off, other young women proved willing to indulge the number one contender. As the uncrowned world heavyweight champion, the twenty-two-year-old Louis approached the Schmeling match grossly over-confident. For the first time since he began his career, he did not listen to his trainer Jack Blackburn, cut his training short, and focused much more on his new passion, golf, than on the task at hand. Despite Blackburn's warnings that playing golf in the sun would dehydrate him, Louis ignored the advice, and as a result lost eighteen pounds. His camp was too close to New York, and reporters, chorus girls, musicians, and sporting figures were there all the time. As Louis noted, he took Schmeling lightly, and his "spoiled" attitude nearly cost him his career.[31]

When the two fighters arrived in New York on June 18, they were forced to cool their heels. A rainstorm delayed the match for one day, but as evening of June 19 neared, both German and American fans were excited. Back in Germany, a poem in *Der Angriff,* "I'll Keep My Fingers Crossed," expressed some of the German fans' expectations. "Go to it like a son of Troy/ Like Hector at the Bulettes!/ As for me, I count it as certain/ Your opponent will catch hell." Although promoter Mike Jacobs expected an audience of 80,000, only 45,000 showed up, discouraged, perhaps, by talk of an anti-Nazi boycott of Hitler's athletes, the rain delay, and more probably, by the prediction by 99 percent of boxing experts that Schmeling would be a sure knockout victim. Still, when the gong rang at 10 P.M., an eerie silence fell over the crowd. "The tension is unbelievably dramatic," noted the *Völkischer Beobachter,* "and holds everyone of the thousands and thousands of spectators spellbound." In the middle of this "inferno of heat, amidst fevers and shakes, two men take their places for the murderous battle—our Max Schmeling and Joe Louis." For Schmeling, declared the Nazi Party newspaper, bent on taking the next step to the championship, "this match was a boxing event of the greatest propor-tions." It turned out to be "one of the most unforgettable experiences we have lived to see." Black spectators sprinkled lightly throughout the stadium and heavily up in the highest bleachers confidently expected that their hero would annihilate a boxer deemed over the hill.[32]

Entering the ring as a 10:1 underdog, Schmeling followed his plan. He stood in against Louis's jabs for the first three rounds, waiting to land his right cross. So bad was it that one eye was nearly closed. "It is almost like the opening of a music composition, a symphony. The themes are announced, Joe Louis' left jab, my right cross." According to Schmeling's account, the third round was his worst. "I take a good licking. But it is also the round in which I win the fight." After absorbing innumerable lefts, "for the first time it happens the way I want it. He jabs his left and pulls it back for another, and I cross my right over and smash him on the side of the jaw. And for that I take another good beating. But I don't care. My left eye is closed, but I don't care either. I have him. . . . The plan is right." According to novelist James T. Farrell, who covered the bout for *The Nation*, "Louis was no longer the graceful, panther-like animal prancing around, in sure expectation of the kill."[33]

Having gained his confidence, Max took charge in the fourth. As the bell sounded, the crowd yelled for blood. Joe hit him with a left hook, and Max crushed him with a right, forcing Louis away from the hook and back to the jab. With Louis feeling safer to jab, Schmeling smashed over with a right cross, which staggered the Bomber. Immediately, Max went after him and put him down with a powerful right. Louis got up at the count of two, a bad mistake, and Max poured in more right-hand punches. "Kill him, Max!" a woman shouted hysterically from the grandstand. Sensing an upset in the making, the crowd cheered and exhorted Schmeling, calling for blood. After the fourth, Louis did not know where he was. He fought back, but the pattern repeated itself with Schmeling firing in his powerful right and Louis seemingly helpless to stop it. At the end of the fifth, Max let go another right just as the bell rang. While Louis dropped his hands at the bell, Schmeling's punch came crashing through. If there were any telling blow, that was it. "That punch was the turning point of the fight," declared Nat Fleischer. "Neither the referee nor the fighters had heard the bell and so powerful was the punch that it made Louis's legs take a rubber appearance and befuddled Joe's brains to such an extent that he never came out of the stupor."[34]

The Brown Bomber fought on, but the outcome was no longer in doubt. Many in the stadium, disappointed by the shocking turn of events, began yelling that Louis could not take it. After each gong he wobbled about, scarcely able to find his own corner. Loud and gleeful voices announced that the black boy was out on his feet. The superman of pugilism had been turned into a "bum" by one knockdown and a pounding succession of drives from Schmeling's right hand. Groggy for two rounds, he woke up in the seventh and attacked and had the

In an amazing upset, Schmeling knocked out Louis in the twelfth round. Here is Louis trying to raise himself from the canvas, only to roll over and be counted out. With this victory, Hitler and Goebbels turned the German boxer into an Aryan racial hero, a symbol of the new German man and the new German nation. (Acme, Library of Congress)

mob on its feet, ready to shift its allegiance as he banged away at Max. It was his last hurrah. Schmeling continued to land his right hand at will, and while Louis gamely stood up under the attack, his blows were wider and wilder, and they strayed low on several occasions into foul territory. In the twelfth round, a thoroughly exhausted and physically beaten Louis took one last hard right hand and collapsed to the canvas. The superman had fallen. "He is out. It is a clean knockout," Schmeling recalled. "It is over! Yes, I jump high into the air and wave my arms. . . . I tell you, so happy I have never been before."[35]

As James T. Farrell put it, "A long and lusty roar acclaimed the end of one superman and the elevation of another superman to supplant him in the sports columns." Schmeling was clearly the hero of the evening as sat in his dressing room speaking of the "shampionship" in a heavy German accent. Then he broadcast a statement to Germany, and called his wife, who was listening to the bout at the home of Josef and Magda Goebbels. For Louis, the results were written all over his face. Dressed in a loud gray suit, with a straw hat askew on his enormous head, Joe sat with his head bowed, his face sore and grotesquely swollen, dazed and stupefied from punishment. Helpless, he was pushed into a taxi and driven away while the crowd fought with police to get a look at him. As Louis slipped away in shame, the spotlight turned to Schmeling. "It was the end of a perfect night" for him, noted Fleischer. "He had succeeded where others had failed. He had earned for himself a niche in the fistic hall of fame."[36]

Schmeling's dramatic upset of the black superman shocked the boxing world and cemented his place as "unser Max," a German national hero. With his amazing victory, Schmeling laid claim to a title fight against James Braddock in a match that most observers believed would be a sure win for the German boxer. Having defeated the fighter hailed as the marvel of the age, he became the darling of the Nazi regime and of German boxing fans. Poems appeared in many different periodicals, including *Box-Sport*. "My dear Max, we are so proud/ Mighty Joe was knocked out/ So that was the Bomber?/ All Germany rises and celebrates." Even more, congratulatory telegrams flooded in from Nazi officials, all of which were printed on the front pages of German newspapers. Hitler immediately telegraphed his delight to Max and wife Anny for the "wonderful victory . . . of our greatest German boxer." The *Schwartze Korps*, one of the party's paramilitary units, exulted that Schmeling's "shattering fists had smashed all adversaries of National Socialism in the face" and had "saved the prestige of the white race." Reichssportsführer von Tschammer und Osten also chimed in: "In the name of German sports I wish you heartiest congratulations." Now that there was no longer any chance that a black boxer would defeat an Aryan one, Germans celebrated the victory as a racial one. As Goebbels happily wrote in his diary, Max has "fought for Germany and won. The White over the Black, and the White was a German." The

Hamburger Anzeiger added that his victory even made him an American hero to the army of whites that had preferred a white hope all along. Louis may have been a modest Negro, the paper noted, but "he can't help being the representative of a race whose self confidence following great successes promptly turned into arrogance." As a result, Schmeling's victory made him "for Americans, the savior of white boxing supremacy."[37]

The German press also printed congratulatory telegrams from other white racist countries, such as South Africa, and took great delight in noting a celebration that took place on the floor of Congress among white southern representatives once the match was decided. According to the *Leipziger Neueste Nachrichten*, many of the congressmen listened to the fight over the radio, and after the report of victory, "ran into the large Congress hall where indescribable scenes were acted out. The dignified Senators gave Schmeling three cheers, clapped each other on the shoulders, and shook hands with joy." In fact, Germans were pleased to lead an international white front against the brown wave. Party ideologue George Spandau claimed victory in the worldwide racial struggle of superior races against their genetic inferiors. Had Louis won, he argued, colored peoples everywhere would have received encouragement to revolt "in arrogance and bestial cruelty." By his victory, however, Schmeling restored "the prestige of the white race," the "superiority of white intelligence," and the power of white authority everywhere. As the leaders of an international white front, German newspapers scoured the conservative and fascist press in Britain, France, and Italy, and reported their positive reactions to the outcome of the match. Clearly, Germans took great satisfaction in the attention that Schmeling earned for the nation in the eyes of the world. The *Völkischer Beobachter* perhaps put it best: "When Nurmi [the Finnish track star] raced in America and rushed from victory to victory, he secured for his land badly needed credit. Who would deny that we need this ideal credit in answer to a world wide smear campaign and lying prophets."[38]

The elated Nazi regime and the mass of the German people now happily glorified Schmeling as a national hero, and he returned home to an ecstatic welcome. So that the regime could exploit the victory for propaganda purposes, Schmeling was ordered to return to the Reich as quickly as possible. He flew across the Atlantic in a Zeppelin, the fastest mode of intercontinental travel and a marvel of Nazi mechanical and spiritual genius; the flight terminated in Frankfurt where, like an ancient German god, he descended from the skies to a huge reception organized by the local authorities. After local party officials hailed his achievement, Schmeling, his wife Anny, and his mother then flew to Berlin on Goebbels's private plane, where they were greeted by an army of officials at Tempelhof Field as well as by a corps of five hundred amateur boxers who stood at attention.[39]

A three-hour reception in the Chancellery followed, where Schmeling and his family had tea with Hitler, Goebbels, and other top Nazi brass, pic-

Heil Max. A mass reception in Frankfurt for Schmeling after his victory. (Acme, Library of Congress)

Adolf Hitler holds a reception at the Chancellery July 1936 for Schmeling, his wife Anny, and his mother. Hitler was delighted with the outcome of the fight and turned it into a German victory. (Corbis)

tures of which graced newspapers and newsreels for the following week. In a ceremony that marked athletic achievement with national political success, Hitler expressed his thanks along with those of the German people, as he declared, "Every German has reason to be proud." In the more relaxed portions of the visit, Hitler asked to see the films of the match, and as he watched them he grew excited. "Every time I landed a punch," Schmeling recalled, "he slapped his thigh with delight." The Führer immediately saw the propaganda value of the victory and its film record. He told Goebbels that the film would not be just part of the weekly film newsreel, but ordered it to be shown as a main feature throughout the Reich. Arno Hellmis, the premier German sports broadcaster who had announced the fight from New York, noted that "to argue about the value or lack of value of professional boxing is superfluous at a time when a German professional boxer stands at the center of interest of 100 million people. And only one who is familiar with crowd psychology knows what kind of great, vital publicity Max Schmeling provides." Everyone in the United States, Hellmis argued, now knew that Schmeling's name was associated with Germany and its National Socialist regime.

Hitler and Goebbels transformed the individual achievement of a professional athlete into a German triumph by expanding the fight film, adding special inserts to give the bout a political interpretation, and releasing it commercially to enthusiastic crowds in movie houses across the country. A sold-out audience attended the premiere of "Max Schmeling's Victory—a German Victory," at Berlin's Titiana Palace, where the boxer was treated like a movie star. The film was also shown free to youth for educational purposes and its profits went untaxed. The focus of the film was "unser Max," whose victory, the film's narrator Arno Hellmis tells his audience, "was more than just a success by a German sportsman; it was a German victory"; the other emphasis was on Schmeling's racial triumph. "Telegrams poured in from Australia, South Africa, South America and the American south," Hellmis declares, "where the loss of a white man to a black man could be accepted only with clenched teeth, but where the win caused great jubilation." The Nazis also interpreted the victory as a triumph of mind over body. No expert believed Schmeling could beat Louis who had youth and his race's "natural boxing talent." But Max possessed the iron discipline, iron willpower, and strategic intelligence that no black boxer could match.[40]

The special additions to the actual fight film stressed the humiliations that Schmeling had faced in the United States. Using blowups of cartoons that had appeared in the American press, Hellmis showed how America "laughed and degraded him." Sports cartoonist Burris Jenkins, for example, depicted Max tied to a cannon labeled Louis, implying that Schmeling was mere cannon fodder for the powerful Brown Bomber. In another cartoon, a host of boxing experts predict the outcome of the bout by pointing to a bloody

Max, lying on the canvas. But the goal of the film was not merely to show the degradation that Schmeling was forced to undergo in a foreign and hostile land. Rather, the film sought to depict the resurrection of a symbolic German despite the great odds and world opinion against him. The movie depicts Schmeling standing up effectively to these insults to his athletic abilities and to German manliness and national pride. After he knocked out Louis, humiliation turned to respect. "This German had done what no one thought possible!" In his last words of commentary before the actual film of the fight starts, Hellmis tells the audience, "You will see a will as hard as Krupp steel that will accomplish everything." The movie does show Louis fighting bravely to the end, but he is no match for the German's superior courage, strategy, and will. As Hellmis puts it, "The Black Uhlan of the Rhine rides again!"[41]

This tale of German triumph over national humiliation turned Schmeling into a German superhero. Although not a fair-skinned Aryan, Schmeling was the closest thing to a German super athlete the Nazis and the German people possessed. Increasingly, he assumed the role of Siegfried, the pure idealistic hero beset by unscrupulous and conspiratorial enemies in one of the oldest heroic myths in German culture. Schmeling, the man of iron will, tough discipline, and good habits, embodied the warrior ethic. His always-fit body and confident mind were the opposite of the diseased body of the Jew and the instinctual nature of the black man. A man of good and clean habits, known to drink little, smoke not at all, and hunt often, he was happily married and lived in a suburban idyll away from the corruptions of city life. Overall, he demonstrated his superior mental toughness, his willingness to take punishment in a carefully planned strategy. In doing so, he became the perfect Aryan man who embodied the strength and will power of the resurrected nation, a man capable of destroying the racially mixed sign of pollution in the body politic. In a culture that equated money and professionalism with Jews and the commercial corruption of sport, Schmeling, the consummate professional boxer, was reinterpreted as fighting not for prize money, "the dance around the golden calf," but for a noble sportsman's purpose—the comeback. Now that he had triumphed, "unser Max" would do what no one had done before, recapture the heavyweight crown and regain the world's respect.[42]

Schmeling's triumph over the enemies of German honor and national respect found widespread expression throughout German media. A wax recording of the German announcer's blow-by-blow description of the bout played over and over on German radio and on public loudspeakers. The press joined in the patriotic celebrations too. The *National-Blatt*, for example, charged that the victory occurred against "a world of enemies." The *Berlin Zeitung am Mittag* declared that it was wonderful "to gain the conviction of being permitted to call today's most popular athlete in the world a *German*.

Goebbels's press organ, *Der Angriff*, was the most explicit in its political interpretation of the fight. "He succeeded against world opinion," the newspaper announced, because of the Führer. Schmeling "says he would not have had the strength if he had not known what support he had in his homeland," the newspaper declared. "He was allowed to speak with the Führer and his Ministers and from that moment his will to victory was boundless."[43]

For German sports fans this successful boxing achievement was part of the rescue of German pride and manhood, and the triumph of a master race. Indeed, Max's victory came shortly after the reoccupation of the Rhine and the beginnings of German military rearmament. Both Hitler and Schmeling stood as national heroes who overcame the odds and the shame of national humiliation, and it is no accident that their stars rose at the same time. The defeat of German manhood in World War I was a theme that the Nazis were happy to exploit. That French African soldiers had fraternized with the locals in the Rhineland to produce mixed-race bastard children only added to the sense of violation and oppression that many Germans felt at the loss of their colonial empire. Once a major imperial power, the Germans were only recently occupied by black colonial troops. These anxieties of racial weakness and pollution also surfaced in the widespread anxiety about "Jewish-Neger jazz" infecting German youth and weakening racial and national bloodlines. Now, however, Hitler had proven that the Germans had the will to triumph and were on the march again. And with his ring victory, so had Schmeling.[44]

In this climate, the Nazi press portrayed Louis as "a child of nature," who posed no match for a member of the master race. While "it is proven that nature's peoples [*Naturvölker*] possess endurance and toughness," noted *Box-Sport*, the black man "is morally weaker than the white man." Often, their drinking, sexual indulgence, and fondness for celebration led to their defeat. Hans Massaquoi, an Afro-German youth, recalled his teacher's words after Louis's defeat: "Max Schmeling has demonstrated in the most convincing way that a Negro's brute strength is no match for an Aryan boxer with superior intelligence. His victory was a great victory not only for Germany but for Aryan people throughout the world." The teacher's views of Louis flowed easily into his assessment of America's black athletes in the upcoming Olympics. America's "black auxiliaries," as they were often called, were not true athletes, but rather "born runners and jumpers—like horses and other animals." For a German to lose to these "half-civilized people," the teacher said, "is no more disgrace than losing to a horse. Everybody knows a horse is physically superior but mentally inferior to a man. The same is true for Hottentots from America." In fact, black boxers followed the dictates of their race. As Hans Botticher argued in the *Stuttgarter Neues Tagblatt*, Louis "possesses all the advantages of his race, but also all their faults: uncontrolled animal wildness!" Indeed, over and over Germans described Louis fighting by instinct rather than intellect. They also maintained that most Negro boxers could not be "knocked out at the chin or the skull," because one "cannot claim that the skull of the Negro is constructed especially finely and delicately." Schmeling's decisive knockout blows to the face, however, raised questions about these theories. *Box-Sport* explained this contradiction, however, by noting that that Louis "is not full-blooded, he is *mixed*," and hence probably inherited "the white's *normal capacity for endurance*."[45]

Schmeling beat more than a man; he beat someone whom the German press called "Clay-Face." To the Germans, Louis represented American racial miscegenation, which they feared was spreading throughout their own land. For the Nazis, the United States was the scene of "the most unrestrained miscegenation" among poor whites and blacks, surpassed in racial betrayal only by archenemy France. A year before the match, *Box-Sport* noted that most descriptions of Louis described him as "black," but his photo proves that "he is in fact not a Negro, but some *mixture* of black and white." Yet, it is impossible to mistake a Negro because "they 'smell' different" from whites. The mixture, allowed by the United States, was part of the rising anarchy of a black population close to being out of control sexually as well as physically. As the boxing reportage reveals, Germans were appalled by the conditions in Louis's training camp, compared to the quiet, rigorous, and disciplined setting of Schmeling's quarters. Close to the city so Louis's supporters could drop in at will, his camp in Lakewood, New Jersey, also was set up to make money from entrance fees to watch the Brown Bomber train. Not only were there celebrities, gamblers, and the flotsam and jetsam of Harlem, according to German accounts, "Negresses" screamed at all hours in undisciplined displays of enthusiasm. No wonder Louis was defeated.[46]

Schmeling's victory was thus widely hailed as a major cultural achievement that transcended sports. As German ideologue George Spandau put it, athletics should be considered more than mere pastime, for they helped in "rebuilding our nation to a nation of men, orderly and disciplined, and above all fully conscious of their national ties." Yet the attempt to justify a government based on the success of the nation's athletes was new. As Schmeling noted in his autobiography, victories in sports now carried tremendous political value, and he was becoming deeply embroiled in the politicization of sport. He saw the bout "characterized in headlines and newspaper cartoons as a 'Battle of the Races,' and my victory had been turned into a 'German victory.' Congratulatory telegrams and occasional contact with those in power was now being held against me."[47]

While Schmeling gloried in his role as a German national hero, his central place in Nazi culture did not prevent him from earning the ire of high-placed officials. In private he attempted to use his newly acquired status to help friends and associates who found themselves in trouble with the regime. He may have been encouraged in his actions because a grateful Hitler waived his taxes on the fight, and Goebbels decided to make no more fuss about "unser Max's" Jewish manager, Joe Jacobs. Flush with victory in summer 1936, Schmeling tried to save a neighbor, Frau Josef Thorak, from arrest under the Nuremburg Laws of 1935, which forbade intermarriage between Jews and Aryans. A Jew, she had married sculptor Josef Thorak; they divorced to save Thorak's career but continued to live together even though the Gestapo watched their house. Given the situation, Schmeling pleaded her case before Goebbels. "But she's a Jew, isn't she?" Goebbels kept asking. Officials ordered the couple to separate, and Thorak then went on to become one of Hitler's favored sculptors. In 1938, the former Frau Thorak, along with the couple's son, managed to emigrate to France.

In the summer of 1937 Schmeling found himself in trouble again for his friendship with Jews. On a trip to Rotterdam to watch Gustav Eder box, he enjoyed a reunion in a cabaret with old friends, many of whom were Jewish exiles. Two days later the Ministry of Enlightenment and Propaganda complained about a picture that was taken as a souvenir. Schmeling replied, "I conduct myself abroad as would any good German. Those are my old friends and I won't be told how I should treat them!" Later two of those friends were gassed in Auschwitz. While capable of decent and courageous acts in private, acts that marked his distance from the central tenets of Nazi philosophy, Schmeling did little to oppose the regime in public.[48]

While Germans were ecstatic with the outcome of the June fight, African Americans found the devastating defeat of their hero a severe shock. As Schmeling recalled, driving downtown from Yankee Stadium proved dangerous. He saw passing cars spit on and hit with bricks and boards by small groups of disappointed young African Americans. The next day he read that hundreds of people were injured in rioting. In Chicago, he reported, matters were worse. For the most part, however, an eerie, wounded silence fell over black communities everywhere. According to the *Chicago Defender*, "The downfall or collapse of a Race prize-fighter of Joe Louis' caliber gives cause for more grief among the race than any other single event." For the black community as for Germans, a boxer was more than an individual. As a folk hero, Louis symbolized an entire people. He fought for the lowly versus the powerful, and black versus white. If the *Defender* is to be believed, black people took the idea of race ambassador very seriously. And here their champion and ambassador had failed. "A black prize-fighter who reaches the stellar role belongs to the race as a whole," the newspaper maintained. "He is looked upon by thousands of the other group as the sole representative of the black race's ambition, its hope and its pride." Any black man who gained such fame, the newspaper argued, "has a double duty to perform: one to himself; the other to his race. He no longer remains his own property. The public has an investment in his conduct; his successes and his failures."[49]

The deep public investment in Louis appeared in the immediate response to his defeat. Reminiscent of Schmeling's departure for the United States, no crowd waited at the train station to meet Louis when he returned to Detroit. "The fallen Bomber, wearing blue spectacles to hide a damaged eye, pulled up his topcoat collar. . . . In the taxicab, he hid his face with his straw hat." Maya Angelou described what it meant whenever Louis was hurt: "it was our people falling. It was another lynching, yet another Black man hanging on a tree." Singer Lena Horne expressed the feelings of millions who saw their superman destroyed. On the road with the Noble Sissle Orchestra, she was near hysteria and some of the musicians were crying as they listened to the fight over the radio. Joe "was the one invincible Negro, the one who stood up to the white man and beat him down with his fists. He in a sense carried so many of our hopes, maybe even dreams of vengeance."[50]

Aware of the international and racial aspects of the Schmeling bout, many African American commentators linked Louis's defeat to the fall of Haile Selassie and Ethiopia. Writing in despair, the Reverend Adam Clayton Powell, Jr., noted that both Selassie and Louis symbolized the fight against white oppression. Delighted that a black man was fighting a white man in Ethiopia, "the populace became jaunty, carefree . . . even arrogant at times. . . . There was a definite light of a new day shining in our eyes." Then along came the Brown Bomber, "and our racial morale took a sky high leap that broke every record from Portland to Pasadena." But when Addis Ababa fell and Louis lost, "something died . . . we're just shuffling along." Similarly crushed, Roi Ottley linked the battle against race supremacy to the international threats of Fascist Italy and Nazi Germany. With the defeat of Ethiopia and Joe Louis, "white folks still in the lead." White southerners and white gentiles, Ottley declared, could once again celebrate the victory of "Nordic supremacy."[51]

The willingness of the community to identify with "our Joe" as a betting favorite only compounded the disappointment. "Besides the loss of Joe," claimed the *Chicago Defender*, "there was the loss of thousands of dollars, furniture, jewelry, rent and bonuses." When the all-black musical "Blackbirds of 1936" appeared in England, for instance, almost the entire cast bet their meager wages on Louis, and they lost everything. In an extreme example, a black woman in Chicago lost $50 on Joe, and she ended up in a psychiatric hospital. Listening to the bout on the radio, she fell off her chair and fainted when Louis was knocked down in the fourth round. Taken to the hospital, she remained unconscious. Loss of money also led to violence. When a Harlem black man poured salt in the community's wounds by trying to collect on the wager he had made on Schmeling, a number of the black men he had bet with beat him severely.[52]

So great was the disappointment and so hard was it to imagine Louis losing that the black press openly asked if "Joe Louis Was Doped?" The *Defender* charged that Louis's listlessness in the ring was the result of an

injection of some unknown substance prior to the fight. Sports reporter Al
Monroe claimed that evidence of doping fit with his reports from Louis's
camp that something was wrong all along, and certainly on the night of the
fight. When Louis entered the ring, he was in a daze. "Was it a well-organized
plot, faultlessly maneuvered? Or was it a series of strange circumstances that
worked with deadly effect?" The *Pittsburgh Courier's* Ira Lewis, agreed because Louis appeared mentally befogged. He had no evidence, but he reasoned that "it would take more than a punch to make a man of Louis's ability
and stamina, he later showed, to forget all about boxing." In fact, Lewis blamed
the managers for letting their fighter stay in a New York hotel where they did
not exercise supervision over food, water, and the wait staff. "This was a costly
mistake." If it was not dope, then "Did Max or Marva Beat Joe," inquired the
Courier. William G. Nunn, the paper's sports editor, discussed rumors that
Joe was upset on the eve of the fight by a letter from Marva's former fiancé
that threatened to reveal details of their relationship. Whatever the source,
something aside from Schmeling's fists had to account for the weakness of the
strong black hero. Perhaps the fight was fixed, perhaps by whites. "They finally beat Joe Louis!"[53]

Yet the furor quickly passed. As several sportswriters pointed out, there
was no reason to fix the fight since all the betting was on Louis, little on
Schmeling. Moreover, an agonized Louis and Marva denied all charges of
doping and of marital turmoil. To his credit, Louis responded honestly that
"there was no dope in any needle that got into my arm or any other place. But
there was dope in that right of Schmeling." Such plain speaking was a Louis
hallmark. His refusal to make excuses helped him rebound in the public's eye
and would become part of the larger Louis myth. Even more important, the
loss had a long-term effect on the young boxer. For the first time, he recognized how much he meant to black people as a symbol of their hopes and
aspirations. "I let myself down, I let a whole race of people down because I
thought I was some kind of hot shit."[54]

In an experience common to Depression-era heroes, his failure spurred
him to identify more deeply with the fate of the group—in this case the black
community. A fallen idol, he now became a fallible superman, someone ordinary black Americans could identify with because he was not invincible. Shamed
by his ineffectiveness, he vowed to come back and win the crown. "It was like
I had climbed a steep flight of stairs and fallen down halfway." Similar to
classic heroes, Louis's loss to Schmeling would be a test of his character.
Knocked out of title contention, now it was his turn to struggle to come back
from a devastating defeat. After a short period of soul-searching, Louis vowed
never again to be cocky, ignore his trainers, or go "high-hat." As he trained,
every sparring partner was Schmeling. "I had been humiliated and I had to
prove that I was the best heavyweight around." Blacks forgave quickly, for
Louis had experienced the humiliation and loss that they knew every day, but

he had not been defeated by it. The trumpeter and bandleader Louis Armstrong, a huge supporter of the Brown Bomber, wrote to the *Courier*, "Joe Louis is not through." With him when he won, "we should rally around *our* Joe and encourage him in defeat."[55]

Louis's defeat also knocked him off the white press's superman pedestal. Initially, many white sportswriters sounded the themes reminiscent of the German analysis: Louis was reduced to the status of a naïve "boy" who lacked Schmeling's intelligence and skill. Grantland Rice, the dean of American sports columnists, for example, argued that "the near superman of many fights suddenly turned into a duffer with nothing to offer but fighting instinct and a stout heart." As one of the reasons for this, Rice argued in a direct parallel to German racial thought that "his elemental, jungle cunning was no match for a much superior intelligence that happened to size things up—and act on the situation as it was." In sum according to the much-syndicated Rice, "Schmeling had the head and the heart to win." Others asked whether Louis would lose his self-confidence. Davis J. Walsh argued that the defeat had destroyed his self-assurance, and that in "his own eyes, he stands destroyed, demolished, wiped out." Worse than the fact that he cannot take a punch "is that he won't." Many white reporters expressed sympathy for the Brown Bomber, but they were also aware that an idol had fallen. No trumpets lashed the air, noted Walter Stewart of the *New York World-Telegram*. "Trumpets are not for idols with the cracked clay still sticking to their feet—not for men still bruised by the beating."[56]

In the white South, the defeat produced a flood of negative stereotypes, as if people were waiting for Louis to lose so they could unload on him. The *Chicago Defender* did a survey of southern papers and found that "it took the defeat of Joe Louis to uncover this condition [racial prejudice] in boxing." While the press remained neutral, during the past year, race haters had nursed their fears of him in secret, but his defeat unleashed letters to the editor that used "every imaginable type of abuse:" "nigger," "darkie," "coon," "Sambo." Letters to northern papers from the South, moreover, celebrated Joe's defeat and extolled Schmeling for upholding the virtues of white supremacy.[57]

Yet, Louis still had support among many white sportswriters and fans who sympathized with his plight and saw the loss as a sign of an overconfident young man who had not trained well. In fact, many sports columnists found themselves in the same predicament as Louis. As boxing experts, they too had been overconfident in their own predictions that Louis would win handily. Now they stood vilified and shamed in the eyes of outraged readers. Knocked off their own pedestals, many of them continued to predict that Louis would not make the same mistakes twice and that he would come back. For these writers, Louis's modesty, hard work, and seriousness would carry him to the top despite the loss. His failure, then, came to be everyman's failure—a fate common in the Depression. Moreover, Louis's declaration that "I'll come back" was a sign of hope over adversity. As he went on the comeback trail later that summer and all through the fall and winter, he continued to knock out opponents and make new fans. Faced with obstacles common to all larger-than-life heroes, here was a Depression hero who would not quit.[58]

While the political implications of the first Louis-Schmeling fight took on greater life after the match, there were some undercurrents to suggest that boxing all along was embroiled in the international tensions of the era. Even before Schmeling's victory turned him into a full-fledged Nazi hero, Jewish and black groups had taken notice of Nazi racial philosophy, the regime's treatment of Jews, and their attitudes toward blacks. For the past year, anti-fascist groups had campaigned against American participation in the Berlin Olympics, and since the fight took place in New York, Jewish and anti-fascist groups debated whether to boycott Schmeling too. For the most part, they decided there was no need. Louis would win and that would put an end to the Nazi hero. As a result, many Jews and blacks who disapproved of the bout decided to attend. Rabbi Alexander Lyons of Eighth Avenue Temple and the Reverend Dr. Thomas Harten, Negro pastor of Holy Trinity Baptist Church, told an audience of six hundred gathered in Harten's chapel that they would attend the fight to protest Hitler's view that a bout between a German and a Negro was improper. They urged their audience of blacks and Jews to join with "every decent American" in boycotting all German-made goods until "Hitler comes to his senses." Rabbi Lyons declared that the Nazis were not merely anti-Semitic; they were "anti-everyone who has something they want." He pointed to several German Jews in the audience who had been forced to flee their country, and he charged that the Nazi idea of a "pure Aryan race" also discriminated against blacks. "There is no such thing as a pure race any-where on earth," the Rabbi asserted. Both men announced, however, that they planned to attend the fight to root for Louis against Nazi racial theories. As Schmeling became more closely identified with Nazi Germany and as-sumed his place as the logical contender for the heavyweight throne, this sen-timent would produce an organized boycott movement that would play an important role in his quest for a comeback. Despite being athletes who be-lieved in the independence of sport, Schmeling and Louis in the years ahead would find themselves embroiled even more in the rising fervor of national-ism on the international stage. For now, Schmeling prepared himself to fight for the crown, while Louis still had much to prove.[59]

4

THE BRADDOCK AFFAIR AND
THE COLOR LINE

The new champion stands forth as uncontroverted evidence that boxing, as well any other
professional sport, rates fair play above race or
color prejudice.

Edward Van Every, *Ring*, September 1937

We can see from the fact that the Negro Louis
now is proclaimed world champion how little
this American title amounts to. The world's
sportsmen never will recognize this American
world champion. For Germany there is only one
world champion and he is Schmeling.

Der Angriff, June 1937

Max Schmeling's remarkable triumph over Joe Louis in June 1936 propelled him to the height of his fame as a German national hero. Beginning with his victory and ending with the Olympic Games, staged during August in and around Berlin, Germans basked in the sporting victories of their triumphant heroes and their triumphant nation. Confident that "unser Max" soon would be world heavyweight champion the German public also reveled in the fact that the Berlin Olympics riveted the attention of the world on the new German order. During that Olympic summer, German interest in sports reached fever pitch. Schmeling's incredible victory and the Olympic Games were two of the emotional centerpieces of the Nazi era. In recognition of his triumph, the German boxer and his wife received passes to all the games and were guests of honor for the opening ceremonies in August. As they approached the stadium on the outskirts of Berlin, they probably saw the crowds milling around the monumental statue of the noble boxer, sculpted by their neighbor Josef Thorak as a classical warrior for whom Schmeling was the model.

Parallel to Hitler's hopes for German boxing, the Berlin Olympics trained the eyes of the world on a powerful and respectable nation recovered from defeat and depression. Success in international sporting events was equated with successful political systems, and in the mid-1930s the Nazis set out to demonstrate that their political system was stronger than that of the democracies. Almost immediately after Schmeling's return home, for example, German boxing promoters, in cooperation with the highest levels of government, sought to stage his heavyweight title match with the current champion, James J. Braddock, in Germany. While that attempt proved unsuccessful, the regime used the entire power of the national government to create the most elaborate Olympic festival in history. As Hitler put it, "Germany is in a bad and difficult situation internationally. It should therefore try to impress world public opinion by cultural means." The Olympics of 1936 were the first since the reconstitution of the games in 1896 to be fully organized by state authorities. Hitler's participation and his daily appearances in his private box made it seem that he and the regime, not the German Olympic Committee, were the sponsor and patron of the events. The massive sports stadium and the entire Olympic complex, the most modern and expensive in the world at the time, cost more than thirty times the original estimate. Once he recognized the enormous propaganda value of international sporting events, Hitler stinted on nothing to make his summer Olympics a spectacular advertisement for the Third Reich. The enormous statues, the well laid out village for the athletes, the translators and tourist guides, and the lavish ritual and display showed the world that Germany had risen from the ashes. To foster favorable opinion of Germany in the eyes of the world, Dr. Goebbels decreed that for the duration of the summer, Nazi paramilitary groups stop mistreating Jews, all signs disparaging Jews should be removed from shops and streets, and the most rabid of the anti-Semitic newspapers, *Der Stürmer*, should disappear from the newsstands.[1]

Schmeling had been depicted by the Germans as a representative of classical sportsmanship rather than material ambition; similarly, the Olympics was a symbolic expression of the Nazi regime's self-portrayal as the inheritor and protector of the highest ideals of Western civilization. To foster the link with classical Greece, Germans financed the excavation of the original Olympia and inaugurated the torch relay ritual. Three thousand runners carried the fire from Olympia in Greece to the Olympic Stadium in Berlin where they symbolically passed the torch of classical sport and culture to Nazi Germany. In order to showcase the vitality and strength of the nation, German Olympic officials were the first to officially tally the medals to show the number won by nation as well as by individual athlete. As a result, they could claim that Germany's thirty-three gold medals, twenty-six silver, and thirty-six bronze made them the "winner" of the Berlin Olympics over the Americans.[2]

Their overall triumph helped console German officials over the spectacular victories of African American athletes in the track and field events. Jesse Owens, Archie Williams, Mack Robinson, Fritz Pollard, Jr., Ralph Metcalfe, Cornelius Johnson, and Dave Albritton stood at the forefront of the challenge to German notions of racial superiority. Before the games opened, Schmeling sought out Jesse Owens in the Olympic Village as a gesture of international friendship. Years later, though, Owens said that he and his black teammates were angered by how the Nazis paraded the German boxer around the Village. As Owens recalled, "inwardly many of us were trying to atone for Joe's loss." African Americans, Afro-Germans, and colonial peoples took great hope from Owens's four gold medals and transformed him into a race hero after Louis's ignominious defeat. The soft-spoken, friendly, and well-behaved Jesse Owens not only tied the world record in the 100-meter dash; he also set new Olympic records in the long jump and the 200-meter run. As part of the 400-meter relay team, he also helped set world and Olympic records. To a degree, he became an American hero for disproving German notions of Aryan racial supremacy and convincing white Americans that their athletes could defend the honor of the United States and democracy. Adolf Hitler politicized the Olympics by making them a test of Nazi racial theories while also heralding Schmeling's victory as proof that Aryans were superior to athletes of inferior races. His refusal to shake Owens's hand, though more myth than reality, was widely reported in the United States as an insult to the African American people and to American national honor. By disproving theories of Nordic physical supremacy, Owens and the other black athletes on the Olympic team opened the door to a debate over white supremacy abroad—and at home.[3]

The National Socialists assuaged their national and racial anxieties with the notion that the Games were only a temporary phenomenon and Owens merely a unique physical specimen. According to *Der Angriff*, African American athletes were America's "black auxiliaries." A Nazi assistant to Foreign Minister von Ribbentrop told the American ambassador's daughter that the United States had taken unfair advantage by letting "non-humans like Owens and other Negro athletes" compete in the Games. Still, many Germans flocked to watch the black Americans, and they gave Owens huge ovations after his feats. The lasting image of the games lay in the triumphant athletic festival memorialized by Leni Riefenstahl's film, *Olympia*. Overall, many in the world were dazzled, and Germans could see themselves as the perfect hosts: gracious, tolerant, well organized, respectable. Most of all, they were powerful once again.[4]

While many black and white Americans delighted in Jesse Owens and his compatriots astounding the world in an international test of national strength, the success of so many of "Uncle Sam's black athletes" raised thorny questions for the racially segregated United States. The white press treated black track stars as they often did Joe Louis, emphasizing their racial status, quoting them in dialect, and relying on race to explain their athletic success. Remarkably similar to the Nazi view of Owens as a natural athlete, for example, John Kieran declared in the *New York Times* that "apparently it takes time to work up endurance, but speed comes by nature." Some writers, though, criticized their fellows for equating black sport success with the savagery of the African jungle, and some even stressed the training and hard work that went into the making of a top Olympic competitor—black or white. Even more important, the politicization of the Olympics by Germany as a test of national and racial strength heightened the paradox of black sportsmen representing a segregated United States. Some sports reporters, for example, refused to accept blacks as their representatives. Grantland Rice, for one, called black athletes "our Ethiopian phalanx," in language similar to the Nazi view of them as "black auxiliaries." The dean of American sports columnists noted that "the United States will be okay until it runs out of African entries." For Americans, international events such as the Olympics and the Louis-Schmeling match brought the question of American and German racism to the forefront of national consciousness. More to the point, international rivalry politicized sport and played an important role in breaking the color line in the heavyweight division.[5]

Not surprisingly, the political intensification and heightened nationalism of sport had tremendous effects on the world of international boxing. Certainly it was international boxing that Max Schmeling had uppermost in his mind. While the drama of the Berlin Olympics unfolded, Max and Anny could not linger beyond the opening ceremonies. The very next day, they boarded the Zeppelin *Hindenburg* for one more trip to New York City. Max had been promised a contract to fight the champion, James Braddock, but he did not have it in hand. On August 9, 1936, though, he and Joe Jacobs met with Joe Gould, Braddock's manager, and representatives of the New York State Athletic Commission and signed the contract for a title fight scheduled for September 26, 1936, at New York's Yankee Stadium. With little over a month to go, Schmeling and Braddock prepared to open their training camps. As the culmination of his comeback, the German fighter eagerly anticipated becoming the next heavyweight champion of the world. Coming off its triumphant

Olympic Games, the National Socialist regime looked forward to the perfect end to the perfect athletic summer.[6]

Schmeling's hopes for another heavyweight title rested on Braddock, the champion since the summer of 1935 when he took the title from Max Baer in a fifteen-round upset. Despite his crown, however, Braddock found himself in the shadow of Joe Louis, whose spectacular ring achievements attracted most of the attention and gate receipts of fight fans. In part, fans overlooked the champion because bad hands kept him from defending the title and he was aging fast without having much to show for his crown. Most boxing experts expected his first defense to be his last. Now that Schmeling had demolished Louis, however, Braddock stood at the center of German and American interest in the sport. A tough Irish-American with a hard right and a good chin, Braddock and his manager would decide the fate of Schmeling and Louis. Despite his contract to fight Schmeling, Braddock and his manager had their eye on the biggest payday they could find. What if prize fighting's biggest draw, Joe Louis, were available? Schmeling had reason to worry. From August 1936 until June 1937, these three men were entangled in a boxing version of a love triangle.

As Schmeling began preparations in August for his title fight against Braddock, Louis's handlers worked hard to restore the Brown Bomber's self-confidence and catapult him back into the championship picture. There was much at stake. The longer Louis was kept away from fighting for the title, the greater the opportunity for American racists to fortify the barrier against a black heavyweight champion. Concerned also that too long a layoff would be bad for his physical and mental disposition and his box office appeal, promoter Mike Jacobs and Louis's managers vowed to put him back in the ring quickly. As part of their public relations effort, Roxborough, Black, and Jacobs used the defeat to stress a new aspect of the Louis legend. The loss, they emphasized, would only make Louis stronger. Not only would he win the title but he would also redeem himself by defeating Schmeling the next time they met. For African Americans the old question persisted: would whites let another black contender fight for the title or would the color line continue to prevail?[7]

While the sporting public turned its attention to the Olympic Games, Louis's advisors pushed him back into training for his next bout against ex-champion Jack Sharkey, which would occur on August 18, 1936, at Yankee Stadium, only a month after his loss to Schmeling. Determined to get him back on the right track, Jack Blackburn closed Louis's camp at Pompton Lakes, New Jersey, to the public, stepped up the hours of roadwork, and banned wife Marva. Sharkey, the Brown Bomber's opponent, had won the title from Schmeling in 1932 at the age of thirty-three, promptly lost it again in 1933 to Primo Carnera, and gone into retirement. With the revival of the fight game

Sharkey had come back in 1935, but with indifferent results. Still, as an ex-champion he would serve as a perfect test for Louis's comeback. During the publicity buildup to the match, Sharkey confidently told reporters that he had a hex on black fighters, since he had beaten Harry Wills and George Godfrey earlier in his career. Louis would present no trouble.[8]

Blackburn vowed otherwise. Aware that Sharkey would throw a constant barrage of right hands in imitation of Schmeling's victorious strategy, Blackburn had Louis's sparring partners pepper him with rights so that the Bomber could practice his defense. The fight, however, would be the real test. On the day before the match, Louis spoke with William Nunn, sports editor of the *Pittsburgh Courier*. "I won't let my people down," Louis assured him. "They had confidence in me and wanted me to win the heavyweight title. . . . I'm hitting the comeback trail . . . and I don't mean maybe." Still, Louis was uncharacteristically nervous as he listened to the prefight announcements. The introduction of Schmeling, on his visit to nail down his contract for a title bout, and the tremendous applause he received probably fed Louis's uneasiness. Once the bell rang, however, the Brown Bomber proved as good as his word, knocking down Sharkey twice in the second round with a vicious attack before finishing him off in the third, and setting off celebrations in black neighborhoods across the nation. The joyful mood was strengthened by news from the Olympics that Jesse Owens had destroyed the myth of Aryan supremacy by winning four gold medals.[9]

While African Americans celebrated the redemption of their idol, Schmeling's great expectations began to sour. Only days after Louis defeated Sharkey, the Braddock camp announced that the champion had broken his finger and would need an operation. It turned out to be rheumatoid arthritis in his hands, and it became clear that the fight had to be postponed. Although there were rumors that Braddock's injury was a ruse to buy time so that the champion could fight a revived Louis instead, Schmeling refused to challenge a disabled fighter. With the outdoor boxing season coming to a close, the German boxer agreed with the American promoters to put off the title match until early June 1937. Deeply disappointed Max returned home where he consoled himself by hunting on Field Marshall Hermann Göring's private estate outside Berlin. While he held a contract that guaranteed him a championship match, at nearly thirty-two, Schmeling could not help worrying that time was slipping away from him. Instead of fighting for the title, the number one contender was forced to watch events spiral out of control.[10]

As Louis pursued his comeback, a rematch with the man who had recently vanquished him remained uppermost in his mind and in the mind of promoter Mike Jacobs. Jacobs offered the German fighter a bout for the fall since Schmeling had no one to fight until Braddock's hands healed. Jacobs proposed a $300,000 guarantee for Schmeling, but the German prizefighter, who played his cards close to the vest and handled his own business affairs, believed he would be better off waiting for Braddock and the title. If he met Louis and lost, his comeback would have been for naught; Louis could claim that he was the rightful contender for the crown. If Schmeling won, he would have achieved little other than beating the same man twice in a row. When the German heavyweight turned him down, Jacobs reasoned that he could push Louis into contention for a title bout. Hoping to lure the match with Braddock away from Schmeling, Louis's handlers scheduled him to meet a series of opponents during the fall and winter of 1936. After beating Sharkey, the Brown Bomber knocked out local hero Al Ettore in the fifth round on September 22 in Philadelphia, and then blasted out Jorge Brescia of Argentina in two rounds in New York on October 9. In Cleveland on December 14, 1936, Louis dispatched Eddie Simms in twenty seconds of the first round. Although doubts still remained about his vulnerability to a right hand, Louis had fought his way back into the title picture.[11]

At the same time, Mike Jacobs opened negotiations with Braddock and his manager Joe Gould. In the sleazy world of American boxing, as Gould and Jacobs knew, state commissions had little power and money talked louder than contracts. It was clear to Gould that in all probability Braddock would lose the title in his first defense, and Gould wanted to earn as much as possible in exchange for giving it up. The two camps, however, could not come to terms. Braddock was contractually tied to Madison Square Garden and Jimmy Johnston. As a way around the contract, Jacobs proposed a twelve-round exhibition between Louis and Braddock in Atlantic City. Exhibitions were no-decision bouts, and Braddock would lose his crown only if Louis knocked him out. Louis's team was convinced he would accomplish this easily. Even with a $500,000 guarantee, far more than he would make in a fight against Schmeling, Gould wanted more money.

Louis might have been a clean fighter, but boxing still retained its ties to the underworld and remained one of the true vestiges of primitive capitalism. When John Roxborough traveled to New York in December 1936 to check with Jacobs about his negotiations with Braddock, he found matters stuck. Upon leaving Jacobs's office, two hoodlums waited for him. One worked for Owney Madden, the owner of the Cotton Club and the backer of Primo Carnera, and a man who controlled a good deal of New York City's criminal enterprises. The pair drove Roxborough around Manhattan for an hour, without saying anything. The silence began to get to him. Was this a particularly long version of the last ride? They pulled into an alley and led him into the rear entrance of a nightclub, where to his relief Roxborough saw Gould waiting for him. Gould agreed to a twelve-round exhibition with Louis and assured Roxborough that Braddock was sure to lose his title. There was a catch: Gould demanded 50 percent of Louis. Indignant over such a blatant attempt at intimidation, Roxborough refused. He refused again when Gould lowered his demand to 20 percent. Finally, Louis's manager suggested that Gould talk to Mike Jacobs about a share of the promoter's future profits. No decisions were made. Roxborough walked out happy to be alive.

Once rumors of a Braddock-Louis exhibition match surfaced, Madison Square Garden, which controlled the original fight through its contract with Braddock, worked to stop it. Schmeling also grew concerned that the New York boxing world would leave him out in the cold. In December he boarded the *Bremen* and sailed to New York to appear before the New York State Athletic Commission, where he asserted that he had a contract for a title match. The commission considered the German the leading contender for the crown because he had beaten Louis, and it issued a ruling that prohibited Braddock from meeting the Brown Bomber in an exhibition. The commission also ordered Braddock and Schmeling to post $5,000 bonds that they would forfeit if they failed to show up for their scheduled bout on June 3, 1937. Concerned as well that a Schmeling victory might result in his taking the title home to Germany, the commission required him to put up another $25,000 to guarantee that he would defend the title in the United States within half a year if he won. As a result, Gould signed another contract with Madison Square Garden promising that Braddock would not fight Louis before the Schmeling bout. Once more Schmeling returned to Germany optimistic that his quest to retake the title was at hand. It looked like Louis was odd man out.[12]

As German boxing fans looked forward once again to "unser Max" contending for the heavyweight title against James Braddock, they soon found their hopes at the mercy of political forces building against the Nazi regime. On January 8, 1937, the Non-Sectarian Anti-Nazi League to Champion Human Rights, Inc., one of the many left wing anti-fascist Popular Front organizations active during the Great Depression, announced a boycott of the Braddock-Schmeling heavyweight title match. The politicization of international sports unleashed by the Nazi propaganda machine in the wake of Schmeling's defeat of Louis and the successful Berlin Olympics now came home to roost. Dr. Henry Smith Leiper, a minister of the Church of Christ and supporter of the league, put it best: "The clear statement of Nazi policy concerning the place of sports makes it evident that no sport exists in Germany for its own sake. . . . Every sport is part of Nazi propaganda and militarism." The league urged the Madison Square Garden Corporation to stop its plans for the bout. "Our organization is engaged in combating the menace of Nazism," the league declared in a letter, and proposed a boycott to deprive Schmeling, as a citizen of Nazi Germany, of a chance to gain the ring's richest crown. In addition, the league objected to American money finding its way to the coffers of the Third Reich. "We don't want to interfere with the fight itself if the money stays here," league president Samuel Untermyer declared. "We don't want it sent to Germany." A Schmeling victory, the league feared, would also turn into a giant propaganda bonanza for the Nazi regime and aid

a nation now bent on the persecution of the Jews. The leaders of the movement had nearly pulled off an official boycott of the Berlin Olympic Games
and they knew how to work the press. Untermyer and Jeremiah T. Mahoney,
the former head of the American Athletic Union and a major leader of the
Olympic boycott, spearheaded the movement. An impressive list of members
immediately assembled, including New York City Mayor Fiorello LaGuardia,
who served as one of the league's vice presidents. Almost immediately the
league began bombarding the New York State Athletic Commission and the
newspapers with letters and telegrams objecting to the fight.[13]

The idea of the boycott against Schmeling as a representative of the Nazi
regime played strongly with Jewish and leftist groups, especially in New York
City and the surrounding east coast urban areas where the majority of American Jews resided. While the anti-Nazi activity was strongest among American
Jews, a number of Catholic organizations also expressed their opposition to
the bout as a protest against Nazi threats to church independence in Germany. *The Daily Worker*, the communist newspaper, eagerly supported the
league's actions. As the newspaper noted, the movement was "spreading like
wildfire," and had assumed "proportions which made it almost certain that
the fight would be doomed." The Jewish War Veterans, with a membership
of 250,000, for example, along with left wing anti-fascist groups joined the
protests. Among them were 208 New Jersey organizations, which met in
Newark to support the league, along with the Patriotic Men's and Women's
Society, an organization of 42,000 people who met at the Hotel Commodore
to endorse the boycott. Letters and telegrams also went out to athletic and
anti-Nazi organizations in Cleveland, Chicago, and other large cities to prevent the bout being moved out of New York. The boycott, moreover, was
only the tip of growing anti-fascist sentiment in the United States. In February 1937, on the fourth anniversary of Hitler's rise to power, 1,200 people
met at Carnegie Hall to voice their opposition to the Nazi regime. William
Green, president of the American Federation of Labor, placed American labor on record as opposed to Nazi policies. He called upon the American people,
"regardless of creed and nationality, and who believe in freedom, democracy
and liberty," to boycott "German goods and German services so long as persecution, intolerance and repression are imposed upon the working people of
Germany and upon the Jewish race."[14]

In response to the Nazi politicization of sport, the American anti-fascist
coalition transformed Schmeling into a Nazi representative and Joe Louis
into a democratic hero. The glorification of Louis as an anti-fascist symbol
had first emerged during his bout with Carnera, when politicized African
Americans and leftist whites interpreted Louis's win as a victory for anti-
fascism and anti-colonialism against Mussolini's Italy. Now because of Hitler's
actions, Schmeling was perceived on the left, and among Jewish and African
American groups, as a member of the Nazi Party and hence complicit in the

growing crimes of the regime. The interest of black and white leftists in sports was a new phenomenon. Previously the left had viewed sports as an expression of bourgeois capitalism, and boxing in particular as the symbol of dog-eat-dog brutality; now they interpreted athletics as a contested terrain where democracy and ethnic and racial tolerance vied with fascist racism—against Jews and blacks—for allegiance. In order to reach younger workers, the Communist Party sought to speak to them on their own level and about things that they considered truly American: sports and entertainment. As a result, in January 1936, just as the boycott was announced, the *Daily Worker* inaugurated a sports section under the direction of Lester Rodney, another leftist of Jewish background. At the same time, the communist newspaper and the party's magazine of opinion, the *New Masses*, opened their pages to black leftists such as novelist Richard Wright and Frank Marshall Davis. As Marxists, Wright, Davis, and Rodney not only campaigned against the values for which they believed Schmeling stood, but for Joe Louis whom they saw as a democratic hero battling worldwide fascism, white supremacy, and Jim Crow. Claiming that the boxing hierarchy did not want a "Negro champion," for instance, the *Worker* argued that "the public does." Although they continued to see boxing as a brutal sport, these writers understood that it appealed to a pluralistic, working-class audience. Eager to break the color bar and discrimination in American sports, they took the boycott issue onto the pages of the leftist press.[15]

The boycott movement against the proposed Braddock-Schmeling match had an immediate effect on what the *Daily Worker* called "the hard-boiled boys of Fistic Row." Joe Gould, Braddock's manager, who was Jewish, was especially nervous as he contemplated the horror of empty seats at Braddock's first title defense. As soon as the boycott was announced Gould declared that he would not permit Braddock to take part in the fight if the boycott got into full swing. "My job as the champ's business manager," Gould declared, "is to see that Braddock makes some money out of his fights, but as the matter stands now the fight could be held in a telephone booth and probably Jim wouldn't make enough to buy him a taxi ride home." At the same time, Mike Jacobs also expressed concern over the $30,000 he had advanced Schmeling. There was reason to worry. New York City was the largest Jewish city in the world; Jewish fans made up a large part of the audience for boxing, and if Jewish groups decided to boycott the match, promoters stood to lose a huge sum of money. Gould announced that he had polled sportswriters on the depth of anti-Nazi sentiment and that the writers had agreed a boycott would hurt the gate. It might be too risky, Gould claimed, to go on with the fight.[16]

As soon as Schmeling heard the news of the boycott, he sensed that the wind was not blowing in his direction. Deeply upset to learn that his worst fears might be confirmed, he appealed to the American public's sense of fair play. "I believe the American public is too fair to be influenced by a political campaign against a sportsman like me who never went in for politics," he said.

While Schmeling staked his faith on American fair play, the German press reacted to the issue with unanimous indignation. "Schmeling Heckled in Unbelievable Way by U.S.A. Jews," headlined the front page of the Nazi newspaper *Der Angriff*. The paper called the boycott movement "crazy and malicious," while the Berlin *Nachtausgabe* termed it an "evil-minded attempt to blackmail the promoters" into sidestepping Schmeling in favor of a match between Braddock and Louis. "We cannot assume," said the Berlin *Tageblatt*, that the Americans will deny the traditions of fairness and chivalrous treatment of competitors which are common to all Anglo-Saxon nations." *Box-Sport*, however, better understood how American boxing worked. The German boxing magazine reported that American champions "choose from among challengers of equal merit, the one promising the highest income."[17]

While the boycott movement raged, Louis's managers put on a final push to show that the Brown Bomber deserved to fight Braddock for the title. They reasoned that Louis had beaten every top heavyweight other than Braddock and Schmeling, but these two boxers remained out of reach for a match. If Schmeling defeated the champion, as was expected, then Louis might hope to fight Max for the crown in late summer or fall of 1937. But Schmeling might refuse. He had no need to tangle with Louis again. Having beaten him decisively, Schmeling might claim he had nothing to prove and just return to Germany where the Nazis would delight in using the championship for propaganda purposes. The Nazi regime might refuse to allow Schmeling to fight Louis again on racial grounds, or the Germans might insist that the American come to Germany, not a welcome prospect for a black man in 1937. Nor was it beyond reason that white promoters might seize any excuse to keep Louis from his opportunity to fight for the crown. Hence, Louis and his managers kept the pressure on by fighting and winning. In January 1937, the Bomber knocked out Steve Ketchell, and later that month met Bob Pastor, a former football star at New York University, in the Garden. Realizing that mixing it up close in would be a disaster, Pastor used his speed to stay away from Louis. At the end of the ten-round bout the former NYU star remained standing and unhurt. When the unanimous results of a Louis victory were announced, the crowd booed. White sportswriters continued their mantra that Louis was outsmarted by Pastor and was too dumb to adapt to Schmeling's tactics. In his next fight, though, the African American heavyweight contender looked particularly good, knocking out tough Natie Brown in the fourth round in Kansas City. Shortly thereafter, on February 19, 1937, Mike Jacobs and Joe Gould announced that the Brown Bomber would meet Braddock for the championship in Chicago on June 22, 1937.[18]

As soon as the promoters announced their decision to call off the Schmeling bout, the boycott movement proclaimed victory. Frederick L. Dannick, secretary of the Anti-Nazi Department of the American League against War and Fascism, declared, "The Braddock-Louis fight is the natural outcome of the splendid boycott movement against Schmeling." It was clear to the various Jewish and popular front groups that the boycott had made the Schmeling bout economically unattractive. Everyone dreamed of a million-dollar gate, argued the *Daily Worker*, but the opposition to the proposed match made that seem distant. As the financial angle seemed to be the major concern of the Braddock camp it was doubtful the bout would go on because "it will be a profitless" one. They also claimed that their victory was a victory for racial justice. The top managers, the communist newspaper claimed, did not "want a Negro champion," and they would do everything they could to prevent him from the title. Other observers also credited the boycott for Braddock's actions. As sportswriter Hype Igoe argued, "It is no laughing matter and never will be. Max Schmeling is a 'marked' man in New York so far as the Jewish and Catholic patrons are concerned." Asked why they did not oppose the first Louis-Schmeling bout, league spokesmen noted that they had mistakenly believed that "the German would be crushed by a Negro," and "Hitler's oppression would be revenged." Having erred once, they vowed to oppose this bout with all their energy.[19]

The boycott would not have had such force had it not intersected with the Braddock camp's desire for a huge payday. The champ preferred Louis to Schmeling because the Brown Bomber would attract a much bigger gate. Hurt financially by the Depression and by his inactivity since winning the crown, Braddock was looking "for money enough to last me the rest of my life." Because of his ring inactivity, the champ could not avail himself of the benefits of the title: lucrative advertising, radio, and stage contracts. Although well respected, he lacked color and was a poor draw. Most boxing experts predicted that the ring-rusty veteran would lose to whomever he fought, so he "was selling his title," a term used when a champion meets a man he knows he cannot whip. Indeed, this is why his camp insisted on Louis over Schmeling and was willing to overlook the informal agreement among white promoters, managers, and boxers that the heavyweight title was a Caucasian preserve. Louis's exciting boxing style, his many knockouts, and his popularity with whites and blacks meant that a Louis-Braddock title match might earn a million dollars. It is also possible that Braddock's experiences with welfare, working the docks, and putting up with hard times made him less hostile to African Americans who had faced similar obstacles. He certainly did not express any of the racist sentiments so common among boxers, including Sharkey's claim that he had a hex on black fighters. As George Nicholson, one of Braddock's black sparring partners noted, "He was a wonderful guy. Always treated everybody the same. . . . We ate together, showered together, all equals." Still, while Braddock deserves credit for not drawing the color line, his motives were largely pecuniary.[20]

Mike Jacobs played a key role in securing the bout for Louis. He offered Gould better terms, a guarantee of $500,000 or half the gate and radio revenues, whichever was greater. Moreover, he clinched the deal by giving Braddock and Gould 10 percent of his net profits from heavyweight title pro-motions for the next decade should Braddock lose, as was expected. For Braddock and Gould, this meant future paydays, estimated at $150 dollars per week, whether the Irish-American fighter won or lost against Louis. Jacobs paid a high price, but he was after bigger game. If Louis won, Jacobs would finally control the heavyweight title, the weight class that dominated the en-tire sport, and he would also have broken the monopoly over all of champion-ship boxing long exercised by his old enemies, Madison Square Garden and Jimmy Johnston. Jacobs thought this financial deal was in his and Louis's own long-term interest. "Uncle Mike," as Jacobs was called, stood to make a lot of money. The color line would be broken, but not all the reasons were noble.[21]

While many American boxing fans expressed sympathy for Braddock's desire to support his family, Nat Fleischer also recognized the merit of Schmeling's outraged tirade against poor sportsmanship and unscrupulous business prac-tices in the American boxing world. Appearing before the New York State Athletic Commission, Schmeling charged that he had been cheated by Braddock and Gould, as well as by Mike Jacobs. Given that the German had defeated Louis, Fleischer asserted, Schmeling was still the world's outstand-ing heavyweight and deserved the title bout. In fact, *Ring* continued to rank him as the number one heavyweight ahead of both Louis and Braddock, whom they barely ranked third. The prizefight magazine also awarded the German boxer its Merit Award based on his high standing in the field of boxing.[22]

Being ranked number one held small consolation. Schmeling was hurt and frustrated. In his memoirs, he recognized the increased role that interna-tional politics had come to play in boxing. On the German side, he acknowl-edged that his victory over Louis and German triumphs in the Berlin Olympics of 1936 may have played well in Germany, but they had disastrous effects in the United States. Ignoring the accomplishments of Jesse Owens and other black American track stars, Hitler claimed that Germany had "won" the Olym-pic games. Everyone knew that the Führer viewed athletic success as political validation, but "without wanting it," Schmeling recalled, "I too was being pulled into this political aspect." In recognition of his symbolic importance, the Sturmabteilung (SA) attempted to award him the Dagger of Honor and name him an Honorary Commander. After mulling it over, he refused the honor because he recognized that it would cause even more problems for his pursuit of the heavyweight crown in the United States. Schmeling tried to put off these demands by sounding out government officials about joining the Schutzstaffel (SS) instead, a plan of action on which he did not follow through. Yet, while other athletes were being pressed into wearing the SA pin, the Nazi authorities, again acting pragmatically, allowed him to refuse so as not to sully his image in the arena of international sport. As it was becoming increasingly more difficult for Schmeling to separate himself from the politicization of German sport, as far as he was concerned, sports were also being pressed into the service of politics in the United States. A German champion could have been tolerated earlier, in 1930–32, he maintained, but "one coming from Hitler's Germany was acceptable to no one" in 1937. As a young man whose primary goal was to regain the title, "I had tried to convince Hitler of the merits of my Jewish manager, Joe Jacobs, and I wanted to convince Americans of my right to a title bout. Both attempts were equally naïve."[23]

Despite these claims, the "Braddock Affair," as Germans called it, actually drove Schmeling closer to the regime while pushing German and American boxing farther apart. When Gould announced the Louis-Braddock fight, Schmeling realized that the only way to save his championship match was by holding a fight with Braddock in Germany. He got in touch with Adolf Hitler, who agreed to the plan. The National Socialists had long dreamed of capturing the international capital of boxing from New York. Having their own champion fighting in the Third Reich would do wonders for Germany's image abroad. Once boxing in the United States had shown itself to be controlled by unscrupulous Jewish promoters and gangsters, it would be only fitting for Germany's image to break the American hegemony. As with the Olympics, Germany would show that it could stage a spectacular title match and handle business affairs in strict accordance to the international rules of sport. Schmeling would win the title in an ecstatic Germany and raise the nation's prestige in the eyes of the world, while the bout promised to attract sought-after hard currency.[24]

The regime appeared willing to put its full weight behind the effort to capture international boxing. Hitler contacted his old friend Justizsenator Herman Esser in Berlin, who believed that the proposed title match would be a boon to building the German tourist industry. Esser wrote to Reichsminister Dr. Lammers that he wanted to lure to Germany as many foreigners as possible "with a lot of capital" for the "sporting event of the year 1937." In pursuit of prestige and foreign currency, Esser, Lammers, and von Tschammer agreed to guarantee Braddock $350,000 tax-free. In addition, they proposed to hold the fight in Berlin's Olympic Stadium. As Lammers put it, "Schmeling would be boxing before Hitler's eyes and would very likely win." The German government went so far as to set up a Dutch company to control ticket sales and radio and movie rights. "It is understood," wrote the American Consul to Germany, "that Chancellor Hitler has already voiced his general approval of such a match, and the match will be presented to Göring for consideration."[25]

With the details not fully worked out and the German bureaucracy grinding slowly, Schmeling went back to the United States in March where he attempted to lure Braddock to Germany with the offer of a title fight and the monetary guarantee. According to the *New York Times*, there was "not the slightest doubt that the German Champion has the National Sozial Regime behind him [sic]." Yet, the offers did not produce the desired effects. Gould and Braddock had no intention of fighting anyone other than Louis. Still, Schmeling planned to go through with his planned exhibition tour of the United States that March to keep himself before the public eye. He hoped to move public opinion in his favor to ensure that Braddock fight him instead.[26]

American protest groups, however, did not let up. They had vowed to boycott Schmeling's proposed exhibition tour as early as January, and they were as good as their word. Hitler had made sports into a battle between Democracy and Fascism, and leftists and Jewish groups had vowed that in the United States fascism with its virulent anti-Semitism and racial prejudice would not win. In March 1937, for example, the *Daily Worker* crowed that Schmeling's tour of twenty-two cities was in "hot water." Most of the dates were in parts of "the South where Fascist and reactionary forces are in control and where Max will be guaranteed a good reception." There would be no picket lines, the paper declared, "in most of the towns where the Storm Trooper boxes, if and when he boxes." The paper used the supposed receptiveness of the white South to equate Nazism and American racial and political repression. The whole exhibition was a Nazi trick to make Max an idol of the American fight fans as well as those of Germany. "The idea is to make it appear that Max will march through the badlands of America like a conquering lion. Ha-ha! But let the old SA man show his face in the ring of a city where civil liberties still include the right to protest and the Nazis would have to think of another lie to explain his unpopularity." In fact, the *Daily Worker* took as a sign of the boycott's effectiveness the fact that Braddock broke his contract with Schmeling and chose to fight Louis instead. At the end of March 1937, for instance, the paper argued that "the public is quickly learning that they can promote fights against the wishes of the promoters, if they exert enough pressure. The Braddock-Louis fight is the first title fight in the history of the game that has actually been promoted by the fans."[27]

The only recourse left was for Schmeling to plead his case in court and before the New York State Athletic Commission. In and out of the courts, back and forth to the commission, from Germany to the United States and back, Schmeling and his manager Joe "Yussel" Jacobs went, but to no avail. Back in Germany in April 1937, Schmeling described his problems to Dr. Goebbels, who wrote in his diary that "Braddock is cowardly and is always looking for new excuses." In a last desperate attempt to secure the title fight, Schmeling allegedly called Joe Gould via transatlantic telephone to have Goebbels handle the final negotiations to bring the championship bout to Germany. Gould demanded that the Germans deposit $500,000 in a New Jersey bank, and he insisted on an American referee and one English judge. The third point was

Despite being denied the opportunity to contend for the title against Braddock, Schmeling remained enormously popular among the German people. Here he is signing an autograph for a member of the German military. Whatever his fate, Max remained a popular hero to many Germans. (Harry Ransom Humanities Research Center, The University of Texas at Austin)

the deal-breaker. By no means an observant Jew, the hard-boiled Gould nevertheless demanded that "you get Hitler to stop kicking the Jews around. Unless he gives them back full citizenship and property rights, you know what you and Max can do with your fight." Perhaps Braddock's manager had no intention of fighting in Germany anyway, but it is still noteworthy that the policies of the National Socialists had aroused in him enough of a sense of Jewish pride that he would make a demand that would outrage the Nazis. The politicization of sports showed up in surprising places indeed.[28]

Against all odds, Schmeling returned to the United States and began intensive training at his camp in Speculator, New York, in May. He was told by the New York Athletic Commission to get himself into condition for the Braddock match despite the fact that the commission and fight fans around the world knew that the battle would not take place. When he came down to the city for the weigh-in on June 3, he stepped onto the scales before the largest gathering of newsmen and photographers that had ever attended such a ceremony. He was the only one to weigh in. Braddock remained in Grand Beach, Michigan, training to meet Louis later that month. The bout that never was came to be known widely as the phantom fight. The Commission fined Braddock a mere $1,000. The German press was beside itself with rage and so was Goebbels. He confided in his diary, "Schmeling duped by Braddock. He won't fight out of cowardliness. Very American-like!"[29]

Watching from abroad, German fans remained certain that the Americans had conspired to trick their German hero. The events of winter and spring 1937 magnified the German public's view that Schmeling was a Siegfried hero, beset on all sides by foreign enemies who conspired to bring about his and Germany's destruction. Outraged by the insult to their national honor, German fans and boxing authorities proclaimed Schmeling the only true heavyweight champion of the world. While many white Americans concurred, Germans were convinced that their pure hero was destroyed by the lack of sportsmanship in the United States. Schmeling's trainer and friend, Max Machon, reported that each time they came close to a solution, Braddock's camp "wanted money, nothing but money." On the other hand, Machon reported, Schmeling's motives were far more honorable. He noted that the German hero had said that he "would enter the ring against Braddock without receiving a penny for it." In fact, the German boxing establishment, in conjunction with Nazi officials, went so far as to award Schmeling a special honor that recognized his achievements in the face of concerted opposition. At a special amateur boxing festival staged for Winter Relief in April 1937, German boxing authorities awarded him the Golden Belt of the Association of German Boxers and at the same time the title "German Champion of All Classes." *Box-Sport* explained the award. "Max Schmeling has long merited such a distinctive award, after, in his early years, he had to wade through a mire of undeserved offences." These offenses, the magazine declared, "he never deserved and . . . [they] were artificially constructed by people who have not known a sense of fair play (*Fairness*) in sports, or the satisfaction of manly struggle and victory." The magazine pointed out that the Americans once denigrated Germany's greatest boxer because he was the first to win a world championship and because he was in the forefront of a struggle "beyond the frontiers of home"—not just for himself, "but also for his fatherland." The Golden Champion's Belt and the title served to distance Germans "from those ingrates, beneath which one of the best athletic sons of our homeland has had to suffer."[30]

The decision to award Max an official honor arose from a desire to contrast his special character with a debased America taken over and controlled by Jews. His pursuit of the title in the face of all obstacles, *Box-Sport* argued, "against all lack of good sportsmanship . . . shows Max as an athlete of the best character," for he did not fight merely "for money," but for the pure quest of the comeback. In fact, the failure of the American courts to honor Schmeling's contract with Braddock meant that in the United States there was no public honor and government commissions lacked the strength to keep the sport clean and fair. The end result would be anarchy, a falling back to a "level of savagery in the ring (*wilden Ringkämpferei*)." With some justification, German fans were incensed. But what stands out is how obsessively they pored over the insult and the conspiratorial framework into which they put the individual events. In boldface the magazine declared, "There is a conspiracy active in the wings, which asks nothing about right or sporting ethics, which places money above all, which is bare of feeling or fairness, and which has altogether submitted to Mammon." The claim was that American sport had been taken over by pure commercialism, which was an old charge against Americanism, but reflected the deep-seated German conservative fear that an older German culture and way of life was being destroyed by the desire for gold.[31]

Underlying fears of commercialization in the holy arena of sport was a much darker conspiratorial view of the world, the belief that it was the Jewish press and the Jewish powers behind the throne of New York and American boxing that were responsible for Mammon's triumph over American sportsmanship. When the German sporting and Nazi press referred to the conspiracies of businessmen they had the Jewish Joe Gould, Braddock's manager, and Mike Jacobs, Louis's promoter, in mind. Consumed by fear that the commercial world in Germany would swamp traditional organic values, conservative Germans blamed the Jews for their distress. At the same time, they could project onto the American sporting world a "*Judaization*" and—with Louis— a mongrelization of everything they held dear. Indeed, for many Germans, though they admired American technology and efficiency, Americans were entirely consumed with business and commerce. A country without a true culture of its own, America was ripe for infiltration by Jewish interests. The widespread presence of Jewish businessmen, promoters, and managers in boxing, along with the (alleged) Jewish-controlled press, proved that America already had been subverted. On the other side, the Nazis railed against the Jewish boycott too as slandering the good name of the German nation for no good reason other than malicious ill will. "Unser Max," the *Völkischer Beobachter* argued, "had a much greater fight against those led by the lower instincts, that circle of Jewish boycotters who plague the whole world and who thought that through him, the German, they would take on national-socialist Germany." At the bottom of society Jewish boycotters spread Marxist filth while at the top Jewish businessmen perpetrated "Dollar-America." They were responsible for debasing American culture and for insulting the true sporting values as embodied by the Third Reich. A Jewish conspiracy and a lust for money had sidelined the German hero bent on his noble quest and, worse, installed a "Neger" as champion.[32]

June 3, 1937, the date of the phantom fight came and went, and German public opinion grew even more livid. Having trusted the New York State Athletic Commission, Schmeling was irate. He expressed his indignation clearly. "The decision is really a broad joke and no more. It is laughable that a state boxing commission should not have the power to force a *breaker of a contract* to keep his obligations." According to the *Berlin Zeitung am Mittag*, the word was out "to European sports authorities, who must prove that they know how to protect top European athletes from unobstructed American gangster politics." The day of the phantom fight, announced *Box-*

Sport was "a black day for boxing, blacker than any other in the last ten years."[33]

To the dismay of German sports fans and to the delight of African Americans and many leftists and Jews, it was Joe Louis, not Max Schmeling, who met James J. Braddock for the heavyweight championship at Chicago's Comiskey Park on June 22, 1937. Almost a year to the day after his shocking defeat by "unser Max," Louis had rebounded, with the help of international politics, to become only the second black heavyweight to contend for the championship. Not since Jack Johnson lost his title in 1915 had another African American had a chance at the crown. Recognizing the importance of the mixed-race title bout, the chairman of the Illinois Boxing Commission asked that true sportsmanship be displayed and that fans disregard prejudice based on race, color, or creed before, during, and after the fight. The stakes were high. For Louis's army of black fans, the bout had historic implications. Their idol was at twenty-three not only the youngest man to contend for the heavyweight title but he was also "breaking through a barrier that has been placed in the path of Negro heavyweights since champions were recognized in the division." He entered the ring, declared the *Chicago Defender*, "as standard bearer for those who have battled to blot out an unwritten, but emphatic law that stood between a Race man and the chance to win the heavyweight title." The hopes of a people were riding on his shoulders.[34]

The Louis-Braddock bout raised serious issues about American national identity. Such a blatant act of discrimination as denying Louis the opportunity to fight for the title solely because of his color would abrogate the standards of fair play and sportsmanship that Americans claimed to stand for in contrast to the Nazis. But it was not just a matter of importance to African Americans. For many Jewish Americans, Schmeling and the Nazis had come to stand for the opposite of what American values ought to be: a broader civic nationalism that included Jews as well as other groups considered outsiders and inferiors. While profit played a huge role in determining who would fight for the title, sports had become a testing ground for American self-conceptions as the plebian arena of boxing attests. Should Americans bar Louis from the title bout they would be placing themselves on the same level of racism as the Nazis. Moreover, Louis had already surpassed standards of appropriate conduct and proven that he was different from Jack Johnson. For white and black fans, the emerging national values of the United States guaranteed Louis's right to fight for the crown.[35]

Louis's managers, trainers, and sparring partners had called Louis "Champ" from the start of his professional career, but this was his first shot at the title. At his training camp in Kenosha, Wisconsin, "I worked harder for it than for any fight I remember," Louis recalled. Blackburn got him up at 5 o'clock every morning for six weeks so that he could do ten miles of roadwork before the sun came up. Back from the road, he would take a nap, then get up for breakfast around 10 or 11 o'clock. He had a large number of sparring partners, and he would work out with them. His handlers brought in Harry Lenny, a special boxing teacher, to instruct him on how to avoid a right, which, according to Louis, "was Damon Runyon's idea." He knocked off at 5 P.M., had supper, and talked with his entourage until 9. Then he went to bed for eight hours of sleep. "I came around fine. I weighed in the day of the fight at 197¼, just like I figured to do."[36]

Most boxing experts favored Louis to win, but Braddock remained the sentimental favorite of many white fans. At thirty-two years of age, the Irish-American boxer was considered past his prime, and having been out of the ring for two years, ring rust was expected. Yet despite his mediocre record—he had lost twenty-nine fights—and his reputation as a slugger, Braddock was treated as smarter than Louis and thus considered to have an edge in ring craft. Many white fans admired Braddock as a Depression-era hero. The champ had been an underdog his entire life, and his upset of Max Baer was one of the great triumphs of the "little man" during the 1930s. He was also the first Irish-American to hold the championship since Gene Tunney, and the sons of Erin hoped he would continue to hold the title.

The son of Irish immigrants, Braddock was born on December 6, 1905, and grew up in Hell's Kitchen in New York City. A few years after Jim's birth, the family moved to West New York, New Jersey, where he attended Catholic school. He and his pals had their share of schoolyard bouts, and young Jim did well. Leaving school at the age of thirteen, he carried copy for a printing company, and then rode the rails in search of adventure. Three years later, tired of the hobo life, he found a job as a stevedore back in New Jersey on the Weehawken docks, which helped his physical development. At the encouragement of his brother he entered the amateur boxing ranks, and his knockout punch made him a champion. When he turned professional in 1926, he acquired his manager Joe Gould, who stuck with him through the ups and downs of his career.[37]

His career went through a decline just as the Depression deepened its hold on the country. In 1929 he lost a fifteen-round decision to light heavyweight champion Tommy Loughran, and then broke a knuckle on his right hand and could not afford the operation required to fix it. The hand did not heal well and proved troublesome for the rest of his career. Despite the injury, he kept fighting, and from 1930 to 1933 he lost a number of bouts against mediocre opponents. His hand continued to worsen, and by late 1933 he could no longer pass a physical to fight. To make matters worse, his investments failed during the winter of 1933–34. With a wife and three children to feed, Braddock was on the edge of poverty and "not ashamed to exchange the role of fistic celebrity for that of honest laborer." He took any job he could find. He tended bar and worked as a stevedore. A loan from Gould prevented his electricity from being cut off, but he had to apply for welfare. For a while he worked for the Works Progress Administration, one of the New Deal relief agencies. While the time out of the ring hurt him financially, it did give his hand a chance to heal. Coming off the docks in June 1934, Braddock reentered the lists as a sacrificial lamb for fighters on the way up, but he surprised the boxing world by winning a series of surprising upsets against Corn Griffin, John Henry Lewis, and Art Lasky. Ultimately, he went on to win the crucial upset. An 8:1 underdog, he took the title from a clowning, sneering, out-of-shape Max Baer on June 14, 1935, on a decision. Braddock's story, from "forgotten man" to "eating the fat of the land," resonated with fans who were going through similar travails and hoped at least for a similar triumph over circumstances beyond their control. Nat Fleischer called him "a Cinderella man" for his feat, while *Ring* noted the change "from the shadows of defeat and near-poverty to a place in the great white light that beats around the throne." From dockworker to champ, Braddock carried the hopes of white working-class Americans—and certainly Irish-Americans—burdened with family responsibilities and mountains of debt.[38]

Inactive for two years, he finally climbed into the ring against Joe Louis on the night of June 22, 1937, in Chicago's Comiskey Park. More than 45,000 people jammed the stadium, including 20,000 of Louis's black fans up in the bleachers. Most were from Chicago's south side, but some came from as far away as Canada and California, New York and New Orleans, Georgia and Texas to see one of their own win the heavyweight crown. Inside the White Sox dressing room, Braddock and Louis sat on either side of a wooden partition and awaited their entrance into the ring. Braddock made his way first, wearing a green robe with a white shamrock on the back. Louis followed in his lucky blue and red-trimmed robe. The two fighters waited impatiently through the prefight introductions of current and former champions—Jack Dempsey, Gene Tunney, John Henry Lewis, Sixto Escobar, and Barney Ross— and the instructions by referee Tommy Thomas. Then they slipped out of their robes and down to their trunks. Louis wore purple trunks with his initials JL; Braddock wore dark boxing shorts. In Louis's corner, trainer Jack Blackburn told him, "This is it, Chappie. You come home a champ tonight." Braddock crossed himself as the bell rang and walked out to the middle of the ring. The 6' 2", 190-pound champion unleashed a wild right and the fight that Louis had been pointing to for two years was under way.[39]

The decision by the thirty-two-year-old Braddock to come out fighting made the bout one of the most stirring heavyweight title fights in memory. Many experts felt that the champion had only one chance—to stay away from the powerful challenger. Braddock would not have it that way. "Those people came to see me fight, not run away," he declared, "and it was up to me to give them what they came to see." This was also the type of fight that Louis liked,

Joe Louis and champion James J. Braddock, the Cinderella Man, slug it out in the middle of the ring in their title fight in June 1937 at Comiskey Park, Chicago. By winning the title, Louis broke the color line in the heavyweight division to become only the second African American heavyweight champion since Jack Johnson. (Wide World, Library of Congress)

not a running match, "but a he-man's stand-up battle in which each was taking a chance." Both gambled on a knockout, and it looked like Braddock might win when he knocked Louis down in the first round with a right uppercut, but the Brown Bomber bounced right up again. After that mishap, according to Fleischer, "Louis fought a perfect fight." He boxed superbly, sidestepped the champion's big rights as trainer Blackburn had taught him, and then speeded up the pace when Braddock tired. During the second round Louis scored with his jab over and over, and toward the end of the round he hit the champ with several rights and then two more solid left hooks. Braddock was badly hurt, but the bell saved him. Louis came back to the corner confident that the fight was his, but Blackburn preached caution. "Wait . . . take it easy," he said. "He's game, and he knows a lot. Keep sticking and countering. Don't get in too close. Let him do the crowding. He'll come apart in five or six rounds. I'll tell you when to shoot."[40]

   In the sixth Louis blasted him with both hands and had him bleeding from the face and mouth. He then battered him in the seventh, so much so that in Braddock's corner, Joe Gould suggested he quit. Through bloody lips Braddock responded, "If you do, I'll never speak to you again as long as I live." In the eighth, a game but tired Braddock came out swinging in the center of the ring. With his legs and arms gone he was wide open. Just as he unleashed a looping right hand, Louis leveled him with a powerful right to the face. "I laid it solid, with all my body, on the right side of his face, and his face split open. He fell in a face-down dive." Down went Braddock, knocked unconscious in the middle of the ring. After the fight, referee Tommy Thomas said he had never before seen a man travel through space as Jim did when Joe caught him with his right. According to the referee Braddock did not appear to be breathing. "When Gould and I picked him up he was stiff as a board." As Fleischer put it, this was one of the best heavyweight bouts he had seen in thirty years, and "the kind of finish that adds to the romance of the ring."[41]

As soon as the referee finished the count, "demonic pandemonium" broke out in the stadium. "Like maddened horses on the great Arabian desert, the huge crowd leaps from the grandstands and the fields, flows like a torrent through the gates and fills the streets," according to William Nunn, sports editor of the *Pittsburgh Courier*. Out on the streets of the south side of Chicago, thousands of Louis's black fans engaged in exultant celebrations that lasted into the wee hours of the morning. Nunn witnessed ecstatic black people dancing in the streets. They were "swirling, careening, madly dashing from house to house . . . yelling, crying, laughing, boasting, gloating, exulting . . . slapping backs, jumping out of the way of wildly-driven cars . . . whites and blacks hugging . . . the entire world, this cosmic center of the world tonight, turned topsy-turvy, this is the Southside of Chicago." Crowds jumped onto the backs of buses and the running boards of cars, and flowed into the street-cars. "Whites are not sour. Blacks are glad." Braddock may have been the Cinderella man, but "Joe Louis is the SUPERMAN who made good." As Nunn put it, "all the fondest dreams of the 12,000,000 racial brethren of the new champion have come true. He has been a credit to them and now he rides the 'Glory Road.' He has taken them up with him. He is theirs." The celebrations described by Nunn and the racial sentiment about Louis could be found in every major city—and some small towns—where black people lived. As Malcolm X recalled, "All the Negroes in Lansing, like Negroes everywhere, went wildly happy with the greatest celebration of race pride our generation had ever known. Every Negro boy old enough to walk wanted to be the next Brown Bomber." As far away as Lafayette, Alabama, known as "Powder Town," Louis's relatives and other blacks came to town from the Bukalew Mountains to listen to the fight on radio and to celebrate. After it was over, his relatives danced with delight, along with 1,000 other black celebrants, down the main street of the Negro section of town. Louis did the race proud.[42]

Harlem's celebration of the new black champion surpassed the one in Chicago. A slight youth carrying a tremendous green, white, and yellow flag, the banner of Ethiopia, led the way at midnight as a parade of fully 5,000 chanting, dancing celebrators took over Seventh Avenue at 136th Street. As Al Richmond wrote in *The Daily Worker*, "Joe Louis threw a leather-packed stick of dynamite at Jim Braddock's chin and it exploded in Harlem!" Richmond overheard one black woman tell her companion, "I was sick but this made me well!" According to the *Chicago Defender*, "every cloak of restraint was thrown to the winds as bedlam reigned in every conceivable spot, far into the wee hours of the morn." Gin mills overflowed and impromptu parties broke out on every street corner. Everywhere people were happy and without malice in "that moment of spontaneous jubilation over *their* victory." According to Richmond, Harlem was celebrating "something more than just a fight victory." Some in the crowd shouted "'Louis is King!'" and they "meant more than just a pugilist king supported by a pair of dukes." As Richmond explained, "He was a national hero, symbol of national aspiration who with his two fists crashed the myth of white supremacy and tore asunder the noose of discrimination which throttles the Negro people." He kayoed the same discrimination that hurt all talented blacks. This was the joy in Harlem. "It was a celebration of vindication," after the Schmeling defeat. "It was all this pent-up emotion and hope that burst loose in the celebration the like of which has never been seen in Harlem."[43]

Ultimately, Louis upset the idea that blacks could not be champions, that the heavyweight crown was reserved for whites only. By breaking the color barrier that had kept African American heavyweights from the title, Louis confirmed his place, as Fay Young put it in the *New York Amsterdam News*, as "King Louis I." According to Young and just about every black commentator on the fight, "Joe Louis and his managers have just surmounted the most difficult of all barriers, the unwritten law in boxing that said no Race man should fight for the championship." Writing in the *Defender*, David Kellum put the matter clearly. "A sportsman, a gentleman and a citizen," Louis "wants it clearly understood that he will meet all the requirements necessary to bring to the American public proper recognition of the race." If there had been any doubt, by now it was clear that Louis was "our Joe," the man who stood in the arena as a representative of the race."[44]

As they turned the world topsy-turvy with their joy, dancing in the streets to swing bands, black people made the world pay attention to them and the "superman" who had made dreams come true. Louis was the "giant killer," who in the realm of athletics expressed for them what they wanted to do in their own lives—smash the power of white America. As blacks rejoiced in Louis's victory, they participated vicariously in dethroning white physical superiority, white authority, and their own subservient condition. They had found a hero who expressed the manhood of the race, and who was capable within the rules of the larger society of proving his masculinity and the potential power of the community. Blacks could take comfort that they were now a powerful people who on a mass scale had glimpsed images of freedom in the urban north. As *Pittsburgh Courier* columnist Earl J. Morris put it, "Joe Louis, superman, is from a super race." After listing a string of similar heroes, he exclaimed, "the gifts of genius of our super race refutes all Nordic supremacy or Aryan line of chatter." That there were still bigger fish to fry, however, emerged in a cheer that was heard in many of the celebrations. "Schmeling's next! Go get Hitler!"[45]

At least one young black Chicagoan equated Louis's advances with broader changes in society. Timuel Black recalled that on the night of the title match, he and some of his friends had gone to the Armory on the south side to see and hear Benny Goodman's orchestra. Along with a racially mixed crowd, they were excited especially by the prospect of seeing Goodman's integrated swing quartet composed of African Americans Lionel Hampton on vibes and Teddy Wilson on piano, along with Polish-American Gene Krupa on drums and the Jewish Goodman on clarinet. As the band played "Moon Glow," Joe Louis and his entourage walked in, fresh from his victory. "The relief of seeing those, it's not unusual now, but for us then, relief of seeing those two star musicians in this mixed band and the same night having a black man become the champion of the world, boxing champion, was quite a thrill. It inspired us." Young people, he asserted, felt that if black athletes and musicians could break the color bar, then they could do it too. "Just not being a doctor or lawyer, those of us who did not have those backgrounds could look forward to accomplishing something in another kind of way."[46]

The welling up of black pride also drew on the masterly way Louis won the fight. Black fans had endured a steady barrage of criticism from white boxing fans and experts that Louis was not smart enough to outwit Schmeling, Bob Pastor, or Braddock. These echoed the deeper white belief that African Americans were merely instinctual, fun-loving, expressive animals incapable of exercising their full rights as citizens. Before the fight, for example, R. G. Lynch, the sports editor of the *Milwaukee Journal*, described Louis at his training camp as a typical "darkie." "The hulky, lazy brown boy might have been lolling in a cabin doorway down in Alabama, listening to somebody inside making mouth music." In response, black fans and black sportswriters gloried in the tough physical way Louis fought, and the intelligent and crafty manner in which he bided his time. "They said Joe was slow," declared the *Courier*'s Nunn, "was dull of mind and easily bewildered." While "there was something inhuman in the lad as he went to work," Louis had "a plan of action," and he carried it out. Another *Courier* columnist concurred. Joe's victory proved wrong the "thousands who had previously said he could not think for himself by outwitting, out-guessing, outthinking and outfighting the Irishman." Instead, his "superlative judgment" proved his greatest asset.[47]

The *Courier*'s William Nunn also noted that while blacks were understandably overjoyed, "whites have a similar feeling." Louis "has been a boon to the game," and he brought the entire sport of boxing to new heights. Re-markably, little racial animosity on the part of whites was expressed toward Louis and his breaking the color line in the heavyweight division. Unlike what happened after Jack Johnson gained the title in 1908, there was little hue and cry for a "white hope" to defend the honor of the white race. Ironically, one of the few people who made any positive noises about white hopes was former champion Johnson, the subject of the whole controversy in the first place. Johnson declared that he was "starting to look for white hopes right now." He would find "a white man who can beat Joe. Every white man I see that's as tall as six feet, I will try to test him out to see if he can fight good." It was not that he did not like Louis, "it's just that white hopes are good for boxing."[48]

No one else seemed to think so. *The Illinois State Register* in Springfield, Illinois, a city that had experienced a deadly race riot in 1908, noted how little racial resentment surfaced. "The victory of Louis, a Negro, over Braddock, a white man, last night removed the criticism that race would prove a factor in the determination of the referee and the judges." However, it was a clean fight, and "America hails the new champion with the conviction that the bet-ter fighter won." Some went even farther, noting that the whole idea of a white hope had diminished in intensity among boxing fans. *Ring* magazine was particularly strong in attacking the white hope idea and upholding the notion that boxing, and by extension all sport, should be color-blind. As Ed Van Every declared, "The new champion stands forth as uncontroverted evi-dence that boxing, as well as any other professional sport, rates fair play above race or color prejudice." Daniel M. Daniel, an associate editor of *Ring*, more-over, noted that most people acted as if nothing had happened. "It would be folly to say that all the Whites got up and cheered when the Negro became the champion of the world." Still, "the world has changed." When a black man whips a white man, it no longer meant that "all the men with black casts of countenance could whip all the men with white casts of countenance, and that the fistic victory immediately establishes one race over another." In 1937, he declared, "we are willing to dissociate one activity from another." As a result, there has been no violence and "we face the reign of Joe Louis not only with equanimity, but with a certain feeling of satisfaction."[49]

Equally remarkable, Louis was only one of three black champions who had emerged at about the same time. In 1937, the impoverished Henry Armstrong emerged from years of fighting on the West Coast and in Mexi-can rings to take the world featherweight title, followed in 1938 by the world welterweight and then world lightweight titles. He was the first boxer in his-tory to hold three separate titles simultaneously. Similarly, John Henry Lewis, fighting out of Pittsburgh, won the light heavyweight crown in 1936. While the color line had applied primarily to the heavyweight division, there had never been three black champions at the same time, and certainly at no time did three men control five separate division championships as occurred in the late 1930s. *Ring*'s Ted Carroll noted "the surge of Negro fighters to the front line of the Fistic Parade." In fact, the "ancient barriers" that blocked colored heavyweights seemed to have fallen "before the box office magic, magnetic appeal, subdued personality and lethal powers of young Mr. Louis, and what was once barren land for boxers of his race, has turned into a veritable happy hunting ground." Things were easing up for black fighters, Carroll noted, in 1937. The huge financial success achieved by Joe Louis, "the disappearance of old prejudices, and the transition of the fighters themselves" from the boisterous illiterates of the past, to "the polished, educated, and quiet Negro pugilists of today, are the reasons" for the progress of black boxers.[50]

Carroll was onto something in his reasons for the collapse of boxing's color barrier. The primary reason was that Louis made it clear that he could make a lot of money for everyone in boxing. Whites would come out to see blacks fight, and the staging of a theatrical race war in the ring did not as a usual matter extend beyond the confines of the arena. After the financial catastrophe in the boxing world of the early 1930s, there were forces in the sport's establishment that would accept anyone who could make money. Coupled with this was the promotional war between Madison Square Garden and Mike Jacobs's Twentieth Century Sporting Club. It was clear, moreover, that fans would accept black boxing champions more readily in the 1930s than in the 1910s and 1920s. In part it had to do with the crafted image of each of these champions. All were modest, none got into trouble publicly, and perhaps most important, they had little to say about America's racial system. Many whites assumed that the violence in the ring did not extend beyond it because the champions were not politically active or outspoken on the subject of race. In addition, during the growing battle with Nazism and fascism it was relatively easy to hold up black champions as exemplars of American democracy and the United States as a more racially and religiously tolerant nation than Nazi Germany.

Although there was a good deal of hypocrisy associated with this belief, it still represented an important step. During the New Deal era, the movements for working-class solidarity, such as the Congress of Industrial Organizations, were also multiracial. While white workers did not abandon their racism, they looked upon Joe Louis and other black champions as working-class men who had come up from poverty, or as with Louis, had come out of the auto plants where so many of them still worked. Moreover, despite all his money and fame, the new champion refused to set himself above white or black workers, adopt a celebrity personality, or act as though he had a swelled head, as had Max Baer. By their actions—or inaction in the ring—previous white champions had undermined the idea that the title somehow belonged by right to white men. Their power had proven hollow, and boxing fans were willing to support a tough champion, regardless of race, who promised action in the

ring and the ability to destroy his opponents—all accomplished with a sense
of masculine grace and dignity. Whatever the cause, the door had opened to
black boxers to contend for and win championships, and to become idols of
the race and of many different types of Americans. Although many white observers assumed that the effects of black champions were relatively modest
outside the ring—and hence easier to take—the tremendous assertion of black
pride and the demand for African American access to opportunities in other
arenas of life proved them mistaken.

As reporters rushed to interview the new champion after his triumph, Louis
declared, "I want you to thank all my friends through the *Courier*, Ches, for
being with me and sticking by me tonight just like they stuck by me when I
lost to Schmeling. And I hope to some day to wipe out that defeat." Understandably, Louis believed that he would not really be champion until he had
avenged his loss to Max Schmeling. The Brown Bomber also declared that he
wanted to set a new precedent. "None of that one-fight-a year stuff for me,"
he told those assembled in his crowded dressing room. "I'm gonna be the
fightingest champion that ever was." Other title holders had proclaimed the
same thing, but for the most part they followed the dictum established by
promoter Tex Rickard that champions fight only once a year so as not to dull
their drawing power. Louis, however, had been a very active challenger, and
he would go on to fight over four times a year as champion. That his managers felt he had to do this because as an African American he had to constantly
prove that he was the best was not mentioned. According to *Ring*, moreover,
there was "the quite unusual spectacle of the champion challenging the challenger." He had hardly assumed the heavyweight throne before he began
demanding, "'I want Smellin'. Get me Smellin'." Despite his horrifying loss
to the German, the Brown Bomber remained confident that he would win
the rematch. He realized that while he was officially the champ, as long as
"the Black Uhlan remains unvanquished, his heavyweight crown can never
glitter the way it should." According to *Ring*, Louis "was never one to dodge
the issue."[51]

At the same time, Schmeling and his many German and American supporters maintained that he was the legitimate champion. In Germany, Louis's
title was met with skepticism. After all, Schmeling had destroyed "the myth
of Joe Louis." In German sporting and political circles, "unser Max" was the
real champ and Louis merely the so-called (*sogenannte*) champion, or only "an
American heavyweight champion," deprived of his title by the continuing Jewish conspiracy against the German hero and the underhanded tactics of American promoters. Despite Louis's victory, argued *Box-Sport*, "in Braddock the
best heavyweight of the white race did not stand opposite the Brown Bomber."
It would take another year for the rematch to take place and settle matters. In
that time the international situation heated up dramatically, racial and reli-

gious issues became even more prominent, and the representatives of both Germany and the United States would meet in a boxing match of international proportions. Until that time, however, the battle between the American and the German heavyweights continued to take place outside the ring.[52]

After Louis won the title, Mike Jacobs attempted to arrange a rematch with Schmeling as soon as possible. The promoter offered the frustrated German heavyweight the normal challenger's fees of 20 percent, but on the assumption that he had already beaten Louis and had been robbed of the title by Jacobs, among others, Schmeling demanded 30 percent of the box office. Negotiations broke down. It looked like the German would have to wait even longer to achieve his goal of doing what no heavyweight had ever done: reclaim the title.[53]

Schmeling had an alternative. In their eagerness to establish "unser Max" as the true champion, German government officials made plans for a heavyweight title between their "moral" champion and a leading contender. With Hitler's direct participation, they chose the winner of the match between Walter Neusel, German heavyweight, and Tommy Farr, the Welsh coal miner who was heavyweight champion of the British Isles. When Farr won, Hitler and his current Reichsminister and chief of the Association of German Boxers, Dr. Franz Metzner, had the bout declared a European world championship, and made plans to organize excursions so that as many Germans as possible could attend the match in London. Along with legions of German fans, *Box-Sport* was delighted that Max would be back in action, although its editors remained disappointed that he had not gained the rematch with Louis. Placing Germany at the forefront of European athletic culture, the magazine declared, "We are happy that boxing Europe has finally intervened in the crooked situation of heavyweight world championships and therewith given a proper shot on the nose to international racketeering." Americans, they charged, would be surprised how quickly the "Old World" had leaped to keep boxing alive, "even if in the United States it is supposed to be sacrificed to money."[54]

Having rejected the rematch, Schmeling began preparations for Farr. Here too, the German boxer was outmaneuvered. Filled with resentment toward the American boxing world, he wanted to beat Farr, declare himself European champion, and then reopen bargaining with Jacobs on much more favorable terms. Yet Farr reportedly began to balk at the terms of his agreement since Schmeling had arranged to get the better deal. Sensing an opening, Jacobs sent his lawyer and cousin, Sol Strauss, to London to make Farr a counteroffer. Strauss offered Farr a much more lucrative guarantee ($60,000) to meet Louis in New York on August 26, 1937. The deal nearly doubled what Farr could make in a fight with the German, and offered the Welshman a crack at the title accepted by most of the world. He chose to meet Louis.[55]

Louis's victory vindicated him in the eyes of his many African American fans. In this picture a huge crowd in Harlem celebrates with carnival-like energy. When Louis beat white fighters, black Americans took vicarious pleasure in the defeat of a symbolic aspect of white supremacy. The pride and sense of community power are evident in the happy faces. This took place after the Farr fight in fall 1937, a bout that Schmeling thought was his. Note the trumpet player. (Acme, Library of Congress)

Once more a dispirited Schmeling traveled abroad, this time to attend the Louis-Farr bout in August 1937. His frustration was immense. Cast aside again, forced to stand outside the ring as a spectator for the second time, he could only hope that his turn would come eventually. One month short of his thirty-second birthday, Schmeling had not fought in over a year, and he could feel the title slipping away. At Pompton Lakes, he and Louis talked and posed for photos to work up the gate for their probable rematch. Although Farr was next, Louis wanted to erase the one blot on his record. He wanted Schmeling. He knew that it was his own failure to train seriously that had cost him the first fight. Now he was the champion. He and Jacobs had tried unsuccessfully three different times to arrange bouts with the German, and Louis was anxious to meet his one conqueror in the ring. Aware that Schmeling believed himself the better fighter, Louis resented the German's air of confidence and superiority. He was determined to beat him.

Louis's fight with Farr was anything but easy. The ex-coal miner had great stamina and, like Pastor, used his speed to stay away from the champion's powerful punches. Confounding the experts, he lasted fifteen rounds. The small crowd booed when the announcer declared Louis the winner. Immediately after the hard-fought victory, however, Louis and Schmeling finally came to terms. Concerned that he might never get to fight for the championship, Schmeling agreed to accept 20 percent of the box office plus a percentage of the radio and movie rights. The bout would take place the following June in Yankee Stadium. For the German public, the perceived insult to their hero and to the German nation would make their second bout in June 1938 a grudge match with tremendous political and international overtones. Both men would have to wait for the rematch to settle who was the true champion. As black journalist Roi Ottley put it, winning the title "was only a rehearsal for the event on which the whole world had its eyes focused—the return match between the Brown Bomber and the Black Uhlan."[56]

5

THE GREATEST FIGHT
OF OUR GENERATION

> Joe Louis killed the idea of Nazi supremacy. All
> the horses of 'King Hitler' will never put it on
> its feet again. He laid to rest the idea of the su-
> premacy of any racial or national group over
> another. The 'color line' in the boxing game
> may be revived again, but only with the great-
> est difficulty.
>
> William L. Patterson

Joe Louis and Max Schmeling finally had the opportunity to square off against each other in a rematch of epic proportions. On the evening of Wednesday, June 22, 1938, the long-anticipated bout brought the competing aspirations of Americans and Germans to a head and transformed Louis from a primarily African American hero into an all-American idol. Facing each other in the ring once again, both combatants stood as an idealistic symbols, Siegfried and Galahad, fighting for the honor of their respective nations. The international tensions surrounding the match stimulated fan interest to new heights. According to Joe Williams, sports columnist of the *New York World-Telegram*, the usual domestic race angle of white versus black could be downplayed in the publicity for the fight, because "here's a hate motif ready made. . . . Those who view in Schmeling a political symbol will be desperately hopeful for his downfall." In a period when Adolf Hitler's politicization of sports and aggressive military intentions were increasingly

Joe Louis, reigning champion. Once again dead-pan, Joe awaits his second battle with Schmeling. His slight crouch and his shuffle step allowed him to knock out an opponent with either hand. (Frank Driggs Collection)

clear, Schmeling became a convenient symbol of Nazi Germany. Democracy and fascism were set to go at each other in the ring. While many Germans hoped for vindication of their champion, "unser Max," and their nation, black Americans prayed that "our Joe" would knock out this embodiment of white supremacy. Blacks were not alone. White Americans and descendants of European immigrants worried about Hitler's aggressive designs on their nations, and Jews were especially terrified about Hitler's virulent anti-Semitic policies.

All of these groups rooted for the African American boxer as a patriotic champion of American democracy.[1]

For the boxers, of course, individual goals came first. Since the German had upset Louis in twelve brutal rounds two years earlier, the American had become heavyweight champion; Schmeling, following his humiliation by the American boxing establishment during "the Braddock Affair," more than ever hungered to be the first heavyweight boxer ever to regain the crown. Meanwhile, Louis, who had been "humiliated" by Schmeling in their first bout, "had to prove to everybody that I was the best heavyweight around." Each boxer wanted to show the world that he was the real champion.[2]

Befitting a match that radio announcer Clem McCarthy called "The Greatest Fight of Our Generation," New Deal officials, governors, mayors, senators, socialites, and stars of stage and screen clamored for ringside seats in New York's Yankee Stadium. Among those present were boxing notables such as former champions Gene Tunney, Jack Dempsey, and James J. Braddock, along with Postmaster General James Farley, Director of the FBI J. Edgar Hoover, United States Attorney General Homer Cummings, and one of President Roosevelt's sons. The list of celebrities included Gary Cooper, Clark Gable, Robert Taylor, and a young Gregory Peck. Overall 70,000 fans paid $940,096 to see the fight. Adding in radio and film revenues, the bout turned into the first million-dollar gate since Louis beat Max Baer in 1935. Perhaps 20,000 African Americans, almost a third of the paying gate, arrived from Harlem as well as from cities across the nation to root for their "national" hero. "Every train into New York had disgorged thousands of fight fans," noted Roi Ottley. "For days people had been pouring into the city by airplane, ocean liner, bus, and private car. Betting was brisk; Louis was favored but plenty of Schmeling money was about. Black America was in a rare pitch of excitement." An estimated 70 million listeners, second only to those who tuned into President Franklin D. Roosevelt's formal speeches, huddled around their radios for the NBC broadcast, anxiously awaiting the outcome of the most dramatic fight in over ten years, and the most significant since the Johnson-Jeffries battle of 1910. As a sign of the worldwide interest, thousands of foreign press and radio reporters were in attendance. Their newspaper reports and radio broadcasts in English, Spanish, Portuguese, German, and French transformed the boxing match into an international media event. A contingent of 1,000 Germans, meanwhile, took advantage of special excursion prices to journey to the United States to join their German American compatriots in rooting for "unser Max." The bars, saloons, and restaurants of German American areas were packed. In Germany and other European countries, people stayed up until the wee hours of the morning to listen to the radio broadcasts.[3]

As a sporting event, the fight had much to recommend it. In many ways it was a grudge match. Louis had won the championship, but he still had to beat his challenger to erase the one smirch on his otherwise sterling record. Every fight fan, and even members of the general public, realized that this was the most important fight of his career. When a boxer is knocked out, he is often not the same—and certainly not when he meets the man who performed the original knockout. For months the press wondered whether Louis suffered lingering fears of Max's right hand. As the champion, he now possessed greater self-confidence and ring experience. At twenty-four he was also just reaching his peak as a boxer, while Schmeling at thirty-two, going on thirty-three, might be over the hill. Could the German duplicate his awesome feat or was his first victory merely a fluke? Moreover, could a good right hand beat a fighter with dynamite in both hands? Both men were highly motivated. Louis held the title but he would not receive his full due as the champion unless he beat his former conqueror. To Schmeling and the German people, he was the true champion, but had been cheated of the chance to do what no other heavyweight in history had managed to accomplish: come back and regain the title. As a result of the bad blood between them, both men had scores to settle. As white sportswriter Bill Corum put it, "This is the most important battle in the lives of these two men . . . the climax and cross-roads of their careers."[4]

The international tensions that had risen since the first Louis and Schmeling bout gave the rematch an extra electric charge. With his party firmly in power and opposition brutally suppressed, Adolf Hitler no longer felt compelled to placate world opinion as he had when he first became chancellor in 1933. Secure enough at home, he not only militarized Germany, but he also stepped up aggressive territorial demands on his neighbors. Military support for General Franco's fascist revolt against the Spanish Republic proved only the beginning. Increasingly Germany allied with Mussolini in an informal Rome-Berlin Axis, which resulted in their joining together with Japan in the Anti-Comintern Pact of November 1937. In March 1938, just three months before the bout, the German troops rolled into Austria in what was called the Anschluss. Buoyed by this successful expansion of German power, Hitler continued to foment strife in Czechoslovakia by stirring up the Germans in the Sudetenland to demand reunification with Germany. All of this fed American fears about Germany's aggressive intentions toward the rest of the world. Even more frightening, days before the bout eighteen American citizens were indicted as Nazi spies. The rising sense of German threat heightened the concerns about the Nuremberg Laws passed in 1935 and the quite public anti-Catholicism and anti-Semitism that reemerged with renewed vigor after the Berlin Olympics of 1936. In the United States, moreover, the German American Bund, which had some support in German American communities throughout the East Coast and Middle West, increasingly began to echo Nazi doctrines. The Bund was led by its own führer, a naturalized American and World War I German army lieutenant named Fritz Kuhn. Kuhn expressed the common fascist theme at a Bund rally in 1939 where he denounced President Roosevelt, Secretary of Labor Francis Perkins, and Treasury Secretary Henry Morgenthau. In a declaration of purpose, the führer announced that the Bund was fighting for "a socially just, white, Gentile ruled United States." The virulence of domestic fascism and anti-Semitism among such orators as Father Coughlin, Gerald L. K. Smith, and groups such as the Silver Shirts added to the fear among many Americans that a worldwide fascist onslaught was in the making and that democracy was imperiled.[5]

Both Louis and Schmeling noted a different atmosphere surrounding the fight. As Louis recalled in his memoir, "the whole world was looking to this fight. . . . Germany was tearing up Europe, and we were hearing about the concentration camps for the Jews. A lot of Americans had family in Europe and they were afraid for their people's lives. Schmeling represented everything that Americans disliked and they wanted him beat and beat good." American Jews were firmly in his camp. This was understandable, but white Gentile support proved a surprise. "White Americans," the Brown Bomber recalled, "even while some of them were lynching black people in the South—were depending on me to K. O. Germany." President Roosevelt, who was already keenly aware of the threat posed by Nazi Germany, stoked the patriotic fervor. While Louis was making an appearance at the Colored Elks national convention in Washington, D.C., in spring 1938 he received an invitation to the White House. "Joe," the president declared while feeling Louis's arm muscles, "we're depending on those muscles for America." Newspapers expanded on this statement to say, "Joe, beat Schmeling to prove we can beat the Germans." Louis was thrilled. "Now, even more, I knew I had to get Schmeling good. I had my own personal reasons, and the whole damned country was depending on me."[6]

Having enjoyed the support of large numbers of white Americans in 1936, the German contender expressed shock at the dramatic shift in public opinion. Protesters met his ship with signs calling him an "Aryan Show Horse," a symbol of the "Master Race," and demanded that Americans "BOYCOTT NAZI SCHMELING!" Up until the day of the fight he also received thousands of hate letters signed "Heil Hitler." The German boxer tried to explain that he was a sportsman not a politician, but he was badly hurt by the Nazi propaganda that had transformed him into an Aryan icon and by his contacts with Hitler and Goebbels since the first fight. For example, when Mussolini visited Berlin in September 1937, Schmeling's appearance at the reception for Il Duce appeared in the *New York Times* as "Schmeling Steals Show at a Tea for Mussolini." When Germany held a referendum on the annexation of Austria, Schmeling signed a petition, published in the *12-Uhr Blatt*, urging Germans to go to the polls and vote for Hitler as he supported boxing. Whereas in 1936 reporters had wanted to know whether he feared Louis, now they asked him about Hitler's racial policies. Although he still identified himself as primarily a sportsman, Schmeling reluctantly made statements common to many Germans, that Hitler had improved the economic and social climate of Germany, had ended political strife in the streets, and enjoyed the overwhelming support of the German people. The city that had cheered him two years earlier now turned hostile. Even old friend Marlene Dietrich refused to meet with him. Because of Hitler, Schmeling recalled in his memoirs, "No one wanted to see me win the title." The boxer's rhetoric hurt him too. According to the *Pittsburgh Courier*, the "Nazi" boxer referred to the three black champions currently enjoying success in the United States—Henry Armstrong, Joe Louis, and John Henry Lewis—and said that "the black dynasty of pugilism must come to an end." Having beaten Louis once, he argued that he had "a strong psychological superiority over the Negro" and had instilled strong fear in "a man of Joe's race." In response Louis sneered, "I only hope Schmeling will have plenty of that psychology around to use for salve when I knock him on his pants."[7]

Fueling the political aspects of the bout, the Non-Sectarian Anti-Nazi League announced a boycott of the fight. Ten women appeared with picket signs outside Mike Jacobs's office. Concerned about the fight's future, Jacobs met with a delegation from the American Jewish Committee who urged him to cancel the match. They explained that if Schmeling won the heavyweight title, the Nazis would rush to exploit it for propaganda purposes and it would become a weapon against United States morale. Jacobs replied that Schmeling would become a martyr if he were denied his rightful opportunity to meet for the title and his martyrdom would be used to curry favor among the world's nations. Instead of giving in to their demands, Jacobs assured the committee that Louis would destroy Schmeling in the ring, avenge European Jewry, and at the same time deliver a momentous defeat to the Nazi regime. To undermine the boycott, Jacobs promised to donate 10 percent of the gate to a nonsectarian refugee group set up to assist those who had been forced to flee Nazi Germany. Some members of the group wanted Schmeling to award a percentage of his earnings to the Anti-Nazi League, but this never happened. While Hitler and Goebbels fumed that Schmeling was now fighting to aid Jews, Jewish fans rooted for Louis as their avenger. Several newspapers warned that the Bund would create a riot at the fight, but Jacobs pressed on. Although no sizable demonstration by Nazis appeared at Yankee Stadium, communists handed out flyers urging fans to cheer Louis and boo Schmeling, while members of the Non-Sectarian Anti-Nazi League passed out leaflets calling for a boycott of German goods.[8]

The international aspects of the bout dominated the prefight publicity. Indeed, given the real concerns that were on people's minds, it did not take much for the fight's publicists to use the Nazi versus Democracy, Germany versus United States theme to ballyhoo the event into a million-dollar gate. Despite the hype, white Americans found themselves having to choose between supporting a white Nazi or a black American. Reporter Joe Williams noted that the Nazis were using their German boxer, just as they had exploited the Olympics, to "accent the racial superiority of the Nazi" and to "confirm the claim of the Nazi government that the German race is superior to all other races." Their virulent racism, argued others, was the very opposite of American ideals. The Beckley, West Virginia, *Post-Herald* held that Hitler's treatment of the Jews and his threats to world civilization forced the newspaper, and presumably some of its white readers, to "choose Joe Louis, an America Negro, to beat the ears off Max." Fearful of Nazi intentions and taken aback by the outspoken racism against all but Aryans and Nordics, white Americans viewed the bout as a test of American national strength. Two years before, whites had viewed Louis primarily as a black boxer. Now many whites appointed him the standard-bearer of American democracy. Even many white southerners, with long memories of the German enemy during World War I, tacitly supported Louis over the German. In a scripted article Louis accepted his new role as an American national hero. He fought not only to avenge his one loss, he said, "I fight for America against the challenge of a foreign invader, Max Schmeling. This isn't just one man against another or Joe Louis boxing Max Schmeling; it is the good ole U.S.A. versus Germany."[9]

Some commentators downplayed what was at stake, calling the bout just another prizefight. Sports and politics had nothing to do with each other, they argued. Myrtle S. Weigand's letter to the *New York Times* on June 18 not only expressed this view but it also revealed that the proponents of fair play were in fact arguing against the dominant trend. In "Let's Be Americans," she recounted that she had heard boos for Schmeling and cheers for Louis when both men were introduced prior to the recent Barney Ross-Henry Armstrong title match. She pleaded with Americans to follow their democratic instincts, which included being fair and hospitable toward foreign guests. "Let us be above 'common politics' and use greater wisdom in these trying times by endeavoring to promote more harmonious relationships wherever international affairs touch our country." Weigand argued that the present circumstances in Europe should not be allowed to "contaminate our intelligent sporting blood." In essence, Americans should leave European problems to Europe and stick to the American ideals of fair play and good sportsmanship. By treating Schmeling as an individual sportsman rather than as a representative of a country or political system, Americans would be upholding the highest ideals of American sport and democracy. While many other Americans shared her views, the dominant opinion held that American national values were at stake.[10]

Surrounded on every side by political drama, both fighters trained for the battle of their lives. Up in Pompton Lakes, New York, Nazi Bundists visited Louis's camp where they watched him train and laughed "like jackasses." Visitors to both camps relayed to Louis that Schmeling was saying that Germans were a super race and no Negro could stand up to them. In all probability, the sportswriters, aided by his managers, did it to provoke him, but after hearing it many times, Louis "knew it was true." Schmeling's apparent remarks fed Louis's anger. In fact, he told one biographer, "In all my fighting I never got a real hate on another fighter, but I didn't like that Schmeling." Despite the political distractions, the Brown Bomber bore down, giving up golf and women for the duration. A serious mood pervaded his camp this time, and his dedication paid off. He showed strength and speed, and his lefts were better than at any time since the Max Baer fight in 1935. His footwork was agile, and he parried right hand punches with ease. Louis's training had one main object: to prepare him for Schmeling's devastating right that had brought about his defeat two years earlier. Every one of his sparring partners had instructions to hit him as hard and as often as possible with a right. Louis still remained vulnerable to a right hand, but his defenses were much better. During camp Jack Blackburn and Louis decided on a fight plan. Joe would attack from the start. Taking a page from Schmeling's book, they watched films of the first bout and saw that Max needed time to set himself before throwing the right hand. When Louis went on offense in the early rounds, he had easily backed up his opponent. Only when he went on defense and attempted to counter did Max have time to set and counter his right over Joe's left. This time, Louis would pressure him the entire fight. The day before the match, expectations were that Louis would use body punches and a relentless attack to disconcert the German challenger. A supremely confident Louis told sportswriter Jimmy Cannon that he would knock out Schmeling in the first round.[11]

When he arrived at his training camp in upstate Speculator, New York, located in the rural isolation of the Adirondacks, anti-Nazi pickets greeted the German heavyweight, but state troopers denied them access. Inside, Schmeling worked hard physically and even harder mentally to block out the pickets and the hate mail that he continued to receive. His visitors told Max that "Louis had worked himself into a rage of retribution" and that he was training harder than ever against a right. Still, by the end of his training, Schmeling declared, "I have reached a physical condition that I cannot have bettered in any way. For two years I have prepared for this fight." Not just in training camp but in "real, tough fights." Indeed, in December 1937 he had knocked out Harry Thomas, then won by a decision over Ben Foord in January 1938 and a knockout of Steve Dudas in April. Having ended his inactivity, he expressed confidence that he would knock out Louis once again. So did most Germans. Two days before the match, the Führer himself cabled, "To the coming World's Champion, Max Schmeling. Wishing you every success. Adolf Hitler." Dr. Franz Metzner, the Reich's Bureau Minister of Boxing, cabled too: "With Germany as your boxing family the whole German people's (*Volk*) thoughts are with you, beloved comrade Schmeling."[12]

When the two fighters wrapped up their prefight preparations, expectations ran high in both camps. The consensus was that both men had trained hard and were in top shape. Acting as if he had not a worry in the world, Max Schmeling on the day of the fight rejected the advice of his handlers and flew rather than drove from Speculator to New York City. Meanwhile, an equally self-assured champion traveled by car for the weigh-in with his entourage. As they drove into New York, the normal laughter was absent. "Chappie and Mr. Roxborough knew what this fight meant to me. They didn't try to make it something light." At eleven the two fighters appeared at the New York Athletic Commission's office. As reporters and photographers milled about, taking notes and firing periodic questions, the two men nodded to each other, not speaking. Schmeling weighed 193 pounds, Louis 198½. Except in Germany, the odds favored Louis. The die was cast.[13]

As they waited in their dressing rooms later that night, the weeks of turmoil took their toll on Schmeling. "I was nervous," he recalled. He was also without several key members of his ring support team. His American manager Joe Jacobs had been suspended by the New York Athletic Commission because of his ties to Tony Galento, a heavyweight boxer out of favor with the commission. Doc Casey, who had served as Schmeling's trusted corner man for years, begged off because he feared that the political turmoil surrounding the match would result in violence. As Schmeling put it, "I had never before felt so alone before a fight." In his locker room, an eager Louis warmed up for half an hour rather than his usual ten minutes. He had a thin sheen of sweat all over his body. He told Blackburn that he was going to let it all out for three rounds. It would be all or nothing. Mike Jacobs made an appearance. He told Louis that he had promised the protest groups that Joe was a cinch to knock out the German and vindicate the Jews. If he did not win, both careers might be over. The last thing he said was "Murder that bum, and don't make an asshole out of me." Louis reportedly replied, "Don't worry about a thing. I ain't going back to Ford to work, and you ain't gonna go back to selling lemon drops on the Staten Island Ferry."[14]

After the preliminary bouts, the two fighters made their way to the ring in the center of the stadium. Louis entered first to tepid applause and a few boos, followed by a smiling Schmeling surrounded by police to protect him from the missiles and debris fired at him by the crowd. On the way to the ring, "all hell broke loose." It "was like walking a gauntlet. . . . I was . . . hit by cigarette butts, banana peels, and paper cups." A squad of police had to station itself around the outer edges of the ring to protect Max from any further assaults. Ring announcer Harry Balogh introduced the ex-champions and prominent contenders in attendance, among them Jim Braddock, Jack Sharkey, and Max Baer. As he introduced the featured boxers, the crowd cheered, but the applause was louder for Louis. In a direct contrast to the Jack Johnson "white hope" bout with Jim Jeffries in 1910, when "All Coons Look Alike to Me" was played, the crowd at Yankee Stadium stood for the "Star-Spangled Banner." American flags flew in abundance, but no swastikas were evident. The symbolism could not have been stronger. Whatever the deepest racial attitudes of those in the audience, the fight itself was playing out in the minds of Americans as a drama about nation more than about race. After the introductions of the two combatants, the arena went breathlessly quiet. At the bell, a great roar erupted from the crowd. The "Fight of the Century" was under way.[15]

As the two fighters met in the center of the ring, they circled each other warily. To get his bearings, Louis feinted for several seconds, and then did what he had promised—he launched an attack and never let up. He threw two hard left hooks that rocked Schmeling's head back. Then followed a series of rights and lefts that soon had Max bewildered. He backed up toward the ropes, covering as well as he could, but the punishment continued to rain on him with devastating force. Louis then caught him with five big left hooks, followed by a powerful right to the chin. Max's legs began to wobble. As he started to fall, Schmeling caught the top strand of the ropes and held on for dear life. His arm was locked around the upper strand and his body faced sideways. He kept blinking his eyes and his face was ashen, filled with pain. Louis then moved in to deliver the heavy blows. With Max caught on the ropes, the Brown Bomber unleashed a terrific right hand to the body. To avoid its full impact, Schmeling twisted out of the way, and the blow fell on the area just below the ribs. The pain was unbearable, and Max let out a scream that was heard across the ringside seats. "I was paralyzed from that point on," Schmeling said later. The action in the ring electrified the crowd. Everyone leaped up, people were standing on their chairs, and wild yells rang out. "Kill him," "Kill the Nazi," roared the crowd as Louis battered the German.[16]

Aware of Schmeling's plight, referee Arthur Donovan dragged Louis away from his helpless victim and pointed him toward a neutral corner. The referee then began a count of one, but Schmeling came off the ropes ready to fight again. Louis came in with a fury, and Schmeling could only feebly protect himself. Throwing rapid-fire blows, Louis hit Max with hard lefts and rights. In total, the Brown Bomber threw an avalanche of forty-one blows, of which thirty-one landed solidly. Fourteen crashed against the chin, and like a pendulum, Schmeling's head went back and forth as Louis battered him. When Joe went downstairs, Max lowered his hands. In a flash, Louis shot up a big right hand to the jaw and the German was back on the ropes. The champion sensed the kill. "The revenge for which he had been looking for two years was now within his grasp," wrote Nat Fleischer, "and he had no intentions of letting it slip away. Like a tiger, Joe was at him. He wasted no time and only a few punches. Those that missed didn't matter much. Too many were landing with telling effect." With Max again on the ropes, Louis punished him from

Louis has his revenge in the second fight. His overwhelming power drove Max to the ropes within a few seconds of the first round, where the latter got hung up and could not move. Trying to twist away from Joe's devastating punches, Max left himself open to a punch that landed on or near the kidneys, setting off a controversy in Germany and the United States. After this punch, he was helpless. (Acme, Library of Congress)

every angle. Backing away slightly, Louis found an opening and with all of his power he drove a vicious right to Schmeling's jaw. The German went down. He rolled over on his back, but rose at the count of three.[17]

Louis came tearing in again. A left to Schmeling's mouth started blood flowing, then a left and a right to the jaw, followed by another crashing right to the jaw and the challenger was down again. He got up at two, groggy and bleary-eyed, a pathetic sight. Unable to defend himself, Schmeling staggered backward, but his jaw stood out as a ready target. Louis unleashed his best shots. With the German barely able to stand, the Brown Bomber hit him with a left and then a right to the mid-section, and then banged him with a volley of rights and lefts. Few if any missed. Then came the coup de grace. Louis crashed a powerful right against Max's jaw and he toppled over. As Schmeling tried to rise, a desperate Max Machon threw in a white towel, a token of defeat in many states, but not in New York. Donovan hurled the towel onto the ropes and turned to pick up the count at four. When the timekeeper hit eight, Machon ran into the ring to rescue his fighter. Donovan could do nothing more than wave his arms, a signal that the match was over, a TKO. In total, the lopsided match took only two minutes and four seconds, the shortest heavyweight title fight in history.[18]

In his dressing room, a dejected Schmeling told the NBC radio audience that "I have not much to say. I very sorry, but, I won't make any excuse, but I get such a terrible hit, the first hit I get in the left kidneys, I was so paralyzed I couldn't even move. And then after it was all over, you know." Both Machon and Joe Jacobs claimed that he had been hit with a foul to the kidneys. Max also claimed that he was fouled. Then Machon and Jacobs packed him up and took him off to Polyclinic Hospital, where he underwent X-rays and observation. A series of tests determined that he had suffered several broken vertebrae and would have to remain immobilized in the hospital for ten days. He was not allowed visitors. When Louis came to pay his respects, Machon and Joe Jacobs, still bitter, refused to admit him. His wife Anny, who stayed behind in Berlin, was distraught when she heard the news. The only German official to visit him in the hospital was the German Ambassador, who asked Schmeling if he wanted to lodge a formal claim that he was felled by an illegal punch. Having reclaimed his senses, Max realized that to press the issue would only make him look bad. Moreover, it was clear that even if the blow had landed on his kidneys, it was not illegal under American rules. Still, the furor that his remarks unleashed in Germany and the United States hurt his reputation badly in American boxing circles, and old memories of his having won the title in 1930 on a foul surfaced once again. After spending ten days in the hospital, he was carried aboard ship and sailed home in defeat. In many ways he returned to Germany a disgrace in American eyes and something of an embarrassment to Nazi officials.[19]

Louis knocks Max to the canvas and TKOs him in the first round in an amazing 2:04 seconds of round one. The speed and ferocity of Louis's attack surprised and shocked Germans and delighted Americans who now saw Louis as a national hero who had defended American democracy and national honor. Many whites and blacks considered the outcome a devastating blow to Nazi theories of racial supremacy. (Associated Press, Library of Congress)

For his part, Louis remained calm after the bout. Still uneasy around reporters, he smiled and then declared, "I'm sure enough champion now." *Life* magazine carried an account of the body punch that hurt Schmeling. "I just hit him, tha's all. I hit him right in the ribs and I guess maybe it was a lucky punch but man, did he scream! I thought it was a lady in the ringside cryin'. He just screamed, tha's all." In a later recollection, Louis said he felt, "'How's about those, Mr. Superrace?' I was glad he was hurt. That's what I wanted." He told reporters assembled in his dressing room that he had been angry at Schmeling for the way "he kept posing as the uncrowned champion and the way he claimed I fouled him before." When a reporter asked him if he would fight Schmeling again, he responded, "What for? Didn't I just beat him?" But for Joe, at least, this fight was different. "It wasn't just Joe Louis defending the championship against Max Schmeling. It was international, like the Olympic games. I just couldn't let that crown get out of this country and I aim to keep it here for many years." Not only did Louis establish himself as a defender of the American nation, a constant theme from now on, but the devastating nature of the victory erased from the minds of most Americans the first defeat at Schmeling's hands. His championship confirmed at last, Louis established "himself as the hardest hitter and greatest heavyweight that ever pulled on a glove." For the *Pittsburgh Courier*, the victory was even more special. The previous Sunday he had promised the newspaper that he would "redeem himself in the eyes of those he 'let down' when he lost to Schmeling." He kept his promise, by "unleashing one of the most murderous barrages in fistic history." Not only did he avenge his only blemish, he also "proved his right to the title of King of Kings of the fistic forests." He was in a class by himself and would remain so for another ten years. Even his most persistent critic, former heavyweight champion Jack Johnson reversed himself to declare that Louis had fought a great fight.[20]

Schmeling's shocking and overwhelming destruction by a member of an "inferior race" stunned his German fans. Many of them took the defeat almost personally. According to Dr. Goebbels, who listened to the fight over the radio, it was "a crushing defeat. Our papers had too readily predicted a victory. Now the entire country is depressed." In Hamburg, the city where Max grew up, "Nestor" conveyed the general incredulity in a poem: "Quietly we feel the tragedy of this hour/ As if we ourselves received a painful wound/ And still feverishly searching for a reason/ For this defeat." The editors of *Der Angriff* claimed that "not just America was gripped by boxing-fever. We too sat excited in our editorial offices and tensely awaited the telegrams from the USA." The broadcast by Arno Hellmis of the shockingly quick and destructive defeat left them "speechless." A report of Berliners listening to the bout gave the same impression. After waiting at a Berlin café until the early morning, "Our faces are extremely tense. The Negro punches savagely, and Maxie, unser Maxie, on whom we have placed all our hopes, goes down on his knees. Is this really possible?" Even the radio announcer, the article says, could hardly comprehend it. Announcer Arno Hellmis "is almost crying and just keeps saying, 'Max, take your time, Max, take your time!'" The crowds in the café by now "were speechless, we still hardly believe this outcome." From all the bars that played the fight, men staggered out, "staring gravely into the morning. Only slowly do they all find their voices again." Among those who went to bed deeply disappointed was Adolf Hitler who listened to the brief bout at the Berghof in Berchtesgaden. At Max's beloved Sport-Bar in Berlin, his many friends were in a gloomy mood.[21]

In Yorkville, Ridgewood, and other German sections of New York City, as well as in other German American enclaves of the country, the mood was just as depressed as in Germany. Along Eighty-sixth Street all the bars and restaurants had geared up for the big night. Crowds were everywhere and the beer flowed. However, Yorkville awoke with "a terrible hangover." German Americans, looking to assert their ethnic pride, had hoped for a victory by

Schmeling. Unfortunately, they sang a different tune: "Bei mir bist du shame!" German-Americans bet heavily on Schmeling and gave two to one odds as well. In the Lorelei, one of the popular halls, the mood was dead and unhappy. One fellow said that it was unfair and unsporting. The referee should not have allowed Louis to hit Schmeling on the ropes. Several people declared that "Max's food was poisoned," or that Max Machon had thrown the fight for $10,000. Adding fuel to the fires of despair, African American jokesters made several phone calls to bars and restaurants along Eighty-sixth Street. "Hello. Is there a Mr. White there?" "Mr. White. He's a Negro!"[22]

To find explanations for the unbelievable defeat of their hero, German boxing fans blamed the savage animal nature of Louis that triumphed over the superior mental ability of Schmeling. Max was seen as a paragon of Aryan values. Unlike other boxers, noted *Der Angriff*, Schmeling "did *not* let himself be blinded by money, did not succumb to the petty cravings of life." Rather than pursue wealth, he was "a perfect example of athletic ambition and inner strength of character." He was not beaten fairly but in an underhanded way, by "the wild drumfire of the Negro." Indeed, before and after the bout, Louis was described as fighting wildly, as opposed to Schmeling's cool mental style. The day of the fight, the *Völkischer Beobachter* ran caricatures of the two combatants. The newspaper depicted Schmeling carrying his weapons: a compass, T square and triangle, all signs of strategy and mental ability. Dressed in a leopard skin outfit, by contrast, Louis carried a club and had claws instead of fingers. His weapons were "instinct and brute strength." This was the dominant theme in Germany. According to the *Berliner Tageblatt*, for instance, it was a "victory of hate-filled wildness over a cool, reasoned temperament, which did not have enough time to fully develop its power." After the fight, the *Stuttgarter Neues Tagblatt* summed up best: "Whoever saw the short murderous bout with his own eyes experienced the victory of a savage fighter over a cooler, more level-headed temperament." As if a black man could not figure out his own strategy, the paper claimed that former champion Gene Tunney acted as "a spy in service for Joe Louis," and advised him to attack furiously. If Schmeling was beaten by a savage barely removed from the jungle, there was little reason for Germans to question their ideas of racial superiority.[23]

The kidney punch controversy raged in Germany as another, more convenient excuse for the defeat of the German hero. One story claimed that X-rays of Schmeling proved that he was damaged by a kidney punch. The *Berliner Tageblatt* concurred, reporting that doctors had proven that a kidney blow had done the damage "beyond doubt." The German press also quoted Schmeling's statement that he had lost because of an unfair punch. "It was the Negro's first punch that hit me. To be more precise it was a right haymaker that landed exactly on the left kidney. I was immediately paralyzed," and "could no longer think and lost all control." The noble German hero, the epitome of sporting values, was not unmanned on the field of battle in honorable combat, his countrymen argued, but lost through typical American chicanery and lack of true sportsmanship.[24]

Nazi propagandists were so disturbed by the effects of the defeat on national morale that they refused to allow the actual fight footage to be shown in Germany. The man responsible for the ban, Dr. Goebbels, reported to his diary that he examined the films of the fight, and concluded, "He is beaten up terribly. Not to be shown." Daniel M. Daniel, a regular contributor to *Ring*, took it much farther. He noted that the movies of the fight would not be shown in Germany because it would be offensive to show "Max being knocked out by a Negro. That sort of thing would be contrary to the principles of the Aryan philosophy of the Nazi government." An angry John Roxborough charged that the Germans had produced a phony fight film that showed Schmeling winning until the kidney blow. While the furor raged, Schmeling's refusal to lodge a formal protest had serious consequences. "After this defeat," he wrote in his memoirs, "I no longer existed for Hitler and Goebbels ... my name simply disappeared from the newspapers."[25]

Underlying all their charges, Germans blamed "certain unfair machinations" for their hero's defeat. According to the *New York Herald Tribune*, one German newspaper explained that American businessmen should be blamed for Schmeling's defeat. It was said that they "hindered the fight to the point where ... only a miracle would enable Germany to win." Another member of the German press corps, as paraphrased in the *New York World-Telegram*, pointed out the exact nature of the machinations. "The world title must be kept in the United States, which is the reason for all the maneuvers against the German, who repeatedly insisted on fighting Louis." Although that claim was not fully accurate, the author of the statement argued that Schmeling was prevented from fighting until an older Max was no longer "a great menace anymore." The Nazi press also blamed American media persecution for attacks "of the most malicious kind" against Schmeling and Germany. In their self-image, the Nazis were true sportsmen, upholding the highest ideals of athletic culture and civilization. It was "the persecuting press of America" that made Schmeling "into a representative of Nazi Germany, who is said to be an important asset to German propaganda."[26]

Still, the German press maintained that while they were disappointed, "the defeat of a boxer means no loss of national prestige; it is a battle lost always for the boxer himself alone." Of course, this was a pre-arranged viewpoint that Goebbels's propaganda office had insisted on for the German press: this was a sporting, not a political, affair. Yet had Schmeling won, it is inconceivable that the Nazi propaganda machine would not have made tremendous political capital out of the victory, much as it had after the first fight. At the very least the regime would have cooperated with the champion to hold some of his defenses in Germany and made much out of the strongest man in the world being a German. Moreover, while the German press refrained from calling the fight anything other than a sporting match, they could not leave the racial dimension alone. The *Völkischer Beobachter*, in its fight preview, did not claim that the bout was Democracy against Nazism, but "age against youth, right against left," and then, "brain against muscle, black against white." In denying that it believed in the racism it evoked, the paper claimed that the "southern states of the USA, all South America, South Africa and Australia" regarded "the fight as a confrontation between our era's best man of the white race and the Negro." *Der Angriff* also resorted to racist stereotypes in predicting that Max would win because Joe was a "primitively thinking child of nature" who fought only for money, while Schmeling fought for the more noble goal of the comeback and national honor.[27]

The theme of Negro savagery not only dominated the descriptions of Louis, it also influenced the coverage of the celebrations by African Americans in honor of their hero. The *Stuttgarter Neues Tagblatt*, for example, described the "Negro quarters of American big cities" as having engaged in violent and anarchic behavior, which was not an accurate depiction of what actually occurred. In Harlem, "the Negroes threw milk and whiskey bottles high in the air for sheer pleasure, without consideration whether these projectiles would hit any one when they fell back down." They claimed that twelve policemen were hurt, one badly. In Cleveland, they reported, police were forced to shoot tear gas into a crowd of 12,000 Negroes. This was little different than descriptions of Harlem the day before the fight. Then, wrote W. G. in the *Hamburger Anzeiger*, Harlem "is besides itself." Tourists were discouraged from going there because of the danger. Blacks were throwing stones at buses. Rounding out their picture were Negro women wearing Louis's picture as an amulet. Younger blacks raged and yelled like wild demons, "shrieking for joy in a way that could only be expected from the descendants of African ancient forest Negroes." While the New York City Chief of Police declared the crowd peaceful and good-natured, the Hamburg newspaper saw Harlem as its worst nightmare come true—an area filled with racial inferiors emboldened and made wild by Louis's victory over a man of the "superior" race.[28]

American reaction to these charges was swift and bitter. German complaints, argued American sportswriters, were part of the typical deceit practiced by the Nazi regime. In the American view, "America" was responsible for Schmeling's defeat, all right, but it was less the machinations of businessmen and more that Joe Louis was an American who had risen to the top of his profession in a "free" society. As a representative of American democracy, Louis had defeated the Black Uhlan as a symbol of German Nazism. As Jewish-American columnist Sid Ziff put it in the *Los Angeles Herald and Express*, "bitter the gall for Max Schmeling today and for the fanatics who made of his bout with Joe Louis last night more than a mere prize fight. His was a disgrace unequaled in the archives of the boxing game." For a "man of destiny," it was "a tragic finish." He would now have to explain himself to the Nazi authorities. In this atmosphere of heightened nationalism, Schmeling's loss was a defeat for Germany. Nowhere was this argument made more forcefully than in the *Neue Volkzeitung*, a liberal German American newspaper opposed to Hitler. The newspaper blamed Hitler's abasement of Germany for the politicization of sports. "The insane racial theories and the overdone nationalism, the method of considering every sporting event from the perspective of national prestige," the newspaper argued, gave the German press the opportunity to turn the boxing match into a "propaganda world war." Under Goebbels's orders, German newspapers pitted "the pure German hero against the dark foreign power, the representative of National Socialist Germany against the judaized, negroid, democratic America." For the 150 percent Nazi, the issue was never in doubt. After all, how could a racially inferior Negro beat a proud Aryan? Because the Nazis made boxing a political event, they expected confirmation of their racial theories, and acted as if German national pride was at stake; "the disappointment now is especially great."[29]

Conversely, Louis's triumph became one of the greatest symbolic victories in boxing history. African Americans saw Schmeling as an embodiment of white supremacy in its most virulent form. Louis's personal victory over someone who was perceived as having trumpeted his mental superiority over their race

The greatest of the Louis fight celebrations occurred after the second Schmeling fight, June 22, 1938. African Americans across the country took to the streets to glory in the defeat of the greatest White Hope of all. The political issues that surrounded the bout are evident in the sign: "Oust Hitler's Agents and Spies." This celebration took place in Harlem. (Acme, Library of Congress)

proved sweet revenge against all forms of racism at home and abroad. In fact, novelist Richard Wright interpreted the match as a racial and political drama in miniature. The Louis-Schmeling fight, he wrote, was "a drama which manipulated the common symbols and impulses in the minds and bodies of millions of people." In his view, those who followed the fight saw a puppet show in which two distinct ways of life found representation in either a black or white puppet. Sharply different in "race, creed, and previous condition of servitude," the two protagonists made "their partisans wax militantly hopeful." For his part, Schmeling was a friend of Hitler and a supporter of the Nazis, whose propaganda machine had declared the German's prior victory proof of Negro inferiority. Yet "contrary to all Nazi racial laws," the black boxer punched the white one "so rapidly that the eye could not follow the blows . . . his blows must have jarred the marrow not only in the white puppet's but in Hitler's own bones." Out beyond the walls of Yankee Stadium, moreover, there were twelve million black people to whom the black puppet symbolized "the living refutation of the hatred spewed forth daily over radios, in newspapers, in movies, and in books about their lives." Joe Louis was their answer to the exploitation, oppression, and segregation that they encountered. He was a champion of and for black America.[30]

Indeed, in city after city, African Americans once more streamed into the streets, and victory poems poured into the offices of black newspapers. As one poem stressed, "Der was a man named Maxie Schmeling/ When he got tagged he started yelling/ He tried to stop Joe Louis's punches/ And that spelled doom to Hitler's hunches." African American reporter Frank M. Davis recorded that "shouts of joy rang to the stars," as blacks spilled out of their apartments into the streets of Chicago. "It was as if each had been in that ring himself," as if all of them "had dealt destruction with his fists upon the Nordic face of Schmeling and the whole Nazi system he symbolized." This was, for Davis, more than an athletic victory; it was "the triumph of a repressed people against the evil forces of racial oppression and discrimination condensed—by chance—into the shape of Max Schmeling." This was a victory over racial oppression in all areas of American life. Such was the great hope.[31]

In Richard Wright's opinion, the intense public celebration after the second Louis-Schmeling bout, far more intense than those after his previous victories, figured as "the largest and most spontaneous political demonstration ever seen in Harlem." Overjoyed that Louis "wiped out the stain of defeat" and feeling of inferiority in the face of white power, blacks "threw off restraint and fear" and defied police and property with "an impulse which only the oppressed can feel . . . the earth was theirs as much as anybody else's." Mary McLeod Bethune, president of the National Association of Colored Women, wrote the *Pittsburgh Courier* that she had prayed for "our Joe Louis." In her estimation, his win aided all Negroes, for they "feel inspired to get to the top" in all fields of endeavor now that Louis had fought with "the courage, the grit and the persistence that will get any of us to the top." By defeating the German he had proven himself not just a black hero. He had shown himself as an American hero defending the most important ideals of the nation against a foreign invader. "Joe Louis, son of America, son of Alabama, Black American and fighting champion," declared the *Courier*'s sports editor William Nunn, "WE SALUTE YOU!" Within the rules of the ring, as historian Lawrence Levine points out, Louis proved his manhood and the potential power of the community as blacks and as black Americans. By defeating a foreign invader and a symbol of white supremacy, Louis laid claim to full American citizenship for all his people.[32]

It is no accident that African Americans made a successful fighter a symbol of the community, for boxers fought and defeated white opponents, while carrying the banner of the race. Moreover, in the day-to-day competitive world of the United States, in which white competitors had all the advantages, Louis showed that they could be defeated honorably and thoroughly. And he did it not just with his fists, but with his mind. Although the white press emphasized the primitive, panther-like way Louis attacked, many blacks praised him for his cool-headedness. African American fans made a point of Joe's ability to change his tactics after the first fight. His determination to overcome his vulnerability to a right hand showed that he and blacks in general were not mentally inferior to whites. According to black attorney William E. Lily, Joe's taciturnity had led many blacks and whites to consider him "stupid or dull," but these views did not accurately account for champion Joe. He had tremendous punching power, to be sure, but there was "such an obvious method and precision in their delivery that we know there is a thinking man back of them." In many ways, Louis's victory promoted a counter narrative of masculine power and pride that subverted the dominant white stereotypes that black Americans faced every day. In a society where few opportunities existed in the public arena to express black strength and cultural pride, Louis's victory—and his whole career—allowed average black people to envision alternative, more powerful selves.[33]

But this power was not limited to the individual level. In the black community public awareness of its own potential and power was emerging on a mass level. This is the message of the celebrations. Blacks poured into the streets in Harlem, Chicago, Indianapolis, Baltimore, Portland, Gary, and all across the nation. While the violence was limited, shots were fired, young blacks defied police authority, and interracial conflicts occurred that resulted from black self-assertion in the face of white power. In Indianapolis, for example, "thousands of Negroes and many Jews paraded back and forth screaming 'we won', and proceeded to stage a Mardi Gras carnival. The feverish excitement spread to the residential district and quiet, staid Capitol Avenue seemed to pulsate with one rousing 'whee, we won.'" Communal celebrations in Harlem "were marked by political and international implications which the people read into the victory of their idol." Everywhere one looked, there were "placards denouncing nazism and fascism." They announced the knockout "a victory for democracy" and proof that "democracies must fight fascism everywhere." As one sign declared, "Louis wins, Hitler weeps."[34]

In Baltimore, reporter Russell Baker witnessed blacks writing a new script for themselves after Louis's triumph. As soon as they heard the radio announcer declare Louis the victor, black residents "seized by an instinct to defy destiny," streamed out of their homes and their segregated section of the city, into white neighborhoods where their presence had been prohibited. "Joe Louis has given them the courage to assert their right to use a public thoroughfare. . . . It was the first civil rights demonstration that I ever saw, and it was completely spontaneous, ignited by the finality with which Joe Louis had destroyed the theory of white supremacy." As blacks rejoiced, they participated vicariously in dethroning white physical superiority, white authority, and their own subservient condition. In the largest sense, Louis's victory was an important assertion that blacks no longer were a colonized mass but full American citizens, proud of a black and American national hero.[35]

Across the globe the fight attracted boxing fans, but even more dramatically, it drew the attention of "colored" peoples who saw in Louis a Pan-African hero fighting against colonial oppression. Claudius Leo, for example, heard the fight over the radio in Puerto Armuelles, Republic of Panama. In the *Pittsburgh Courier* he described the great joy among the "race population" which Louis's victory unleashed. Black Africans also followed the fight. The Lagos, Nigeria, *West African Pilot* covered the exploits of black American athletes. Shortly after the Louis-Schmeling bout, they printed Louis's picture along with photos of an American track star and African cricketers, tennis players, and boxers. They celebrated Louis as "the impregnable Joe who is the idol of sportsdom." *The Bantu World*, a newspaper for black South Africans, also showed a vivid interest in Louis and Jesse Owens. Indeed, the *World* had used the victory of Owens to attack the segregation of South African rugby. "This 'nigger' who is blithely oblivious of the supremacy of Springbok athletes, is JESSE OWENS of America." Then they cited black American heavyweight boxer LeRoy Haynes who had kayoed Primo Carnera, "Mussolini's giant carpenter." This led them to ask, "Do our Springboks still think that Pigment, or lack of it, makes them superior athletes–beings multiplied to the tenth decimal point?" If they do, the *World* ironically declared, "they must be VERY SUPREME." While athletics gave Bantu readers a chance to challenge white notions of racial supremacy, no one drew their attention as much as did Louis. The newspaper carried news of his major fights, pictures of him and his opponents, and accounts of his championship bout with Braddock, and of course gave extensive coverage to the Louis-Schmeling match and the joyous African American celebrations that followed it. As the paper put it, "Negroes dance in the streets."[36]

Marcus Garvey, founder and leader of the Universal Negro Improvement Association, emphasized that Louis's victory was a triumph for black people worldwide in their battle against racism and colonialism. Although now the leader of a smaller movement than in its heyday of the early 1920s, the black nationalist figure and long-time fight fan still had a following scattered across the African Diaspora. In a front-page editorial in his *The Black Man*, Garvey called Louis "one of our messengers of goodwill throughout the world." After losing to Schmeling, Louis took the time to reflect and appreciate "the responsibility our race has placed upon his shoulders." For the second bout, he delivered the punches "that are typical of our race in action. In that knock out blow the hopes of the German people were shattered and a Negro rose triumphant in the great wilderness of prejudice." As an athlete occupying a great place in American sports, Louis was "our international leader." It was clear that the fight took place as much outside as inside the ring. After all, the German people and Hitler, argued Garvey, did their utmost to "make him feel not only inferior but a worm." In every way, black Louis proved himself a worthier man than the white Schmeling.[37]

The victory not only produced tremendous pride in the worldwide African Diaspora; it also transformed Louis into a patriotic American standard-bearer against a foreign foe. This raised questions about American national identity in the minds of white Americans. In an international conflict between American fascism and German democracy, white Americans were forced to choose between their racial and their national sympathies. Columnist Dan Parker expressed the general white American dilemma when he wondered "how Americans can work up enthusiasm for [Max] to beat Joe Louis, an American boy. . . . One hundred per cent Americans who can't see any merit in an athlete if his skin happens to be of darker pigmentation . . . are hereby reminded that some of Joe's ancestors, the Cherokee Indians, were here long before the forebears of most of the so-called 100 per centers." Looking in from abroad, the *Manchester Guardian* noted that the international situation was forcing Americans to choose between race and nationalism, and found them "torn between wishing that a white man would win the title and not wanting the German to win." Apparently many white Americans followed their nationalist urgings. As the *Chicago Defender* noted, many whites celebrated the victory "because the Bomber, even if black, is an American, and his victory was not one for his race alone, but for millions of Americans anxious to see the title remain in this country."[38]

Concerned about the threat that an aggressive and militaristic Nazi Germany posed for the United States and the rest of the world, white Americans transformed the nation's defender into an American hero, despite his race. White cartoonists, for instance, were quick to point out Louis's role as a national savior and living proof that the formidable Nazi military machine could be defeated. A cartoon in the *Baltimore Sun* portrayed Louis mocking a dejected Hitler. The Führer, wearing a swastika armband, stands with fists cocked in a boxing pose as if he is about to attack. From behind, the champion holds up a huge gloved hand in a Nazi salute, proclaiming, "Heil, yo' all." Another in the *Chicago Daily News* had an explicit military motif. An airplane, named the "Brown Bomber," drops its load on the head of a startled Adolf Hitler. "A Wash Out on the Line," in the Pittsburgh *Post-Gazette*, shows a shirt labeled Schmeling with two gloved hands stamped with swastikas, leaning over the ring dripping wet. The cartoon also says that this is "Brown Shirt Championship Material." At the bottom of the picture another caption says that this is "Lightning Laundry Work by Joe Louis." Moreover, the *New York Post*, depicted Hitler crying, carrying wilted flowers and a swastika in his hands, waiting forlornly for Germany's champion. Of course, the *Daily Worker* had a field day with cartoons. The day after the fight, a badly beaten Schmeling, walking on crutches and wearing a swastika armband, limps off "to Germany" with a "Made in U.S.A." bandage on his badly swollen jaw. On the editorial page another cartoon shows Louis walloping Schmeling, in the shape of a swastika, into oblivion. The title reads "What a SWAT-sika."[39]

As the man whose physical prowess defended the nation against international threats, moreover, Louis's visual depiction in the white press underwent a deeper transformation to an image more suitable for a national hero. Folklorist William Wiggins, Jr., has found that before the second Schmeling fight, many white cartoonists expressed their racial ambivalence toward a powerful black man by depicting Louis as they had Jack Johnson: a lazy Sambo, with savage, ape-like features, dark skin, kinky hair, speaking in dialect. As with the blackface minstrel, Louis was too slow and simple to take care of himself and hence he did not have the requisite character and will power to be a self-made or self-directing citizen of a democracy. After Louis won the title in 1937, and certainly after he decisively vanquished the foreign foe in 1938, his image became more humane and realistic.[40]

The shift occurred in two significant stages. In the first place, white cartoonists began to portray Louis more realistically, befitting the fact that he had both earned the heavyweight championship and had thus proved his manliness and shown himself a worthy representative of the nation. Yet, white cartoonists continued to project the sambo image onto others in his entourage, mostly trainer Jack Blackburn, who took on greater ape-like features and was caricatured as a southern darkie. In phase two, white cartoonists simply abandoned the sambo image entirely. For example, a cartoonist who had perpetrated the worst racist caricatures of Louis reversed his former style starting in 1937 and much more forcefully in 1938. Prior to 1938, Ed Hughes of the *Brooklyn Daily Eagle* was known for his portrayals of Louis as a big-eyed, big-lipped minstrel darkie, as occurred in "Another Case of 'Bad Hands'" in August 1935. Not only did the picture highlight Louis as a grotesque but his

The Wrong Man, a cartoon of June 22, 1938, reprinted on the same date in 1939, with more explicit attention to the political and international implications of the bout. Other cartoonists made the equation between Hitler and Schmeling explicit at the time. Louis became an all-American hero as a result of this bout, the first time in history that an African American male enjoyed such widespread devotion and popularity. Boxing and nationalism had merged in new ways. (Library of Congress)

speech was all dialect: "You aint seen no bad hands—Mistah Baer—until you've felt these!!!" After the second Schmeling fight, however. Hughes depicted the champion as a handsome young man with a powerful body.[41]

Contemporary white viewers could not avoid the fact that Louis's victory struck a blow against Aryan race supremacy. The *Dallas Morning News*, for instance, declared that "the drama of the thing lies less in the fact that Louis, knowing or unknowing, was a symbol." His blows sent "a message to the fairy story of Nazi Aryanism for which poor Schmeling stood." Another American newspaperman commented that Louis had defeated the notion that Nazis and Aryans were invincible. "The Aryan idol, the unconquerable one has been beaten, the bright, shining, shimmering symbol of race glory has been thumped into the dust." Bill Corum made the point clear when he addressed Schmeling directly. "You learned Wednesday night . . . that not all the so-called supremacies and 'Kultures' of which men prate can withstand an exploding punch. It is only an accident of birth that the greatest fist fighter in the world today . . . has brown skin."[42]

Communists and other members of the Popular Front left proved instrumental in promoting Louis's victory as a triumph over Nazi ideas of Aryan racial supremacy as well as American white racism. Liberal columnist Heywood Broun believed that "the decline of Nazi prestige began with a left hook delivered by a former unskilled automobile worker who had never studied the politics of Neville Chamberlain." Even more, William L. Patterson, an African American secretary of the American Communist Party, considered the fight filled with deep import. Having taken up the fight to save the Scottsboro Boys in the early years of the Depression, Patterson was well aware of the violence that lay behind white supremacy in the United States. For him, the fight against Nazism bore dividends against American racism too. In his view, the fight was a political event in which "Joe Louis killed the idea of Nazi supremacy" and "laid to rest the idea of the supremacy of any racial or national group over another." Patterson had grounds for hope that the defeat of the color line in boxing, a key linchpin of white American racism and segregation, would make the struggle against it easier in other fields of sport and in all aspects of American life.[43]

Novelist Richard Wright, a member of the Communist Party and editor for *New Masses*, also linked the victory over international fascism to the battle against domestic white supremacy. Wright maintained that a victory against Nazi racial ideas symbolized by Schmeling would challenge those ideas at home too. Because Louis was black, argued Wright, southern racists had warned against allowing a Negro to defeat a white man for fear of making blacks prideful and "intractable." Calling Schmeling "a friend of Hitler and a supporter of the Nazis," Wright asserted that reactionaries in Germany, Italy, Japan, and the United States had championed Schmeling as one of their own. They believed that he would win because of the superior mental ability of the Aryan races. This implied that Negroes in the United States and in colonized nations were inherently backward "and should be conquered and subjected for the benefit of mankind." Given these blatant views, according to Wright, even poor whites of the Deep South rooted for Joe, "something unparalleled in the history of America." Ordinary blacks seemed to recognize the political implications as thousands yelled, "Heil Louis!" This was Harlem's taunt to fascist boasts of the "superiority of 'Aryans' over other races," to "show how little they feared and thought of the humbug of fascist ritual."[44]

The questioning of white supremacy as an American national ideal went beyond African Americans and communists, however. Louis's victory also opened the door to a new conception of American identity: civic nationalism and ethnic and racial pluralism. *The Ring*, for example, which all along had raised questions about the color line in boxing, declared Louis a courageous champion in avenging his only loss, and his victory symbolized the complete deflation of "claims to natural supremacy of any particular group." As the implications of Nazism became clear, the magazine equated the virulent anti-Semitism of the Hitler regime with the color barriers faced by African Americans. But it was not just those in what the Nazis would call the "Jewish press" who began to question white supremacy. Burris Jenkins, Jr., one of the *New York Journal American*'s most distinctive sports cartoonists, framed the issue of Louis and Schmeling to highlight the racial dimension of the fight. The two boxers face off against each other under a searchlight labeled "politics." A shadowy figure (a ghost of the past?) and a scroll reading "Nordic Supremacy" hovers over the German, while above Louis stands the shadow of Abraham Lincoln and a scroll: "That All Men Are Created Equal." Even the *Louisville Courier Journal* noted that "the ludicrous Nazi myth of racial superiority suffers a knockout at the fists of Joe Louis."[45]

To a large extent, the drama of Louis versus Schmeling was also framed as a battle against anti-Semitism everywhere. The fight against Nazi racial ideology thus made an enemy of all kinds of racial superiority. Promoter Mike Jacobs's cooptation of the Jewish boycott led Jewish sports fans to root for Louis as an anti-Nazi champion. Former champion James Braddock put it best. For every Jewish fan who stays away, there were "ten who will go to see Schmeling get his block knocked off." In the process, Jewish sports fans could celebrate Louis as a pro-Jewish American hero who championed tolerance toward all religions and races. In a parallel to African Americans, they could see the fight as a battle for group dignity and national acceptance as Americans.[46]

In recognition of the increasing mutuality of interest between blacks and Jews in facing a common enemy and promoting a common national ideal of tolerance and pluralism, the *Chicago Defender* reprinted the *Jewish Daily Courier*'s tribute to Louis, which also included a photograph of a determined and serious champion. In a laudatory article, the *Courier* commended Louis's triumph in a way "characteristic of Jewish sentiment throughout the country as this group was solidly behind Louis as against the Nazi German." The *Defender* summed up Jewish hostility toward Schmeling as the result of "the ruthless persecution of Jews by Hitleristic Germany." At many of the public celebrations, moreover, various black people shouted out, "I bet the Jews are happy tonight!" Equally important, the black press recognized that Nazi anti-Semitism was linked to a general fascist racist program that also threatened African Americans. Increasingly, the northern white press also recognized that Nazi philosophy was racist and hence at odds with American national values. Nazism, declared Royce Brier in the *San Francisco Chronicle*, "is founded upon racial pride, and this pride has reached such explosive force that it has become a world scandal in its anti-Semitic phase, and blows up time and again at the slightest jostle from a 'non-Aryan.' It is not that the Nazis hate America; they hate American democracy's tolerance of a Negro."[47]

By defending America against the Nazis, Louis transformed himself from a race hero into the first black all-American icon without losing his African American following. For many white Americans, Louis opened a space to begin the questioning of the myth of white supremacy, just as Jesse Owens had at the Berlin Olympics of 1936. Along the way he had won a measure of acceptance as America's national representative, something that no black figure had ever before accomplished. This was a revolutionary development, impossible during the days of deepening segregation in sports and the hysterical reaction to the displays of black physical and sexual power around Jack Johnson. As a sign of his widespread acclaim, moreover, a host of civic officials went out of their way to express their support for Louis. Before the fight, for instance, Governor Frank Murphy sent a letter to Louis at Pompton Lakes expressing the support of the people of Michigan for the state's first heavyweight champion. After the match, the governor visited Louis's dressing room to congratulate him on his successful battle. Similarly, Mayor Reeding of Louis's home city of Detroit, burst into the dressing room, embraced Joe, and said, "You son of a gun, we are all proud of you, sitting out there." When the champion returned to Chicago, Mayor Edward J. Kelley, along with his family and three children, welcomed Louis and co-manager Julian Black to city hall. Crowds all but blocked the corridors waiting for a glimpse of the champion. Even First Lady Eleanor Roosevelt, commented favorably on the bout in her column, "My Day." Of course, these Democratic officials did not act entirely out of ideological motives. It can be assumed that they were in the process of wooing a growing part of the party's urban constituency—African Americans—just as they might other American ethnic groups.[48]

Although Louis's star rose to unprecedented heights among whites as a result of his victory, not all whites stood behind him. The white southern press generally congratulated him in measured tones, stressing patriotism rather than racial advancement as their theme. Many southern whites did not go that far. Jimmy Carter recalls an episode that occurred during his childhood in Plains, Georgia, where his father, Mr. Earl, owned a peanut farm staffed by black tenants. The forty or fifty tenants respectfully asked to listen to the radio broadcast, and Mr. Earl, following the racial etiquette of the segregated South, allowed them to listen to the radio from out on the porch, while he listened from inside. "The fight had heavy racial overtones," noted Carter, and his all-white school supported the German over the African American. "My father was deeply disappointed in the outcome," recalled Carter. As soon as the bout ended, he snapped off the radio. The tenants, with "masks" firmly fixed, walked silently back to their cabins. When they were safely inside, "pandemonium broke loose." Mr. Earl's tenants knew that he and many other southern whites were in no mood to join in celebrations of an African American racial hero over a white—even if foreign—opponent. While joyous celebrations took place in the North, southern blacks knew better than to celebrate too openly or too loudly.[49]

But while many whites were at best ambivalent about Louis's victory, even racists recognized that something had changed. Former champion Jack Dempsey, who had refused to defend his title against blacks and usually questioned Louis's ring intelligence, admitted that Louis equaled "the best heavyweights of modern times" and had proven that he was not just an instinctual fighter. "He can hit like a mule," Dempsey noted, "and he is also clever." General Hugh Johnson, past head of the National Recovery Administration, a prominent New Deal agency, noted that although Nazi propagandists had boasted of a race victory, Schmeling's loss had disproved "this nonsense about Aryan physical supremacy." Johnson demonstrated that he, like many white Americans, was not free of racism. He declared that whites were smarter than blacks because the latter were closer to the jungle, yet blacks were physically stronger for the same reason. This was a common notion of the day. Various physical anthropologists measured black athletes to declare that their physical makeup was substantially different from that of whites and this explained their perceived superiority in sports. Still, Johnson declared, "it is nothing for us to weep about and seek white hopes. . . . These black boys are Americans."[50]

The acceptance of Louis as an American hero was only the first step for whites on the long and difficult road to redefining American national identity as ethnically and racially diverse, but we can see the beginnings of a new civic awareness in the opinions that followed the fight. In "Joe and the Aryan Issue," for example, the unidentified author declared that this was the first bout "in which a prizefighter delivered left hooks and right-hand smashes for democracy, the equality of peoples, and the brotherhood of man, while supposedly he was merely fighting for his cut." Then the author thanks Louis for giving "we Americans" a lesson in not taking a fellow at his own appraisal. The sports editor of the *Detroit Times*, Bud Shaver, went even farther. Louis, he said, "has white, Indian and Negro blood in him, and to me that is all good American blood." Recognizing race mixture as a national ideal, especially when compared to the Nazi insistence on racial purity, Shaver argued that Louis was "far more than a superbly competent fighter. He is a challenge to tolerance in an intolerant world." In fact, Shaver revealed to his readers that Louis's whole image of modesty was a mask designed to counteract white racial attitudes about blacks. It was for this reason that he saw him as a beacon in a dark world. The *Boston Globe* also used the fight to question American racial values. The newspaper noted the irony that "brown Joe was accepted by multitudes as the representative of world democracy . . . [which] is strange when the undemocratic treatment of Negroes by many who boast of their own attitude toward freedom and equality is recalled."[51]

Equating Schmeling with Goebbels's "Aryan superiority campaign" and Louis with American democracy and racial and religious tolerance not only opened up a discussion of American national ideals but it also led to some concrete changes in the world of boxing. In one of the major shifts in American sport, Louis's victory marked the end of the white hope concept in boxing. Although exploitation in prizefighting continued and white contenders were still valued for their ability to attract white fans, the urgency for racial revenge lost its steam, and the linking of the heavyweight title to racial and national honor lost its central place in American discourse. Indeed, the desire for racial revenge because of ring victories by blacks had been fading throughout the 1930s. The Great White Hope himself, Jim Jeffries, for example, declared in 1935, as Louis became the new "Black Menace," that he saw no point in the idea any longer. As writers in *Ring* magazine put it several years later, few people in the world of boxing assumed that "the fistic victory immediately establishes one race over another." In a revealing cartoon, moreover, *Boxing News* showed "The White Hope Trail" filled with white boxers bent on fighting Louis, who stood at the center of a United States map, a giant of a national ideal surrounded by regional pygmies. Referee Arthur Donovan, the man who oversaw the Schmeling bout, wrote that he heard "no cry of outraged racial pride. . . . Perhaps we're a trifle more civilized than when . . . we thought pictures of a Negro slapping a white man down were dangerous to the republic, and prohibited them."[52]

In a related development, Louis's heroism, as historian Jeffrey Sammons shows, helped end the federal ban on prizefight films. Louis's clean-cut image and reassuring public demeanor eventually convinced Congress to lift the twenty-seven-year ban on the interstate transportation of prizefight films. Instituted in the wake of the riots allegedly spurred by the showing of the films of the mixed-race "White Hope" bout between Jim Jeffries and Jack Johnson in 1910, Congress had banned the films in 1912 to stop race riots, especially on the part of blacks. Underneath their decision, however, was the desire to prevent the mass distribution of images of black male strength triumphant over white men. Although flouted often, the law was a symbolic statement that American nationalism as embodied in male strength in general and boxers in particular was tied to whiteness. When Congress finally repealed the ban on fight films in the wake of Louis's victory over Schmeling, the members recognized at the very minimum that male athletic strength, racism, and nationalism should be decoupled.[53]

Senator Warren Barbour of New Jersey, a former boxer and prominent fight fan, had offered a bill to legalize fight films in 1935, with support from Congressman Emmanuel Cellar of New York, but it did not go through. In 1938 Barbour tried again. In two days of hearings the Senate focused on four issues: the common flouting of an unpopular law; the acceptance and legalization of boxing in every state; the changed racial conditions of the country, personified by Joe Louis; and the expectations of television as a new mass visual medium. Two of the most important factors considered had to do with the role of women and blacks in the sport. Various witnesses testified that numerous women had attended prizefights in 1938, including more than 10,000 at the recent Louis-Schmeling bout, while others noted that women enjoyed the fights as much as did men. One boxing broadcaster, writer, and promoter testified that his mother enjoyed boxing matches, "not because she has a barbaric spirit," but rather because "it is a contest between two evenly matched men, and she has a little red blood still in her corpuscles." Whereas Progressive reformers and moral critics of boxing had considered women potential victims of lustful black champions such as Jack Johnson, now boxing promoters and the sport's proponents considered them potential paying customers.[54]

As to race, Abe Greene, chairman of the New Jersey Boxing Commission, explained that "the measure came into being in the midst of a boxing contest which involved racial feuds; it was conceived at the time that the showing of such films might fan the flames of racial hatred." At present, he testified, "there is now, and for a long time there has been, no such condition, with the result that prize-fight films have been shown in various states in violation of the law." Senator Barbour extolled Louis as a key reason that the films should be legal. He was the "first Negro heavyweight," Barbour declared, "who was so respected across the country that fight films could be sent interstate." Other prominent boxing figures, like Gene Tunney, John Reed Kilpatrick, and Jack Dempsey, concurred. Joe Louis's fights did not upset racial "tranquility." Despite some unease among white southerners that the films could encourage black rebellion, on June 13, 1939, the Senate unanimously passed a bill to permit interstate shipment of prizefight films. In the future, black and white fighters and promoters could hope to earn at least some percentage of the revenues accrued from the showing of their fights in theaters across the country.[55]

Equally important to the decline of the color line in boxing, white and black fans proved willing to watch Joe Louis fight against a black challenger in 1939. Earlier in his career, Louis did not engage in any matches with other African American boxers, as his managers wanted to keep him from falling into the black heavyweight ghetto. Unlike Jack Johnson, who, having fought many black heavyweights on the way up, drew a color line after he became champion, Louis agreed to fight John Henry Lewis, the former light heavyweight champion once he became champ. A heavyweight title fight would provide Lewis with probably the best payday of his career. Both boxers could rely on their army of African American supporters, but they also appealed to white fans. Louis also fought a number of exhibitions against black boxers during World War II, and title matches in the late 1940s.[56]

There was another fallout of Louis's victory. While many whites continued to treat the Brown Bomber condescendingly, increasingly they expressed admiration for him as an exemplar of the common man. In part, this forced an admission that he had the intelligence to beat Schmeling. Prior to the fight, white Americans saw the match as a battle between "brains and brawn." That this matched the way the German press portrayed the matter should alert us to the similarity in the racist thinking exhibited by both nations. Grantland Rice, for instance, wrote, "Louis was an instinctive fighter. I don't think he can be taught anything that is even slightly new." After the bout, opinion shifted. "Joe Louis is credited with never thinking about anything," wrote Tom Cribbs, Jr., to the *New York Post*. "It is an obvious slander thus to put him in the class with so many of our statesmen." Yes, he had a blank mask and might be a jungle god. "But he must have been thinking on Wednesday night for two minutes and four seconds." Everyone saw that he fought in a fury, but now commentators acknowledged that the fury was part of a well-conceived plan laid out in training and followed to a tee. Moreover, for many whites the issue was moot. It was not how smart he was, but whether he was a good fighter. Comparing Louis to that other, fictional champion Joe Palooka, the *San Francisco Chronicle* noted that the whole issue was beside the point. It was said that Max might win by "superior generalship, that is brains. Joe handled that by knocking the brains out of the superior general. That is, Joe rendered Schmeling's brains useless." Equally important in the white reassessment of Louis was his deep-rooted "sincerity." He did not, declared *Ring*, say anything more than he meant, and everything he said he meant sincerely. Louis was honest, straightforward, and fair. His pithy sayings were quoted repeatedly as sports folklore and common wisdom. For example, when asked by reporters if he wanted to see movies of the first Schmeling bout, Louis replied, "No, I saw the fight." After 1938 and during World War II, Louis rose to a new level of status. He became what one sports writer called a credit to his race—"the human race."[57]

On the night of June 22, 1938, Joe Louis stood at the pinnacle of what would be a long and spectacular career as heavyweight champion of the world. Public adulation was at its peak, and the opponents he would now face seemed of lesser caliber. Former champion Jim Corbett once said that in the life of every champion there came a night when he had everything. Such a night occurred for Louis against Schmeling. His annihilation of a strong, confident, and crafty veteran led fans to compare him to Jack Dempsey, Jack Johnson, John L. Sullivan, and all the rest of the ring greats. Whereas Louis stood atop the world, however, Max left the ring a "battered, brain-fogged, tortured victim." Once again knocked off the pedestal of public recognition and acclaim, Schmeling would face the depression and self-questioning that he had experienced during the early 1930s. How could he come back from that? Even more important, what would be his fate in Nazi Germany now that he had lost to a Negro?[58]

6

THIS IS THE ARMY

Entering the ranks of their respective nation's
armies, it was fitting that these two fighters
should typify so perfectly the conflicting principles and characteristics in back of them.

Willis N. (Jersey) Jones, "Two Fighters,"
1943

The spectacular battle between the Brown Bomber and the Black Uhlan
transformed the lives of both men. While Joe Louis's victory turned
him into a national hero, Max Schmeling's devastating defeat strained
his relationship with Nazi officials. His new status was apparent as soon as the
German boxer returned home. When he staggered off the boat at
Bremerhaven, reported *Ring*, there was no public celebration, and no official
came for the man who nearly had been injured fatally in his battle "with the
Negro." Only his wife and mother, anxious over his health and well-being,
waited to meet him and transport him to a private clinic in Berlin, where he
enjoyed a room filled with flowers from his friends and fans. None came from
the Reich Ministry of Sport or the Chancellery. Except for Albert Speer,
Hitler's chief architect, moreover, officials failed to pay their respects to the
man who had carried the nation's banner into the ring. Seemingly forgotten,
Schmeling brooded during the six weeks that he remained in the clinic. The
physical injury to his vertebrae pained him, but the mental torment drove
him toward feelings of depression and guilt. Not only had he let his country

and his fans down, he also could not grasp how he had been destroyed so quickly and so thoroughly. After years of campaigning for another title shot, he now faced the likelihood that he had ruined his last chance to recapture the crown.[1]

Shocked and disappointed by the embarrassing defeat of the Aryan hero, Dr. Goebbels immediately moved to halt the damage at home and abroad. As the overseer of German mass communications, the Minister of Propaganda ordered the nation's media not to dwell on the match as a blow to German national prestige. Schmeling may have lost, Goebbels decreed, but he was merely a boxer; in no way was German national honor involved. Even as the German boxer lay in a New York hospital, Goebbels decided that Schmeling represented too big a propaganda liability. While the press could still cover the boxer's activities, this would occur on the sports pages rather than the first two news pages. Similarly, after viewing films of the fight on July 12, three days after Schmeling's return to Germany, Goebbels noted in his diary that the film should not be shown because it depicted the defeat in graphic and undeniable terms. Hitler agreed. Equally important, government officials stepped back from promoting Schmeling as their athletic champion in the international arena. Nursing his wounds, the Black Uhlan realized that he was isolated from the regime in Berlin and the boxing world of New York. Chancellery receptions, national honors, and trophies were a thing of the past. In an effort to pull back from public life, the boxer and his wife sold their large Berlin apartment and took a smaller one for their increasingly infrequent trips to the capital. More and more they spent their time at their Ponickel estate near the Polish border.[2]

Despite Goebbels's orders, however, the German press could not completely ignore a man as internationally famous as Schmeling and as popular a hero at home. While the boxer remained out of the public eye, the international media circulated rumors that he had been arrested on his return to Germany and sent to a concentration camp. In September, fresh rumors appeared that Max had shot his wife and then killed himself, or that they both had fled to Czechoslovakia. In order to deny these reports, the authorities asked Schmeling to appear at the ten-year anniversary of the National Socialist Party in Benneckenstein, where he met with the Gauleiter of Thuringia. Officials also arranged for him to appear as a guest of Hitler at the Nuremberg party rallies of 1938, after which he traveled to Königsberg to hunt with Field Marshall Göring. As much as they wanted to downplay Schmeling's cultural significance, German officials had to bring him before the public to disprove rumors that he had fared badly in the Nazi regime.[3]

Not only was he increasingly isolated from the government, Schmeling also realized that political events threatened his circle of friends and rendered criticism of the regime increasingly dangerous. On September 29, 1938, while Hitler was meeting with other European leaders in Munich to resolve the

Czechoslovakia crisis, his aggressive policies roiled the normally peaceful precincts of Roxy's Bar, Schmeling's favorite Berlin haunt since the 1920s. The discussion in the bar grew quite heated when director Rolf von Goth and Heinz Ditgens, the owner of Roxy's, criticized Hitler's warmongering and the dangers of a full-scale war. Outraged, another old friend, opera singer Michael Bohnen, jumped to his feet to declare, "I won't tolerate this type of conversation in my presence!" Bohnen then reported his friends to the Gestapo. Van Goth was later picked up and Ditgens was told not to leave town. In his memoirs, Schmeling emphasized that the incident was a sign that his group of friends was breaking up under the pressure of political events. Although Schmeling was not actually present, Ditgens asked him to intervene on their behalf, a role that the German boxer had played on several occasions in the past. Schmeling replied that he no longer had any pull, but he called Heinrich Hoffman, a friend and Hitler's photographer, who berated Schmeling for trading on his status as a sports hero to help possible traitors. Eventually Goebbels smoothed things over, but the days of approaching German officials on anyone's behalf were coming to an end. Moreover, the incident left bad blood everywhere. The *Stammtisch* broke up, and friends were now suspected of being Gestapo agents. Even the Schmelings became objects of scorn in the Roxy Bar.[4]

The increasingly dangerous situation for Germany's Jews also put Schmeling in a difficult spot. Isolated as he now was from his political contacts, he could no longer use his influence on behalf of individual Jews. He could still act privately and in secret, which he did during Kristallnacht, November 9, 1938, when he protected two Jewish youngsters from Nazi mobs that attacked individual Jews and Jewish synagogues and shops. In response to a desperate appeal from his tailor, David Lewin, Schmeling agreed to hide his two sons Henri and Werner, aged fourteen and fifteen, respectively. The boxer and the elder Lewin, who was well known in Berlin's sporting and entertainment circles, had been friends since the mid-1920s. Schmeling had purchased suits from Lewin's fashionable clothing shop, eaten at his restaurant, stayed at his Aristocrat Hotel in Potsdam, and had been a guest in his friend's home. When David Lewin asked for help, Schmeling secreted the two boys for four days in his apartment in Berlin's Excelsior Hotel, despite the risk of imprisonment or worse had he been discovered. When the violence subsided, he spirited the boys to a safe haven, from which they eventually escaped the country. Only in 1989 did Henri, then a successful Las Vegas hotel operator, reveal the German boxer's role in the episode.[5]

His own reputation in ruins, Schmeling could not help feeling envy while *Ring* awarded Louis its Most Valuable Boxer Award for 1938 and ranked him with such greats as Jack Dempsey and Jack Johnson. Unwilling to retire with such a crushing defeat as his lasting memory and confident that his one-round TKO was a fluke, early in 1939 Schmeling mounted his campaign for a rematch. In a visit to Paris, he confidently told his old hero, French boxer Georges Carpentier, that he would fight Louis in September. Just the mention of such a fight alarmed Berlin. Dr. Franz Metzner, the German boxing minister, was stunned at the fighter's audacity. He wrote to von Tschammer that he found it impossible that Schmeling would contemplate a rematch against the Negro after his catastrophic defeat, especially now that he was another year older. Convinced that "unser Max" had no chance, Metzner and von Tschammer alerted Hitler to what was afoot.[6]

Before anyone could stop him Schmeling and his trainer Max Machon once again traveled to New York, hoping to secure a third Louis fight. Their greeting in New York proved friendlier than in June 1938. Introduced at the Billy Conn-Fred Apostoli light heavyweight match at Madison Square Garden, Schmeling received a sustained round of applause. His greeting by promoter Mike Jacobs was friendly too. In response to the German boxer's request for another match, Jacobs advised him first to redeem himself by winning several European bouts, and then a title fight might be arranged in summer 1940. While this held out a ray of hope, Nat Fleischer was more pessimistic. He had nothing against the German personally, *Ring*'s editor declared, "but in the face of what is taking place in Germany, I think that the American public will be more grateful to Uncle Mike if he lets good enough alone and refrains from importing Schmeling." Moreover, the Black Uhlan did not meet with his American manager Joe Jacobs. Their contract had expired, and for reasons that have not come to light, there appears to have been a breach in their relationship. Achieving a third title fight without "Yussel the Muscle" could prove daunting. Aware that his work was cut out for him, "unser Max" returned to Germany prepared to take on the top European heavyweights.[7]

In March, shortly after he and his trainer returned from New York, matters came to a head. Metzner summoned Machon to his office and informed him that Hitler would not approve another fight against Louis. An official letter followed: "the Führer made it known through his adjutants that another campaign for you in America is not desired." It was obvious to Schmeling that the regime did not wish to suffer another racial and political embarrassment and hence wanted his international career over, but he refused to take the news lying down. He asked whether the decision was made for political reasons or because in Hitler's eyes he was no longer a capable boxer. Put on the spot, Metzner responded that Schmeling was too old for the ring. Despite this discouragement, the German boxer still attempted to maintain good relations with the Führer in hopes that the situation would change. Schmeling was convinced that if he could fight in Germany he could convince Hitler and his countrymen that he still had something left. He would also find out once and for all if he were too old.[8]

In an attempt to do a favor for Germany's most prominent fighter, Metzner proposed the idea of a German championship bout with Adolf Heuser. On

July 2, 1939, Schmeling met Heuser in Stuttgart's Adolf Hitler Stadium before 60,000 fans. Convinced that Max's best days were behind him, most German fans put their money on Heuser. Surprising the doubters one more time, Schmeling proved overwhelming, knocking out his opponent in seventy-one seconds of the first round and leaving him unconscious for several minutes after the bout ended. In interviews, "unser Max," now Germany's Heavyweight Champion, declared himself back on track and feeling like a twenty-five-year-old again. More important, having beaten his opponent faster than Louis had beaten him, Schmeling felt confident that he had recovered fully from defeat. He requested an audience with Hitler, but there is no record of what transpired at the meeting in Munich in mid-July. However, two weeks later Schmeling canceled a trip to New York to fight Tony Galento or Lou Nova, as arranged by Mike Jacobs, so it is probable that Hitler continued to oppose any further American ventures. Instead, Schmeling agreed to fight Walter Neusel in Dortmund on October 1, 1939. On September 1, 1939, however, the German army invaded Poland to start World War II. By mid-September, just as he planned to head to his Westphalia training camp, the fight was called off. Managers and promoters had been drafted. Back in shape, his chances for fistic redemption hanging by a thread, Schmeling, with Machon in tow, headed for Lisbon to travel to the United States where he desperately hoped to arrange a fight with Louis. When the two reached Madrid, they found Hitler's orders to return to Germany immediately. The regime had other plans for Schmeling.[9]

Like other top German athletes, Schmeling was expected to put his career on hold for the duration and enter the armed forces as an example of his nation's fighting spirit. When three-time Olympian Alfred Schwarzmann distinguished himself in the attack on Holland, a pleased Reichssportführer von Tschammer und Osten declared, "My best athletes should also be my best soldiers." As in peace so in war, Goebbels planned to mobilize the full force of German radio, press, newsreels, and film in a carefully controlled propaganda campaign to highlight Schmeling's military service. As the number one sports icon in Germany, the fighter in uniform would encourage others to support the war fully, serve as a role model for German youth, and demonstrate that even the most privileged celebrities were eager and willing to do their duty.[10]

Unbeknownst to the German public, however, Schmeling sought to avoid military service. He was incensed that alone among German athletes he was drafted into the paratrooper corps in 1940—although for propaganda purposes the regime declared it was voluntary—at his age. "No one had expected that. Not only were prominent artists, actors and athletes usually exempt," he asserted in his memoirs, "but I was also, at thirty-five, well over draft age." Because he no longer had prospects of becoming world champion, he lacked the protection of officials high up in the regime. The dismayed boxer believed that it was von Tschammer who was responsible for his fate. The

Max Schmeling as a paratrooper, 1941. In 1940 Schmeling was drafted into the paratroopers, and despite his reluctance to serve, was used to promote the German war effort. He became the face of the enemy to the allies. (Associated Press, Library of Congress)

Reichsportsführer had not forgotten their run-ins over manager Joe Jacobs, Schmeling's refusal to hold his championship matches in the Third Reich, and his intervention on behalf of individual Jews. It was von Tschammer, Schmeling maintained, who had personally arranged, with Hitler's approval, his induction into the German army. Moreover, the Reichsportsführer prevented him from boxing during the war. Convinced that he was the subject of a personal vendetta, "unser Max" appealed to his many contacts, but to no avail. Everyone in the Chancellery knew him for his appeals on the part of Jews. In fact, in 1940 he spoke up for an Austrian boxer who had a child with his Jewish lover and hence had committed *Rassenschade*. The charges were dropped unexpectedly, but the incident did little for Schmeling's reputation.[11]

When he was drafted, Schmeling believed that he would serve not as a regular soldier, but as an exercise and sports instructor for young recruits. Initially assigned to an antiaircraft unit in East Prussia, he did his basic training, earned a promotion to corporal, and then took his airborne training. After assignment to a combat unit, in early 1941 he was sent to Greece, where he believed himself out of the action. But as Anny told him, "Max, you've been had . . . you're a regular soldier now!" Numerous photos of him in full paratroop regalia about to jump from a plane appeared in newspapers, newsreels, and magazines around the globe. He became the face of the German army at war.[12]

On May 20, 1941, his unit jumped into Crete in the face of heavy British fire. To avoid becoming sitting ducks, the troopers jumped from about 450 feet. There were still heavy losses, however, as some parachutes failed to open, a number of men smashed to the ground, and others were raked by machine gun fire. Schmeling landed safely in a vineyard, but hitting the ground hard, he re-injured the vertebrae that he had fractured in the Louis fight. "I could barely move," he recalled, and the British targeted him with heavy fire. He lost his sense of orientation, got cut off from his unit, and only found his way back the following night. Taken to a field hospital suffering from severe dysentery, he needed to be separated from the other patients. Soldiers all around him died as he lay outside in a field. On the third day after the landing, Schmeling was flown to Athens. German POWs captured on Crete told their British captors that Max had been wounded, and soon both the United Press and Reuters reported that he had "fallen in the fighting on Crete," and was thought killed. It took until May 30th for Anny to learn that her husband was still alive. For his actions, Schmeling received an Iron Cross, second-class medal.[13]

Goebbels hoped to use the Crete incident as part of an international propaganda campaign, but Schmeling's failure to cooperate led to an irredeemable break. The propaganda minister planned to undermine British reporting by showing that the foreign press had gotten the story of Schmeling's death wrong and hence could not be trusted for reliable war news. In addition, he wanted Schmeling to confirm that British soldiers had abused and tortured German POWs after the German victory in order to justify German retaliation. In pursuit of these aims, Goebbels arranged with CBS reporter Harry Flannery to interview the German boxer. However, Schmeling declared that English troops had fought fairly and that he had not heard of any cases of British cruelty toward German soldiers. Asked about a possible war between Germany and the United States, which had not yet entered the conflict, he replied, "For me that would be a tragedy. I have always seen America as my second home." The interview received positive attention abroad, but enraged German authorities suppressed it at home. As Goebbels wrote in his diary "One hears nothing very good from Schmeling. He gave an American journalist a considerably poor and childish interview." He confided that boxers should fight rather than sit in Athens giving out interviews.[14]

From then on Goebbels considered Schmeling a dangerous loose cannon. In a speech to a group of actors and directors at the propaganda ministry, Goebbels ranted that the German boxer had exposed himself as "the most pathetic weakling." Yes, he jumped into Crete, Goebbels admitted, but "we know from eyewitnesses that Schmeling hid himself under a large ledge and from there watched how his comrades were slaughtered without involving himself in the fight." For a time the propaganda minister tried to bring him before a *Volksgerichtshof* [National Socialist People's Court] on charges of treason, but as a soldier only a military court could try him. In just such a Berlin military court, the judges found no cause for action since the United States was at that time neutral. Still not satisfied, the propaganda minister had the boxer's name struck from German newspapers. According to Schmeling's memoirs, Goebbels's order to the press declared, "The interview with Max Schmeling is not to be printed. The Schmeling matter will disappear from press (good boxer, bad politician)." Still, his picture continued to circulate in *Box-Sport* and other periodicals because he was too useful an example of the athlete at war to be completely forgotten. The German public, however, knew little of his difficulties.[15]

Eventually released as physically unfit for military service in spring 1943, Schmeling planned to resume boxing. Still European champion, he hoped to fight Walter Neusel once more. While the authorities placed no restrictions on Neusel during the war, the Ministry of Sports, certainly at the behest of von Tschammer, and perhaps with Gobbels's concurrence, officially banned Schmeling from the ring. Fed up, he surrendered his last title and retired from the sport he had loved since his youth. At the age of thirty-seven, with Joe Jacobs dead, Schmeling returned home. Although out of favor with the Nazis, he remained popular among German soldiers and boxing fans, and was hailed as the perfect boxer-warrior hero by *Box-Sport*, because he had fought for his country like other German men. Despite his celebrity status, he had proven his bravery on the field of battle. As a private citizen, moreover, he continued to serve his country, but now it was to raise morale. This too ensured his reputation among the German population. With the permission of the German army, he aided the International Red Cross by visiting prisoner of war camps, where he went out of his way to cheer up American and British soldiers. He also appeared at boxing exhibitions in Paris and elsewhere to keep up the spirits of German soldiers.[16]

His image in the United States, however, hardened into that of an out-and-out Nazi as the world descended into war. In 1940, for instance, after the fall of France, the *New York World Telegram* reported that the German-controlled Vichy government had banned all professional sports except cycling. The newspaper explained this development by recalling Louis's victory over Schmeling. "Still suffering from the shock of Max Schmeling's summary dismissal by the Negro, Joe Louis," along with their failure to destroy the United States in the Berlin Olympics, the Nazis "no longer admire the democratic idea in sports" and imposed their views on the French government. The following year, the *Rochester Democrat and Chronicle* reported that Schmeling had become a dedicated Nazi soldier. The newspaper described the German's introduction at a Louis bout as a "parachute troop volunteer" in the German army. According to the report, "he clicked his heels in true Prussian fashion, and snapped out a Nazi salute to the four sides of the hall." That he had come to embody Nazism led to the rumor in the United States that he had served for over a year as the commandant of the Osciecim Prison Camp in Poland, "one of the most brutal concentration camps in Europe." Just as he had transformed "unser Max" into an Aryan god during peacetime, Goebbels's wartime propaganda campaigns had turned his best fighter into his best soldier, an enthusiastic volunteer in the parachute corps. As a sign of his prominence as a symbol of the Nazi enemy, Schmeling's body became a celebrated token for allied troops. From Crete to Norway, rumors circulated throughout the war that the German boxer had been killed. Allied soldiers searched for his remains as proof that they, like Louis, had defeated their symbolic enemy. They found no body, of course, because Schmeling remained alive, although like Germany, badly wounded in spirit. Although the Nazis had pursued him for propaganda purposes, his accommodation to and identification with the regime made him a suitable villain for Americans during the war. His loss to Louis came to symbolize that the Nazis, like Schmeling, could be defeated. As a wartime article about the two boxers put it, "a lot of other Max Schmeling's in Berlin are learning what one Max Schmeling learned in a New York ring nearly five years ago."[17]

In the boxing world, his hardening image emerged in a series of letters to *Ring* magazine. In February 1941, an outraged German American wrote to denounce the "abusive and so vile" treatment of Schmeling in particular and Germans in general in the pages of the magazine. The responses were fierce. Nat Fleischer wrote that "the quicker the world gets rid of Hitler, the quicker peace will reign." Many readers defended Fleischer as "a 100 per cent American, ready to fight for this country's rights." In fact, said one, "he brought Max Schmeling to America," and helped other foreign boxers make their way, while another, John Bruen chimed in that Schmeling was not a super fighter but had just gotten lucky in catching Louis at a weak moment. Perhaps no one put it better than Private Johnny Irish McGrath, a former boxer, who now proudly served his country. "This fight [World War II] won't end in a disputed decision, or a draw. It will be a knockout victory that will surpass Joe Louis' K.O. victory over the German, Max Schmeling."[18]

As Schmeling witnessed the decline of his reputation, Louis's victory and his activities during the war made him a full-blown American hero. Seemingly a permanent champion, Louis offered African Americans a model of self-confidence and fighting spirit and white Americans the image of a protector. As humorist Art Buchwald recalled, kids in his town believed in three certainties: "Franklin Roosevelt was going to save the economy," "Joe Dimaggio was going to beat Babe Ruth's record," and more than anything else, "Joe Louis was going to save us from the Germans." With Louis leading the way and radio publicizing his bouts, boxing in 1939 was probably more popular than it had been in the glory days of the 1920s. As a fighting champion, moreover, he mowed down the opposition regardless of race, creed, or color, giving all contenders a chance, from the over-age Jack Roper to the fighting Italian American bartender Tony Galento and the former African American light heavyweight champion John Henry Lewis. His record number of defenses and the weakness of the opposition led the press to dub his opponents "Bums of the Month." Louis appeared invincible, as firmly fixed a part of the American scene as was FDR. Only former light heavyweight champion Billy Conn gave him trouble. A confident Conn bragged that he was smarter and faster than Louis, and predicted victory. When asked when he hoped to catch Conn, the Brown Bomber sneered, "I hope to catch him with his mouth open." On June 18, 1941, in one of the most exciting fights of the era, Conn stuck and moved, peppering Louis with rights and lefts, piling up points as the bout progressed. On the verge of taking the title, however, he tried to slug it out with the Brown Bomber in the thirteenth round and ended up another knockout victim. For his efforts on behalf of boxing, Louis received *Ring*'s Fighter of the Year Award for 1938, 1939, and 1941. He was in "a class by himself, the champion of champions."[19]

Increasingly at ease as champion, Louis entered the political arena in the 1940 presidential election to campaign for the Republican nominee, Wendell Willkie. Black Americans had only begun to vote for Democratic nominees during the 1930s and many remained loyal to the party of Lincoln. Determined to appeal to blacks as key swing voters in northern cities, Willkie campaigned on a progressive civil rights platform that included an anti-lynching

Louis campaigns for Wendell Willkie, Republican candidate for president in 1940.
Using his prestige as champion, Joe supported Willkie, much to the dismay of
many African Americans, because he believed that President Franklin D. Roosevelt
had not supported the anti-lynching bill. This move prefigured the black
community's demands for the desegregation of defense industries and the
American army in 1941. (Associated Press, Library of Contress)

bill that southern Democrats had consistently stalled. White and black Democrats expressed dismay at Louis's actions, but so too did NAACP leaders who increasingly aligned themselves with FDR's "common man" rhetoric and the New Deal's work relief programs. While Jack Dempsey charged that Louis was "talking against his race and his people," the Brown Bomber in fact stood at the forefront of the African American challenge to FDR that the following year would flower into protests against the segregation of the army and the defense industry. As a sign of growing black political self-confidence that he had helped engender, the champion told northern black crowds that the president had had two terms to show what he could do, "but didn't give us an anti-lynching law." In New York, he announced, "I am not thinking so much about my people up North. I am thinking about my people down South." As the *Pittsburgh Courier* asserted, his actions "caused more comment" in the black community than any other subject. White and black reporters alike criticized Louis for his political naïveté and for speaking about political matters at all. While his speeches on economic issues were garbled, there was no mistaking his fervent belief that the Roosevelt administration, by ignoring the lynching issue, had not fulfilled its promises to African Americans. Usually quiet on race issues, Louis demonstrated that the issue of civil rights was coming to the fore as the nation prepared for war and that he would speak his mind.[20]

When the United States entered the war, government officials expected Joe Louis, as a symbol of America's fighting strength, to join the armed forces. In a direct parallel to Schmeling, boxers and other athletes were expected to demonstrate that American manhood had the strength to prevail over a determined enemy. No less than five world champions and 4,000 boxers overall entered the military. Even forty-six-year-old Jack Dempsey eventually secured a commission as a lieutenant commander in the Coast Guard, making him the highest-ranking professional fighter in the armed forces, while Gene Tunney, returned to the Marines as a captain. Other fighters helped on the home front. James J. Braddock took charge of boxing for the United States Civil Defense, and Jack Johnson helped raise a record $3,000,000 for the Brooklyn War bond campaign. Boxing promoters did their part too, arranging special war bond tournaments, putting on shows for defense workers, and pledging a 2 percent levy on boxing purses and managers for the war effort. As National Boxing Association president Abe Greene admitted, "We want to be able to do our part so that when the role of sports is recalled at the close of the struggle it will be found that boxing has played the part well in the true American style." With Joe Louis as its chief exemplar, and thousands of other boxers in service, boxing became more than a rough, often corrupt sport; it became a symbol for all that was best in American society.[21]

As the heavyweight champion of the world, no athlete was more important to the war effort than Joe Louis. Already considered a race hero by blacks and a patriot and acceptable black boxer by many whites, Louis rose to the

Steel workers of the Serbian Club listen to the Louis-Conn fight in June 1941.
Radio was an important sports medium and served to unite white and black
working class Americans behind Louis in a national sound community. (Library of
Congress)

height of respect and acceptance during World War II. In the simple way he
spoke patriotic sentiments, in his selfless actions for the nation, Louis became
a symbol of the common man whom the Americans were fighting to defend.
As a black man, moreover, he embodied what historian Gary Gerstle called
American civic nationalism, which the war brought to its height. Forged in
the Great Depression, this form of nationalism emphasized that the United
States was a nation where no deserving individuals, regardless of ethnic or
racial background, would be denied economic opportunity or assistance should
they need it. As the first man to knock out a Nazi, Louis symbolized the
growing recognition of the new inclusiveness toward the children of Catholic
and Jewish immigrants and the black migrants from the South. The growing
tide of fascism in the world, which the Louis-Schmeling fights had highlighted,
spread a new self-definition of the United States as an ethnically and racially
tolerant nation. In many ways, American propagandists framed the war as
another Louis-Schmeling fight, only on a worldwide scale. At the same time,
as a black man Louis also faced the deep-seated racial nationalism of American society that forced him and millions of other African Americans into segregated branches of the military. As he performed his military duties admirably,
he also expressed the heightened demands for racial justice on the part of

African Americans at the crossroads of a war for greater freedom and democracy and a war for racial supremacy.[22]

The solidification of Louis's stature as a national hero flowed from his fervent support of and sacrifice for his nation at war. The most notable example was his selfless participation in a benefit bout for the Navy Relief Society on January 9, 1942, two days before he volunteered for the United States Army and only one month after the Japanese attack on Pearl Harbor. Staged at a flag-bedecked Madison Square Garden, the charity match featured Louis against Buddy Baer, Max's huge younger brother. For the benefit of the families of naval personnel killed or wounded at Pearl Harbor, the Heavyweight Champion of the World risked his title and donated his earnings of $47,000, while promoter Mike Jacobs donated all of his profits, $37,330, and challenger Baer turned over $4,081. The fight stirred controversy in the black community because the navy was the most segregated branch of the service. Realizing the futility of stopping the match, Walter White of the NAACP complimented Louis for acting "bigger than the Navy" and hoped that his example would force the navy to include blacks in roles other than mess boys. He then organized NAACP Youth Councils to distribute leaflets advocating the removal of discrimination to fight fans entering the Garden.[23]

Despite the criticism by African Americans, Louis upheld his commitment. Many things were wrong with the United States, he said, "but Hitler won't fix them." In response to reporters' asking why he would risk his title for nothing, he replied, "I ain't fighting for nothing, I am fighting for my country." Promoter Mike Jacobs did his part to frame the fight and Louis's efforts as part of a battle against discrimination. As he put it, "There is no place in America for discrimination. What Joe Louis and the 20th Century Sporting Club are doing is for a worthy cause and if it is found that any member of the Navy is discriminated against in this case, we will throw in the sponge." Jacobs did more, however, because as a Jew, he framed the war as one against Nazi racial ideology and in favor of greater ethnic and racial pluralism and acceptance. "My people are discriminated against as much as yours," he told the *Pittsburgh Courier*'s Billy Rowe, "so you know I'm against any such practice. This may help to make the Navy open its eyes."[24]

As 17,000 fans sat on the edge of their seats, the Brown Bomber demolished Baer in one round. Sportswriter Dan Parker described the action. "Fighting for the U.S. Navy," he wrote, "Joe Louis made Buddy Baer the symbol of the Japanese race last night . . . with the most devastating broadside he has ever fired at an opponent, blasted him out of action in 2 minutes and 56 seconds of the first round." Using a full palette of colorful war imagery, Parker noted that Joe, "the trim, fast cruiser converted the huge battleship Baer into a wrecked hulk with point blank salvos after flooring him three times." According to *Ring*, this was Louis's best fight since his defeat of Schmeling. "Joe had everything. He was magnificent. He was a whirlwind on attack, a master on defense, a terror with his devastating punches." Nat Fleischer also stressed war imagery. Conceding forty-four pounds to the behemoth Buddy, Louis "tackled his opponent as the Yankees will shortly do to the sneaky, slimy, yellow boys of Japan, once the Yanks get going."[25]

The impact on the nation was immediate. "Because of his utterly unprecedented act of generosity in turning over the entire purse to the Naval Relief Society, Joe was an almost unanimous favorite with the crowd," noted *Ring*. Several months later Louis repeated his feat by beating Abe Simon in a benefit match for the Army Relief Emergency Fund. A sports cartoon that accompanied the story on the navy benefit revealed a good deal about the transformation of Louis's image. Entitled "Everyone's Sitting Pretty Here," the cartoon shows a brown Louis and a white Baer sitting atop two bucktoothed, bespectacled Japanese soldiers. In one corner, a white mother and her two babies look on with affection at the two American boxers. "They're our buddies," the mother and her children say. Clearly, Louis had become the defender of American civilization in the guise of the American family hurt by the Japanese attack, and a central part of national self-definition. As a sign of his heroic status, Louis was included in some of the persistent racial nationalism aimed at the Japanese and thereby signaled the ambivalent nature of the American war effort. While the war in Europe aimed to defeat Nazi ideology and those individuals, like a Schmeling, who were presumed to promote it, the war in Asia aimed to defeat a thoroughly racialized enemy. During World War II, Joe Louis and African Americans remained at the center of two competing visions of American nationalism.[26]

Louis's enlistment in the United States Army as an ordinary private soon after the Navy League charity event raised his star even higher. He could have secured a family exemption, but, in his words, "What could I say? 'I have to be exempted so I can work so that my wife can pay the housekeeper?'" There were also indications that Louis had personal reasons for joining the army. After the Schmeling bout his record-setting title defenses tired him on fighting, and the army posed a way for Louis to get away from endless training and endless fights, and a way to experience something new. Various civil rights organization officials attempted to secure him a commission as an officer, but Louis refused. "No way I could be an officer. I'm not the type: I didn't have the education." Instead, he preferred to "be just a plain, ordinary G. I. I'd feel closer to people like me. If I had to spend time with all those men, give me somebody who I could talk with and laugh with." Despite his celebrated status, Louis entered the army no different from any other private.[27]

His willingness to serve his country earned Louis almost universal adulation. United States Senator Prentiss M. Brown of Michigan praised his patriotism, while bandleader Lucky Millinder memorialized his enlistment as an ordinary private in "Joe Louis Is a Mighty Man." Even the white South approved. As the *Birmingham News* declared, "There never has been a champion like Joe Louis in the ring." Yet few people realized that his managers attempted to stall his induction for months in order to keep the profits rolling in. Only when it was clear that he faced the draft did Louis and his managers accede to government officials and volunteer. Administrators of several federal government departments, along with the representatives of various lobbying organizations such as the NAACP, had discussed Louis's military role as early as September 1941. Once the Navy League match was set, officials believed that induction immediately after the fight would bolster public morale in the aftermath of the Japanese attack on Pearl Harbor. Roy Wilkins of the NAACP warned that public reaction would be "very unfavorable" if Louis avoided the draft, and he and Walter White urged him to volunteer. The leaders of the NAACP worried that people might take offense at his enormous income and compare him with Jack Dempsey, who endured criticism for failing to serve in World War I. Instead, they would be "greatly impressed" if Louis served as "a private just like Joe Doakes earning $18 a week" and did not accept "some soft berth" made possible "through the pull with Army higher-ups."[28]

The public believed that Louis freely chose to give up the private and comfortable life of a champion, risk his life, and defend his country. Knowing of the segregated military only made his selflessness even more impressive, and the press reflected this image. In 1935, influential columnist Paul Gallico of the *New York Daily News* had expressed the common view that Louis was a primitive puncher barely removed from the jungle. After his benefits for the navy and army, and his enlistment as a private, the sportswriter called him "a simple, good American," a man who "had found his soul." Over the years he built a spectacular record, but perhaps his greatest fight, Gallico repeated, was the second match with Schmeling, by 1938 "an out-and-out Nazi." Many sportswriters consider this his turning point as a man, highlighting that after the victory Louis shifted from a taciturn, sullen athlete to a pleasant and friendly young man. His sacrifices were real, noted Gallico, because it was likely he would be too old to retain his title after the war. As Gallico summed up, "Citizen Barrow has set us a lesson." Jimmy Powers of the *New York Daily News* was just as ecstatic about Louis's sacrifices. "You don't see a shipyard owner risking his entire business. If the government wants a battleship, the government doesn't ask him to donate it. The government pays him a fat profit. . . . The more I think of it, the greater a guy I see in this Joe Louis." The *Journal-American*'s Burris Jenkins, moreover, drew a cartoon of Uncle Sam holding Louis's right hand up in a sign of victory. The caption referred to Louis's risking his title and his winnings for "the most priceless prize ever won in the world of sports." The prize was in the cartoon's headline: "The Undying Admiration of His Countrymen."[29]

His boxing style and his reputation for fair play also made him a perfect symbol for America at war. Gallico and other sportswriters highlighted Louis's actions against Billy Conn, his toughest opponent since Schmeling. When he met the ex-light heavyweight champion in June 1941, Louis was in severe danger of losing his title to his faster opponent. Still, he refused to hit Conn when Billy threw a punch that left him off balance. Instead of pouncing on the challenger, Louis stepped back and waited for Conn to recover. He had, in Gallico's words, acted in a chivalric manner. Whether chivalric or not, he certainly embodied the concept of fair play as the American national ideal as the country went to war. When he heard of the sneak attack on Pearl Harbor, Louis angrily declared, "Hell, this is my country. Don't come around sneaking up and attacking it. If a fighter had done that to me, I would have smashed him. I'm strictly for fair deals and open fighting."[30]

His actions and his statements on behalf of the war effort made Louis a hero to whites and blacks alike, but as a black American, he was forced to serve in a segregated military unit. Part of the upsurge of black political and cultural activity since the middle 1930s, Louis also stood at the barriers where black political pressure proved ineffective. A. Philip Randolph's call for the desegregation of defense industries was successful, but the demand for the integration of the armed forces was met with adamant refusal on the part of Secretary of War Henry L. Stimson and top military leaders. Not only did Stimson and the top brass hold prejudiced views about the fighting spirit of African Americans, they also feared that any experimentation with racial integration of the armed forces during a total war would seriously damage national morale. As a result, Louis said, "They gave me my uniform and sent me over to the colored section." Although he was thus forced to serve in the segregated armed forces, the Brown Bomber periodically made clear that he preferred otherwise. As he told the *Pittsburgh Courier*, "I sure hope our boys will get their opportunity in the Navy equal with the other boys. I think we deserve our chance because our country is united now, and those Jap bullets don't have any prejudice in 'em." As Louis put it, "Those shells never stop to ask you whether you're white or colored. That's why this war should put an end to all this foolish discrimination."[31]

Although the War Department and the federal government in general were reluctant to integrate the military, officials were keenly aware that they needed black support for the war. The conflict between the stated war goals of pluralism, tolerance, and democracy and the realities of racial segregation and oppression created concern that enemy propaganda could exploit American racism and undermine a unified war effort. Small but vocal groups of African Americans maintained that this was a white man's war and that blacks had no reason to fight. In addition, the military brass worried about racial conflicts at army posts wherever black and white soldiers gathered. As a result of these concerns, the Office of War Information (OWI), the Treasury Department, and other government agencies created a massive propaganda campaign to elevate Joe Louis as a black hero who would help in securing African American loyalty. Government officials feared that mention of racial discrimination and racial equality might spur blacks to demand their full rights, so they decided that American propaganda would feature prominent blacks as symbols of the benefits of living in the United States under a democratic form of government. As a result, rather than turn to overtly militant black individuals, the American government turned to culturally successful African Americans, such as musicians like Duke Ellington and athletes like Joe Louis, and highlighted their symbolic role in American life and society.[32]

While Louis preferred to serve as an ordinary private, the army, the OWI—and the NAACP—had other uses for him and ordered him to the Morale Branch, where he advanced to the rank of sergeant. Like Schmeling in Germany, Louis's role as a symbolic American made him part of radio broadcasts, bond promotions, and other propaganda efforts even before he completed basic training. His image as a symbolic African American now became part of the government's efforts to win the war. Instead of focusing primarily on his boxing, now newsreels showed the champion as a symbol of national unity and marked his presence even when he was just a spectator at an event. Repeatedly, they presented him as did the U.S. Army film, *The Real Joe Louis*, as "the true American," with "his simplicity of faith, loyalty to country and to his race," and his belief in the "sanctity of Democracy." Louis also gave speeches at numerous patriotic events, all of which the newsreels gladly covered. In May 1942 he appeared at an "I Am an American Day" celebration in New York's Central Park, attended by 1,260,000 people, including more than 150,000 African Americans. As part of the national broadcast celebrating 50,000 immigrants who had gone through the naturalization process, Private Louis, dressed in his khaki uniform, positioned himself as a common American citizen too. "I'm glad I am an American citizen. It's sure better than being a citizen of Berlin or Tokio." He also offered his hopes for the postwar world. "All I want to say is that after the fire is out . . . I hope the spirit of 'I Am an American Day' will be celebrated all over the world . . . with liberty and justice for all." Whether he knew it or not, Louis had endorsed the basic premise of the Double V campaign inaugurated by the *Pittsburgh Courier* and black civil rights organizations: blacks would defend their country abroad in exchange for liberty and justice at home after the war.[33]

When the champion spoke to the Navy Relief Society on March 10, 1942, he stunned his audience with a few simple words. Although not known for public speaking, the champion rose to the occasion. Without notes he declared, "I'm only doing what any red blood American would do. We gonna do our part, and we will win, because we are on God's side." These simple words became the subject of much national discussion. President Franklin Roosevelt wrote to congratulate him on his remarks because he had asked reporters to find a name for the war. He had received many suggestions, but Louis's comments made the war "God's war." The president's former challenger in 1940, Wendell Willkie, noted that being on God's side was a distinct departure from the German "*Gott mit uns*," rather a more humble American belief in modest service to a higher being.[34]

The champion's remarks found a ready listener in Carl Byoir, a New York public relations counsel, who wrote a poem for *Collier*'s entitled "Joe Louis Named the War." In an unprecedented national broadcast, actor Conrad Nagel read the poem over NBC, as the black gospel quartet, the Deep River Boys, sang the background music. As the radio announcer put it, Joe had "just said what was in his heart. He did not realize that folks would remember his simple words . . . would carry his message home with them." No one put such deep emotion into his message as Louis did, and "it's so warm and human, and expresses so well . . . what all Americans are thinking about these days." Lest anyone forget, songwriters Sammy Cahn and Jule Styne included his memorable words in the patriotic war tune "Keep Your Powder Dry."[35]

The full-page poem carried a powerful message. Byoir lionized Louis as an American citizen who named the war, and then probed the depths of the champion's commitment to freedom. The name of the war had to arise from humanity's deep-seated desire "to establish the rights/ That we are fighting to keep now." Joe's words came from his heart and from the depths of the slave experience. Byoir imagined that the words were Joe's grandfather's, born free, but "then someone brought him to America/ And made a slave out of him." Because he knew the bitterness and agony of slavery, Louis's grandfather "knew the value of freedom/ And wanted it again." Byoir then cites the Emancipation Proclamation as having made the United States a truly free country, where it did not make any difference "about a man's race or creed or color." On the other side, there had always been people like Hitler or Hirohito who thought they were either God or "bigger than God." Being on God's side, however, meant standing for the "rights of free men." In Byoir's estimation, Louis reminded everyone "that freedom is part of God's plan for mankind." By linking Louis to the slave past, the poem acknowledged how much freedom meant to ordinary African Americans, and elevated the meaning of World War II as a freedom struggle for African Americans at home as well as abroad.[36]

Louis's famous words quickly found their way into one of the most memorable World War II posters, a dramatic departure from standard wartime racial iconography. Dressed in full combat gear, a fierce-looking Brown Bomber thrust his rifle, armed with a bayonet, directly at the viewer as he stated, "We are on God's Side." The poster was rare in portraying a black soldier in an aggressive stance. Fearful of offending white southerners with depictions of black troops or war workers, government censors eliminated most pictures of black male aggression. Instead, the few posters that portrayed black workers aimed at racial harmony and sacrifice, and deliberately avoided any hint of

Private Joe Louis Says: 'We Are on God's Side'. (National Archives)

racial militancy. As a national hero, though, Louis's history allowed him to be presented in ways no other black man could. Despite his image of racial moderation, here was the Brown Bomber in a pose anathema to the white South: a black soldier ready for combat, a strong male figure ready to kill for his country with a rifle in his hand. Not since Reconstruction had black men been depicted in such a violent phallic pose that undermined the traditional demands for black humility and passivity. Created to spur black enlistments and foster black loyalty, the poster glorified a black man willing to use violence to fight his enemies.[37]

As a national hero, Louis played a crucial role in other forms of propaganda, such as the wartime film version of Irving Berlin's *This Is the Army*, the biggest money-making movie of 1943. Designed to stir patriotism and stimulate national unity, the film dramatized the desires of Americans from many ethnic and racial backgrounds, including Jews, Irish Americans, and African Americans, to pull together to defeat a foreign foe. As the country's best-known black man, Louis was portrayed as contributing his strength to the national effort. After hitting the speed bag, he appeared in a song-and-dance number, "What the Well Dressed Man in Harlem Will Wear," along with comedian Jimmy Cross. While the song and dance bit highlighted black patriotism, it also served as a critique of black zoot-suiters who most whites considered disloyal and disruptive, more concerned with their individual pleasures than national sacrifice. Standing in front of a stage set depicting gaudily dressed and wildly jitterbugging zoot-suiters, black G.I.s sang, "If you want to know, just look at Bomber Joe," dressed in his patriotic khaki. At the end of the sketch, with the rest of the black G.I.s behind him, Louis salutes both the flag and the audience. "Joe's appearance in the picture," noted *Ring*, and "the appearance of so many other Negro soldiers—comes at an opportune and important time. It will help to educate where education in matters of race relationships is needed so badly." Louis may have played a patriotic role in *This Is the Army*, but his sequence was almost entirely separate from the rest of the film. Many musicals made during World War II had distinct sections for black entertainers that could be readily snipped out by offended white southern censors. Yet the movie at least made an attempt to showcase the role of African Americans, as did a host of other films that have been dubbed the "multi-ethnic platoon movies."[38]

Liberals and conservatives vied with black lobbying groups to make Joe Louis a symbol of the war and to shape the war effort to appeal to blacks. Would Louis advance the racial struggle toward equality, or would he merely serve as a defender of the nation and its racial status quo? As a result, the image of Joe Louis and of African Americans in general during the war was not only the subject of fierce debate but it also had to walk a fine line. Still, however much officials tried to manage Louis's image, he stood out as bigger than any construction because he had already beaten a "Nazi" when he triumphed so dramatically over Max Schmeling. As a black man, Louis embodied a war against ideologies of race supremacy abroad and at home. In that sense, his inclusion in propaganda made him, and by extension all blacks, American citizens, and set up an undercurrent of tension and conflict with the official policies of armed service segregation.[39]

These tensions emerged in official government propaganda films that featured Louis. *The Negro Soldier*, the first large-scale effort to appeal to African Americans to support the war, was created as part of the *Why We Fight* series under great pressure by the NAACP and other liberal groups, together with the War Department and the OWI. Troubled by race riots in 1943 and by fears that black revolt might detract from the war effort, the army brought out the film in 1944 at an opportune time. The film opens with a black minister, played by leftist screenwriter and actor Carlton Moss, delivering a sermon about the Negro role in the American military to a large middle-class African American congregation. In his sermon, the minister uses the second Louis-Schmeling match to frame World War II, just as films of the fight fill the screen. "An American fist won a victory," intones the minister, but a final victory will take longer. In the present war, "those two men are matched again in a far greater arena and for much greater stakes." No longer merely a prize-fight "between man and man," the battle now was for a real world championship "between nation and nation." Would "their way or our way" survive? From clips of Louis destroying Schmeling the film glides into scenes of the two men in the uniforms of their respective nations: Joe in khaki and Max as a German paratrooper, being made into a machine by the Nazi war juggernaut. To make the contrast explicit, the minister quotes *Mein Kampf*'s references to blacks as "born half-apes." Just as Louis was now placing his body at the service of the American nation, the film shows the sacrifices of African Americans in all previous wars. Moreover, America had also produced black judges, surgeons, singers, conductors, and Jesse Owens in the Berlin Olympics. "The tree of liberty has borne these fruits," the minister says, "for every American regardless of race, color or religion." Yet the film altogether ignores slavery and racial discrimination, in large part because these topics would have both offended southern whites and raised doubts about America's commitment to racial equality. Still, by focusing on the contributions of black heroism in previous wars, the movie challenged older concepts of the black fighting spirit. Even more, *The Negro Soldier* was probably the first government propaganda effort to recognize the necessity of black contributions to the nation's defense and hence kept African American hopes alive that the nation would reward their loyalty.[40]

As part of the effort to create national unity and prevent racial clashes in the army, the film was eventually shown as an orientation feature for all servicemen, although black G.I.s were the initial targets. African American reaction was highly positive. For the first time blacks were treated inclusively as

American citizens and they were portrayed as normal human beings in contrast to the usual Hollywood stereotypes. Thomas Webster, the executive secretary of the Kansas City Urban League, declared, "Every citizen, white and black should see this picture, for embodied in it are all the principles for which we are now fighting." In the *Chicago Defender*, moreover, poet Langston Hughes noted, "It is the most important film of Negro activities yet brought to the screen. . . . it portrays, without the customary Hollywood stereotypes, the heroic role of the Negro throughout."[41]

Despite the best attempts of the OWI to stress unity rather than equality, government propaganda often carried deeper political messages. The symbolism of Louis and his bouts with Schmeling became a key part of the government's plan to sell the war to blacks. The pamphlet for the OWI, "Negroes and the War," written by African American publicist Chandler Owens, attempted to promote black patriotism and support for the war effort. The pamphlet stressed that Hitler's snubbing of Jesse Owens encapsulated Nazi racism toward blacks. Chandler Owens had to explain away the dismal situation in the United States as showing progress, but the heart of the pamphlet lay in the description of the second bout with Schmeling, in which "our champion knocked out the German champion in one round. Sergeant Joe Louis is now a champion in an army of champions. Joe Louis doesn't talk much, but he talks truly. He talks for 13,000,000 Negro Americans, for all American citizens, when he says: 'We're going to do our part, and we'll win 'cause we're on God's side.'"[42]

Although the American armed forces were segregated, several Hollywood films attempted to include images of black servicemen doing their part to win the war. The NAACP and Hollywood leftists and liberals worked with the OWI to pressure the studios to "show colored soldiers in crowd scenes" and "occasionally colored officers," and to sometimes create images that went beyond demeaning stereotypes. But while American propaganda depicted Louis positively, not all such efforts showed African Americans in the same light. Despite growing images of inclusiveness in World War II movies, the sexual hygiene films produced by the army replicated racist images of black sexuality. *Easy to Get*, for example, included Joe Louis, Ralph Metcalfe, and Jesse Owens as symbols of clean-living African Americans. Over and against these admirable individuals, however, the film depicts a whole Negro section of a southern town as possibly infected with venereal disease. A black soldier is shown at risk through dating a nice middle-class girl who gives him gonorrhea. A "bad girl" also appears, prowling a seedy saloon, where low-down music fills the soundtrack, lewd and lascivious dancing takes over the screen, and black pimps cruise the room. Later the black soldier is shown sick in bed because he forgot to use his prophylactic kit. He is treated by white-coated, white-skinned doctors. In this film, the army was composed of two factions: a black, hedonistic, and sick one and a white, healing and healthy one. During a segment of Joe Louis annihilating Max Schmeling in their second match, the narrator proclaimed that "this massacre could not have taken place if Joe hadn't kept himself clean." Louis and the other black athletes may have symbolized clean living, but they could not erase the image of a whole black population at risk from unhealthy and dangerous habits.[43]

It was perhaps the Treasury Bond campaigns that utilized to the fullest Louis as a symbol of positive black achievement in the United States. In response to his appearances on stage and radio in various bond drives, African Americans purchased a large numbers of bonds, and black pilots named their planes the "Brown Bomber." Using Louis, along with other prominent black entertainers such as Marian Anderson and Duke Ellington, was part of the philosophy behind the bond campaigns—to create national unity and show democracy in action. The Treasury Department sought to sell bonds to blacks in order to convince them that they were valuable citizens and that their loyalty was essential during the war. To fulfill its goals, the Treasury Department appointed William Pickens, an official with the NAACP and a vocal critic of both the Garveyites and the New Deal, to head the Interracial Division of the campaign. The Treasury Department believed that Pickens could enlist blacks in the campaigns without having to promise them equality, while also appealing to liberal whites and various organizations interested in interracial tolerance and harmony. Sports figures played key roles, and among these, boxers assumed tremendous importance. After all, much of the excitement in the sport lay in its participants of many different ethnic and racial backgrounds upholding the hopes and aspirations of their various groups. Long one of the more rough-and-tumble pluralistic institutions of American popular culture, boxing now stood out as a model of racial pluralism, seemingly a living form of the multi-ethnic platoon. Using black celebrities such as Louis proved to have widespread appeal to both blacks and whites. When Private Louis spoke to a predominantly black gathering of 20,000 of his fellow Detroiters, for example, they bought bonds amounting to $275,000. He was also effective in his appeal to whites. At a Tam O'Shanter golf tournament in Detroit, he raised $933,000 worth of bonds from the 65,000 white patrons in attendance.[44]

Among boxers and celebrities, Louis was the most visible supporter of bonds. After his title defense against Billy Conn, for example, he invested all of his prize money ($89,000) in defense certificates. His appearance in *This Is the Army*, moreover, was part of a hugely successful attempt to sell war bonds, which audience members bought after every screening. Underlying the many appeals, though, was a sense that if blacks were promoting it, the war had a democratic goal. Entertainers sold loyalty to country and to their race despite the indignities of present segregation. In doing so, they advanced the central proposition of the Double V—that they were loyal American citizens whose loyalty would be rewarded with greater equality and freedom in the postwar world. Certainly their participation in the bond drives proved that the nation acknowledged that for the first time, blacks were a central part of wartime unity.[45]

So popular was Louis that all sorts of civic groups demanded his presence at rallies and events. In Detroit, unions at Ford Local 600 requested that Louis appear at the patriotic rally they sponsored. Malcolm S. MacLean of Hampton Institute advised that Louis should visit black colleges and uplift R.O.T.C. students with his simple talks. In July 1943, while Louis was on leave, he was given permission to take part in the Fourth Annual American Negro Music Festival at White Sox Park in Chicago. Along with Paul Robeson, pianist Dorothy Donegan, and a massed chorus of three thousand voices directed by Thomas A. Dorsey, Louis appeared at "one of the greatest examples of interracial goodwill" before an audience of 35,000 whites and blacks. Louis's message of greeting was broadcast during a thirty-minute hookup over the Mutual Broadcasting network. Moreover, Walter White requested Louis for various NAACP events, attempting to use the champion as a political symbol in the organization's increased battle for civil rights during the war.[46]

Worried about what messages he might convey, however, government officials carefully monitored Louis's activities. Concerned about having him become a civil rights symbol that could be used to challenge segregation in the army and in American society, they preferred that Louis appear only to represent a more generic symbol of unity and inclusion. As a result, only the request of the United Auto Workers seems to have been favorably welcomed by government officials. As a result of the government's continuing commitment to racial segregation, the goals of the war and the Double V stood on a collision course.[47]

While Louis spoke at various army, government, and civic events and performed in films, perhaps his most effective work was through the boxing exhibitions he conducted as part of the Morale Branch of the Army. Along with George Nicholson, Sugar Ray Robinson, and George J. (Jackie) Wilson, the Brown Bomber toured with an all-black unit under the Special Services Division to army camps across the United States and around the world. Beginning August 30, 1943, he spent four months boxing in front of thousands of soldiers, visited wounded service personnel in hospitals, lectured on good health, and sparred two or three rounds daily in front of black and white soldiers. In 1944, he and his troupe toured the British Isles, France, Italy, and North Africa, returning home in October of that year. All together, Sergeant Louis and his boxing troupe traveled for fourteen months, covered 30,000 miles, entertained 2,000,000 troops, and fought nearly 200 exhibition bouts overseas. Servicemen were delighted to have this touch of home. Of all the entertainment available, boxing shows proved the most popular. Soldiers were

Cartoon of Sgt. Joe Louis (National Archives). GI Joe may be a hero, but he also had to serve in a segregated army. The tensions between American ideal and American reality angered Louis and helped spark a wider civil rights movement after the war. (National Archives)

excited to see him fight, "exchange quips, act in skits or just talk," while the visits to hospitals had a heartening effect on the wounded.[48]

Aside from training and entertainment, officials hoped that the army camp tour would promote interracial goodwill. Louis, Robinson, Nicholson, and Wilson not only fought exhibitions; they also helped soldiers of both races develop their boxing skills and refereed countless boxing contests among the troops. In *Life* magazine's story of the tour, for instance, Louis and his mates are shown interacting with black and white soldiers at army camps, hospitals, and canteens. Not only did it have educational and morale building values, the magazine announced, but it was "also a quiet parable in racial good will, for hard-working Joe makes a good impression and hundreds of white soldiers, officers and men, are proud to shake his hand." In addition, the special tours would show the G.I.s that their country cared about them. In arguing for the tour, for instance, Mary McLeod Bethune noted that soldiers would see the boxers fly "across thousands of miles of enemy infested lands and waters," and this would make them "glad to be fighting for a country so thoughtful" of them. The larger goal, however, was to break down the existing conflicts at training camps between segregated black and white soldiers. As a result, the boxing unit entertained audiences of both races. According to one proposal, the tour would include a number of individual and team events to improve morale and promote democratic values through regulated competition. Athletics could thus undermine "the myth of race inferiority" and provide soldiers with "a better understanding of what we are fighting for."[49]

Letters from the troops reflect how much G.I.s appreciated Louis's efforts. Black soldiers, for instance, requested his appearance to boost their morale and help with race relations on their bases. A black G.I., Private F. K. Winant, asked the champion to visit his Greensboro, North Carolina, air base because the post was "undergoing a great change from white personnel to colored." So moved was white Private Tom Ephrem that he wrote to *Ring* magazine about Louis's visit to Europe. "After watching him and his troupe perform" for the men in camp and the wounded in field hospitals, "I daresay that his trip overseas has done a world of good for the morale of our boys. His popularity has been attested by the tremendous ovations he has received wherever he has appeared." Moreover, "no movie star has been greeted by our fighting men with more enthusiasm than that displayed when the Brown Bomber got into action." Louis and his troupe appeared at a field hospital filled with wounded returning from the D-Day landing, related Ephrem. One seriously wounded Tennessee G.I. who had his injured eyes blindfolded to keep away damaging light, asked a nurse to remove his bandages. "Let me have just one look at him." The G.I. said, "I'll take my chance with my eyesight." When he had a chance to see the champ in action and shake his hand, he declared, "This is the happiest moment of my life." As Ephrem exclaimed, "That's what makes Louis' tour so worthwhile. What a champion!" At a plane crash site in England, moreover, Louis raced down the field to provide first aid, and cradled the head of a wounded airman while waiting for help to arrive. It was clear to Ephrem that Louis "has proved himself a great soldier in more than one way. True he has not shouldered a gun . . . but he has accomplished far more for the morale of our boys than any amount of gun-toting would have done."[50]

There were a few exceptions to these positive evaluations. For example, Major Robert Lough complained that the troupe was often late and missed trains, which often disturbed the plans of officers and soldiers. As a result he considered the project a "waste and an operation unbecoming the military." Lough scolded the Special Services for giving Louis and the other boxers unfair advantages. In addition, some journalists argued that it made no sense to waste the fighting ability of such a manly champion. Louis, they maintained, should take part in the normal risks of war as a soldier. Yet it is clear from newspaper reactions and comments in *Ring* that most Americans believed Louis had succeeded in fostering interracial goodwill, had uplifted morale (certainly among black G.I.s), and had shown that all Americans—even famous athletes—were willing to do their part for victory.[51]

Although Louis proved a perfect symbol of interracial goodwill and national unity, his experience also highlights the deep racial conflicts that lay at the heart of World War II. Despite the best hopes of civil rights leaders, the armed forces of the United States remained segregated. In fact, the war heightened racial expectations and the conflict between the newly expanded civic nationalism and its older, deeply rooted racial variety. The war may not have integrated African Americans into the multi-ethnic platoon or the multi-ethnic society, but it did bring black Americans from many backgrounds and parts of the country together in the same units. During basic training, Louis had the opportunity to meet and live with all types of black G.I.s. Some, according to the Brown Bomber, now lived better than ever. All, however, found that they had a "common enemy—Nazi Germany. All those guys could relate to that. Wasn't a black man there who didn't understand what the Jews were going through." Moreover, "they could place their own lives into what was happening over there, and a lot of them, for real, wanted to get to Hitler." The outrages against the Jews and the Nazi ideology of racial supremacy served to highlight similar racial ideologies in the United States and helped to delegitimate them as part of the same enemy that the Americans were fighting. At the same time, the reality of their situation in the United States was brought home to Louis and his army mates every day. As Louis recalled, "They can't sleep in the same barracks with the white guys or go to the same movies or hardly get in officer's training." The situation, the Brown Bomber noted, "made me start thinking." When black columnist and old friend Billy Rowe covered the Brown Bomber's induction, Louis turned to him and, referring to the segregated sleeping quarters and mess hall, declared, "This is the real battlefield."[52]

In a variety of ways, Louis's thinking on race matured while he served in the segregated army. On a personal level he began to rectify some of the injustices he discovered. For the first time in ages, he was without the guidance—or control—of his advisors and managers. When Jack Blackburn died in April 1942, Louis lost the man he called his "teacher, father, brother, nurse, best pal to me. . . . I'll never get over" it. John Roxborough was indicted for his numbers activities and went to jail, and Julian Black was too far away. So was Marva, with whom he had never been close despite their seven-year marriage, and who now, separated from the champ, embarked on a singing career. In essence, he was no longer sheltered from the experience of racism. He also met new people who were less quiescent about race. When the army transferred Louis to a segregated cavalry unit at Fort Riley, Kansas, he served with former UCLA football and baseball star Jackie Robinson. As Louis recalled, Jackie "wouldn't take shit from anyone." Robinson remarked to Joe that "he felt he was just as good as anybody else." It did not hurt Louis's learning process that Robinson told him that "I was his idol." Louis realized the extent of racism in the service when Robinson complained that neither he nor any other black athlete could join the baseball or football teams. An angry Louis resolved to use his influence. He went to Brigadier General Donald Robinson to ask him about the discrimination in the base's athletic program and told him that he had one of the outstanding football players in the country serving at Fort Riley. The general relented and agreed that Robinson and any other qualified Negro could play on the team. When Louis conveyed the good news to Robinson the latter said, "I'm not playing football unless they let me play baseball, too." With the champ's help the future Brooklyn Dodger wound up powering both the baseball and football teams of Fort Riley, and doors opened up in many other camps for integrated ball playing, even in Georgia and Virginia.[53]

Louis found he could bring about change for the better in another case involving Robinson. An educated and ambitious young man, Robinson and seventeen other black enlisted college men discovered that their applications for Officer Candidate School (OCS) were repeatedly denied. Louis found the situation maddening. He was a man with little education, yet the army had offered a commission to him rather than to the college-educated black men. Back he went to the brigadier. "It's bad enough to have a segregated Army," he wrote in his memoirs, but "at least some blacks should be officers over their own people." Not satisfied with the answers he received, Louis called Truman Gibson, a special aide on race relations in the War Department. After Gibson looked into the matter, Robinson and fifteen other men received permission to attend OCS. Robinson got into trouble in OCS when he lambasted a white drill instructor who called a black G.I. a "stupid nigger son of a bitch." Louis immediately put in a call to Gibson to save Robinson from disciplinary action. Similarly, Louis and Robinson worked together on several segregation issues at Fort Riley. Tired of the constant long lines in the black section of the segregated canteen, the two friends complained to the base commander. In response, Robinson was made the morale officer and more seats in the canteen were given to black soldiers.[54]

The exhibition tours made Louis aware of the miserable conditions under which all African American G.I.s were forced to serve. Initially, the army planned to segregate boxing exhibitions by having Louis's troupe fight before only one race at a time or else have the black troops on any given post sit in the rear. Having performed before black and white fans throughout his career, Louis was not about to take a step backward. He refused to go along with segregated exhibitions or speak to segregated audiences. "Hell, whites and blacks were all fighting the same war," Louis wrote, "why couldn't their morale be lifted at the same theater?" Much to his delight the army agreed with his demands.[55]

Despite his stature, Louis could not avoid segregation while in basic training or on his army trips, but he was not shy about reporting the worst examples to his influential friend in Washington, Truman Gibson. According to Gibson, Joe had a keen sense of justice and would report on conditions in camps he visited in the United States and overseas. "He was responsible for a lot of changes in the army." From Fort Bragg, North Carolina, for example, Louis reported that "they don't let Negroes *on* certain buses." Burning inside, he reported on white southern bus drivers at other bases who used pistols to force blacks to the back of the bus. During a stop at Camp Sibert, Alabama, he and Sugar Ray Robinson were involved in a cause célèbre. The two men were sitting in a camp bus depot when an MP told them they had to move to a "colored" bench in the rear. When both boxers heatedly refused, the MP drew back his billy club as if to attack the champ. "When I saw that," Robinson recalled, "I leaped on the MP. I was choking him, biting him, anything to keep him away from Joe." Eventually, both boxers were arrested. The Provost Marshall told Louis that as a soldier he had to follow orders. In response, the Brown Bomber declared, "Listen, I'm an American, I'm fighting in this war like anybody else, and I expect to be treated like anybody else." Louis announced that he would follow the town's laws of segregation, but not in the army's bus station. Once more he attempted to use his ties with Truman Gibson in Washington, but the army brass would not permit him to call Washington, D. C. Still, the news got out to the black and white press. An embarrassed army ordered that there would be no more Jim Crow buses in army camps. "If I was just an average G.I.," Louis recalled, "I would have wound up in the stockades."[56]

Louis encountered segregation at other bases at home and in England when the troupe went abroad. At Keesler Air Base, blacks told Sugar Ray that the exhibition would be performed for white servicemen only. "Isn't this the United States?" Robinson asked. "No, man," a G.I. told him. "This is Mississippi." After a call to Gibson, the commander allowed a mixed audience to watch the troupe do its stuff. When the troupe went abroad, they found that the discrimination and segregation followed. Told to sit in a "special section" of a theater in England with other black G.I.s, Louis demanded to see the manager, who recognized him and apologized, maintaining that an American military commander had delivered the orders. An investigation, instigated by Louis's report to Truman Gibson, led to the desegregation of the theaters. In England, the Brown Bomber learned, prejudiced officers declared certain places or towns "off limits" to black soldiers to prevent racial disturbances and sexual mingling. In Italy, the troupe visited the all-black 99th Pursuit Squadron, which had performed exceptionally well despite reservations about their fighting and flying ability. At Ramitelli, "several of our men had their pictures made with the champ," recalled Commander Benjamin Davis, Jr. "He was mobbed by hundreds of admirers who were thrilled to be in his presence, shake his hand, and explain what we were doing in Italy." As Louis told a correspondent for the Baltimore *Afro-American*, "I think these fellows over-seas know now that the world is not meant to be ruled by one color," Louis said. "They know that is why we are beating Hitler." When white southern troops came home, their living and working together with black soldiers would teach them "that a lot of stuff they have been taught is not right."[57]

Along with these negative experiences, though, Louis observed some of the positive aspects of World War II for blacks. Wherever he went blacks enjoyed greater opportunities to make money in defense plants in the cities of the North and South. With the money coming in, new places were opening where blacks could spend their money. In his autobiography he mentioned New York's Café Society nightclub as a place he liked to visit. As the first racially integrated nightclub in a "white" part of town, Café Society welcomed blacks on the stage and in the audience, and presented such acts as Billie Holiday, boogie-woogie pianists and the band of pianist Teddy Wilson, along with comedians such as Zero Mostel and Jack Gilford. Similarly, as a swing music fan, the Brown Bomber also gravitated to Fifty-second Street, also called Swing Street, in New York City, the place to go for black and white jazz fans. For Louis and blacks in general, thus, the war years witnessed an opening up of new opportunities and new hopes, while at the same time they were re-stricted in myriad ways by segregation and discrimination. The question was which way would the country go in the postwar world?[58]

The conflict between competing national self-definitions moved blacks and white liberals toward greater militancy. Louis was affected too. According to his son, the champion "in a significant way, changed during the war." Before the conflict, he avoided racially embarrassing situations. Now, however, he had become much more aware of the racial situation and he refused to hide his reactions. Barrow, Jr., notes that once a plane was delayed waiting for Louis's coming from an army exhibition bout in Oklahoma City. A white businessman complained to the pilot, "What nigger is so important that I have to be late for my appointment?" Seeing Louis, the man apologized, but Louis pushed his hand away and looked at him disgustedly. As Louis's son put it, "His experience in the army had crystallized his views. He truly realized how much he repre-sented all blacks." While military and government officials used him to raise black morale and secure their loyalty without disturbing the status quo, Louis's image as a "citizen-soldier" encouraged African Americans to believe that they were entitled to equal rights as American citizens as promised by the ambiva-lent messages of government propaganda campaigns.[59]

When the war came to an end, Joe Louis had earned the praise and adulation of white and black Americans. As a sign of his stature, when he left the service in October 1945, Louis was awarded the Legion of Merit Medal "for exceptionally meritorious conduct." In a speech in his honor, Major General Clarence H. Kells expounded on his value to the morale of the armed forces, while a military review and a national broadcast marked the ceremony at Fort Hamilton, Brooklyn. During his forty-six months in service, he had traveled over 70,000 miles, appeared in front of almost five million servicemen, fought ninety-six exhibition bouts, which "entailed considerable risk to his boxing future as the champion heavyweight of the world," visited numerous military hospitals, and cheered innumerable wounded G.I.s. Yet, for Louis and the nation, his bouts with Max Schmeling remained the focus. After the ceremony, a group of youngsters crowded around for autographs. In his request, one young boy brought the war full circle. "How did you lick Max Schmeling, Joe?" Drawing a parallel between his own fate in the first match and the nation's near knockout at the hands of the Japanese at Pearl Harbor, Sergeant Louis replied, "Remember, little fellow, he beat me, too." In the metaphorical rematch in World War II, however, everyone knew who had won.[60]

As allied forces rolled into Germany, Max Schmeling discovered that he had lost much more than the second fight. Everything he had worked for was gone. In winter 1945, the Soviet Army closed in around his estate in Ponickel,

Max Schmeling detained by British troops in Hamburg at the very end of the war. Identified as a Nazi in American propaganda, how would Schmeling fare in a defeated and occupied postwar Germany? (Acme, Library of Congress)

in the eastern part of Germany. Refugees flooded the property, making it difficult to remain, and in advance of the Red Army, Schmeling decided to take his wife and mother to Rostock. In their hasty flight, the couple had to leave almost everything behind: the house, his championship belt, and all the souvenirs of his boxing career and her acting days. The former boxer tried to go back to Ponickel, but heavy fighting had broken out in the surrounding area and it was clear that the estate was lost. Turning his car around, he headed for Berlin, but what he found was complete devastation in the Reich's bombed-out capital. After performing his last act for the army—visiting British and American POWs—he was forced to flee again as the allied circle tightened around Berlin, this time to Hamburg, his hometown. Throughout the Nazi era he had attempted to walk a tightrope to pursue his individual sporting goals, but he had treaded too close to the fires of Nazism for the allies and too near cosmopolitanism for the Third Reich. It appeared that he had failed on both counts. At the end of the war, Schmeling seemed even more of a Nazi icon than ever before, and his reputation lay in ruins. His future, like that of Germany, would require repudiating the past, a feat seemingly as impossible as achieving another victory over Joe Louis.[61]

7

LAST ROUNDS

Joe Louis is a living tribute to the democratic
ideal.

    Frank Sinatra, May 1947

My life is that of a German in the twentieth
century; or perhaps more precisely, it was a
German-American life, a tie made even stronger through my association with Coca-Cola of
Hamburg.

    Max Schmeling

After World War II, boxing fans of all colors and backgrounds eagerly anticipated Joe Louis's return to the ring and the revival of heavyweight prizefighting that had languished in his absence. To commemorate the Brown Bomber's return to civilian life, Margery Miller magnified his heroic qualities into an American ideal in her biography, *Joe Louis: American*, published in 1945. Not only had Louis annihilated Hitler's representative in history's most important boxing match, she argued, but he also had willingly sacrificed his career in defense of the nation as a "champion citizen." In her review of the book, Eleanor Roosevelt seconded these sentiments, declaring that Louis, "through his work in sports, wanted to win for his people good will among the people of other races and religions." This made him a "citizen." Shortly thereafter, longtime admirer Frank Sinatra added to the adulation. "If I were the government official responsible for the job of making the rest of the world understand our national character and the ideals that motivate us," the singer asserted, "I would certainly make use of the case history of Joe Louis." As far as Sinatra was concerned, the Brown Bomber "personifies one of the ideals which we hold dear—that a man's character and ability do not spring exclusively from the color of his skin or the nature of his religious beliefs." In sum, "Joe Louis is a living tribute to the democratic ideal." While Louis rode this wave of adulation, a disgraced Schmeling struggled to survive, a living embodiment of a defeated Germany tainted by the horrors of its Nazi past. According to *Ring*, both Schmeling and Germany had suffered a horrible knockout, but "the saddest kayo came in 1945." As a defeated nation and a defeated fighter, the fate of Germany and Schmeling were at the mercy of external forces, and the allies appeared determined to keep them from rising to power ever again.[1]

Even before Louis was discharged from the service, boxing fans could hardly wait to see him reassume his championship. Neither could Louis. He had been away from the professional game for nearly four years and he needed money to repay Mike Jacobs the large sums that the promoter had advanced him, to pay off other loans from John Roxborough, and to settle his outstanding tax debt with the Internal Revenue Service. Louis also wanted to lay claim to his title once again because it was a key part of his identity, and a role that the public expected him to play. After the long war, many Americans hoped to reestablish the lives that they had known before the conflict. With Louis as an active champion again, sports fans had one familiar icon whose presence provided reassurance that there would be a smooth transition from war to peace.

As Jacobs and Louis examined the field of potential opponents, one stood out as capable of guaranteeing a million-dollar gate and reminding fans that American life had returned to normal. The challenger was Billy Conn, the former light heavyweight champion from Pittsburgh, a superb boxer with good speed and a handsome Irish American face. Ever since their first fight in June 1941, when a game Conn had given the champion a boxing lesson for twelve rounds, only to be knocked out in the thirteenth, sports fans had speculated endlessly as to who would win a rematch. The two had nearly settled the question in 1942 in a third benefit for the armed forces, but Secretary of War Henry Stimson refused to allow it on the grounds that some of the proceeds would have gone to pay training expenses and to settle a portion of Louis's debts. In the interim, both fighters served in the military, both men fought exhibitions for the armed services, and both were pictured together shaking hands, joking, and smiling as a sign of racial harmony and national unity during the war. The public had waited for over three years for the fight, and now heavyweight boxing—and American life—could pick up where it had left off.[2]

With the outdoor prizefight season fading fast, "Uncle" Mike Jacobs scheduled the bout for June 19, 1946, in Yankee Stadium. The delay between their army discharges and the match allowed both men to get back into shape after their long tours of duty. Louis took the opportunity to fight a series of exhibitions and work off some of the weight that army chow and relative ring inactivity had added to his frame. Those who watched the exhibitions noted that the Brown Bomber had slowed, his body was paunchier, and his hitting, though still powerful, lacked the sharpness that had made him so fearful a ring adversary. While Louis lacked "the panther-like litheness of his best fighting form," Conn, according to Jack Dempsey, showed worse signs of deterioration. Still, expectations ran high: 45,266 fans paid $1,925,564—the second largest amount ever grossed in boxing—to attend the fight, while a small number of viewers at home and in bars had the opportunity to watch the first bout ever televised.[3]

Despite everyone's high hopes, however, the most awaited match of the war years proved to be a yawner. Conn tried to repeat the tactics that had proven so successful in the first fight, but after years in the army he was much slower and his jabs carried less power. For most of the early rounds Louis chased him ineffectually, trying to corner him so that he could unleash his deadly arsenal. Only in the eighth round did he manage to land a series of solid lefts and right to the body and the eye, followed by a terrific right to the jaw that put the challenger down for the count. Declared "the winner and still the world's heavyweight champion" in the twenty-second defense of his title, Louis reassured himself and his fans that he had returned to dominance. Noted Nat Fleischer, "There is no one to challenge his supremacy even though he has slowed up."[4]

Louis not only worked hard to defend his title, he also championed a more aggressive attack on racial discrimination and inequality in the United States. After his years of valuable service to the nation in the belief that a war against Nazi racial supremacy would produce real democracy at home, the intensified racism of the postwar period infuriated him. "I was tired of all this racism shit," he declared, and he appeared ready to join the upsurge in civil rights activism on the part of other African American veterans, social justice groups, and civil rights organizations such as the NAACP and CORE. He was especially disgusted by the brutal attack on black veteran Isaac Woodard by the police in Batesburg, South Carolina. Describing the incident, an outraged Louis angrily announced, they "jugged both his eyes out with that billy stick policemen carried; they attacked him for no reason." The fact that a fellow G.I. who had served his country was so brutally treated led the champion to appear at a benefit for Woodard at Lewisohn Stadium in New York. Clearly moved, Louis was choked up when it came time to speak, but he still managed to assert that "nobody in America should have to go through Second Class Citizenship. Me and a whole lot of black guys went out fighting for the American cause, now we're gonna have to get America to give us our civil rights too. We earned them."[5]

In a speech in late 1946 at the Southern Conference for Human Welfare, he promised to lend his prestige to the struggle for civil rights. Some people had told him to stick to boxing, he said, "but they don't understand that fighting prejudice, disease, and second class citizenship is my business, too. I hate Jim Crow. I hate disease. I hate seeing people kept down because they are colored." Rather than let this hate poison his system, Louis vowed to "help people fight Jim Crow." Looking back at his remarks, Louis recalled how Roxborough and Blackburn "both hoped for an equal chance for all races in America some day." Thinking about World War II and the prejudice he experienced as a soldier as well as the rights that African Americans expected as a result of their service, he compared the fascist enemy to the rankest American racists. As he put it, "I think that the days of the ideas of Hitler, Talmadge, Bilbo and Rankin, the days of bucking one race against the other, are passing." And while he spoke, he recalled the Isaac Woodard case, and two other G.I.s "who were lynched down in Monroe, Georgia." As he summed up his remarks in a ghosted article in *Salute* magazine, Louis argued that "prejudice is weakening. The good people are softening it up. So we can't stop punching now. We have to punch faster and harder. That's the only way to make America a better place for my little boy and girl and all the little boys and girls in our country. I'm going to do my part."[6]

Yet while he sympathized with the freedom struggle, Louis never became a crusader for civil rights. He continued to give money throughout his life to the NAACP and the Urban League, he paid attention to the Henry Wallace campaign's stand on racial equality in 1948, and he appeared in Birmingham at the request of Martin Luther King, Jr., and SCLC in 1963. His usefulness was as the champion, as an African American hero who by example contested the power of white supremacy and the lynching of black bodies. Black people looked to him as a model of aspiration at a time when there were few, and an example of black power when there were none. As champion, he served as a model of the fighting man who spurred his followers on to battle for their rights outside the ring. Of course, that required Louis to hold onto the title, but he discovered that would prove harder and harder as the 1940s wore on. Usually easygoing, the Brown Bomber experienced so many troubles during the postwar era that his mood, like that of the nation, darkened considerably.

As he reentered the ring, the champion found preparing for matches a tremendous grind. In the past Louis had lived to train, but at thirty-two, he resented having to rise early and do ten miles of roadwork. So he cut the distance in half, and reverting to the ways of former champions, he no longer fought every few months. After taking out Tami Mauriello in one round in September 1946, he did not fight again until the following year, when he was greatly embarrassed by journeyman Jersey Joe Walcott. Knocked down twice in that fight, Louis looked paunchy, his belly fat and his chest saggy. He came on in the later rounds to earn the decision, but most fans thought that Walcott won the bout. For the first time, Louis heard boos from a crowd that expected a great deal more from him. "I felt a depression I had never felt before," Louis recalled. "It was one hell of a way to end the year." At the point of losing his title and his reputation to someone he would have beaten easily in the old days, the champ trained hard for the rematch. True to his form of learning from his mistakes, Louis knocked out Walcott in the eleventh round in 1948. On March 1, 1949, he finally retired undefeated as heavyweight champion. He had held the title for twelve years, longer than had any other boxer. As the *Ring* put it, it was "the end of an era."[7]

If he had had his way, Louis probably would have retired sooner. A superb athlete in tune with his body, he knew that his reflexes and his skills had diminished over the course of his army years, but he needed money desperately. During the war, he had run through his earnings. Despite the image he and his managers had crafted for him as a sober saver with secure annuities, in reality Louis spent money faster than he made it. He was always in debt to Mike Jacobs, and always sure he could pay what he owed after his next big fight. Louis also invested his money in various businesses, such as the Joe Louis Chicken Shack in Detroit, Joe Louis's Rhumboogie nightclub in Chicago, a Joe Louis Restaurant and Bar in New York, the Joe Louis Punch Company, and a vocational training school in Chicago, that all failed. His attempt to become the first African American to run a Ford dealership went nowhere, in part because his reputation as a businessman was not good, but primarily because the Ford Motor Company, like most large American corporations, did not want to associate its brand name with an African American. With little or no interest in or aptitude for business, or for working nine-to-five for a living, the Brown Bomber watched one after the other of his ventures fail for lack of a firm sense of leadership.[8]

Having put in years of fighting, Louis expected to live off his fame as champion. Away from the ring he was restless, a pattern into which many other athletes have fallen after their glory days, and with longer periods between fights he lived an ever more peripatetic existence. What he really wanted to do was play golf. Long a fan of the game, he spent hours on golf courses whenever he could. Yet the problem was not golf; it was gambling. Friends report that Louis often wagered $100 a hole. When he was not spending on golf or living well, he was giving money away to his entourage, to down-and-out ex-boxers, or to anyone else who gave him a sad story. "I guess one of my biggest weaknesses was that I was always too generous when it came to my money," he admitted in 1952. "I figured it was all right to try to help make other people happy as long as we had enough for ourselves. It made me feel good whenever I could help out anybody with a dollar or two." His generosity, however, meant that he might give away as much as $1,000 to $5,000 in a day. Nor was Louis embarrassed about this when it came to light. He had been born poor, he said, so he knew what it meant to be broke.[9]

Louis also spent lavishly on women. This proved the major cause of his two divorces from Marva, one in 1945, followed by remarriage in July 1946, and then the final split in December 1949. Coming as his debts were accumulating, these personal disruptions only deepened his emotional turmoil. As a wealthy celebrity, famous for his masculine prowess, the former champion remained a notorious but discreet womanizer. Because of his training, traveling, and philandering, Marva wrote in 1949, "our marriage never worked out simply because I never had a husband or a home life I could really call home." The couple had two children by the late 1940s—Jacqueline, born in 1943, and Joe Louis Barrow, Jr., born in 1947—but even a family could not keep Louis at home. Half the time Marva never knew where he was. He paid for the upkeep of numerous women around the country, and after big fights in New York rented out whole floors of Harlem's Theresa Hotel, where he would

Joe and Marva, with Joe Louis Punch, 1947. Both the marriage and the soft drink company failed and Louis began a long descent from the heights he had known as an American hero during World War II. (Acme, Library of Congress)

stash women in different rooms. While Marva was well aware of his many affairs, it never affected his image because it occurred in black neighborhoods, and because the black and white press maintained a protective attitude toward such a towering sports hero. Like many other star athletes, white as well as black, he indulged himself whenever he wanted, and he paid generously for his pleasures.[10]

While spending on women, businesses, friends, and associates depleted Louis's finances, it was the Internal Revenue Service that kept him fighting long past his prime. The problem built up over the years and came to a head after the war ended. By 1942, Louis owed about $80,000 in back taxes. Automatic withholding on a fighter's purse did not yet exist, so a boxer had to save money to pay the IRS. On the advice of his accountant, Louis did not pay taxes from 1939 to 1941 in the hope of reaching a better settlement once he had accumulated a larger amount of earnings. Because of compound interest and penalties, Louis's tax debt grew during wartime. When his advisors saw the mounting debt, they suggested that Louis fight Billy Conn for another service charity, keeping back enough to cover expenses and the tax bill. The War Department and the Department of the Treasury, however, refused permission for another bout if any of the proceeds went to pay off Louis's obligations. They reasoned that allowing a wealthy celebrity to earn enough money to settle his private financial affairs would set a terrible precedent for the other servicemen and women. If they let Louis work to pay his taxes other G.I.s might demand the right to be excused from duty to pay off a mortgage or save a failing business. *Ring* magazine took the same stance. As a result, by the time Louis left the army he owed the IRS about $115,000 in back taxes. His earnings from his fights could not pay off his back taxes and the interest on them. By 1950 he owed the IRS $208,000. In 1957, his tax bill jumped to $1.3 million.[11]

Louis's financial difficulties did not end there. The cost of his generosity toward black G.I.s and his taste for the high life far surpassed the $28 a month he earned as a sergeant in the army. To make up the difference, he was forced to do as he had done throughout his career. He borrowed money from Mike Jacobs and John Roxborough, thinking that he would pay them back as soon as he had another title fight. By the time he was discharged he owed Jacobs $150,000 and Roxborough another $40,000. Moreover, in a seedy move after the war, Jacobs structured the payoff from the Conn fight so that he would be paid first, rather than the IRS, although all the income would be subject to tax when and if the IRS discovered the maneuver. The champion was now in the position of having to borrow constantly against future purses, especially as he continued to run through his winnings. Just released from prison, Roxborough could not help. Julian Black refused to lend Louis any more money, and the two had a falling out. Black's ten-year contract with Louis for 25 percent of his earnings was up, and Louis made a disastrous decision. As part of his alimony settlement he apportioned Black's share (25 percent) of his future earnings to Marva, who for tax purposes was listed as a co-manager. Unfortunately, when the IRS learned of this maneuver in 1950, they refused to allow her earnings to be deducted as a business expense. To them it was an alimony settlement pure and simple. Hence, Louis not only owed the IRS for the taxes on the full amount of his earnings, but he also had to pay Marva her portion of his purses. In an attempt to safeguard his fighter, Louis's new manager, Marshall Miles, urged Mike Jacobs to put aside the champion's winnings of $103,000 from the Mauriello fight for the 1947 tax bill. When he came for the money, Miles found out that "Uncle Mike," weakened by a recent stroke, had let Louis have all but $500. The shocked Miles discovered that Louis had invested $43,000 in the Rhumboogie and blown the rest on women, golf, and travel.[12]

As a result of his debts, the champion fought on through the late 1940s, but the thrill was gone. The second Conn match earned almost two million dollars, the second largest gate in boxing history, but the money went to his managers and the IRS and Louis remained in debt. He had the opportunity to earn a million dollars tax-free by throwing a bout, but he had too much pride in his title, his reputation, and what such an act meant for his standing among his own people. He turned it down. Instead, he kept on fighting honestly and honorably, an aging lion still willing to take on all comers. When Louis whipped Walcott in the rematch he told the radio audience that it was his last fight. Unfortunately, it was not. With his tax bill mounting and his various investments failing, Louis had to go back into the ring. In 1949, he signed up four contenders for his crown, and then sold the rights to the title fight to the newly established International Boxing Club for $150,000. In the process, Louis aced out ailing Mike Jacobs and the 20th Century Sporting Club and helped deliver control of Madison Square Garden and heavyweight boxing in the United States to the IBC. As part of the deal, Louis was supposed to receive 20 percent of IBC stock and an annual salary of $20,000 for promotional duties, a job that he did not take seriously. But the IRS remained an implacable foe, gobbling up his assets, including the trust funds for his two children, and even fees for refereeing that he had donated to charity. With an overwhelming tax bill due in 1950 for the years 1945–1949, Louis was more desperate than ever.[13]

At the age of thirty-six, the Brown Bomber came back in August 1950, against Ezzard Charles, who had replaced him as champion. Weighing 218 pounds against a much younger and lighter opponent, Louis looked slow and sluggish. With his reflexes gone, he took a beating for fifteen rounds. Although he said he would retire again, he left the door open. What else could he do? Again he came back, winning a string of bouts against mediocre competition. Then came the last fight. On October 26, 1951, the aging Louis met the up-and-coming contender, Rocky Marciano from Brockton, Massachusetts, at Madison Square Garden. Presumably the winner would meet the new champion, Jersey Joe Walcott, who had taken the crown from Charles. Although he did well in the early going, by the eighth round Louis had run out of gas. Marciano knocked him through the ropes and out of boxing for good. Men and women at Madison Square Garden wept openly and sportswriters penned columns that read like obituaries. It finally was the end of Louis's boxing career. Afterward, as if in ironic counterpoint, the television audience watched the film of his one-round knockout of Max Schmeling. It hurt to see the Bomber lying on his back, wrote Arthur Daley, sports columnist for the *New York Times*. "Better by far is it to remember the Dark Destroyer in the supreme moment, his annihilation of Max Schmeling. That is the one which will be forever treasured here."[14]

While Louis continued to enjoy a measure of celebrity during the 1950s, new black sports heroes emerged in the late 1940s to join him as important heroes among African Americans and as crucial symbols of racial advancement. In 1945, immediately after the war ended, the Brooklyn Dodgers made headlines across the nation by signing Jackie Robinson to their Montreal farm team. To some extent the signing of Robinson represented the passing of the torch of African American athletic stardom. When the Dodgers signed Robinson, owner Branch Rickey asked Paul Robeson, Bill Robinson, and Louis to speak with Jackie about how to comport himself in the white big leagues. Louis did not feel it necessary because he knew from their wartime service that Robinson was prepared to take the insults and setbacks silently in order to advance the cause of blacks in organized baseball. "He knew he'd have to be strong and take the shit, or he'd close the door for black people in baseball for Lord knows how many more years." For his part, Louis wrote in his autobiography, "I felt real good when Jackie said that if it wasn't for me and Jesse Owens, he wouldn't be where he was." To a great extent, that is true. Whatever he did in private, Louis had demonstrated to the white world that blacks could break through and achieve some of their dreams in a white-dominated world if given a chance. By being well behaved and following the rules of deportment in public, he demonstrated that blacks deserved to be judged on their skills and abilities. Louis did this in the individual sport of boxing, where formal segregation never existed and where it was relatively easier to forge a new path. Once he established the precedent, it was inevitable that the assault on the other sports, and especially the national game of baseball, would increase in intensity.[15]

Robinson acknowledged Louis's role in the desegregation of sports. In a *Pittsburgh Courier* column, he declared, "I have said many times before that I only hope I can do half as much for my people as he has done." In another

Joe's last fight. In 1951 the former champion, on a comeback trail, was knocked through the ropes and out of boxing by up-and-coming contender Rocky Marciano. Many fight fans considered the fight the end of an era. (Library of Congress)

column, Robinson noted, "He's been an inspiration to all of us. . . . Joe has made it easy for me and the other fellows now in baseball. I'm sure his example had a lot to do with my breaking into big league ball." While the pressure for the integration of baseball started in the communist and black press before the war, after World War II, black and white sports columnists in greater numbers came out in favor of the desegregation of baseball. Now they claimed that black G.I.s, like Louis and Robinson, had fought and died for democracy during the war and thus deserved their full rights in American society as only proper in a nation committed to the ideals of fair play. On

August 25, 1946, on radio station WJZ and the ABC national radio network, Jimmy Cannon denounced baseball as a "game of prejudice, played and dominated by bigoted men with Jim Crow for an umpire." As he put it, "Having Jim Crow as an umpire in organized baseball is laughable when you realize what a fine champion Joe Louis has been."[16]

In fighting the Nazi threat, Louis had demonstrated the full claim of blacks to their American inheritance. At the end of his career, white sportswriters always mentioned his unalloyed selflessness in serving his country in World War II and his defense of its values in the fights against Max Schmeling and "Nazi arrogance about the superiority of the Master Race." The anti-Nazi imagery carried over to baseball. When he joined the Dodgers, Robinson was pictured in his army uniform. During the late 1940s, black newspapers maintained that Louis had influenced the attitudes of the white public for the better. In an open letter to Louis in the *Pittsburgh Courier*, William Nunn wrote, "You made white America realize that Negroes were Americans, too. You let them see that Negroes had feelings . . . had patriotism . . . had loyalty . . . had decency . . . had a sense of humor." As Nunn continued, "You shamed White America into realizing that they had to do better by their 'forgotten tenth.' You were our representative, Joe . . . and no finer, grander representative could have been wished for. You did the right things."[17]

Furthermore, Louis's impact as a race model was unblemished by his recent problems. A *Chicago Defender* editorial written after Louis's retirement in 1949 said, "No one will ever know how much Joe Louis really meant to Negro youth in America. Nevertheless, we are certain that Louis has inspired more of our youth and given them more confidence than any of our leaders no matter how great their prestige. He was a living symbol of greatness which was achieved in the right way and his actions in the ring made him a model of American fairplay."[18]

Even as Louis's skills declined, his example continued to have a major impact on fields of sport other than boxing. Starting in the late 1940s, most professional sports in the United States followed the example of boxing to desegregate their ranks, except in the South. College teams in the North increasingly recruited black players, too. Even professional golf came under the direct influence of avid golfer Joe Louis, who personally pressured the PGA circuit to accept black players. However, rooted as it was in fancy country clubs and intimate socializing and business affairs, as well as sports, the PGA took longer than other sports to accept black players on the tour. Not only did the numbers of black athletes in formerly segregated sports increase, but athletics from then on also stood at the cutting edge of civic nationalism and racial integration as a symbol of American fair play and inclusiveness in a Cold War world. Moreover, Louis could take some pride in the fact that his wartime service also contributed to the desegregation of the United States Armed Forces in the late 1940s, a change that drew on the reevaluation of

African Americans as American citizens who had done their duty when their nation called.

While advances in sports preceded advances in politics and society, the example of Joe Louis, Jesse Owens, and Jackie Robinson also showed the weakness of the integrationist model. The acceptance of Louis came at the expense of having to wear a mask of social acceptability. He and other aspiring African Americans had to prove their acceptance of white middle-class standards. Had Louis's sexual transgressions and financial difficulties become public while he was still boxing, it is unlikely that he would have received the opportunities he did. Moreover, Louis and other blacks had to earn their rights in the United States, rights they deserved as human beings no matter how they conducted themselves. In addition, it took an exceptional athlete such as Louis to break the color barrier in boxing. If his experience were any guide, then all black people would have to be twice as good as whites to succeed in a white-dominated world.

In his day, Louis suffered from the deep-seated discrimination and segregation that existed in and out of the ring. Even when he was the champion, few white firms would give him endorsements or business opportunities for fear of contaminating their product in the white South. He was relegated to a series of businesses and products aimed at the black market. Certainly not much of an entrepreneur, he found few outlets in the white world. In the 1960s, Muhammad Ali and other black athletes would confront the continuing segregation and discrimination in American sport—at the level of management, coaching, ownership, treatment, and endorsements. They would raise the question of whether black athletes were full members of the American team or merely, as Nazi ideologues and some American commentators put it, America's "black auxiliaries." Joe Louis broke some barriers but was defeated by others. While many obstacles remained for future black athletes, it is important to remember that by breaking forever the color line in the heavyweight division, he opened the door for other African American athletes to fight for their equal place on the field of play.

While his example lived on, Louis's personal life continued its downward spiral. In 1953 he suffered the loss of his mother, Mrs. Lillie Reese Brooks, a key figure throughout his life. In December 1955 he married Rose Morgan, the owner and operator of a beauty-supply business in Harlem, but marriage did not stop his nomadic ways. She believed that her husband's name would help raise capital for her business, but the former champion believed that his wife's income would be enough to pay for his indulgences. It was not a happy union. In 1956, a promoter convinced Louis to take up professional wrestling for a guaranteed $100,000. Rose Morgan was appalled. As she noted, "Joe Louis was like the President of the United States. How would you like to see the ex-President of the United States washing dishes? That's how I feel about

Joe wrestling." Many others tried to convince him that he was degrading himself, but Louis replied, "It beat stealin' don' it?" In the South he faced other
black wrestlers in segregated arenas, which so disgusted him that he gave his
share of the gate in Miami, $248, to the NAACP. His new ring adventure
came to an end, however, when Rocky Lee, weighing 320 pounds, fell on
Louis while he was still on the floor and broke two of the Brown Bomber's
ribs and bruised the muscles of his heart. As if things could not get worse, in
1957 he and his wife separated and in 1958 filed for an annulment.[19]

By the early 1960s, his third wife, Martha Jefferson, an attorney in Los
Angeles, whom he married in 1959, finally managed to work out a deal with
the IRS to tax only Louis's current earnings. Yet the damage was already
done. Too many blows to the head and too much fear of the taxman made
Louis search for relief in sex, cocaine, and alcohol. Despite his many affairs,
the strong-willed Martha, one in a series of strong women that Louis leaned
on, stood by him. By the late 1960s, though, Louis began to show signs of
paranoia, believing that his Mafia enemies were trying to poison him with
deadly gas. In this state he would travel incessantly or lie in bed at home too
lethargic and depressed to move. Ultimately, his wife Martha and son Joe, Jr.,
were forced to institutionalize him for three months in a Colorado psychiat-
ric facility in 1970. For the rest of his life, he suffered from periodic bouts of
paranoia, but with family and friends surrounding him, he kept the worst
episodes under control.[20]

When he left the hospital, his friend Ash Resnick set him up as a greeter
at Caesar's Palace in Las Vegas at $50,000 a year. Many have depicted Louis's
role as a doorman, a bellboy, or some other demeaning menial job. That was
not how his son saw it. Louis was a professional sports celebrity, he was the
champ again, and everybody wanted to meet him and shake his hand. As the ex-
champion put it, "Call me a greeter. I go round talk to people about the hotel,
go to golf tournaments and that sort of thing." For a man who did not want to
do conventional work, he had found a suitable job. At the center of the action
once more, appreciated by show business people and high rollers, the Brown
Bomber played golf, gambled, and hobnobbed with the aristocracy of American boxing now centered in the Nevada desert. He may have been down, but
he was not yet out.[21]

Improbably enough, neither was Max Schmeling. Like their countrymen and
women, he and Anny had to start over from scratch after World War II. In
the "hunger years" immediately after the war, everyone's most pressing task
was to acquire food and shelter and a means to support themselves now that
the regime was lost, the economy destroyed, and the cities bombed. Seemingly too old for boxing, living in the ruins of Hamburg, the city where he was
raised, how would Schmeling earn a living? Ondra had retired from her movie

career in 1942, but even had she been willing to work, the German film industry lay in ruins. While his economic difficulties linked the former champion to the common problems of the occupied German people, his ties to the Third Reich created special troubles. The British military controlled the city of Hamburg, and they were bent on de-nazifying Germany. The British worried about Schmeling's reputation as an Aryan icon and his influence on the people, especially the youth, of the defeated nation. When Max and Anny attended a circus, for example, he was introduced to great applause. While Schmeling found it heartening to know that the German public had not forgotten him, the British were concerned that he was rekindling the flame among the Nazi faithful and they sought to prevent him from exercising his influence in a public capacity.[22]

Desperate to find a means to support Anny and himself, Schmeling planned to start a magazine with his friend, John Jahr, a former printer and longtime Nazi Party member, and Axel Springer, who had published several newspapers under the Nazis. When the British authorities learned of the ex-boxer's involvement, however, they denied the group a publishing license. The authorities were especially concerned about the trio's plan to reeducate German youth in a new spirit. Yet, Springer and Jahr were allowed to go forward, while Schmeling, considered a favorite of Goebbels and Hitler and an Aryan symbol, was forced to withdraw so that his friends could obtain their license. Furthermore, Max was arrested and on September 5, 1945, had to appear before a military court to answer charges that he had made false statements in telling a British reporter that he already had the license. While the court found him not guilty, it was clear that the British authorities considered Schmeling a Nazi show horse and thus an unsuitable role model for German youth. Deprived of work in publishing, he and Anny continued to live from hand to mouth.[23]

The British view of Schmeling only worsened when American historian Waverly Root reported the old rumor that Schmeling had been commandant of a concentration camp in "The Secret History of the War." No friend of the "Nazi boxer," the *Daily Worker*, the newspaper of the American Communist Party, ran the story, and then German newspapers reported the news as well. Schmeling issued no denials, but his former trainer Max Machon came to his defense. Writing that the German boxer had never acted as a commandant of a camp nor joined the Nazi party, Machon admitted that Schmeling had attended several party rallies in Nuremburg, but so had other artists and the various stars of the theater and the movies. No one refused der Führer too many times. Schmeling's trainer and friend also argued that there was very little that Max could do to avoid being used by the Nazis for propaganda purposes. No one, charged Machon, had condemned the mixing of sport and politics as much as Max did. The German communist newspaper, *Deutsche Zeitung*, however, responded that it did not matter whether he was a party member; Schmeling had been a Nazi tool. For many allies, Schmeling's role as a Nazi role model for young people was too much to countenance. As a result of these attacks, it appeared as if he had no future, only a discredited past.[24]

With few avenues left, the Black Uhlan returned to boxing as a referee. As he related in his memoirs, Germany after the war was in the grip of boxing fever. Reminiscent of the period after World War I, young German men attempted to avenge defeat and hopelessness by glorifying male battles in the ring. Suffering from feelings of weakness and lacking direction, Schmeling was eager to join them. From refereeing to returning to the ring as an active combatant was only one short step. Yet by the time he finally resumed prizefighting in 1947, "unser Max" had not boxed in eight years, had suffered serious injuries during his army service, and was over forty years old. But, like Louis, he had no other way to earn a living. Starting from scratch, he returned to the days of isolated training. "Once again self-denial was the ruling principle, but now without the stimulating mix of hope, youth, passion, and impatience," he wrote. Just as Louis had found training much more difficult the second time around, so too did Max. Fighting against time, trying to reclaim skills long gone, he had to force himself into shape.[25]

Concerned about Nazi influences on German youth, the British authorities banned amateur boxing, which had deep links to the Hitler Youth organization, but they permitted the professional game to continue. In order to regain his boxing license, however, Schmeling had to appear before the denazification commission and answer a lengthy questionnaire. Schmeling recognized that the British were especially interested in his service on Crete, where British forces had been defeated by the Germans in bitter and bloody battles. He wrote that this event had hurt his public reputation in Germany, as well as his professional and military careers. Especially troublesome was the interview with the American reporter, for it had led to Goebbels accusing him of treason. The German boxer also included a letter from film director Veit Harlan, the disreputable creator of the anti-Semitic film *Jüd Süss*, in which Harlan claimed that Goebbels had bitterly complained about Schmeling's cowardice on Crete and had expressed his regret that the boxer had been awarded the Iron Cross. Schmeling also argued that "in every way and in every circle I tried to fight the Nazis' untruths and irregularities and to undermine the authority of the leading personalities. In addition I have, wherever possible and wherever I had the opportunity, [tried] to help harassed people." He then listed a number of people he had aided, including boxers Paul Noack and Heinz Lazek, Graf Helldorf (who had been executed for his role in the plot to kill Hitler), the actor Rolf von Goth, "Roxy" owner Heinz Ditgens, and two others. In support of Schmeling, Friedrich Grosskopf, an assistant to Admiral Canaris, one of the plotters against Hitler in July 1944, testified that the boxer had indirectly aided the group who had tried to assassinate Hitler by visiting them in prison and securing better treatment for them. The British had their doubts that Max had been a true anti-Nazi, and a report in *Vorwärts*, the socialist newspaper, fanned their suspicions. In a story entitled "Secrets of Max Schmeling's Villa," the newspaper charged that Schmeling had been a member of the SS, that he had associated with other high ranking Nazis, and that he and his wife had acquired Jewish valuables from Pomerania with the aid of the Nazis. While his associations with high-ranking Nazis were well known, *Vorwärts* could muster only two harmless letters to support its other charges. Nothing illegal against Schmeling could be proved.[26]

While the de-nazification officials could find no reason for opening a case against him, the British occupation authorities were still not convinced that Schmeling was completely innocent. With some cash that he had rescued, and perhaps money raised through the sale of Anny's jewelry, Schmeling and Ondra bought a piece of property in Hamburg, where he began to construct a garden house out of wood. When the authorities found him building without a permit, they stopped the construction and brought him up on charges before a military court. According to Schmeling's biographer, Volker Kluge, the British probably did this to appease the mass of people who were living without adequate food and shelter. By making an example out of prominent figures with Nazi pasts caught breaking the rules, they hoped to forestall mass unrest. Schmeling was shocked by the judgment. On May 14, 1946, he received a 10,000 mark fine and a three-month jail sentence. It took years before he could look at his release document, which he kept above his desk, without anger. Ironically, while he served his sentence, the de-nazification committee for sports met, declared him innocent, and approved his application for a boxing license.[27]

Reunited once more with trainer Max Machon, Schmeling returned to the ring on September 28, 1947, his forty-second birthday. His ultimate goal, the *New York Times* reported, was to get in shape for a third bout with Joe Louis, which Schmeling had longed for since 1939. His first opponent was twenty-six-year-old Werner Vollmer. Staged in Frankfurt, in the American zone where United States occupation officials were friendlier to Schmeling, the bout attracted 40,000 G.I.s who greeted him by singing "Happy Birthday." He then proceeded to knock out Vollmer in the seventh round. Not only was Schmeling pleased by his victory, he was delighted to be among Americans once more. Unlike their British counterparts, American Army officers befriended him, urged him to relive his bouts against Joe Louis, and offered him vacations free of charge. Yet, he knew that his reflexes had slowed considerably. He was fighting on borrowed time. Even more troubling, several newspapers charged that some of Schmeling's bouts were fixed. As he fought on, the world of German professional boxing was tainted by charges of

"Das ist Alles." Max calls it quits after a brief comeback. Having lost everything, he returned to the ring, only to ultimately go down to defeat against Riedel Vogt on October 31, 1948. While Louis struggled financially after he left boxing, Schmeling became a successful farmer and then Coca-Cola executive, a key figure in the German economic miracle. (Associated Press, Library of Congress)

corruption and so was he. Yet he fought four more opponents, including Walter Neusel, to whom he lost on May 23, 1948. When he lost to Riedel Vogt on October 31, 1948, Schmeling announced that this was his last fight.[28]

The 43-year-old former champion took his winnings, bought a farm in Hollenstedt in northwest Germany outside of Hamburg, and retired from boxing. Promoters continued to invite him to their major boxing events as a lure for German fans, but Schmeling turned most of his energy toward farming to provide a more secure financial future for him and Anny. With the same dedication, intelligence, and business sense that he had demonstrated during his ring career, the ex-boxer read American trade literature on fur animals, a lucrative form of farming that he had learned about in the United States. He began with fifty nutrias and eventually increased the number to 2,000. In addition, he raised 2,000 hens, sold cognac under his own name, and bought into a German wine and champagne company. Soon he added tobacco to the mix. By the early 1950s it was clear that profit lay in mink, and Schmeling sold off the nutrias and concentrated on raising the animals for

mink coats. When the German economy began to take off under the stimulation of American aid and the German desire to rebuild after the war, German
businessmen bought mink coats for their wives. "Every prosperous burgher,"
wrote *Vend* magazine, wanted "to [dress] his wife in mink as a prestige symbol." Schmeling's star began to rise again. This time, however, it was as an
example of German ability to fight back from economic destruction.[29]

As soon as he was back on his feet, Schmeling attempted to return to his
"second home, America." He might have traveled sooner, but money was still
tight and his links to the Nazis had hurt him in the United States. When he
applied for a visa in 1948 to pursue his comeback in the United States where
he was still well known and prizefighting remained lucrative, Republican congressman John McDowell of Pennsylvania asked the State Department to
look into the matter. A member of the House Committee on Un-American
Activities, McDowell found it "a rather shoddy scheme to bring an over-age
fighter who certainly has been useful to the Fascists into this country to exploit" its sports fans. He never objected to "being idolized by the Nazis as
proof of their master race theories," McDowell charged. Whether it was the
visa issue or money matters, not until early 1954 was Schmeling able to fulfill
his ambition to return to the United States. By then it was in the interests of
the United States to allow a former citizen of an enemy nation to rekindle his
ties with acquaintances in the United States that he had not seen since 1939.
In the mid-1950s, American consular officials who granted him his visa confirmed that he had no Nazi-era taint.[30]

Schmeling's return to the United States was part of the transformation of
German American relations as the Cold War settled in after the Berlin block-
ade and airlift. Germany became a formally divided country and West Germany quickly became a partner with the United States in an anti-communist
alliance. By 1949 the allies lessened their attempts to de-nazify Germany
and bring former members of the Third Reich to justice. Through the
Marshall Plan, the United States poured millions into West Germany. In
part this was to revive the economies of Western Europe and prevent the
breeding ground for poverty and economic want from producing commu-
nism; in part, it encouraged Europeans to buy American goods and provided a new frontier for American economic expansion. At the center of a
divided Europe, Germany became a showplace of the American way of life.
That millions of American troops remained in Europe only spread the taste
for American goods and services.

To tap the growing market in Europe, the Coca-Cola Company, which
had sold its beverage in Germany during the 1920s, sought to reopen markets
for its American product that had languished during the war. In 1949, Coca-
Cola's Essen plant received permission to import the special syrup that went
into the soft drink and begin production for civilian consumption. With its
slogan, "Coke ist wieder da!"—Coke is back again—Coca-Cola became a

bridge to the past and a partner in rebuilding Germany. While in New York in 1954, Schmeling met with top executives of the soft drink company. In this instance, his past helped him as much as it hurt. The head of Coca-Cola's export operations was an old acquaintance, James A. Farley, the former United States Postmaster General and before that president of the New York State Athletic Commission. Farley planned to expand the company into West Germany and the rest of Europe and sought a well-known German, preferably a celebrity, to promote his product. He must also have been impressed by Schmeling's success with mink farming and his ancillary businesses. Whereas Hitler had used the German boxer to validate Aryan supremacy and the strength of the German nation, Farley sought a non-Nazi who could promote the German-American nature of his American soft drink. That Schmeling remained the biggest sports celebrity in Germany proved enormously attractive to the company. Beginning in the fall of 1957, the former boxer received a license for the Hamburg and northeastern area of Germany, and together with a partner, opened his own company, Getränke—Industrie Max Schmeling und Company.[31]

Cleared by the allied authorities, Schmeling was now ready for a larger role as a German goodwill ambassador for Coca-Cola and American influence in Germany. His company began by delivering the soft drink to stores and individual consumers, but in 1963 Schmeling took over the factory responsible for producing and bottling the soft drink in his area. Since the war, and stimulated by the presence of American troops on German soil, American soft drink sales increased dramatically, but Schmeling believed he could duplicate the American market on a per capita basis by using "American vending techniques," which he learned from contacts with the home office. As the German economy took off and began to grow again, Schmeling was at the forefront of introducing vending machines into the offices and factories that were fueling the German economic miracle.

By the late 1950s and early 1960s, Schmeling not only ran a major soft drink business, he was also the best-known pitchman for Coke, appearing on numerous television programs and at sports events with bottle in hand. His business success made him a wealthy man once again. His achievement reflected not only his business acumen but also the power of his personal image. His fame went back to Weimar, and he and his wife Anny, to whom he had been married since 1933, fed the need for some sense of a stable German culture that had links to the past that preceded the Nazi era. As an active and successful survivor of both the Nazis and the war, he demonstrated that there was a German tradition that went back before the Third Reich. The sense of German willpower and determination that was so much a part of Schmeling's image also proved that Germans could survive the troubled period of hunger and desperation and rebuild. As a German sports celebrity, moreover, Schmeling's presence as the public face of Coca-Cola helped Germans associate the soft drink with their own past love of the beverage and temper its association with the United States.[32]

While France and other European countries worried that Coca-Colonization threatened the very existence of their cultural integrity, Germans enthusiastically took to the soft drink. By the mid-1950s, even before Schmeling's involvement with the company, sales had jumped 600 percent yearly, outstripping the booming economic miracle twelvefold. By 1965, Germany was the biggest market for the beverage outside the United States. Part of the reason lay in the company's imperial mission. In the minds of Coca-Cola executives and advertisers, "The Gospel of Refreshment" had a missionary role—it spread youthful vitality, promoted relaxation, and encouraged the harmony of all peoples. Popularized again by American G.I.s who served in the occupation after the war, Coke helped turn the world from hatred and war to friendship and hospitality. According to historian Jeff Schutts, this gospel played a unique role in postwar German society, one in which Schmeling contributed a significant part. Coca-Cola's return matched Schmeling's in the sense that both marked the revival of an older German spirit and the notion of beginning again with youthful energy. His willingness to start over in boxing, in farming, and in 1957 in Coca-Cola bottling reflected in the minds of many West Germans the ability to rebuild in a totally new world but with links to the German past. As a boxer known for always being in shape, moreover, Schmeling was synonymous with the qualities of hard work, self-discipline, and self-confidence that were needed to bring German society and its economy back from ruin.[33]

With Schmeling leading the way, Coca-Cola also helped West Germans redeem themselves on an individual basis. In 1955, the company unleashed a new advertising slogan that surprisingly found great favor with the public. "Mach mal Pause" (take a break) touched on the German work ethic and the stress that went with constant effort. The slogan did not view a break from work as hedonistic exercise but rather a way to take time out so Germans would feel refreshed when they returned to their labors. At the heart of this campaign was the effort to tap "the world's biggest undeveloped market for vending machines." By the end of the 1950s and early 1960s, in part under Schmeling's direction, vending machines appeared in the cafeterias of offices and factories across Germany. Germans could thus continue to work hard but also build new identities that allowed for leisure and consumption.[34]

Not only did Germans need to rebuild from the rubble and regain their self-confidence, but they also sought redemption in their own eyes and the eyes of the world. Here too Schmeling provided a perfect face for the company. While many wanted to forget the nation's war crimes, Schmeling attempted to atone for the past through his travels to the United States to visit the grave of his former manager, Joe Jacobs, and his former foe, Joe Louis. As a German with a cosmopolitan reputation who publicly stated on many occasions that America was his second home, Schmeling showed that there were Germans who were willing to accept democracy and reject war and fascism, together with its racist content. Whether or not most Germans shared these feelings, they found in Schmeling's example a way to forget the Nazi era and look to a more democratic Weimar past. In their adulation of "unser Max," moreover, many Germans found someone who mirrored their own roles under Hitler: loyal Germans who had good private instincts, perhaps, but were afraid to speak out publicly. On another level, the symbol of Schmeling in the modern era allowed many Germans to excuse their own weaknesses. In addition, by consuming Coca-Cola, they had an opportunity to demonstrate a willingness to vote for consumerism rather than war. As Schmeling put it, his life "is that of a German in the twentieth century; or perhaps more precisely, it was a German-American life, a tie made even stronger through my association with Coca-Cola of Hamburg." At the center of the "Coca-Colonization" of the world, Schmeling helped promote the German economic miracle. Tied to American economic might and its most identifiable product, he also pointed the way to overcome defeat. By adapting to the power of the victor, Germany would be linked to the success of the American way of life.[35]

As a key figure in the transformation of West Germany during the Cold War, Schmeling once more rose from the ashes to become a hero in a new setting. As he put it, his life "es immer rauf und runter ging (it constantly rose and fell)." Together with Axel Springer, a friend and the publisher of the popular newsmagazine *Der Spiegel*, Schmeling also endeared himself to West Germans with his public support of a reunified German nation. Once associated with Hitler's Winter Relief Charity campaigns, by the late 1950s the ex-champion was one of a number of socialites and celebrities who attempted to raise money to open the Brandenburg Gate. When the movement failed, he spoke out against the communists and emphasized that despite all political obstacles, Germans remained a united people. A capitalist and an anticommunist the former sportsman articulated the views of many other Germans in his hope for a free, united, and democratic Germany. As a result, his stature continued to rise. When he published an earlier version of his autobiography in 1956, it was a big hit, selling 250,000 copies by 1965. More recently voted one of West Germany's "Athletes of the Century," Schmeling has watched his meaning grow among his citizens. Indeed, on his seventieth birthday, September 28, 1975, the president of West Germany, Walter Scheel, named him "Germany's Number 1 Sportsman for Life."[36]

The making of a transatlantic alliance in the Cold War took place not only between nation-states and international economies but also on the level of personal relations. Schmeling's return to New York in 1954 did more than help him open business negotiations with the Coca-Cola Company. The journey also was an attempt to repair personal relations disrupted by World War

II and embittered by his ties to the Nazis. It was an emotional trip. In New York, he stopped off at Jack Dempsey's Restaurant, one of boxing's great haunts, where he met up with Cashwell Jacobs, Joe Jacobs's brother and one of Schmeling's former bodyguards. Together, they went to a Jewish cemetery in Brooklyn so that he could pay his respects to his former manager, who had died during the war. Schmeling also wanted to repair relations with Paul Damski, Walter Neusel's Jewish manager who had been forced into exile by the Nazis. Damski was bitter about the ex-boxer's association with Hitler and Goebbels and initially he refused to meet with his old friend. When Damski finally consented to see him, Schmeling convinced him that he had not willingly supported the Third Reich and had at one time thought of poisoning Adolf Hitler.[37]

On the same trip, the ex-boxer traveled to Chicago to meet the man with whom he had made boxing history. Without calling ahead, he showed up at Louis's apartment on the south side, where Rose Morgan, the Brown Bomber's second wife, called him home from the golf course. In a way, the meeting of Max Schmeling and Joe Louis continued the international ties not only between the two boxers but also between Germany and the United States. Whether or not Schmeling and Louis were thinking of larger political issues when they met in Chicago, they did bury their old enmity. The German believed that during the Nazi era, journalists, propagandists, and officials of the two governments "had sought to play us off against each other, forever trying to put hateful or insulting words in our mouths." Over coffee, the two old foes discussed their past battles and the bitter political atmosphere that had surrounded them. Schmeling brought up how people on both sides tried to turn opponents into enemies through concerted propaganda campaigns. "I just want you to know," he began, but Louis cut him off immediately. "Forget all that," the Brown Bomber said, downplaying the fact that he had built up a good deal of enmity toward a man he believed had disrespected his athletic abilities, his intelligence, and his race. "For a long time people tried the same thing with me. There were times when I believed what they wrote. But today I know better." The two former enemies talked late into the evening, rekindling a relationship that had been strained by politics and war. They talked about the great fights, as old opponents often will, and they caught up on old friends. "It was only then," Schmeling realized, "that I realized how much it had bothered me over the years that the hatreds of the times had managed to separate us."[38]

The two subsequently met each other perhaps thirteen times, including a surprise appearance by Schmeling for a *This Is Your Life* television episode in 1960 honoring Joe Louis, and a reunion held in Germany on September 6, 1966, on the occasion of the Cassius Clay-Karl Mildenberger fight. As the *New York Times* put it, times had changed: "Joe Louis and Max Schmeling, who once mauled each other in the ring, held a friendly reunion here today." Although they probably never became close friends, they did become friendly,

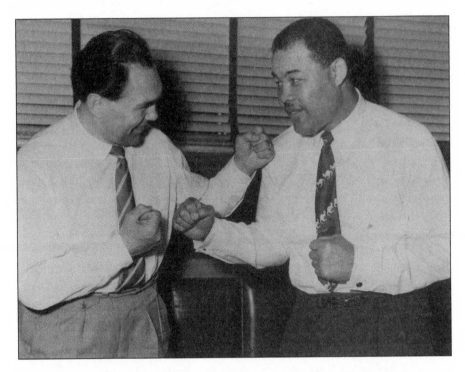

"Two Old Warriors" 1954. As part of Schmeling's first trip to the United States since the war, he held a reunion with Louis, one of many the two old warriors would have until Louis's death in 1981. Often they were asked to recreate their former fighting pose, but now the two old antagonists were friends not foes. This transformation in their relationship followed the alliance between Germany and the United States against a new international threat. (Associated Press, Library of Congress)

and when Max learned of Joe's financial difficulties he quietly sent him money. In these ways, Schmeling hoped to lift the burden of the past that weighed on him heavily and find a place for himself once more in America. To a large extent, the reunions played well in a Germany hungry for redemption in the eyes of the world and in a United States eager to cement its postwar alliance. When the two attended the Sportsmen's World Awards dinner in Beverly Hills, California, in June 1967, the *Times* printed two photos. One showed the two as opponents at the weigh-in for their "revenge match," and then at the dinner. The headline read, "The Years Turn Bitter Enemies to Honored Friends." When Schmeling came to Las Vegas in 1971 to attend a testimonial dinner to mark Louis's fifty-seventh birthday, the two were photographed feigning an arm wrestling match. The caption says, "No Hard Feelings."[39]

The high point of these reunions occurred in August 1973 when the two old foes met again in New York to mark the thirty-fifth anniversary of their June 22, 1938, bout. They, along with the original referee Arthur Donovan, appeared at Nassau Veterans Memorial Coliseum on August 9 as part of the meeting of West German and United States amateur boxing champions in ten Olympic-style bouts. The entire event was staged to "show the bond between the United States and West Germany." To mark the contrast between past enmity and current amity between the two nations, the two boxers entered the ring and squared off against each other once more in mock fighting poses. Preceding the ten amateur bouts, the film of their second fight was shown. As an indication of how much had changed since the boxers last fought, newspapers covering the story asserted that "there were none of the political or racial overtones that marked their last meeting." According to the press reports, the entire narrative of their relations had changed. "We were friends from the first fight," said Louis. "After the fight Max sent me a beautiful clock from Germany." According to Louis, "It never was a personal thing between us." Schmeling concluded, "You know a lot of the talk was just publicity. I had a manager who was a Jew. You shouldn't mix sports and politics together." That the reunion had deeper political meaning in the context of the Cold War could be discerned in the statement of Dr. Leonard Milton, president of the People-to-People Sports Committee, which received United States Information Agency money to promote international friendship through sports. Ignoring the past between the two men and their respective countries, Milton declared, "Here are two men who served their countries well—each was in the service. They fought, but through sports they became good friends."[40]

At the end of their lives, the reversal of fortunes experienced by Max Schmeling and Joe Louis could not have been more pronounced. When Louis died on April 12, 1981, of a massive heart attack, his body had atrophied, his fortune had disappeared, and his fame had dwindled. The Brown Bomber had been sick for years, confined to a wheelchair as a result of a cerebral hemorrhage that he suffered during the late 1970s.

Max Schmeling, on the other hand, who lived on until February 2, 2005, had been destitute and reviled at the end of World War II, but since the late 1950s had become a wealthy businessman and a revered figure in Germany and a rehabilitated one in American life. While their personal fortunes diverged dramatically, they remained linked together through their epic battles in the ring in an arena heightened by international global tensions and the politicization of sport. They had once been the standard-bearers of Democracy and Nazism, civic nationalism and racial nationalism, and the clash between the two men and their respective ideologies opened the door in the United States to a widespread questioning of white supremacy and anti-semitism. Despite the personal reversal of fortunes that they had experienced, their great bouts and their ideological importance still linked them together. At the end of their lives, the "Greatest Fight of 'Our' Generation" had been transformed once again by international currents.

EPILOGUE
WINNERS AND LOSERS

Five days after Joe Louis died on April 12, 1981, from a massive heart attack, his body lay in state at Caesar's Palace Hotel and Casino in Las Vegas. As the fight capital of the world, this oasis in the Nevada desert was the type of nightlife, sports, and gambling town that was a fitting last home to the peripatetic Louis. It took donations from his former antagonist Max Schmeling and singer Frank Sinatra, a contemporary and long-time admirer, to pay for the funeral. As a sign of the enduring importance of the Brown Bomber, black and white boxers, high rollers, small-time gamblers, the sporting crowd, and members of the Rat Pack all came to deliver their respects to the champion of their generation. Former and current champions Muhammad Ali and Larry Holmes, respectively, served as pallbearers, while Sugar Ray Leonard, Floyd Patterson, Bill Cosby, and Alan King stood by. Sammy Davis, Jr., one of the many African American entertainers who had idolized the champion and his accomplishments over the years, sang a tribute, "For the Winners." In the few words he spoke, an emotional Sinatra noted Louis's significance for boxing, calling the Brown Bomber a "champion of champions who introduced dignity to the sports square with the ropes around it."[1]

In a fitting gesture, the Reverend Jesse Louis Jackson delivered the eulogy. Born in 1941, Jackson was named in honor of the two idols of his parents' generation, Jesse Owens and Joe Louis. It was no accident that Jackson fought the good fight in the arena of civil rights, for that was the lasting legacy of both of these towering sports heroes. "We are honoring a giant who saved us in time of trouble," Jackson declared, introducing the theme that Louis helped lift all America from "its Depression psychology," but even more, the Brown Bomber served as a savior for black Americans at a low point in their history. In the darkest days of the Depression, "with lynching mobs threatening our existence, we were defenseless without legal, political, military or economic protection." As Jackson put it, "He was our Sampson. He was our David who slew Goliath. With toughness he destroyed the enemy, and with kindness and tenderness he soothed the wounds and revived the soul, the psyche of the people." Usually a champion rides on the shoulders of the nation and its people, Jackson noted, but in this case, "the nation rode on the shoulders of the hero, Joe." Jackson also touched on Louis's role as an ambassador of his race. He answered the call of his people "when we were in a valley and seemingly couldn't hear nobody pray. When we were vulnerable with the stench of the Depression still in our clothes, God sent Joe from the black race to represent the human race." As a key part of Louis's legacy, Jackson of course singled out the fight with Max Schmeling, for "what was at stake was the confidence of a nation with a battered ego and in search of resurrection, and the esteem of a race of people."[2]

The eulogy also redressed the common idea that Louis had ended up a loser, a "poor Joe," broken at the end. Jackson would have none of it, for what Louis had meant to black and white Americans was so much bigger than his sad state at the end of his life. "For the children of '37 who crowded around the radio, hanging from the trees in the fields and watching the newsreels, they don't understand 'Poor Joe.'" Those who "danced in the streets" when he became champion, "they don't understand 'Poor Joe.'" In the reverend's estimation, "Joe was not dumb, he was generous. Dumb people get tricked out of education. Dumb people cheat. Dumb people bring shame to themselves. Dumb people fix fights. Dumb people steal jobs. Tell them Joe was not dumb. He was *generous*." And, as Jackson made clear, Joe had given of himself to advance the cause of all of his people. He was their champion. At the close of his remarks, Jackson threw back his shoulders and rose to his full height. "We all feel bigger today because Joe came this way. He was in the slum, but the slum was not in him. Ghetto boy to man. . . . Alabama sharecropper to champion. Let's give Joe a big hand clap. This is a celebration. Let's hear it for the champ." At the reverend's urging, the audience of three thousand stood and clapped for the fallen champion.[3]

Several days later, mourners attended formal burial rites at Arlington National Cemetery, made possible by special permission of President Ronald Reagan, where speakers at the gravesite celebrated him as a true American hero, a symbol of black liberation, and a fighter against white racial supremacy. The minister read from the New Testament: "I have fought the good fight. I have finished the race, I have kept the faith." After the dignified ceremony, many who attended the service were moved to recall the fights with Max

Schmeling as central to the Brown Bomber's mythic importance. Seventy-two-year-old Hosea Lindsey recalled "my mom crying when Joe lost to Max Schmeling in 1936." Listening to the decision over the radio, his mother exclaimed, "There goes the savior of our race!" Lindsey replied, he told the reporter for the *New York Times*, "'Mom, Joe will come back.' And he did, oh he did." Other fans, some of them Jewish, also remembered the second match with Schmeling as the battle between America and Hitler. "He broke the myth of the master race," Rabbi Joshua O. Haberman of Washington Hebrew Congregation, an exile from Nazi Germany, said at the chapel. "For that alone, Joe Louis deserves to be blessed, and even more so for his quiet humility." After the honor guard blew taps, an unidentified black man rang a cowbell. A soldier told him it was time for a low profile. "We been low profile a long time, brother," the man responded. "This is the bell of liberty, ringing for Joe Louis."[4]

At his death, mourners celebrated Louis as a psychological savior of black America and of Depression and wartime Americans. They interpreted his battles with Schmeling as a challenge to racist ideology and as a defense of the nation as war clouds gathered. Downplaying his decline from greatness, they returned to his central role as a harbinger of black liberation and a more tolerant nationalism. Although many young people today have only a vague sense of Joe Louis, his significance endures. Shortly after Louis's death, the young painter Jean Michel Basquiat painted his homage to Louis, "St. Joe Louis Surrounded by Snakes" (1982), which shows a young Louis surrounded by the unsavory people who let him down at the end. Similarly, in 1974, the Crusaders, a long-time soul jazz group, had released their composition, "A Ballad for Joe (Louis)," which celebrated his highs and lows and his connection to the world of black music and entertainment. In Detroit, where he and his family moved during the Great Migration, city fathers named the hockey stadium Joe Louis Arena, and a large fist, symbolic of Louis's power, graces the entrance. These continued the pattern of seeing his life in mythic terms: poor black boy, born the grandchild of slaves, who rose from southern sharecropping to northern urban-industrial poverty to the Heavyweight Championship of the World. Many Americans would like to think that his ability to rise represents the opportunities made available in the United States, others point out that his decline represented an America that still does not provide full and equal rights to its African American citizens.

But his story is not merely one of image. Louis and his managers confronted the strong racism of their day and devised a strategy to break the color line. To accomplish a task that seemed impossible in the early 1930s, Louis put on a mask of "the good Negro," a mask that later generations of African American athletes and black people now scorn. Yet he kept his dignity through it all, never becoming an Uncle Tom, never groveling before white power. With his tough guy deadpan and his fists of dynamite, he also conveyed a sense of black male power that expressed the desires of his community and challenged the dictates of the dominant society. By doing so, he broke barriers that had barred black men from holding the heavyweight championship, he exacted a measure of black revenge on white power, and he demonstrated that blacks were equal to or better than whites when given the opportunity to compete fairly. In an era of segregation, he broke a significant color bar, reduced the idea of the white hope to a mere financial term, and set a precedent that allowed later generations of black athletes to compete in almost all fields of American sports. They, however, would have greater freedom to express the full dimensions of their identities no matter what whites expected or the black middle class hoped for. As a fighter, he spurred others to battle the boundaries of segregation and discrimination that had marked his life. Joe Louis placed his stamp on the ring for a good fifteen years, bringing a measure of dignity to a sordid sport, and creating a sense of poetry in motion and explosive power that few other heavyweight champions, black or white, have managed to equal.

The man most linked with Louis throughout his career, Max Schmeling, died in far different circumstances on February 2, 2005, at the ripe old age of ninety-nine. Having made a fortune as a Coca-Cola bottling executive, Schmeling had been feted every year on his birthday by West German celebrities, sports figures, and even presidents since the 1950s. He and his wife attended the major business, sport, and social events until her death in 1987. By the early 1990s, Schmeling removed himself from the public eye and chose to live out his remaining days on his estate in Hollendstedt outside of Hamburg. He had only one dream left to fulfill, he told the last of his interviewers: to live to be one hundred years old. Still lucid almost to the end, capable of riding his exercise cycle to stay fit, he almost made it. As with so many other aspects of his life, however, his reach exceeded his grasp.[5]

The reaction to Schmeling's death in Germany and the United States summed up his entire career, but it was clear that the high points were the matches with Louis. Both the German and American press ran just about the same story. Far overshadowing his championship victory over Jack Sharkey in 1930, *Der Spiegel* recalled that Schmeling's most famous fight was his knockout triumph over the unbeaten Louis in their first match. Two years later, of course, Louis had his revenge. In the United States, the AP wire story hit the same note: "Schmeling's extraordinary career will be remembered for his two fights with Louis, which produced a lasting bond between the two boxers despite the politically charged atmosphere surrounding the bouts." More than the Germans, however, the American reaction noted that the Nazis had trumpeted his victory as a sign of "Aryan Supremacy." Viewed as a Nazi symbol, he was knocked out in the return match. As the *Chicago Tribune* noted, it is the rematch "that is remembered by everyone who knows boxing. And by many who don't." It was a battle of good against evil, noted the *New York Times*, "with the Nazis looking to project Schmeling as an Aryan Superman."[6]

Yet it was clear that by the time of his death there was no doubt that Schmeling had managed to redeem himself in American eyes. Most seemed to agree with the *Chicago Tribune*'s sub-headline on his obituary calling him "a good fighter and a great man." Schmeling, it appears, got the last word in the end. "I'm almost happy I lost that fight," Schmeling is quoted as saying in 1975. "Just imagine if I would have come back to Germany with a victory. I had nothing to do with the Nazis, but they would have given me a medal. After the war I might have been considered a war criminal." The obituaries noted that he differed with the Nazi regime from the start. They mentioned his defense of Joe Jacobs and his role in saving the Lewin brothers on Kristallnacht. From there it was on to his success as a Coca-Cola executive. The pictures in the *Tribune* tell the story. The first one shows him celebrating his twelfth round knockout of Louis, the second shows Louis the winner, and the third has Max and Joe together in Las Vegas in 1971. The two foes were now friends. As many of the stories mentioned, Schmeling provided aid to the destitute Louis and helped pay for his funeral. All in all, most Americans considered Schmeling a man wronged. It was also apparent that as Louis's image ebbed, Schmeling's only gained greater luster as a successful business executive with a happy marriage. It was almost as if at his death Schemling got his wish for a third fight with Louis and this time won it.[7]

Most of the commentary stopped at the second fight and then hurried on to Schmeling's redemption, skipping almost blithely over his ambiguous relationship with so many members of the regime and how he had accommodated himself to it for the sake of his career. One confused old man, however, reacted to "unser Max's" death by plunging back into time as he wrestled with what the German boxer had meant to him. Upon hearing of the ex-boxer's death, Benjamin Dovzinsky, a holocaust survivor living in Israel, recalled a heretofore unknown incident in Schmeling's life. In Berlin in December 1938, the Berlin Sportpalast hosted a boxing competition between Germany and Poland with Hitler, Göring, Goebbels, and many other notable Nazis in attendance. The Polish contingent, the old man noted, included a young Jew. That night all traffic stopped in Poland as Poles listened to the fights on the radio. Each German defeated his Polish opponent. At the peak moment, Shabbatai Rotholtz, the Polish Jew, squared off against Schmeling, "the symbol of German power." As they sat glued to their radio sets, the Jews of Poland prayed for a miracle. Suddenly, Dovzinsky recalled, Rotholtz knocked out Schmeling. At that, Hitler and his entourage "stormed from the hall with angry faces." This incident remained engraved in his memory, especially after the destruction of the Jews during World War II. Several days later, another letter to *Ha'aretz* pointed out that there had been a German-Polish tournament, but it had taken place in Cracow without Schmeling. For

Dovzinsky and many other Jews, Schmeling had been a potent symbol of Nazi power, and his defeat meant so much to oppressed peoples everywhere. In 1930s America and other parts of the world, Jews and other ethnic groups, along with African Americans, found a symbolic savior in Joe Louis.[8]

The increased awareness of Schmeling's actions to help Jews improved his reputation among many Jews in the United States and Israel. While it was long known that he had stood by his Jewish manager Joe Jacobs, only in 1989 did Schmeling's intervention on the part of the Lewin brothers become common knowledge. Writing in *The Jerusalem Report* shortly after Schmeling's death, Eric Silver noted that Yad Vashem never honored Max Schmeling for being a Righteous Gentile, but in his opinion it was deserved. The proof of his righteousness lay in his saving of Henri and Daniel Lewin on Kristallnacht 1938. The rescue remained secret until 800 of the most famous names in boxing attended a gala dinner in Schmeling's honor in Las Vegas in 1989, at which Henri revealed Schmeling's courageous role in saving him and his brother from Nazi mobs. As Silver concludes, "Whether or not he met Yad Vashem's criteria for a Righteous Gentile, he remained a mensch."[9]

In Germany Schmeling had become a larger than life figure by the time of his death. Germans revered him as an example of fair play and rectitude, of dedication to the principles of sport, and as a person who retained cosmopolitan leanings and contact with the wider world even under the Nazis. After the war, many Germans looked upon him as a man who held that certain principles were more important than his own career. He became, according to historian Siegfried Gehrmann, "a kind of witness for a better Germany in a time of darkness." Although he had not been brave enough to publicly challenge the regime, he kept alive the private wish of German honor. In his boxing career, Schmeling "fought honorably and fairly with a sense of personal dignity that rivaled that of his most famous opponent, Joe Louis." In the 1970s he established the yearly Fair-Play Prize for German sport. After Anny's death, he created the Max Schmeling Foundation to aid people in distress. Like so many others, he was a decent, but at times weak man caught up in horrific events beyond his control. This perception of decency grew as his contributions to Joe Louis became known over the years. The German press always remarked that Schmeling had atoned for the past racism of his country and his past ties to the Third Reich.[10]

While the course of the twentieth century witnessed a reversal of roles for Louis and Schmeling, the fact that every obituary places their two fights front and center in their story forces us to recognize how sporting events can become social and political dramas that transcend sport. The Ali-Foreman "Rumble in the Jungle" of 1974 was one such bout, wrapped up as it was in Black Power, the Black Cultural Revolt, and the attempt to link black Americans to their African roots. Similarly, the Johnson-Jeffries match of 1910 was also larger than sport because it touched on the themes of racial honor, black transgressions of white physical power and hence white supremacy. The Louis-Schmeling matches rose to that level because the bouts and the boxers became enmeshed in the Nazi politicization of sport and the tense international struggle between nations. Eager to prove that German sporting and political success was based on Aryan racial purity, Dr. Goebbels transformed Schmeling's victory in the first fight into a German national victory. The trumpeting of German racial supremacy raised the specter of black racial inferiority. For African Americans, this was a deep insult made all the worse because their national hero had gone down to ignominious defeat.

The maneuverings in the world of boxing, some of it motivated by American nationalism and a good deal prompted by profit, spurred German views of a conspiracy, led by the Jewish press and Jewish promoters, to besmirch German honor. This deepened the political meaning of the rematch in 1938, the "greatest fight of 'our' generation." On both sides, national honor was at stake. With German help, Schmeling was transformed by an outraged and fearful United States into a Nazi show horse. On the other hand, Louis, became not only a black idol but also an American national standard-bearer against the Nazi threat. When the bell rang, warring nationalisms went at it in the ring. The German remained rooted in blood and race while white Americans had to choose between supporting a man of their race versus supporting their nation. Although there was much ambivalence over viewing a black boxer as a national hero, even in the white South, many white Americans chose nation over race.

The second Louis-Schmeling bout also carried so much cultural and political weight because it was a media event broadcast around the world by radio and covered by newspapers and magazines in many different countries. Although a myth, many people believe that Hitler had German radio cut off when it was clear that Schmeling would lose. This speaks to the importance of transnational sports radio, for in the United States and Germany, as well as in numerous other countries, the fight was a highly popular media event. Media events have the ability to provide space for societies to construct imagined and collective identities and solidarities. American newspapers and radio broadcasts stressed the theme that Schmeling was a Nazi and Louis represented democracy. In Germany, while the regime tried to downplay the racial imagery in case of a loss, it was clear that a German was fighting an African American and that German national honor and Aryan supremacy was at stake. Radio and newspapers created a narrative in each country that gave the bout additional drama. By pitting two different individuals against each other—one black, one white, one American, one German, one the representative of an underdog race and one the representative of the master race—the media helped shape a dramatic conflict. In both countries, that conflict pitted democracy versus Nazism, and the winner of the match foretold the fate of the world. In the United States, the radio broadcasts helped unite the nation around an ideal of fair play and open competition in which the best man won. That this democratic ideal included in theory the African American hero who won the day helped create a powerful national ideal that could be used to battle the racial realities that actually existed in a segregated nation.[11]

Boxing was a perfect sport to dramatize larger international issues because it had a long tradition of transnationalism, and it was also an arena in which ethnic and racial rivalries had long found a home. Even more important, however, boxing pits individuals rather than teams against each other, and as in any drama, it was relatively easy for each man's supporters to focus their national and racial ideology on an individual, who in heightened form, became their nation in the eyes of the world. The equation of masculinity with nation, moreover, often occurs in a period of aggressive nationalism. As masculine ideals, both boxers came to stand for fighting images of their nation in a surrogate war. The Nazis made this explicit. The heroic ideal of the Nazi state was the warrior male, capable and willing to wage war on his own lesser impulses and on men in other nations. The glorification of Schmeling's physique was surpassed only by the glorification of his will, his determination to win, and the mental superiority he used to accomplish his triumphant upset over an "inferior" Louis in 1936.

Americans had celebrated masculine physical power since the 1890s, but usually that meant glorifying the white male body, often in ways that bore a striking similarity to Nazi philosophy. When Jack Johnson proved that white physical supremacy was a fiction, he threatened white racial power outside as well as inside the ring. With the prize being white women, white men did all they could to put the genie of race back in the bottle. That lasted until the emergence of Joe Louis. While he had to compromise a critical element of his masculinity—his sexuality and his freedom to speak freely on the subject of race—to assuage white and black middle-class fears, Louis quickly demonstrated much more effectively than Johnson that white physical power was a lie. Despite their ambivalence, moreover, white Americans for the first time on a mass scale could celebrate a black male body. When he beat Schmeling, Louis's masculine prowess became associated with the American national ideal.

That the emergent national ideal was heavily masculine should be no surprise given that one of its important arenas of creation was the male sport of boxing. When Louis was making his way, he knew he was serving himself and his people, but he had a limited conception of women doing the same outside the role of homemaker or wife of a celebrity. His casual sexual behavior, like that of many famous men, would be called into question by black and white feminists in the future. On another level, some of the poignancy of Louis's last years and the way he has been portrayed as another black victim of America, speaks to the disappointment that so many black—and some white—Americans feel about the slowed pace of civil rights in this country. In this, he represents the ways that race has continued to be the weak link in civic nationalism and in the triumphant vision of the American nation that emerged from victory in World War II.

For Germans, the second bout continues to have tremendous resonance for different reasons. The Nazis were tremendously disappointed in Schmeling's loss to a Negro, but the continuing story that Germans tell is that looking back, Schmeling was happy to have lost. Losing meant disassociating himself at a deep level from the Nazi regime and its racial ideology. As a man who admitted at least some of his mistakes, Schmeling stands as the representative of a defeated nation capable of rising above its defeat. Although he went onto success with Coca-Cola, becoming a symbol of international harmony against another totalitarian enemy, Schmeling continued to convey that losing the fight of his life saved his soul. And losing the war certainly made Germany a better country than it had been under Hitler. All of the publicity of Schmeling's financial assistance to Louis, moreover, not only demonstrates his "good" qualities, but it also suggests the lessons of defeat to the victorious Americans: winning is not inevitable, losing happens to all individuals and nations. One of the measures of a good man and a good state, moreover, is that it assists those who are down on their luck. In this the losers have a good deal to teach the winners.

Louis and Schmeling were more than boxers. They carried some of the deepest political and social tensions of a period wracked by political, racial, and national conflicts. Because of the transnational nature of boxing, their bouts became world dramas, which moved the racial basis of American and German nationalism to the forefront of American politics and national identity. As their second bout became a metaphor for World War II in the United States, it also served to identify official American war goals with ethnic and racial pluralism. Under different international circumstances in a Cold War world, the Louis-Schmeling bouts and the relationship between the two men became a symbol for the shift in German-American relations. The transatlantic currents that had once made the relationship between Schmeling and Louis one of bitterness, hatred, and heightened national competition now created a relationship in which past bitterness was forgotten and international amity was to reign. In this atmosphere, the Louis-Schmeling relationship underwent its last transformation. But when it comes to the still incomplete racial transformation of the United States, it is apparent that heroes may die, but their battles live on.

NOTES

ABBREVIATIONS

AN   *Amsterdam News*

B-S   *Box-Sport*

CD   *Chicago Defender*

DA   *Der Angriff*

DW   *Daily Worker*

HA   *Hamburger Anzeiger*

JLS   Julian Black Collection of Joe Louis Scrapbooks, National Museum of American History, Smithsonian Institution

NYT   *New York Times*

PC   *Pittsburgh Courier*

SNT   *Stuttgarter Neues Tagblatt*

VB   *Völkischer Beobachter*

INTRODUCTION

1. Heywood Broun, "It Seems to Me," *New York World-Telegram*, 24 June 1938, n. p., in JLS, vol. 56. For more on the international excitement, see Nat Fleischer, "Fleischer Picks Louis to Top Schmeling," *Ring* (22 June 1938), JLS, vol. 51.

2. Alan Gould, "Ring Experts Dizzy Trying to Pick Bout," *New Orleans Times-Picayune*, 21 June 1938, 17, lists the applications for press passes. "Joe Louis Bleibt Weltmeister," *SNT*, 23 June 1938, 1, notes the crowd at the fight.

3. C. L. R. James, *Beyond a Boundary* (New York, 1987), 192. On the dramatic nature of all boxing matches, see Joyce Carol Oates, *On Boxing* (Garden City, 1987), 8. For another view of the bout as political theater, see William L. Patterson, "Joe Louis Killed Nazi Supremacy Theory," *PC*, 24 June 1938.

4. Barbara Keys, "Dictatorship of Sport: Nationalism, Internationalism, and Mass Culture in the 1930s" (Ph.D. diss., Harvard University, 2001), analyzes nationalism and the internationalization of sport in the 1930s. Kristin Hoganson, "Cosmopolitan Domesticity: Importing the American Dream, 1865–1920," *American Historical Review* 107 (February 2002), 55–56, surveys historians' incorporation of transnational events into United States history. Eric Foner, "American Freedom in a Global Age," Presidential Address, *American Historical Review* 106 (February 2001), 4, 10–11, emphasizes that the rise of transnational culture had a powerful effect on American society, especially in the area of race, as well as on the rest of the globe.

5. For the Heenan-Sayers bout, see Elliott J. Gorn, *The Manly Art: Bare-Knuckle Prize Fighting in America* (Ithaca, N.Y., 1986), 148–60.

6. For superheroes in the Depression, see Lawrence Levine, "American Culture and the Great Depression," in Levine, *Unpredictable Past* (New York, 1993), 227–28, and Bradford W. Wright, *Comic Book Nation: The Transformation of Youth Culture in America* (Baltimore, 2001), 1–29. George Mosse, *Nationalism and Sexuality: Respectability and Abnormal Sexuality in Modern Europe* (New York, 1985), 153–80, emphasizes the Nazi preoccupation with masculinity. For Schmeling's enduring importance in Germany, see Hans Joachim Teichler, "Max Schmeling—Der Sportler des Jahrhunderts im Dritten Reich," *Sportzeit* (2000), 7–33; Siegfried Gehrmann, "Symbol of National Resurrection: Max Schmeling, German Sports Idol," *International Journal of the History of Sport*, 13 (1996), 101–13; and Robert Weisbord and Norbert Hedderich, "Max Schmeling, Righteous Ring Warrior?" *History Today*, 43 (January 1993), 36–41. For a discussion of the German reaction to having been vanquished in World War I, see Wolfgang Schivelbusch, *The Culture of Defeat: On National Trauma, Mourning, and Recovery*, trans. Jefferson Chase (New York, 2003; orig., 2001), 196–238.

7. Declan Kibard, *Inventing Ireland* (Cambridge, Mass., 1996), shows how the Irish cultural revival preceded the successful political rebellion against Great Britain. For Louis's heroic role in the black community see Lawrence Levine, *Black Culture and Black Consciousness* (New York, 1977), 420–40, and Thomas R. Hietala, *The Fight of the Century: Jack Johnson, Joe Louis, and the Struggle for Racial Equality* (Armonk, N.Y., 2002), 168–90. On the cultural roots of the African American awakening, see Gena Caponi-Tabery, "Jump for Joy: The Jump Trope in African America, 1937–1941," in *Prospects* 24 (1999), 521–74. Caponi-Tabery equates Louis's championship with the victory of A. Philip Randolph's Brotherhood of Sleeping Car Porters in 1937. For more on the union victory, see Susan Eleanor Hirsch, *After the Strike: A Century of Labor Struggle at Pullman* (Urbana, 2003), 128–55. Lauren Sklaroff, "Ambivalent Inclusion: The State, Race, and Official

Culture, 1930–1950" (Ph.D. diss., University of Virginia, 2002), argues that New Deal cultural programs promoted African American rights and equality, though in ambivalent ways, far more successfully than did the New Deal political agenda. For more on political and cultural changes originating in the 1930s, see John Higham, *Civil Rights and Social Wrongs* (University Park, Pa., 1997), and Patricia Sullivan, *Days of Hope: Race and Democracy in the new Deal Era* (Chapel Hill, 1996). Gregory S. Rodriguez, "'Palaces of Pain'—Arenas of Mexican-American Dreams: Boxing and the Foundation of Ethnic Mexican Identities in Twentieth-Century Los Angeles" (Ph.D. diss., University of California, San Diego, 1999), discusses how boxing offered black and brown boxers a public forum for displaying masculinity and group pride. Clifford Geertz, "Deep Play: Notes on the Balinese Cockfight," in *Myth, Symbol and Culture*, ed. Clifford Geertz (New York, 1971), 1–37, provides the basis for treating boxing as a revealing cultural ritual.

8. For interpretations of New Deal–era popular culture as conservative, see Warren Susman, "The Culture of the Thirties," and "Culture and Commitment," in his *Culture as History* (New York, 1984), 150–210; Andrew Bergman, *We're in the Money* (New York, 1972); Robert Sklar, *Movie-Made America* (New York, 1976), 175–214; Richard Pells, *Radical Visions, American Dreams* (New York, 1973); Lawrence Levine, "American Culture and the Great Depression," and "Hollywood's Washington: Film Images of National Politics during the Great Depression," in his *The Unpredictable Past* (New York, 1993), 231–55. On literature as conservative, see Charles Hearn, *The American Dream in The Great Depression* (Westport, Conn., 1981).

Others see popular entertainment as more insurgent during the 1930s and 1940s. See Lizabeth Cohen, *Making a New Deal* (Cambridge, U.K., 1990); David Stowe, *Swing Changes* (Cambridge, Mass., 1994); Michael Denning, *The Cultural Front: The Laboring of American Culture in the Twentieth Century* (New York, 1996); Lewis A. Erenberg, *Swingin' the Dream: Big Band Jazz and the Rebirth of American Culture* (Chicago, 1998); Lary May, *The Big Tomorrow: Hollywood and the Politics of the American Way* (Chicago, 2000); Robert S. McElvaine, *The Great Depression in America, 1929–1941* (New York, 1984), 196–223; Robert Sklar, *City Boys* (Princeton, 1992); Lawrence Levine, "The Folklore of Industrial Society: Popular Culture and Its Audiences," in Levine, *The Unpredictable Past*, 291–319. For modern dance, see Julia Foulkes, *Modern Bodies: Dance and American Modernism from Martha Graham to Alvin Ailey* (Chapel Hill, 2002).

On racial and civic nationalism, see Gary Gerstle, *American Crucible: Race and Nation in the Twentieth Century* (Princeton, 2001). For whiteness, see David R. Roediger, *The Wages of Whiteness: Race and the Making of the American Working Class* (London, 1991); *Towards the Abolition of Whiteness: Essays on Race, Politics, and Working Class History* (New York, 1994); Alexander Saxton, *The Rise and Fall of the White Republic: Class Politics and Mass Culture in Nineteenth-Century America* (New York, 1990); and Matthew Frye Jacobson, *Whiteness of a Different Color: European Americans and the Alchemy of Race* (Cambridge, Mass., 1998). For whiteness as it affected boxing, see Gail Bederman, *Manliness and Civilization: A Cultural History of Gender and Race in the United States, 1880–1917* (Chicago, 1995).

CHAPTER 1

1. Burris Jenkins, Jr., "Carrying the 'Males,'" *New York Evening Journal*, 15 July 1935, JLS, vol. 2.

2. The phrase, "private depression," is from "Almost a New Champion," *Boston Herald*, 27 June 1935, JLS, vol. 1.

3. Wolfgang Schivelbusch, *The Culture of Defeat: On National Trauma, Mourning, and Recovery*, trans. Jefferson Chase (New York, 2003; original 2001), 196–238, maintains that Germans linked World War I, inflation, and the Depression together.

4. For early childhood, see Max Schmeling, *An Autobiography*, trans. George von der Lippe (Chicago, 1998), 3–11, and Volker Kluge, *Max Schmeling, Eine Biographie in 15 Runden* (Berlin, 2004), 11–21. On the absence of boxing in Germany, see Wilbur Wood, "Germans in Boxing," *Ring* 21 (February 1933), 20–21.

5. For his adolescence, see Schmeling, *Autobiography*, 3–11, and Kluge, *Max Schmeling*, 11–21.

6. For Schmeling's time in the Rhine and details of his training and amateur boxing, see Kluge, *Max Schmeling*, 41–55. For more on the history of German boxing, see Knud Kohr and Martin Krauss, *Kampftage, Die Geschichte des deutschen Berufsboxens* (Göttingen, 2000); Birk Meinhardt, *Boxen in Deutschland* (Hamburg, 1996); and Sepp Scherbauer, *Die Grössen Boxsport Stars* (München, 1994).

7. Schmeling, *Autobiography*, 10–11, on commitment, and 12–14, on circus and risk. For the theme of male vitality in boxing and football, see John Higham, "Reorientation of American Culture in the 1890s," in John Higham, ed. Carl Guarneri, *Hanging Together* (New Haven, 2001), 173–97.

8. See Schmeling, *Autobiography*, 17–21, for his Berlin boxing years. Kluge, *Max Schmeling*, 68–107, discusses the role of Machon and Bülow, as does Wood, "Germans in Boxing," *Ring*, 21.

9. Kluge, *Max Schmeling*, 88–92, discusses his role as a national hero, and quotes *B-S*. See Siegfried Gehrmann, "Symbol of National Resurrection: Max Schmeling, German Sports Idol," *The International Journal of the History of Sport* 13 (1996), 101–2 for his rise.

10. Meinhardt, *Boxen in Deutschland*, 14–21, traces the early roots of German boxing. For new boxing language, see John Willett, *Art and Politics in the Weimar Period: The New Sobriety, 1917–1933* (New York, 1978), 102.

11. For the 1932 radio broadcast, see Rumpelstilzchen [Adolf Stein], *Feuilleton*, 23 June 1932, in *Nu wenn schon!* (Berlin, 1932), 36, as cited in Erik Jensen, "Crowd Control: Boxing Spectatorship and Social Order in Weimar Germany," in *Histories of Leisure*, ed. Rudy Koshar (New York, 2002), 83. For beer halls and the Nat Fleischer observation, see Wood, "Germans in Boxing," *Ring*, 21, 20. Meinhardt, *Boxen in Deutschland*, 41–49, notes the role of radio and newspaper coverage in making boxing a mass spectator sport.

12. Willy Meisl, *Der Sport am Scheidewege* (Heidelberg, 1921), 21, as cited in Gehrmann, "Symbol of National Resurrection," 106. Schmeling, *Autobiography*, 29–30.

13. My thoughts on the role of boxing in Weimar culture were stimulated by Gehrmann, "Symbol of Resurrection," Jensen, "Crowd Control," 79–101, and David Bathrick, "Max Schmeling on the Canvas: Boxing as an Icon of Weimar Culture," in *new german critique* 51 (fall 1990), 113–36.

14. Max Schmeling, *Errinerung* (Frankfurt, 1977), 100, as cited in Gehrmann, "Symbol of National Resurrection, 107–8.

15. Gehrmann, "Symbol of National Resurrection," 108–9. On his movie and song roles, see Schmeling, *Autobiography*, 50; on his relationship with Anny Ondra and their home, 67–77. The marriage of these two celebrities has continued to fascinate Germans. For their relationship, see Hans Leip, *Max und Anny: Romantischer Bericht von Aufsteig-zweier Sterne* (Hamburg, 1935), and Dorothea Frederick, *Max Schmeling und Anny Ondra: Ein Doppelleben* (Berlin, 2001).

16. For the poll, see "Vom Sportleben unserer Vierzehnjahrigen," *Die Leibesubungen* (20 June 1930), 339, as cited in Jensen, "Crowd Control," 99.
17. Schmeling, *Autobiography*, 17–18, 25–35. For Berlin as the cultural capital of German during the 1920s, see Willett, *Art and Politics in the Weimar Period*.
18. David Bathrick has made clear the avant-garde fascination with Schmeling in "Max Schmeling on the Canvas," *new german critique*, 113–36. Schmeling recalled his role in Weimar avant-garde culture in his *Autobiography*, 25–37.
19. For "swaying and whirling," see H. von Wedderkop, "Hans Breitenstrater," *Querschnitt* 1 (1921), 137–40, as cited in Bathrick, "Max Schmeling on the Canvas," 126. Wythe Williams, "Germans Welcome Americanization," *NYT*, 7 April 1929, E1. Thanks to Michael Ermath for this source. For one intellectual who witnessed the influence of American sport, see Ilya Ehrenburg cited in Willett, *Art and Politics of the Weimar Period*, 98. For those who promoted its influence, see Bertolt Brecht in Willett, *Art and Politics*, 102–3. See also Frank Thiess, "Die Geistigen und der Sports," *Die Neue Rundschau* 38:1 (1927), 299–302; Herman Kasack, "Sport als Lebensgefühl," *Die Weltbühne* 24:41 (9 October 1928), 557–58; Herman Bahr, "Geist und Sport," *Die neue Jugend* 1 (April/May 1928), all cited in Bathrick, "Max Schmeling on the Canvas," *new german critique*, 116–17.
20. For criticism of boxing as too commercial, see "Schmeling Fieber," in *Vorwärts*, 15 June 1930, n. p., and Jensen, "Crowd Control," 87–88.
21. "Der Kampf um die Amateurtitel in Hannover," *B-S* 5 (1927), 16, as cited in Jensen, "Crowd Control," 85. For the theme of Schmeling as national hero in the 1920s, see Gehrmann, "Symbol of National Resurrection," 109–11. The newspaper quote is from Karl Mintenbeck, *Es began 1848: Der Ruhrgebietssport im Spiegel der Presse* (Essen, 1988), 139, as quoted in Gehrmann, 110.
22. Kluge, *Max Schmeling*, 108–18, discusses the problems with Bülow. On Jacobs, see Schmeling, *Autobiography*, 43–53. On Fleischer's role, see Wood, "Germans in Boxing," 21. For theme of mongrel culture in New York, see Ann Douglas, *Terrible Honesty, Mongrel Manhattan in the 1920s* (New York, 1995), and Lewis A. Erenberg, *Steppin' Out: New York Nightlife and the Transformation of American Culture* (Westport, 1981).
23. On his similarity to Dempsey, see Nat Fleischer, "Max Schmeling, German Heavyweight Menace," *Ring* 8 (April 1929), 10.
24. For the Sharkey fight, see Schmeling, *Autobiography*, 59–70, and Jeffrey T. Sammons, *Beyond the Ring, the Role of Boxing in American Society* (Urbana, 1990), 80–1. For the million-dollar gate, see Wilbur Wood, "Max Schmeling Revives $1,000,000 Gate Talk," *Ring* 8 (June 1929), 5, 19. For other fouls, see Sammons, *Beyond the Ring*, 81–3. For a German description of the fight, see "Schmeling Weltmeister!" *B-S* (16 June 1930), 5–8.
25. Jack Dempsey, "Jack Dempsey Ranks Boxers for 1930," *Ring* 10 (February 1931), 7, for his disparagement of Schmeling. Charles F. Mathison, "Max Schmeling, a Technical Critique," *Ring* 10 (July 1931), 7. For an outright charge of cowardice, see A. D. Phillips, "Popularity Often Eludes Champions," *Ring* 10 (July 1931), 4.
26. See Schmeling, *Autobiography*, 81–83, for the German reaction. For the hit in the testicles, see "Schmeling . . . Weltmeister!," *Vorwärts*, 13 June 1930, n. p. For "Schmeling-humiliated" and related quotes, see Jonathon, "Zum Weltmeister geschlagen," *Vorwärts*, 13 June 1930, n. p. See Kluge, *Max Schmeling*, 158, for the booing; Nat Fleischer, "Sharkey, Stribling or Giant Carnera?" *Ring* 10 (March 1931), 6–7, for the view that Max was evading tough fights. For the Stribling fight and the record low attendance, "Schmeling Weltmeister," *Vorwärts*, 4 July 1931, n. p.

27. See Kluge, *Max Schmeling*, 178–79, for the second Sharkey match.

28. See Schmeling, *Autobiography*, 80–90, for his career low points. "Ende seine Karriere" in *B-S* (June 1933), and *DA*, cited in Ralf Müller, "Max Schmeling: Seine Rolle in nationalsocialistische Deutschland" (Thesis, Deutsche Sporthochschule, Cologne, 1996), 38 and 40, respectively. Demo, "Geht der Boxsport ein?" *Vorwärts*, 16 June 1931, n.p.

29. Joe Louis with Edna and Art Rust, Jr., *Joe Louis: My Life* (New York, 1978), 3–16 for his origins. See also Joe Louis Barrow, Jr., and Barbara Munder, *Joe Louis, Fifty Years an American Hero* (New York, 1988), 21–26. For more on his family background, see Gerald Astor, ". . . *And a Credit to His Race,*" *The Hard Life and Times of Joseph Louis Barrow, a. k. a. Joe Louis* (New York, 1974), 17–21. For his speech problems and his dislike of school, see Joe Louis as told to Meyer Berger and Barney Nagler, "My Story—Joe Louis," *Life* (8 November 1948), 128–29.

30. On the move to Detroit, see Louis and Rusts, *Joe Louis*, 10–14; Louis quoted, 12–13. See also Barrow and Munder, *Joe Louis*, 21–26, and Louis with Berger and Nagler, "My Story," 129. See James R. Grossman, *Land of Hope: Chicago, Black Southerners and the Great Migration* (Chicago, 1989), for an analysis of the Great Migration to the north.

31. On the Depression, Louis and Rusts, *Joe Louis*, 15–17, and Barrow and Munder, *Joe Louis*, 21–26. See Robert S. McElvaine, *The Great Depression, America 1929–1941* (New York, 1993), 43.

32. For his lack of education, see Alexander Joseph Young, Jr., "Joe Louis, Symbol, 1933–1949" (Ph.D. diss., University of Maryland, 1968), 39. On his speech impediment, see Barrow and Munder, *Joe Louis*, 43, 32, and Louis and Rusts, *Joe Louis*, 6–8.

33. Chicago Recreation Commission, *Chicago Recreation Survey, 1937* (Chicago, 1937), 2:79, cited in Gerald Gems, *Windy City Wars: Labor, Leisure and Sport in the Making of Chicago* (Latham, Md., 1997), 225–26; 193–97 argues that by the 1930s sport both reinforced ethnic working class culture and helped ease the transition to a revised, more pluralistic American culture. Barrow and Munder, *Joe Louis*, 34–36. Sheil quoted in Gems, *Windy City Wars*, 182; 182–85 discusses Sheil and the CYO. See also Tim Neary, "Crossing Parochial Boundaries: African-Americans and Interracial Catholic Social Action in Chicago, 1914–1954" (Ph.D. diss., Loyola University Chicago, 2003), and "Crossing Parochial Boundaries: Interracialism in Chicago's Catholic Youth Organization, 1930–1954," in *American Catholic Studies*, 114 (fall 2003), 23–37. For the Golden Gloves, see Nat Fleischer, "The Black Menace," *Ring* 14 (May 1935), 14.

34. See Louis and Rusts, *Joe Louis*, 20–22 for amateur boxing; 25 for his dislike of the 'natural' idea. Young, *Joe Louis, Symbol*, 40–41, discusses his amateur record. For a sociological account of the attraction of poor, black, young men to boxing, see Loïc Wacquant, *Body and Soul* (New York, 2004).

35. Louis and Rusts, *Joe Louis*, 26, for the Ford experience. Eric Hobsbawm, "Count Basie," in Hobsbawm, *Uncommon People: Resistance, Rebellion and Jazz* (New York, 1998), 248, discusses the role of athletics and sports for blacks and the working class.

36. Williams quoted on baseball in Louis and Rusts, *Joe Louis*, 44; money for clothes and welfare, 42–43. For McKinney's role, see Louis with Berger and Nagler, "My Story," 132.

37. Louis with Berger and Nagler, "My Story," 132–33.

38. Louis quoted on training in Louis, Berger, and Nagler, "My Story," 134. For other training stories, see Henry Armstrong, *Gloves, Glory and God, an Autobiography* (Westwood, N.J., 1956), 70–71.

39. For murder charge, see Louis, Berger, and Nagler, "My Story," 137.

40. Astor, "*A Credit to His Race,*" 32–33. For the growth of segregation of Detroit's middle class professionals, see Olivier Zunz, *The Changing Face of Inequality* (Chicago, 1982), 393–96. For growing white racism and violence in Detroit, see Kevin Boyle, *Arc of Justice: A Saga of Race, Civil Rights, and Murder in the Jazz Age* (New York, 2004), and Phyllis Vine, *One Man's Castle: Clarence Darrow in the Defense of the American Dream* (New York, 2004).

41. Astor, "*A Credit to His Race,*" 33–35.

42. For Roxborough's role in the community, see Astor, "*A Credit to His Race,*" 35–36. On the example of his managers, see Louis and Rusts, *Joe Louis,* 30, 39, 42–43. See also, Barrow and Munder, *Joe Louis,* 42–43. On Roxborough's background, see Chris Mead, *Champion Joe Louis: Black Hero in White America* (New York, 1985), 54–55. For his role as a model and as a second father, see Roxborough, "How I Discovered Joe Louis," *Ebony,* 66.

43. Roxborough quoted in Astor, "*A Credit to His Race,*" 38.

44. Astor, "*A Credit to His Race,*" 39–40.

45. Louis and Rusts, *Joe Louis,* 29–34. Roxborough, "How I Discovered Joe Louis," *Ebony,* 65–6. Roi Ottley, "Good Business Knows No Race," *AN,* 20 June 1936, JLS, vol. 21. Astor, "*And a Credit to His Race,*" 40–2.

46. Wilbur Wood, "Happy Days Are on Their Way," *Ring* 12 (October 1933), 4–5, 31.

47. Sammons, *Beyond the Ring,* 86.

48. Mead, *Champion,* 45–6. "Freak" is from Nat Fleischer, "What Next in Struggle of Heavies?" *Ring* 10 (August 1931), 2. For the fixed fights, see Sammons, *Beyond the Ring,* 87–88.

49. Sammons, *Beyond the Ring,* 90. For the equation of the stock market, business corruption, and crime in boxing, see John Lardner, "Lardner on Sports," *Morning (Portland) Oregonian,* JLS, vol. 1.

50. Blackburn quoted in Louis and Rusts, *Joe Louis,* 35–36.

51. For Molineaux and Jackson, see Fleischer, "The Black Menace," *Ring* 14 (May 1935), 15. For more on Jackson, see David K. Wiggins, "Peter Jackson and the Elusive Heavyweight Championship: A Black Athlete's Struggle against the Late Nineteenth Century Color-Line," *Journal of Sport History,* 12 (Summer 1985), 290–93. For Sullivan, see Michael T. Isenberg, *John L. Sullivan and His America* (Urbana, 1988). See also Elliott J. Gorn, *The Manly Art, Bare-Knuckle Prize Fighting in America* (Ithaca, 1986), 19–21, for the Crib-Molineaux matches.

52. My thoughts on the color line have been influenced by Gregory S. Rodriguez, "'Palaces of Pain'—Arenas of Mexican-American Dreams: Boxing and the Foundation of Ethnic Mexican Identities in Twentieth-Century Los Angeles" (Ph.D. diss., University of California, San Diego, 1999), especially 3–6, 23–28, and Sammons, *Beyond the Ring,* 31–47, 76–78, 96–129. For an overview of race in American sport, see Jeffrey T. Sammons, "'Race' and Sport: A Critical Historical Examination, *Journal of Sport History,* 21 (Fall 1994), 203–78.

53. Mead, *Champion,* 22–31, describes the fight, the riots, and general white reaction to Johnson. Thomas R. Hietala, *The Fight of the Century, Jack Johnson, Joe Louis, and the Struggle for Racial Equality* (Armonk, N.Y., 2002), 3–128, is insightful on

racism and Johnson's challenge to white supremacy. For other excellent discussions of Johnson, see Gail Bederman, *Manliness and Civilization: A Cultural History of Gender and Race in the United States, 1880–1917* (Chicago, 1995), 1–10, 41–42; Al-Tony Gilmore, *Bad Nigger! The National Impact of Jack Johnson* (Port Washington, N.Y., 1975); Randy Roberts, *Papa Jack: Jack Johnson and the Era of White Hopes* (New York, 1983); Geoffrey C. Ward, *Unforgivable Blackness: The Rise and Fall of Jack Johnson* (New York, 2004).

54. For the preference of foreigners over black contenders, see Sammons, *Beyond the Ring*, 73–78. On the British Home Office, see Patrick F. McDevitt, "May the Best Man Win: Sport, Masculinity and Nationalism in Great Britain and the Empire, 1884–1933" (Ph.D. diss., Rutgers University, 1999).

55. On Dempsey, see Randy Roberts, *Jack Dempsey, the Manassa Mauler* (Baton Rouge, 1979), and Sammons, *Beyond the Ring*, 67–72. For more on Tex Rickard, who deserves a biography, see Nat Fleischer, "Rickard Five Years Gone," *Ring* 13 (February 1934), 34–35.

56. On Wills, see Randy Roberts, *Jack Dempsey*, 141–45, Francis Albertine, "Harry Wills, Giant Negro Gladiator, Credit to the Game," *Ring* (August 1922), cited in Roberts, *Jack Dempsey*, 142. For the attitude of the New York State Athletic Commission on the color line, see Wilbur Wood, "Muldoon Maps Out Plans for Tunney's Successor," *Ring* 8 (October 1929), 7. Sammons, *Beyond the Ring*, 74–75, analyzes the Siki case in depth. For Fleischer on George Godfrey, see Nat Fleischer, "The Black Menace," *Ring* 14 (May 1935), 55.

CHAPTER 2

1. Roi Ottley, "Joe Louis and His People," in *New World A-Coming* (New York, 1943), 186–89.

2. Chester L. Washington, "Chez Says 1935 a Joe Louis Year," *PC*, 4 January 1936, sec. 2, p. 5.

3. Nat Fleischer, "The Black Menace," *Ring* 14 (May 1935), 14.

4. Ottley, "Joe Louis and His People," 186–89.

5. Joe Louis and Edna and Art Rust, Jr., *Joe Louis: My Life* (New York, 1978), 58. For a political cartoon that makes the themes of David and Goliath, Ethiopia, and black boxing explicit, see Holloway, "Loaded," *PC*, 3 August 1935, 10. "Dooley: Selects Joe Louis to Climb over Alps to Victory," *Philadelphia Record*, 25 June 1935, JLS, vol. 1. Ottley, "Joe Louis and His People," 186–89. Cheryl Greenberg, *Or Does It Explode: Black Harlem in the Great Depression* (New York, 1991), discusses the Harlem riot of March 19, 1935.

6. Will Rogers, "Rogers Figures Joe Louis Could Lick Il Duce, Too," *Cleveland Plain Dealer*, 27 June 1935, JLS, vol. 1. H. G. Salsinger, "Fury Grips Joe, He Ends Fight Quickly," *Detroit News*, 26 June 1935, JLS, vol. 1. Brisbane, and Balogh cited in Chris Mead, *Champion—Joe Louis: Black Hero in White America* (New York, 1985), 58–59. See "Police Squads to Guard Louis," *The Baltimore Sun*, 25 June 1935, JLS, vol. 1, for discussion of first big money mixed fight, the police, and the guards around Louis.

7. Ottley, "Joe Louis and His People," 186–89.

8. "What Now among the Heavyweights," *Ring* 14 (September 1935), 10. "Almost a New Champion," *Boston Herald*, 27 June 1935, JLS, vol. 1. George Clarens, quoted in the *Boston Transcript*, 25 June 1935, JLS, vol. 1. Richards Vidmer, "60,000 See Louis Knock Carnera Out in 6th Round," *New York Herald-*

Tribune, 26 June 1935, JLS, vol. 1. H.G. Salsinger, "Joe Louis Favored by Salsinger," *Detroit News*, 25 June 1935, JLS, vol. 1.

9. For restrictions on black contenders, see Nat Fleischer, "The Black Menace," *Ring* 14 (May 1935), 55. For fears of another Jack Johnson, see Grantland Rice, "Goals," *Birmingham News*, 25 June 1935, JLS, vol. 1, and "Richards Vidmer's Classic Comment on Joe Louis," reprinted in *PC*, 6 July 1935, sec. 2, p. 5.

10. "Paul Gallico—*New York Daily News*," reprinted in *PC*, October 1935, sec. 2, p. 5. For "Africa, the dark continent," see Davis Walsh, "Louis Possesses Punch and Science of Masters," *Birmingham News*, 26 June 1935, 10. Grantland Rice, "Carnera Crushed," *New York Sun*, 26 June 1935, JLS, vol. 1. Frank Graham column, *New York Sun*, 25 June 1935, JLS, vol. 1.

11. "Kinky head," in Joe Williams, *Cleveland Press* (perhaps), 27 June 1935, JLS, vol. 1. William H. Wiggins, Jr., "Boxing's Sambo Twins: Racial Stereotypes in Jack Johnson and Joe Louis Newspaper Cartoons," *Journal of Sport History*, 15 (winter 1988), 242–54, for cartoons.

12. Gerald Early, "The Black Intellectual and the Sport of Prizefighting," in *The Culture of Bruising: Essays on Prizefighting, Literature, and Modern American Culture* (Hopewell, N.J., 1994), 5–12. On puncher and boxer, killer and craftsman, see M. Jill Dupont, "The Self in the Ring, The Self in Society: Boxing and American Culture from Jack Johnson to Joe Louis" (Ph.D. diss., University of Chicago, 2000), 2:327–54. Nat Fleischer, "The Black Menace," *Ring* 14 (May 1935), 14.

13. Nat Fleischer, "Better Get Those White Hopes Ready!" *Ring* 14 (September 1935), 2.

14. For hybrid movie heroes, see Lary May, *The Big Tomorrow: Hollywood and the Politics of the American Way* (Chicago, 2000), 55–99. On self-possession, see Susan Douglas, *Listening In* (New York, 1999), 208. Poker face from *Philadelphia Tribune*, 10 January 1935, as cited in Thomas R. Hietala, *The Fight of the Century, Jack Johnson, Joe Louis, and the Struggle for Racial Equality* (Armonk, N.Y., 2002), 162.

15. On his management team, see Louis and Rusts, *Joe Louis*, 29–34. Roxborough, "How I Discovered Joe Louis," *Ebony*, 65–66. Roi Ottley, "Good Business Knows No Race," *AN*, 20 June 1936, JLS, vol. 21. Letter to Editor, *PC*, 11 May 1935, sec. 2, p. 2.

16. Louis and Rusts, *Joe Louis*, 4. Roi Ottley, "Good Business Knows No Race," *AN*, 20 June 1936.

17. Louis and Rusts, *Joe Louis*, 4, 47–48. Ottley, "Good Business Knows No Race."

18. On the advice and example of his managers, see Louis and Rusts, *Joe Louis*, 30, 39, 42–43. Blackburn quoted in Gerald Astor, ". . . *And a Credit to His Race*," *The Hard Life and Times of Joseph Louis Barrow, a. k. a. Joe Louis* (New York, 1974), 42. Roxborough quoted in "How I Discovered Joe Louis," 67. Mead, *Champion*, 51–54, discusses the crafting of Louis's image, as does Thomas R. Hietala, *The Fight of the Century*, 158–64.

19. For Louis's marriage, see Marva Louis, "Why I Quit Joe," *Ebony* (December 1949), 61–62, 64–71.

20. Roxborough cited in Astor, "*And a Credit to His Race*," 42. Nat Fleischer, "Louis' Rise Revives an Old Topic," *Ring* 14 (May 1935), 3. John Roxborough, "How I Discovered Joe Louis." For Blackburn, see Louis and Rusts, *Joe Louis*, 35–37. For the image of his handlers as naïve and idealistic, see Steve Hanagan, "Black Gold," *Saturday Evening Post*, 20 June 1936, JLS, vol. 23.

21. For Roxborough's desire to do good, see Joe Louis, *My Life Story* (New York, 1947), 196–97. On the black dolls, see Louis and Rusts, *Joe Louis*, 39. The watermelon story is from an interview by Chris Mead with Harry Markson and Barney Nagler, as cited in Mead, *Champion*, 57. The craps photo is cited in Hietala, *The Fight of the Century*, 161.

22. *Philadelphia Tribune*, 10 October 1935, as cited in Hietala, *The Fight of the Century*, 161. Jonathon Mitchell, "Joe Louis Never Smiles," *New Republic* (9 October 1935), 239. For deadpan, and the absence of buffoonery, see Daniel M. Daniel, "Sepia Socker Louis Mauler with Mission," *Ring* 14 (September 1935), 6.

23. For humor and practical jokes, see Astor, *And a Credit to His Race*, 194–96.

24. On the speech impediment and general upbringing, see Joe Louis Barrow, Jr., and Barbara Munder, *Joe Louis, Fifty Years an American Hero* (New York, 1988), 43, 32; Louis and Rusts, *Joe Louis*, 6–8.

25. Dan Burley, "The Love Life of Joe Louis," *Ebony* (July 1951), 22–26, 28–32, 34.

26. Davis J. Walsh, "Louis Possesses Punch and Science of Masters," *Birmingham News*, 26 June 1935, 10. For white support of Louis, see Russell J. Cowan, "Solid South Decides Joe Louis Must Be Somebody," *CD*, 13 April 1935, 11. Quote is from "Daily Press Wants Louis as Champion," *CD*, 6 July 1935, 13. Jimmy Johnson, *Richmond Times-Dispatch* 19 June 1936, JLS, vol. 21. Vidmer quoted in "Richards Vidmer's Classic Comment on Joe Louis," reprinted in *PC*, 6 July 1935, sec. 2, p. 5. George Clarens, "The Pulse," *Boston Transcript*, 26 June 1935, JLS, vol. 1.

27. "Dooley: Selects Joe Louis to Climb over the Alp to Victory," *Philadelphia Record*, 25 June 1935, JLS, vol. 1. Daniel, "Sepia Socker," 6–7.

28. Robert McElvaine, *The Great Depression in America, 1929–1941* (New York, 1984). Daniel, "Sepia Socker," 6. For the plan and his Brain Trust, see Nat Fleischer, "Better Get Those White Hopes Ready!" *Ring* 14 (September 1935), 2. *Philadelphia Tribune*, either 10 January or 8 August 1935, n. p., as cited in Hietala, *The Fight of the Century*, 160.

29. Goodwin quoted in *CD*, 13 July 1935, n. p. *The Crisis* (June 1935), cover (August 1935), 241. Roi Ottley, *New World A-Coming* (Boston, 1943), 189. "Owens and Louis, Our Ambassadors," *PC*, 8 June 1935, n. p. This paragraph owes a good deal to Hietala, *The Fight of the Century*, 158–63. For citizen, see Daniel, "Sepia Socker," 44. C. L. R. James, "Joe Louis and Jack Johnson," in *C. L. R. James on the 'Negro Question,'* ed. by Scott McLemee (Jackson, Miss., 1996), 60–62.

30. Lester Rodney, "What Has Revived the Boxing Game?" *The Daily Worker*, 7 June 1938, 8. Jack Copeland, "Looking 'Em Over with Jack Copeland," *Wichita Beacon*, 23 June 1937, JLS, vol. 38.

31. Max Schmeling, *An Autobiography*, trans. George B. von der Lippe (Chicago, 1998), 89–90. See also Arno Hellmis, *Die Geschichte eines Kampfers* (Berlin, 1937), 26–30.

32. Volker Kluge, *Max Schmeling, Eine Biographie in 15 Runden* (Berlin, 2004), 211–13. Schmeling, *Autobiography*, 101.

33. "Schmeling schlägt Neusel," *B-S* (20 August 1934), 5, 8. For party activity at the bout, see Ralf Müller, "Max Schmeling: Seine Rolle in nationalsozialistischen Deutschland" (thesis, Deutsche Sporthochschule, Köln, 1996), 68–69.

34. For the role of the authorities in the Hamas match, see Kluge, *Max Schmeling*, 218. Johnston quoted on Hamas bout in *B-S* (14 January 1935), 3. The quote from *DA* is from 9 March 1935, 14.

35. For Hitler's economic and social policies, see John A. Garraty, "The New Deal, National Socialism, and the Great Depression," *American Historical Review*, 78 (1973), 907–44; David Schoenbaum, *Hitler's Social Revolution* (New York, 1966); Richard Grundberger, *The 12-Year Reich, a Social History of Nazi Germany 1933–1945* (New York, 1971), 28–31. George Mosse, *Nazi Culture, Intellectual, Cultural and Social Life in the Third Reich* (New York, 1966), analyzes the Nazi effort to transform German culture and earn the nation respect in the world.

36. For his role in the Olympics and other contacts with Hitler, see Schmeling, *Autobiography*, 81–95

37. Schmeling, *Autobiography*, 86–88.

38. For the notion that the Depression and resultant turmoil made Germans psychically return to the traumas of the post–WWI era, see Wolfgang Schivelbusch, *The Culture of Defeat: On National Trauma, Mourning, and Recovery*, trans. Jefferson Chase (New York, 2003), 196–238. Peter Lowenberg, "The Psychohistorical Origins of the Nazi Youth Cohort," *American Historical Review*, 76 (December 1971), reprinted as "The Appeal to Youth," in *The Nazi Revolution*, ed. by John L. Snell (Lexington, Mass., 1973), 93–116, argues that the Depression awakened traumas in German youth of abandonment by fathers during the war and subjection to starvation.

39. Schmeling, *Autobiography*, 87–95. See also Robert Weisbord and Norbert Hedderich, "Max Schmeling Righteous Ring Warrior?" *History Today* (January 1993), 36–41, and Frank Deford with a special report by Anita Verschoth, "Almost a Hero," *Sports Illustrated* 95 (3 December 2001), 64–74.

40. For Nazi ideas about race training and boxing, see Joseph Goebbels, quoted in Clarence Lusane, *Hitler's Black Victims: The Historical Experiences of Afro-Germans, European Blacks, Africans, and African Americans in the Nazi Era* (New York, 2003), 215. For Hitler's views on physical education training and boxing, see Adolf Hitler, *Mein Kampf*, trans. Ralph Mannheim (Boston, 1971), 407–9; for boxing, 409–10. See Schmeling, *Autobiography*, 102, for models for German youth. See Bruno Malitz, *Die Leibesübungen in der nationalsozialistichen Idee* (München, 1934), 12, for the health of the volk. For more on this subject, see Müller, "Max Schmeling," 41–44. For physical education, see Hajo Bernett, *Unterricht an der nationalsozialistische Schule: Der Schulsport an den höhern Schulen Preussens 1933–1940* (Sankt Augustin, 1985), G. A. Carr, "Sport and Party Ideology in the Third Reich," *Canadian Journal of History of Sport and Physical Education* 5 (1974), 1–9, and Grundberger, *12-Year Reich*, 287–88. John Hoberman, *Sport and Political Ideology* (Austin, 1984), 94–95, 162–69, discusses the attempts to create the new fascist man. Barbara Keys, "Dictatorship of Sport: Nationalism, Internationalism, and Mass Culture in the 1930s" (Ph.D. diss., Harvard University, 2001), 138–47, analyzes the Nazi shift to include international sports.

41. For Hitler's views on boxing, see Hitler, *Mein Kampf*, 409–10. See Schmeling, *Autobiography*, 139, for Hitler's use of sports as political validation.

42. Hitler, *Mein Kampf*, 409–412. For the virile young man, see Hoberman, *Sport and Political Ideology*, 94. The appeal to boxers by Erich Rüdiger, Reichsfachamtsleiter, is in *B-S* 16 (23 March 1936), 17.

43. For the reorganization of sports, see Hans von Tschammer und Osten, "German Sport," in *Germany Speaks* (London, 1938), 219–28, and G. A. Carr, "The Synchronization of Sport and Physical Education under National Socialism," *The Canadian Journal of History of Sport and Physical Education* 10 (1979), 15–35. On changes in boxing, see Müller, "Max Schmeling," 41–43, 51–61. The rules

were printed in *B-S* (4 April 1933). See also Kluge, *Max Schmeling*, 192. Sander Gilman, *The Jew's Body* (New York, 1991), 38–59 and 169–93, discusses the perception of Jewish physical traits as distinctive and degenerate. Arnd Krüger, "Der Einfluss des faschistischen Sportmodels Italiens auf den nationalistichen Sport," in *Sport und Politik, 1918–1939/40: Proceedings, ICOSH Seminar*, ed. Megan Olsen (Otta, 1998), 226–32, notes that the Nazis abandoned democratically elected sports clubs for the Italian fascist model of party-run hierarchical sports federations.

44. For lists of Jewish, Gypsy, and Afro-German athletes affected by the new rules, see Lusane, *Hitler's Black Victims*, 217, and Kluge, *Max Schmeling*, 192–96.

45. Nat Fleischer, "Nat Fleischer Says," *Ring* 14 (August 1935), 24. "Negroes Who Starred in 1936," *Ring* 16 (February 1937), 21, and Ted Carroll, "Colored Boxers Make Progress," *Ring* 16 (March 1937), 29, 44. Nat Fleischer, "Nat Fleischer says:" *Ring* 12 (June 1933), 8, and 14 (October 1935), 18–19.

46. Clarens, "The Pulse," *Boston Transcript*, 26 June 1935, JLS, vol. 1. Steven Hanagan, "Black Gold," *Saturday Evening Post* (20 June 1936), JLS, vol. 23.

47. Nat Fleischer, "Nat Fleischer says," *Ring* 14 (January 1936), 14.

48. For the white southern press, see Jeffrey T. Sammons, "Boxing as a Reflection of Society: The Southern Reaction to Joe Louis," *Journal of Popular Culture*, 16 (spring 1983), 22–23.

49. Steven Riess, *Sports and the American Jew* (Syracuse, 1998), 21–22. See also Peter Levine, *Ellis Island to Ebbets Field, Sport and the American Jewish Experience* (New York, 1992), 144–89.

50. For Fleischer, see Nat Fleischer, *Fifty Years at Ringside* (New York, 1958), and Riess, *Sports and the American Jew*, 21–22.

51. Nat Fleischer, *Black Dynamite: Story of the Negro in Boxing*, 4 vols. (New York, 1938).

52. Louis and Rusts, *Joe Louis*, 49–52; "True hustler," quoted, 49. Hanagan, "Black Gold," *Saturday Evening Post*, JLS, vol. 23. Barrow and Munder, *Joe Louis*, 45–47. Mead, *Champion*, 35–46, has the best discussion of the battle between Jacobs and Madison Square Garden. For a skimpy biography of Jacobs, see Daniel M. Daniel, *The Mike Jacobs Story* (New York, 1949). For the Johnston quote, see Joe Louis as told to Meyer Berger and Barney Nagler, "My Story—Joe Louis," *Life* (8 November 1948), 142.

53. For Jacobs's machinations, see Astor, *A Credit to His Race*, 66–80, and Mead, *Champion*, 35–46.

54. "You and Joe are colored," quoted in Barrow and Munder, *Joe Louis*, 47; Johnston "a bigot," from Nagler, *Brown Bomber* (New York, 1972), 43–44, as quoted in Mead, *Champion*, 38–39. Louis's account of Jacobs's lack of prejudice is from Louis and Rusts, *Joe Louis*, 134. For outsiders, see Mead, 44. Hanagan, "Black Gold," *Saturday Evening Post*, JLS, vol. 23.

55. Harvey Thorne, "Baer and Carnera," *Ring* 14 (September 1935), 18–19. For a discussion of Baer, see Jeffrey T. Sammons, *Beyond the Ring: The Role of Boxing in American Society* (Urbana, Ill., 1990), 91–95, and Mead, *Champion*, 66–74.

56. For details of the bout, see Mead, *Champion*, 70–71.

57. McCarthy and Baer quoted in Mead, *Champion*, 71.

58. Shirley Povich, column, *Washington Post*, 25 September 1935, as quoted in Mead, *Champion*, 73–74. Ed Frayne, "Ed Frayne—*New York American*," reprinted in *PC*, 5 October 1935, sec. 2, p. 5.

59. B. Weldon Hayes, "Letter to Editor," *AN*, 5 October 1935, JLS, vol. 8. Theophilus Lewis, 'The Man We Want to Be," *AN*, 5 October 1935, JLS, vol. 8.

60. C. L. R. James, "Joe Louis and Jack Johnson," in *C. L. R. James on the 'Negro Question,'* ed. Scott McLemee (Jackson, Miss., 1996), 60–61. Thanks to Jeffrey Kerr-Ritchie for this source.

CHAPTER 3

1. Adolf Hitler's remarks are quoted in Max Schmeling, *An Autobiography*, trans. George von der Lippe (Chicago, 1998), 111. See *B-S* (15 July 1935) and (August 1935) for the magazine's view of Louis. "Schmeling Weighs Offer for Louis Fight; Nazi Reaction on Racial Grounds Involved," *NYT*, 9 July 1935, JLS, vol. 2. Roi Ottley, *New World A-Coming* (New York, 1943), 195. For the press decrees, see *NS Presse an Weisungen der Vorkriegszeit Edition and Dokumentation*, Bd. 4/II: 1936 (Munich, 1993), 645–46. *VB*, 6 June 1936. For "German character," see Ludwig Hayman, "Schmeling oder Louis?" *VB*, 18 June 1936.

2. "Schmeling's Departure," *NYT*, 16 April 1936, JLS, vol. 16.

3. Schmeling, *Autobiography*, 87–95, discusses how flattered he was by Hitler.

4. Schmeling, *Autobiography*, 147, for the film company; 105, for knowing people forced out. Robert Weisbord and Norbert Hedderich, "Max Schmeling Righteous Ring Warrior?" *History Today* (January 1993), 39–40, has an in-depth discussion of Schmeling's friendships with Jews.

5. All quotes are from Schmeling, *Autobiography*, 109–12.

6. Schmeling, *Autobiography*, 101–2.

7. Schmeling, *Autobiography*, 101–3. See Weisbord and Hedderich, "Max Schmeling," 39–40 for more on Jacobs, and Frank Deford, with a special report by Anita Verschoth, "Almost a Hero," *Sports Illustrated* 95 (3 December 2001), 64–74.

8. Schmeling, *Autobiography*, 102–3.

9. Daniel M. Daniel, "Sepia Socker Louis Mauler with Mission," *Ring* 14 (September 1935), 44. Nat Fleischer, "Up the Ladder for Max; Down the Chute for Max," *Ring* 14 (December 1935), 3, 4. Nat Fleischer, "Nat Fleischer Says," *Ring* 15 (March 1936), 18.

10. Daniel M. Daniel, "Slugging Louis Eager for Vacation Days," *Ring* 15 (April 1936), 2–3, for Dempsey and Johnson skepticism, and racial opinions. Hype Igoe, "Dempsey or Louis," *Ring* 15 (May 1936), 2–5, for Johnson's comments. Johnson repeated his criticism in Jack Johnson, "Louis Analyzed," *Ring* 15 (July 1936), 14, 45.

11. For these and other press stereotypes of Louis, see Chris Mead, *Champion—Joe Louis: Black Hero in White America* (New York, 1985), 87–89.

12. Harry Stillwell Edwards quoted in Mead, *Champion*, 89. Ed Van Every, *Joe Louis, Man and Super-Fighter* (New York, 1936), as cited in Mead, 90–91.

13. Hype Igoe, "Max Won't Be Able to Tag Jim So Easily," *Ring* 15 (September 1936), 11. Other favorable comments on Schmeling cited in Mead, *Champion*, 93–94.

14. Harrington, "Fight Prophecy," New York *AN*, 6 June 1936, JLS, vol. 19. Harrington, "When and If Joe Louis Loses," *AN*, 20 June 1936, JLS, vol. 21. "Execution" quoted in L. E. Harrington, "Schmeling Won't Come Out for 4th," *AN*, 20 June 1936, 4.

15. Eric Foner, *The Story of American Freedom* (New York, 1998), 207–10, discusses the positive and negative aspects of the New Deal for African Americans. For the battle against the Pullman Company, see Susan Eleanor Hirsch, *After the Strike, a Century of Labor Struggle at Pullman* (Urbana, 2003), 128–55.

16. For the upsurge of black popular cultural activity, see Gena Caponi-Tabery, "Jump for Joy: The Jump Trope in African America, 1937–1941," *Prospects*, 24 (1999): 521–74.

17. For Louis as a folk hero, see Levine, *Black Culture and Black Consciousness*, 420–28, and William H. Wiggins, Jr., "Joe Louis: American Folk Hero," in *Sport and the Color Line: Black Athletes and Race Relations in Twentieth-Century America*, eds. Patrick B. Miller and David K. Wiggins (New York, 2004), 127–46. For Louis as a model of fair play, see Sez Chez, "History's Highest-Price Inch," *PC*, 20 April 1935, sec. 2, p. 4. For Joe Louis as a messiah figure, see Wilson Jeremiah Moses, *Black Messiahs and Uncle Toms: Social and Literary Manipulations of a Religious Myth* (University Park, Pa., 1982), 155–82.

18. "Writes Song for 'Bomber,' " *PC*, 20 June 1936, sec. 2, p. 4. J. S. Hayes, "What I Think about Joe Louis and His Future Fights," *PC*, 26 April 1936, sec 2, p. 4. Ad for Louis Statue, *PC*, 6 June 1936, sec. 2, p. 5. "Louis Spends $25,000 to Keep Faith with Kid-Fans," *PC*, 6 June 1936, sec. 2, p. 5.

19. For black audience estimates, see Al Monroe, "Fight Sidelights," *CD*, 28 September 1935, 14.

20. "*Defender* to Issue Louis Fight Extra," *CD*, 21 September 1935, 1, 4.

21. For ads, see *PC*, 22 June 1935, sec. 2, p. 5; *PC*, 22 June 1935, sec. 1, p. 7.

22. Examples of the letters are in Russel J. Cowans, "Joe Louis' Fan Mail Keeps Large Office Force Busy," *CD*, 24 August 1935, 13, and Cowans, "Fan Mail Piles Up for Joe Louis," *CD*, 13 July 1935, 14.

23. For "patron of swing," see Mercer Ellington and Stanley Dance, *Duke Ellington in Person: An Intimate Memoir* (New York, 1979), 79. Information on Cross comes from Lary May, whose mother had a long-term relationship with the comedian.

24. Dizzy Gillespie with Al Fraser, *To Be, or not . . . to Bop* (Garden City, 1979), 288–89. Billy Rowe, "Billy Rowe Places Blame for Armstrong's Failure on Air at Door of Program's Sponsors," *PC*, 10 July 1937, 21. Paul Oliver, *The Meaning of the Blues* (Toronto, 1963), 324–25. "Joe Louis 'Glorified' in Song Hit," *PC*, 10 July 1937, p. 13. I transcribed these songs from the CD, *Joe Louis: An American Hero*, Rounder Records (82161-1106-2, 2001), with liner notes by Rena Kosersky and "Reflections on the Joe Louis Recordings," by William H. Wiggins, Jr.

25. *Joe Louis: An American Hero*, Rounder Records.

26. George S. Schuyler, "Joe Louis Performed Like a Master Surgeon," *PC*, 21 December 1935, Sec. 2, p. 5.

27. Richard Wright, *Lawd Today* (Boston, 1986), 52, 146–47.

28. Richard Wright, "Joe Louis Uncovers Dynamite," *New Masses*, 17 (October 1935), reprinted in the *Richard Wright Reader*, ed. Ellen Wright and Michael Fabre (New York, 1997), 32–34.

29. "Courier Gets Exclusive Interview with Schmeling," *PC*, 9 May 1936, 1, 4.

30. Max Schmeling as told to Paul Gallico, "This Way I Beat Joe Louis," *Saturday Evening Post* (29 August 1936), 5–7, 40–41. For study of fight films, see Schmeling, *Autobiography*, 111, for "I saw something," 112–13.

31. Joe Louis and Art and Edna Rust, Jr., *Joe Louis: My Life* (New York, 1978), 82–84. Mead, *Champion*, 81–86, has an excellent discussion of Louis's slack training regimen.

32. "Schmeling hat wieder heimgenfunden," *VB*, 21 June 1936, JLS, vol. 22. "Ich halte den Daumen," *DA*, 19 June 1936, 16.

33. On the drama of the bout, see Nat Fleischer, "The Fall of the Mighty!" *Ring* 15 (August 1936), 6. This description of the fight is from Max Schmeling as told to Paul Gallico, "This Way I Beat Joe Louis," *The Saturday Evening Post* (5 September 1936), 3, 10–11, 32, 34–35; James T. Farrell, "The Fall of Joe Louis," *The Nation* (27 June 1936), 834–35; and the film, *Max Schmeling's Sieg—Ein Deutscher Sieg*, 1936, Bundesfilmarchiv, Berlin.

34. Schmeling as told to Gallico, "This Way I Beat Joe Louis," 3, 10–11, 32, 34–35. Farrell, "The Fall of Joe Louis," 835–36.

35. Schmeling as told to Gallico, "This Way I Beat Joe Louis," 3, 10–11, 32, 34–35. Farrell, "The Fall of Joe Louis," 835–36. Nat Fleischer, "The Fall of the Mighty!" *Ring*, 6, describes the blow after the fifth round as the critical one. Based on my viewings of various film versions of the bout, I agree.

36. Farrell, "The Fall of Joe Louis," *The Nation*, 836. Fleischer, "The Fall of the Mighty!" *Ring*, 6.

37. Ralf Müller, "Max Schmeling: Seine Rolle in nationalisozialistischen Deutschland" (thesis, Deutsche Sporthochschule, Köln, 1996), 95–98. For the poem, see H. O. Wegener, "Joe ist k.o.!" *B-S*, 22 June 1936, 10. AP quote from Ottley, *New World A-Coming*, 195. For Goebbels's remarks, see Hgb Elke Froelich, *Die Tagebücher von Joseph Goebbels*, Teil I, Bd 3/N.2 (München, 2001), 20 June 1936, 112. Hicks, "Rund um den grössten Knock-out," *HA*, 27/28 June 1936, 48.

38. For Congress and some international reaction, see "Schmeling's Sieg ein Deutscher Sieg," *Leipziger Nueste Nachrichten*, 21 June 1936, JLS, vol. 23. George Spandau, "Schmeling's a Cultural Victory," *Der Weltkampf*, as reprinted in English in *Crisis*, 43 (October 1936): 301, 309. "England an Schmeling's Sieg," *B-S*, vol. 16 (1 July 1936), 21. For comment on French and Italian reaction, see "Der Führer beglückwünscht Schmeling an Der sensationelle Sieg des deutschen Boxer," *HA*, 20–21 June 1936, JLS, vol. 23. For Nurmi quote, see "An Schmeling's K. O. Sieg," *VB* 21 June 1936, JLS, vol. 22.

39. On the receptions, see "Max ist wieder in Berlin," *VB*, 21 June 1936, 1–2, and "Luftschiff 'Hindenburg' bringt den Sieger Schmeling Heim," *VB*, 21 June 1936, 1–2.

40. All quotes are from "Max Schmeling Sieg—Ein Deutscher Sieg," 1936, Bundesfilmarchiv, Berlin. For more on the premiere, see Kluge, *Max Schmeling*, 256.

41. Hellmis quoted in the film, "Max Schmeling Sieg—Ein Deutscher Sieg."

42. For the Siegfried myth, see E. H. Gombrich, "Myth and Reality in German War-Time Broadcasts," *Film and Radio Propaganda in World War II*, ed. K. R. M. Short (Knoxville, 1983), 19–20. For his refusal to "dance around the golden calf," see "Schmeling ist Sportsmann," *DA*, 24 June 1936, 15. For the early view of Schmeling, see "Schmeling boxt doch," *B-S* vol. 10 (10 March 1930), 5–6. The Jewish press was a constant target. See "Echoen von Schmeling's Sieg," *Deutsche Weckruf und Beobachter* 25 June 1936, n.p.

43. Richard Mandell, *The Nazi Olympics* (Urbana, Il., 1987; orig., 1971), 121 discusses the loudspeakers and radio. For the press see, the *National-Blatt*, 6 July 1936, *Berlin Zeitung am Mittag*, 27 June 1936, and *DA* as reported in the *NYT*, 21 June 1936, as cited in Mandell, *Nazi Olympics*, 120–1. For the German reaction to the American "insults" to German honor, see "Die Pressestimmen Amerikas," *B-S*, vol. 16 (1 July 1936), 2.

44. For the concern about World War I defeat, national humiliation, and racial pollution, see George Mosse, *Nationalism and Sexuality: Respectability and Abnormal Sexuality in Modern Europe* (New York, 1985). For the decisive role of World War I in shaping the young people attracted to Nazism, see Peter Lowenberg, "The Appeal to Youth," in *The Nazi Revolution*, ed. John L. Snell (Lexington, Mass., 1973), 93–116. For jazz as racial pollution, see Michael H. Kater, *Different Drummers: Jazz in the Culture of Nazi Germany* (New York, 1992), and Berndt Ostendorf, "Subversive Reeducation? Jazz as a Liberating Force in Germany and Europe," *Revue d'Etudes Americaines*, ed. Bernard Vincent. Hors Series: " 'Play It Again Sim'. . . . Hommages a Sim Copans" (December 2001), 54–72. For the anxiety over with mixed-race unions, see Kenneth L. Kusmer, "Toward a Comparative History of Racism and Xenophobia in the United States and German, 1865–1933," in *Bridging the Atlantic: The Question of American Exceptionalism in Perspective*, ed. Elisabeth Glaser and Hermann Wellenreuther (Cambridge, England, 2001), 161–62. Goebbels saw Hitler and Schmeling's achievements as triumphs of the will—they achieved the impossible. See Ralf Georg Reuth, *Goebbels*, trans. Krishna Winston (New York, 1993), 164.

45. Emil Volkmer, "Negers in Boxen," *B-S*, vol. 16 (23 March 1936), 2. Massaquoi, *Destined to Witness: Growing Up Black in Nazi Germany* (New York, 2001), 115–18, 120–21. Hans Botticher, "Schmelings Anlauf zur Z. Weltmeisterschaft," *SNT*, 15 June 1936. For the black head as hard, see "Die Stimmen an Schmeling-Louis," *B-S*, vol. 16 (1 July 1936), 2–3, "close to nature," 5.

46. For "clay face," see "Schwarz oder Weiss? Joe Louis vs. Max Schmeling Kampf," *B-S*, vol. 16 (12 June 1936), 3. For the Nazi view of the United States and miscegenation, see Ivar Lissner, "Glück liegt nirgends auf der Strasse," *DA*, 13 May 1936, 3–4. "News aus Amerika," *B-S*, vol. 15 (19 August 1935), 9.

47. Spandau, "Schmeling's A Cultural Victory," *Der Weltkampf* (August 1936), as reprinted in *The Crisis* 43 (October 1936), 301. Schmeling, *Autobiography*, 139–40.

48. Schmeling, *Autobiography*, 144–47.

49. Schmeling, *Autobiography*, 127. "Despite Alleged Plot, Joe Must Mend His Ways," *CD*, 27 June 1936, 1, 4.

50. "Louis Downcast and Sullen over Defeat," Helena *Daily Independent*, 22 June 1936, JLS, vol. 23. Maya Angelou, *I Know Why the Caged Bird Sings* (New York, 1993), 111–15. Lena Horne, and Richard Shickel, *Lena* (Garden City, 1965), 75. See also Milt Hinton as quoted in Ira Gitler, *Swing to Bop* (New York, 1985), 11. "Joe and Wife in Firm Denial of Dope Yarn; Jealousy Is Blamed," *Chicago American*, 14 July 1936, JLS, vol. 23.

51. Adam Clayton Powell, Jr., "No Joe Louis Eulogy," *AN*, 27 June 1936, JLS, vol. 23. Roi Ottley, "Hectic Harlem," *AN*, 27 June 1936, JLS, vol. 23.

52. Al Monroe, "N. Y. Random Thoughts," *CD*, 27 June 1936, 12. The Blackbirds of 1936 example is from Philip Furia, *Skylark: The Life and Times of Johnny Mercer* (New York, 2003), 90. Thanks to Kent Mullikin for the reference. For the woman who lost $50, see "$50 Wager Puts Woman in Asylum," *CD*, 27 June 1936, 1.

53. Al Monroe, "Probe Report that Joe Louis Was Doped," *CD*, 27 June 1936, JLS, vol. 23. Ira F. Lewis, "Was Joe Louis Doped?" *PC*, 27 June 1936, sec. 2, p. 4. "Did Max or Marva Beat Joe?" *PC*, 4 July 1936, JLS, vol. 23.

54. Louis and Rusts, *Joe Louis*, 90–93. Edgar T. Rouzeau, "Harlem in Mourning over Louis Setback," *PC*, 27 June 1936, sec. 2, p. 5.

55. Louis and Rusts, *Joe Louis*, 90–93. Warren Susman, "Culture and Commitment," in Susman, *Culture as History* (New York, 1984), 184–210, analyzes shame and commitment as a theme of the 1930s. Louis Armstrong, "Says Joe Louis Took It like a Man, So Should We," *PC*, 4 July 1936, sec. 2, p. 7.

56. Grantland Rice, "The Sportlight," *New York Sun*, 22 June 1936, JLS, vol. 23. Davis J. Walsh, "Writer Claims Joe Louis Is All Washed Up," *Rockford Register-Republic*, 23 June 1936, JLS, vol. 23. Walter Stewart, "Joe's Future in Own Hands," *New York World-Telegram*, 22 June 1936, JLS, vol. 23. Bill Corum, "Louis's Loss Was Boxing's Gain," *New York Evening Journal*, 22 June 1936, JLS, vol. 23, was sympathetic, but saw Louis's defeat as devastating.

57. C. Cecil Craigne, "Louis' Defeat Gives South Chance to Tell How It Felt," *CD*, 4 July 1935, vol. 23.

58. For the many writers who predicted Louis would win a rematch, see Paul Mickelson, "'Experts Dying Hard' on Max's Victory; They Give Some Views," *Rocky Mountain News*, 21 June 1936, JLS, vol. 22. S. T. Holland, "I'll Come Back," *PC*, 27 June 1936, 1. Joseph Campbell, *The Hero with a Thousand Faces* (Princeton, N. J., 1968), 97–109, discusses the trials and obstacles that the hero must undergo in classic mythology.

59. Boycott mentioned in "Lessons from the Fight," *AN*, approx. 26 June 1936, JLS, vol. 23. "Rabbi, Negro Pastor Will Cheer for Louis in Schmeling Fight," *Brooklyn Daily Eagle*, 20 April 1936, JLS, vol. 16.

CHAPTER 4

1. For the Berlin Olympics, see Richard Mandell, *The Nazi Olympics* (Urbana, 1987). For the festival aspect in the Games, see Moyra Byrne, "Nazi Festival: The 1936 Berlin Olympics," in *Time Out of Time: Essays on the Festival*, ed. Alessandro Falassi (Albuquerque, 1987), 107–21. On the suspension of Jew-baiting, see Arnd Krüger, "Germany: The Propaganda Machine," in Arnd Krüger and William Murray, eds., *The Nazi Olympics, Sport, Politics, and Appeasement in the 1930s* (Urbana, 2003), 17–43. Barbara Keys, "The Dictatorship of Sport: Nationalism, Internationalism, and Mass Culture in the 1930s" (Ph.D. Diss., Harvard University, 2001), 131–67 analyzes the Nazis' promotion of nationalism through international sports, especially the Berlin Olympics. Hitler quoted in conversation with Goebbels, 10 October 1936, recorded by Theodor Lewald, quoted in Arnd Krüger, "The 1936 Olympics-Berlin," in Peter J. Graham and Horst Überhorst, eds., *The Modern Olympics* (New York, 1976), 178.

2. Mandell, *The Nazi Olympics*, 200–208 discusses the counting of the medals. The Germans were particularly keen to outpoint the Americans who had dominated previous Olympics and were only slightly less chauvinistic than the Germans.

3. William J. Baker, *Jesse Owens: An American Life* (New York, 1986), 84, for black athletes' reaction to Schmeling's presence.

4. Baker, *Jesse Owens*, *Der Angriff*, n.d., quoted, 100. See Martha Dodd, *Through Embassy Eyes* (New York, 1939), 212 for the remarks by the assistant to the German foreign minister. On German self-image, see Krüger, "Germany: The Propaganda Machine," 17–43. For an example of the argument that African American athletes were viewed as "like horses," and "Hottentoten," see Hans J. Massaquoi, *Destined to Witness, Growing Up Black in Nazi Germany* (New York, 1999), 120–21.

5. "Uncle Sam's black athletes," cited in "Three First Places Make Ohioan No. 1," *CD*, 8 August 1936, 1. Chris Mead, *Champion—Joe Louis: Black Hero in White America* (New York, 1985), 104–06 discusses these issues and quotes Kieran and Rice.

6. Ralf Müller, "Max Schmeling: Seine Rolle in nationalsozialstiche Deutschland" (thesis, Deutsche Sporthochschule, Köln, 1996), 105–6.

7. Thomas R. Hietala, *The Fight of the Century, Jack Johnson, Joe Louis, and the Struggle for Racial Equality* (Armonk, N.Y., 2002), 178–79.

8. For training camp, see "Joe Louis in Camp; Starts His Workouts," *CD*, 8 August 1936, 13.

9. Fight details in Allan McMillan, "Murderous Right Ended Sharkey," *CD*, 22 August 1936, 13. William Nunn in *PC*, 22 August 1936, as cited in Hietala, *The Fight of the Century*, 179–80.

10. Müller, "Max Schmeling," 104–5, and Volker Kluge, *Max Schmeling: Eine Biographie in 15 Runden* (Berlin, 2004), 260–62.

11. Mead, *Champion*, 108–113, discusses the complicated wrangling and the details of these fights and provides the basis for the next two paragraphs.

12. The $25,000 guarantee is mentioned in Kluge, *Max Schmeling*, 262.

13. For material on the boycott, see *NYT*, 9 January 1937, 2; 10 January 1937, 40; 12 January 1937, 9; 14 January 1937, 46. Leiper quoted in *DW*, 12 January 1937, 8.

14. *NYT*, 9 January 1937, 2; 10 January 1937, 40; 12 January 1937, 9; 14 January 1937, 46. For a boycott of a proposed exhibition tour, see *DW*, 27 January 1937, 8. "Green Bids Nation Back Ban on Nazis," *NYT*, 1 February 1937, 5.

15. Arthur S. Evans, "The Jim Braddock-Max Schmeling Affair: An Assessment of a Jewish Boycott of a Professional Prizefight," *Journal of Sport and Social Issues* 6 (Summer 1982), 1–12. The "Jewish press" was a consistent target. See "Echoes of Schmeling's Victory," *Deutsche Weckruf und Beobachter*, 25 June 1936. For Lester Rodney's views of Joe Louis and sports, see Irwin Silber, *Press Box Red, The Story of Lester Rodney, the Communist Who Helped Break the Color Line in American Sports* (Philadelphia, 2003). For the "public does," see Doc Daughterty, *DW*, 17 January 1937, 15.

16. For the effects on boxing, see Doc Daugherty, "Louis-Pastor Bout Key to Title Mixup," *DW*, 17 January 1937, 15, and "Garden Ban Asked on Schmeling," *NYT*, 10 January 1937, 40. Gould cited in Joseph Smith, "Fight Boycott Growing Fast," *DW*, 11 January 1937, 8.

17. For his statement, and the German newspapers, see "Schmeling Asks 'Fair Play," *NYT*, 10 January 1937, 40. *B-S*, 7 December 1936, 2, as in Müller, "Max Schmeling," 107.

18. Mead, *Champion*, 111–12.

19. Dannic, quoted in Joseph Smith, "Illinios O.K.'s Louis Fight in Chic." *DW*, 2 February 1937, 8. Joseph Smith, "Fight Boycott Growing Fast," *DW*, 11 January 1937, 8. Doc Daughtery, "Louis-Pastor Bout Key to Title Mixup," *DW*, 17 January 1937, 15. Hype Igoe, "The Schmeling-Braddock Aftermath," *Ring*, (August 1937), JLS, vol. 39.

20. On Braddock's lack of a draw, see Nat Fleischer, *Black Dynamite* (New York, 1938), vol. 2, 66. For "selling the title," and Braddock's desire to meet Louis, see "Braddock Eager to Meet Joe Louis," *CD*, 31 December 1935. George Nicholson cited in Gerald Astor, *"...And a Credit to His Race": The Hard Life and Times of Joseph Louis Barrow, a.k.a. Joe Louis* (New York, 1974), 156. For another account of Braddock's motivation, see "Braddock May Still Find Wolf at Door," *CD*, 26 June 1937, 18.

21. For Jacob's reasoning, see Mead, *Champion*, 113–14.
22. Nat Fleischer, "Nat Fleischer Says: Schmeling Has Good Reason to Be Peeved," *Ring* (August 1937), JLS, vol. 39. For a defense of Braddock's desire to pursue a large payday, see Hype Igoe, "The Schmeling-Braddock Aftermath," *Ring* (August 1937), JLS, vol. 39.
23. Schmeling, *Autobiography*, 139–40. Hans Joachim Teichler, "Max Schmeling— Der Sportler des Jahrhunderts in Dritten Reich," *Sportzeit* (2001), 16, 22 discusses the easing of opposition to Joe Jacobs and the SA award incident.
24. See Müller, "Max Schmeling," 111–114.
25. Esser and Lammers cited in Müller, "Max Schmeling," 111. For other details, see Kluge, *Max Schmeling*, 266. Report on "Financing of a Proposed Braddock-Schmeling Bout for the World's Championship in Berlin this Summer," Donald Jenkins, American Consul General, Berlin to State Department, 1 February 1937, State Department Decimal Files, National Archives, 862.4066/1, as cited in Keys, "The Dictatorship of Sport," 137, n22.
26. *NYT*, 11 March 1937, n. p., as in Müller, "Max Schmeling," 113.
27. "Boycott Ruins Schmeling Tour," *DW*, 7 March 1937, 14. "Anti-Nazi Boycott KO's Schmeling; He Leaves U. S.," *DW*, 24 March 1937, 1, 8.
28. Goebbels quoted, *Die Tagebücher von Joseph Goebbels, Teil I Aufzeichnungen, 1923–1941*, April 1937, 93. Gould's words are taken from a Budd Schulberg article in *Collier's* (6 May 1950), as cited in Barney Nagler, *James Norris and the Decline of Boxing* (Indianapolis, 1964), 14.
29. For the weigh-in for the phantom fight, see Fleischer, *Black Dynamite*, vol. 2, 67. For German accounts, see "Wer boxt mit Schmeling?" *DA*, 16 May 1937, 2. Germans also saw the bout as the fight with a phantom. See Arno Hellmis, "Schmeling lehnt Kompromisse ab," *DA*, 2 June 1937, 14, and "Ein Mann im Ring," *DA*, 20 May 1937, 20. Goebbels quoted, *Die Tagebücher von Joseph Goebbels*, June 1937, 169.
30. "Schmeling wieder daheim," *B-S*, 17 (5 April 1937), 2. For the award, see "Harmonie im Sportpalast," *B-S*, 17 (19 April 1937), 2–4.
31. Erwin Thoma, "Im Fegefeuer der Intrigen," *B-S*, 17 (18 May 1937), 2–4.
32. See Michael Ermarth, "'Judamerika' and German Counter-Modernity: The Fateful Fusion of 'Americanization' and 'Judaization' 1880–1945 (unpublished paper, 2004), used with his permission. For German views of the boycotters, see *VB*, 16 December 1937, 8, as cited in Müller, "Max Schmeling," 124. For further discussion, see "Geshäft triumpert über Sport: Machtlosigkeit in U.S.A.," *B-S*, 17 (7 June 1937), 2–5. For moral champion and true champion, see "Max Schmeling moralischer Weltmeister," *B-S*, 17 (14 June 1937), 3–4, and "Der VDF erklärt Schmeling moralischer Weltmeister," *VB*, 16 June 1937, "Braddock will nicht!" *B-S*, 17 (1 June 1937), 2–3. Denmark's *Idroetsbladet* quoted in "Scharfe Worte aus dem Norden," *B-S*, 17 (14 June 1937), 4. The Nazis created new medals and awards to honor the Reich's heroes, who were seen as representing the entire Volk or nation. For an example, see Dr. Peter von Werder, "Der Weltkampf," *Nationalsozialstiche Monatshefte*, 102 (September 1938), 42–49.
33. For Schmeling's reaction, see *Berlin Zeitung am Mittag*, 4 June 1937; for "gangster politics," see *12-Uhr Blatt*, 4 June 1937; all cited in Müller, "Max Schmeling, 116–17.
34. For "breaking through a barrier," see Lonnie Harrington, "After Years of 'Run-Around,' Louis Is First to Get Crack at Heavyweight Title in U.S," *PC*, 5 June 1937, 16. David W. Kellum, "Louis Plans Active Career as Ring Champion,"

CD, 26 June 1937, 1–2. Nat Fleischer, "Louis' Improvement Amazes," *Ring* (September 1937), JLS, vol. 40. For the announcement on prejudice, see John Whitaker, "Speculating in Sports," *Hammond (Indiana) Times*, 23 June 1937, JLS, vol. 38. Monroe, "Right Punch Sends Jim to Doom in 8th," *CD*, 26 June 1937, 20. Burden of smashing color line is from Al Monroe, "Speaking of Sports," *CD*, 19 June 1937, 22.

35. See *PC*, 27 February 1937; *Syracuse Post-Standard*, 22 June 1937; *St. Louis Star Times*, 22 June 1937, as cited in Hietala, *The Fight of the Century*, 181–82. In these pages, Hietala discusses the complicated racial, ethnic, and national loyalties that were transforming American boxing during this period.

36. Joe Louis as told to Meyer Berger and Barney Nagler, "Joe Louis' Story Part Two," *Life Magazine* (15 November 1948), 130.

37. Biographical details comes from George T. Tickell, "Dame Fortune Smiles on Braddock," *Ring* 14 (July 1935), 12–15, 46.

38. For the Depression, see Tickell, "Dame Fortune Smiles on Braddock," *Ring*, 12–15, 46, and Nat Fleischer, "Braddock's Amazing Feat Sets Fistic Mark," *Ring* 14 (August 1935), 2–4, 9.

39. Nat Fleischer, *Black Dynamite* (New York, 1938), vol. 2, 68–71, describes the fight, as does Mead, *Champion*, 122.

40. Fleischer, "Louis' Improvement Amazes," *Ring* (September 1937). Blackburn speech cited in Mead, *Champion*, 123.

41. Joe Louis as told to Meyer Berger and Barney Nagler, "Joe Louis' Story Part Two," *Life Magazine* (15 November 1948), 130. Braddock's comments to Gould are from Gerald Astor, *"And a Credit to His Race,"* 158. Al Monroe, "Right Punch Sends Jim to Doom in 8th," *CD*, 26 June 1937, 20. Fleischer, "Louis' Improvement Amazes," *Ring* (September 1937).

42. Young, "King Louis I," *AN*, 26 June 1937. 40. "South Side Goes Wild as Louis Wins," *Chicago Daily Tribune*, 23 June 1937, JLS, vol. 38. William G. Nunn, "Nunn Describes South Side as It Goes Mad after Joe Louis Victory," *PC* (26 June 1937), 16. Malcolm X with Alex Haley, *The Autobiography of Malcolm X* (New York, 1966), 23. For Powder Town, Alabama, celebration, see "Detroit Hails Louis's Victory," *New York Sun*, 23 June 1937, JLS, vol. 38.

43. Al Richmond, "Nine . . . Ten—And Then There Was Bedlam," *DW*, 27 June 1937, 5. W. Thomas Watson, "Harlem Goes Wild as Joe Wins Crown," *CD*, 26 June 1937, 1–2.

44. Fay Young, "King Louis I," *AN*, 26 June 1937, JLS, vol. 40. David W. Kellum, "Louis Plans Active Career as Ring Champion," *CD*, 26 June 1937, 1.

45. Description of Chicago and Harlem is from "South Side Goes Wild as Louis Wins,"*Chicago Daily Tribune*, 23 June 1937, JLS, vol. 38. Ethiopian flag, Schmeling, and Hitler are mentioned in "Jack Johnson Is Hunting a Jess Willard for Joe," *New York Post*, 23 June 1937, JLS, vol. 38. Earl J. Morris, "Grand Town," *PC*, 3 July 1937, 20.

46. Timuel Black interview, Chicago Historical Society. Thanks to Elizabeth Fraterrigo for this source.

47. R. G. Lynch, "Maybe I'm Wrong," *Milwaukee Journal*, 20 May 1937, JLS, vol. 32. William G. Nunn, "'Jim in a Fog,' Declares Nunn," *PC*, 26 June 1937, 1.

48. "Jack Johnson Is Hunting."

49. "Joe Louis Champion," *Illinois State Register* (Springfield), 23 June 1937, JLS, vol. 38. Ed Van Every, "Louis' Rise Meteoric," *Ring* (September 1937), JLS, vol. 40. Daniel M. Daniel, *"The Ring's* Globe Trotter," *Ring* (September 1937), JLS, vol. 40.

50. Ted Carroll, "Colored Boxers Make Progress," *Ring*, 16 (March 1937), 29, 44.

51. "Champ Joe Wants Max," *PC*, 26 June 1937, 1. Ted Carroll, "The Fighting Champion," *Ring* 16 (September 1937), 1, 44.

52. "Louis knockt Braddock aus," *B-S*, 17 (1 July 1937), 2–3.

53. Mead, *Champion*, 131.

54. For the proposed Farr-Schmeling fight, see Müller, "Max Schmeling," 121–23. For "crooked situation," see "Weltmeisterschaft Schmeling-Farr," *B-S*, 17 (1 July 1937), 4–5.

55. Mead, *Champion*, 131. For details on Sol Strauss, see Hype Igoe, "Schmeling Gets His Chance," *Ring*, 16 (November 1937), 2–3.

56. Roi Ottley, "Joe Louis and His People," in *New World A-Coming* (New York, 1943), 197.

CHAPTER 5

1. For the international aspects of the bout, see Nat Fleischer, "Fleischer Picks Louis to Top Schmeling," *Ring*, 22 June 1938, JLS, vol. 51. Joe Williams quoted in Chris Mead, *Champion—Joe Louis: Black Hero in White America* (New York, 1985), 133. For the match's symbolic import, see Anthony O. Edmonds, "Second Louis-Schmeling Fight: Sport, Symbol, and Culture," *Journal of Popular Culture* 7 (Summer 1973), 42–50, and Michael Wollny, "Im Sog der Politik: Die Boxkämpfe von Joe Louis und Max Schmeling in den Jahren 1936 und 1938" (Magisterarbeit, Amerika-Institut, Universität München, 2004).

2. Joe Louis with Edna and Art Rust, Jr., *Joe Louis: My Life* (New York, 1978), 92.

3. McCarthy quoted in Mead, *Champion*, 148. "Interest High in Amsterdam," *NYT*, 24 June 1938, JLS, vol. 54. On the million-dollar gate, see Nat Fleischer, *Black Dynamite*, vol. 2 (New York, 1938), 82. Roi Ottley, "Joe Louis and His People," in Ottley, *New World A-Coming* (New York, 1943), 197.

4. Bill Corum, "Storm Clouds over the Stadium," *New York Journal and American*, 14 June 1938, JLS, vol. 50.

5. Material for this paragraph comes from Gerald Astor, "*...And a Credit to His Race*": *The Hard Life and Times of Joseph Louis Barrow, a.k.a. Joe Louis* (New York, 1974), 166–67. For right wing groups, see Sander A. Diamond, *The Nazi Movement in the United States 1924–1941* (Ithaca, 1974); Susan Canedy, *America's Nazis, a Democratic Dilemma* (Menlo Park, Calif., 1990); and Leo Ribuffo, *The Old Christian Right, the Protestant Far Right from the Great Depression to the Cold War* (Philadelphia, 1983).

6. Louis and the Rusts, *Joe Louis*, 136–39. On expanding of the quote, see Astor, "*And a Credit to His Race*," 169–70.

7. Max Schmeling, *An Autobiography*, trans. George B. von der Lippe (Chicago, 1998), 140, 151–53. For his role at the Mussolini reception and in the 1938 referendum, see Volker Kluge, *Max Schmeling: Eine Biographie in 15 Runden* (Berlin, 2004), 278–80. "Schmeling Steals Show at a Tea for Mussolini," *NYT*, 26 September 1937. "Schmeling Slurs Louis, Negro Race," *DW*, 11 June 1938, 8. Edmund Boyack, "Psychological Superiority Will Beat Joe—Schmeling," *PC*, 21 May 1938, 1, 4. Hype Igoe, "Max Claims Fear Will Conquer Joe," *New York Journal and American*, 10 May 1938, JLS, vol. 49; Louis's response is quoted in Edgar T. Rouzeau, "He Was Plain Lucky When He Fought Me for the First Time," *PC*, 28 May 1938, 1.

8. Astor, "*And a Credit to His Race*, 168–69, discusses Jacobs's comments and his negotiations with the Anti-Nazi League. For leaflets, see Mead, *Champion*, 146.

9. The quotes are in Mead, *Champion*, 140–45. See similar quotes by Westbrook Pegler, as cited in A. O. Edmonds, *Joe Louis* (New York, 1973), 78, and Dan Parker, "Der Fuehrer of Speculator," *Daily Mirror*, 18 June 1938, JLS, vol. 50. William H. Wiggins, Jr., "Joe Louis, American Folk Hero," *Sport and the Color Line, Black Athletes and Race Relations in Twentieth-Century America*, ed. Patrick Miller and David K. Wiggins (New York, 2004), 127–46, discusses how white Americans saw Louis as the defender of American democracy.

10. Myrtle S. Weigand, "'Let's Be Americans,'" *NYT*, 18 June 1938, JLS, vol. 50.

11. For the Bund, see Louis and Rusts, *Joe Louis*, 136–40. For a white man beating a Negro, see Gerald Astor, "*And a Credit to His Race*," 170. For Louis's readiness, see "Max Schmeling," *SNT*, 21 June 1938, 8. For the aggressive strategy, Mead, *Champion*, 138. For Louis's prediction and "I was going to beat Schmeling," see Louis and Rusts, *Joe Louis*, 136–40. For "was true," see Joe Louis as told to Meyer Berger and Barney Nagler, "My Story," Part Two, *Life* (15 November 1948), 133.

12. Reports from Louis's camp, Schmeling, *Autobiography*, 152. Training and readiness, "Max Schmeling," *SNT*, 21 June 1938, 8. For Hitler cable, see Astor, *And a Credit to His Race*, 171. For the Metzner cable, see "Dr. Metzner an Schmeling," *HA*, 22 June 1938.

13. For the mood as they drove into New York, see Louis as told to Berger and Nagler, "My Story," Part Two, 133. Mead, *Champion*, 146, details the weigh-in.

14. Schmeling, *Autobiography*, 153. Louis and Rusts, *Joe Louis*, 139.

15. "Ein Grosser fiel: Max in der 1 Runde k. o.," *HA*, 23 June 1938, describes the bout.

16. W.R., "Max Schmeling im Krankenhaus," *HA*, 23 June 1938, 1. For descriptions of the bout, see Mead, *Champion*, 148–52, and Nat Fleischer, *Black Dynamite*, vol. 2, 82–92. I have also relied on films of the bout, shown frequently on television, and on the radio announcer's account, as heard on "Joe Louis: the Brown Bomber," *Journeys*, WBEZ Chicago, in possession of the author. Thanks to J. Fred MacDonald for a copy of this radio show. Richard Wright, "High Time in Harlem," *New Masses* (5 July 1938), 42. Abe Newman, "Breaks All Precedent with 1 Round KO and Greatest Record Ever," *DW*, 24 June 1938, 8.

17. I have relied on Fleischer, *Black Dynamite*, 82–92, and Mead, *Champion*, 148–52, for this paragraph.

18. Fleischer, *Black Dynamite*, 82–83.

19. Schmeling, *Autobiography*, 155–57.

20. *Life* quoted in Mead, *Champion*, 153. "Mr. Superrace," in Berger and Nagler, "My Story," Part Two, 133. "Mad" and "international" quoted in Gene Kessler, "Joe Louis Tells How He Planned and Won Title Go," *Saint Louis Post-Dispatch*, 23 June 1938, JLS, vol. 54. Chester L. Washington, "Joe Smashes Way to Quickest Victory by K. O. in Fight History," *PC*, 25 June 1938, pp. 1–2. Jack Johnson, "Wrong," *PC*, 25 June 1938, 17.

21. *Die Tagebücher von Joseph Goebbels*, Teil I, vol. 5, 358. Nestor, "Es geschah in der ersten Runde," *HA*, 23 June 1938. "Sprachlos," in Arno Hellmis, "Louis Schlug Pausenlos," *DA*, 24 June 1938, 3. "Yankee Stadium," *DA*, 24 June 1938, 3. "Ganz Deutschland tief enttauscht," A.P. dispatch from Berlin, in unidentified German American newspaper, JLS, vol. 54.

22. Toney Betts, "Blue Thursday in Yorkville," *New York Post*, 23 June 1938, JLS, vol. 54. Also on Yorkville, see Hans M. Hoffmann, "Yorkville will's erst gar

nicht glauben," unidentified German language newspaper, JLS, vol. 54. For poisoned, see Harry N. Sperber, "Die Zuversicht im Camp beim Max war zu gross," unidentified German American newspaper, JLS, vol. 54.

23. "Achtung! Ring Frei! *DA*, 22 June 1938, 3. For the caricatures, see Ludwig Haymann, "Schafft es Schmeling zum zweiten Malve?" *VB*, 6 June 1938,1. "Schmeling hat Pech gehabt," *Berliner Tageblatt*, 23 June 1938, in JLS, vol. 54, refers to "hate-filled." "Referee Donovan Stops the Fight," *SNT*, 23 June 1938. For "wild drumfire," see "Ein Grosser fiel: Max in der 1 Runde k. o.," *HA*, 23 June 1938.

24. "Nierenschlag nahm Schmeling die Kampfkraft," *SNT*, 23 June 1938. "Max Schmeling im Krankenhaus," *HA*, 23 June 1938. "Schmeling hat Pech gehabt," *Berliner Tageblatt*, 23 June 1938, for kidney blow "beyond doubt."

25. *Die Tagebücher von Joseph Goebbels*, Teil I, vol. 5, 358. Daniel M. Daniel, "Schmeling's Squawk Makes Kidney Famous," *Ring* (June 1938), JLS, vol. 54. John Roxborough protested the German film version of the fight. See "Nazis Change Louis-Schmeling Film; Roxborough Cables Protest," *CD*, 30 July 1938, 1–2. Schmeling, *Autobiography*, 154–56.

26. *New York World-Telegram*, 23 June 1938, as quoted in Edmonds, *Joe Louis*, 81. See U.S.A Presse," *DA*, 22 June 1938, and *VB*, 23 June 1938, as cited in Ralf Müller, "Max Schmeling: seine Rolle in nationalsozialishschen Deutschland" (thesis, Deutsche Sporthochschule, Köln, 1996), 130–32.

27. *VB*, 23 June 1938, as cited in Müller, "Max Schmeling," 133–34. For "primitively thinking," see *VB*, 23 June 1938, as in Müller, 136.

28. "Negroes Celebrate the Victory," *SNT*, 23 June 1938. W. G., "Max Schmelings grosse Stunde," *HA*, 21 June 1938. For shrieking like Africans, see Fritz Scharf, "Wildeste Freude herrscht in Harlem," probably *N. Y. Staats-Zeitung und Herald*, 23 June 1938, JLS, vol. 54. For a similar account, see "Ein Grosser fiel: Max in der 1 Runde k.o.," *HA*, 23 June 1938.

29. "Der Kampf Louis-Schmeling," *Neue Volkszeitung*, 25 June 1938, in JLS, vol. 54. Sid Ziff, "Sid Ziff's Column," *Los Angeles Herald and Express*, 23 June 1938, JLS, vol. 54. *Dallas Morning News*, as cited in Edmonds, *Joe Louis*, 81.

30. Richard Wright, "High Tide in Harlem," *New Masses* (28 July 1938), 18–19. Wright's analysis of this sporting event bears a striking resemblance to Clifford Geertz, "Deep Play: Notes on the Balinese Cockfight," in *Myth, Symbol, and Culture*, ed. Clifford Geertz (New York, 1971), 1–37.

31. 'Sez Ches,' "A Promised Fulfilled," *PC*, 2 July 1938, 15. Frank Marshall Davis, "'Sepia America' Goes Wild," *PC*, 2 July 1938, 12.

32. Wright, "High Tide in Harlem," 18–19. Mary McLeod Bethune, "Head High as Victor Answered the Challenge," *PC*, 2 July 1938, 12. William G. Nunn, "Louis Had Knocked Schmeling Out before Referee Stopped Bout," *PC*, 25 June 1938, 1–2. Lawrence Levine, *Black Culture and Black Consciousness* (New York, 1977), 420–40.

33. For an excellent discussion of some of these ideas as they apply to Mexican American and Mexican boxers, see Gregory S. Rodriguez, "'Palaces of Pain'—Arenas of Mexican-American Dreams: Boxing and the Foundation of Ethnic Mexican Identifications in Twentieth-Century Los Angeles" (Ph.D. diss., University of California, San Diego, 1999). Attorney William E. Lily, "A Study of Joe Louis," *CD*, 10 September 1938, editorial page.

34. Charlie Davis, "Hoosiers Jubilant as Louis Triumphs," *PC*, 2 July 1938, 12. *Milwaukee Journal*, 23 June 1938, as cited in Edmonds, *Joe Louis*, 80.

35. Russell Baker, *Growing Up* (New York, 1982), 206.

36. *The West African Pilot*, 16 July 1938, 12. Claudius Leo, "Thanks Joe Louis," *PC*, 16 July 1938, 14. For coverage of Louis and Owens, see "Looking for a 'White Hope,'" *Bantu World*, 13 June 1936, 19; Scorpion, "Jesse Owens The Negro Phantom," *Bantu World*, 8 August 1936, 19; "Jesse Owens Owes His Success to His Heel!" *Bantu World*, 5 September 1936, 19; "Great Boxing Match," 26 June 1937, and "Negroes Dance in the Streets," *Bantu World*, 26 June 1937, 1; "Louis's Great Victory," *Bantu World*, 25 June 1938, 1, 20. Thanks to Timothy Burke, Carol Summers, and Brad Weiss for these sources.

37. Marcus Garvey, "Joe Louis," *The Black Man* 3 (July 1938), 1. See also, David K. Wiggins and Patrick B. Miller, eds., *The Unlevel Playing Field, a Documentary History of the African American Experience in Sport* (Urbana, 2003), 166–67.

38. Dan Parker, "Der Feuhrer of Speculator," *Daily Mirror*, 18 June 1938, JLS, vol. 50. *Manchester Guardian*, 23 June 1938, JLS, vol. 56. "Joy, Tragedy in Wake of Joe's Victory," *CD*, 2 July 1938, as in William H. Wiggins, "Joe Louis," 138.

39. "Heil! Yo' All—!" *Baltimore Sun*, 24 June 1938, JLS, vol. 56; "A Wash Out on the Line," *Pittsburgh Post-Gazette*, 24 June 1938, JLS, vol. 56. Ellis, "What a SWAT-sika," *DW*, 24 June 1938, 6. For more on cartoons, see Edmonds, *Joe Louis*, 80–81.

40. William H. Wiggins, Jr., "Boxing's Sambo Twins: Racial Stereotypes in Jack Johnson and Joe Louis Newspaper Cartoons," *Journal of Sports History*, 15 (winter 1988), 242–54. For a perspective on the white South, see Jeffrey T. Sammons, "Boxing as a Reflection of Society: The Southern Reaction to Joe Louis," *Journal of Popular Culture* 16 (spring 1983), 22–33.

41. Wiggins, "Boxing's Sambo Twins," 242–54. Ed Hughes, "Another Case of 'Bad Hands,'" *Brooklyn Daily Eagle*, 17 August 1935, JLS, vol. 4.

42. The *Dallas Morning News*, the unidentified quote, and Bill Corum are in Edmonds, *Joe Louis*, 82.

43. Heywood Broun, "It Seems to Me," *New York World-Telegram*, 24 June 1938, in JLS, vol. 56. William L. Patterson, "Joe Louis Killed Nazi Supremacy Theory," *PC*, 24 June 1938, JLS, vol. 56.

44. Richard Wright, "High Tide in Harlem," 18–19.

45. Ted Carroll, "A Great Champion Arrives," *Ring* (June 1938), JLS, vol. 54. Editorial, "Joe Stands Supreme," *Ring* (June 1938), JLS, vol. 54. The Burris Jenkins, Jr., cartoon is described in Mead, *Champion*, 142–43. *Louisville Courier Journal*, 24 June 1938, JLS, vol. 56. For civic nationalism, see Gary Gerstle, *American Crucible, Race and Nation in the Twentieth Century* (Princeton, 2001), 3–13, 128–86.

46. James J. Braddock, "Louis to KO Schmeling in Six Rounds," *DW*, 19 April 1938, 8. "Jewish Tribute to Joe," reprinted in Yiddish from the *Jewish Daily Courier*, 25 June 1938, in *CD*, 25 June 1938, 6. Daniel M. Daniel discusses Jewish turnout for the fight in "Schmeling's Squawk Makes Kidney Famous," *Ring* (June 1938), JLS, vol. 54. Billy McCarty quoted in Frances Stan, "Win, Lose or Draw," Washington, D. C. *Evening Star*, 21 June 1938, JLS, vol. 41.

47. Rollo W. Wilson, "Sting of Maxie's Right Unleashes Fury of Bomber," *PC*, 25 June 1938, 17. Royce Brier, "This World Today," *San Francisco Chronicle*, 23 June 1938, JLS, vol. 54.

48. Mead, *Champion*, 159, views Louis's acceptance as a national representative as revolutionary. "Michigan Rooted for Joe," *PC*, 25 June 1938, 12. "Topics of the Times," *NYT*, 24 June 1938, JLS, vol. 54. "City Hall Blocked," *PC*, 9 July 1938, 5. Randy Dixon, "'He Fouled Me', Raves Beaten Max," *PC*, 25 June 1938, 17. Eleanor Roosevelt quoted in "One-Round Fight," *Life* (June 1938), JLS, vol. 56.

49. Jimmy Carter, *An Hour before Daylight* (New York, 2001), 32–34. This episode is also discussed in Al-Tony Gilmore, "The Myth, Legend, and Folklore of Joe Louis: The Impression of Sport on Society," *The South Atlantic Quarterly* 82 (summer 1983), 265–66.

50. Hugh Johnson, ""Finds Hitler's Vaunted Aryanism Took Knockout along with Schmeling," *Chicago Daily News*, 24 June 1938, JLS, vol. 56.

51. "Joe and the Aryan Issue," unidentified newspaper, 24 June 1938, JLS, vol. 56. Bud Shaver, "Joe Louis a Challenge to Tolerance in an Intolerant World," *Detroit Times*, reprinted in *PC*, 2 July 1938. *Boston Globe*, cited in Mead, *Champion*, 158.

52. "Aryan superiority campaign" is from "Goebbels on the Spot," *Scranton Tribune*, 24 June 1938, JLS, vol. 56. Daniel M. Daniel, "The Ring's Globe Trotter," *Ring* (September 1937), JLS, vol. 40. George Winn, "In the Editor's Corner: Heavyweights on Parade," *Boxing News* (June 1938), JLS, vol. 56. Arthur Donovan, "The Referee Fights Three Men," *Saturday Evening Post* (10 September 1938), JLS, vol. 57. Jim Jeffries's criticism of the white hope idea is in "Ring Philosophy," *Peoria Transcript*, 15 August 1935, JLS, vol. 4.

53. Jeffrey Sammons, *Beyond the Ring: The Role of Boxing in American Society* (Urbana, Il., 1990), 118–20. As Sammons points out, there had been many attacks on the fight film ban over the years. Some critics attacked the logic of the law in a technological society where it was legal to attend matches in person or listen to a round-by-round broadcast on the radio. Also, anyone could observe endless newspaper photos. Critics pointed out that state and federal governments already taxed prizefights. If the films became legal, government entities could tap them for greater revenue. Over the years, various courts ruled that exhibition was distinct from transportation, and distribution of such films was not a crime.

54. U.S. Congress, Senate, Subcommittee of the Committee on Interstate Commerce, hearings on legalizing transportation of prizefight films, S. 2047, 76th Cong., 1st Sess., *Congressional Record*, 1939, 38–39.

55. Sammons, *Beyond the Ring*, 120.

56. For a musical description of the fight, listen to John Lee "Sonny Boy" Williamson, "Joe Louis and John Henry Blues," recorded 21 July 1939, on *Joe Louis, an American Hero* (Rounder, 82161-1106-2, Sony Music Entertainment, Inc., 2001).

57. Grantland Rice, "The Sportlight," unidentified newspaper (perhaps *New York Sun*), 18 June 1938, JLS, vol. 49, and "The Sportlight," probably *Denver Post*, 20 June 1938, JLS, vol. 51. Tom Cribbs, Jr., "Letter to Editor," *New York Post*, 24 June 1938, JLS, vol. 56. "Palooka's Big Test to Come," *San Francisco Chronicle*, 23 June 1938, JLS, vol. 55. For sincerity, see Lester Bromberg, "Joe Louis Deplores Lack of Schooling," *Ring* (June 1938), JLS, vol. 56. For "saw the fight," see John Durant, *The Heavyweight Champions* (New York, 1960), 137, as cited in Alexander Young, Jr., "Joe Louis, Symbol, 1933–1949 (Ph.D. diss., University of Maryland, 1968), 127; Cannon's remark, 158.

58. For comparisons of Louis with ring greats, see Frank Graham, "Setting the Pace" column, *New York Sun*, 23 June 1938, JLS, vol. 54. Daniel, "Schmeling's Squawk Makes Kidney Famous."

CHAPTER 6

1. Daniel M. Daniel, "Schmeling's Squawk Makes Kidney Famous," *Ring* (June 1938), JLS, vol. 54. Max Schmeling, *An Autobiography*, trans. George B. von der Lippe (Chicago, 1998; original 1977), 156. Volker Kluge, *Max Schmeling, Eine Biographie in 15 Runden* (Berlin, 2004), 298.

2. *Die Tagebücher von Joseph Goebbels*, Teil I, vol. 5: 1923–1941 (Munich, 1987), 378–79. Kluge, *Max Schmeling*, 291–93. Schmeling, *Autobiography*, 157. Jeffrey T. Sammons, *Beyond the Ring: The Roles of Boxing in American Society* (Urbana, 1990), 116–17, discusses the German reaction to the loss.

3. Kluge, *Max Schmeling*, 305.

4. Schmeling, *Autobiography*, 157. Kluge, *Max Schmeling*, 301, discusses the incident and disputes Schmeling's assertions in his memoir that he was there.

5. Hans Joachim Teichler, "Max Schmeling—Sportler des Jahrhunderts im Dritten Reich," *Sportzeit* (2001), 24. The Lewin incident is discussed in Frank Deford, "Almost a Hero," *Sports Illustrated* (3 December 2001), 74. Robert Weisbord and Norbert Hedderich, "Max Schmeling Righteous Ring Warrior?" *History Today*, 43 (January 1993), 40, and Birk Minhardt, *Boxen in Deutschland* (Hamburg, 1996), 91, form the basis for my discussion of the Lewin incident.

6. "Daniel M. Daniel, *"Ring's* Most Valuable Award to Louis," *Ring* 18 (March 1939), 6–7. Nat Fleischer, "Louis Stands by Himself," *Ring* 18 (April 1939), 4–6, 43, ranks Louis with Dempsey. Teichler, "Max Schmeling—Sportler," 25. Kluge, *Max Schmeling*, 306–8; Metzner an Tschammer und Osten, 2 February 1939, Bundesarchiv R, 1501/5101, cited in Kluge, *Max Schmeling*, 308. Schmeling, *Autobiography*, 158.

7. Schmeling, *Autobiography*, 158. Kluge, *Max Schmeling*, 308. Nat Fleischer, "Nat Fleischer Says," *Ring* 18 (October 1939), 23.

8. Kluge, *Max Schmeling*, 309–11, official letter, Metzner an Schmeling, 13 March 1939, BA R 1501/5101, cited in Kluge, 309.

9. For articles leading up to and including the Heuser bout, see "Schmeling-Heuser-Kampf am 2. Juli in Stuttgart," *B-S* 19 (24 April 1939), 2. "Boxfieber um Schmeling-Heuser," *B-S* 19 (19 June 1939), 2–3. "Stuttgart 24 Stunden vor dem Kampf," *B-S* 3 (3 July 1939), 2. "Schmeling Europameister in genau 60 Sekunden," *B-S* 19 (3 July 1939), 5–6, 19. For his feelings, see Erwin Thoma, "Stuttgarter Nachschau," *B-S* 19 (10 July 1939), 2–4. For his description of the fight, see Schmeling, *Autobiography*, 158–60.

10. Von Tschammer quoted in *B-S* (27 January 1941), 12, as cited in Kluge, *Max Schmeling*, 325.

11. Schmeling, *Autobiography*, 161–62; Minhardt, *Boxen in Deutschland*, 96–97.

12. Teichler, "Max Schmeling—Sportler," 27. Schmeling, *Autobiography*, 162–67.

13. Schmeling, *Autobiography*, 168–69. Kluge, *Max Schmeling*, 332–34.

14. Schmeling, *Autobiography*, 168–69. Goebbels's diary cited in Teichler, "Max Schmeling—Sportler," 27. See Kluge, *Max Schmeling*, 334–39, for his problems with Goebbels, and Minhardt, *Boxen in Deutschland*, 96, for Schmeling's propaganda role.

15. Schmeling, *Autobiography*, 168–69. Goebbels's diary cited in Teichler, "Max Schmeling—Sportler," 27. Goebbels, quoted in Veit Harlan letter to Schmeling, 28 August 1945, BA, Schmeling file, as in *Die Tagebücher von Joseph Goebbels*, Teil I, 370, n.263.

16. Schmeling, *Autobiography*, 171–74.

17. *New York World Telegram*, approx. 1940, and *Rochester (New York) Democrat and Chronicle*, 28 January 1941, as cited in A. O. Edmonds, *Joe Louis* (New York, 1973), 84. For the concentration camp rumor and the equation of all Germans with Schmeling, see Willis N. (Jersey) Jones, "Two Fighters," *Negro Digest* 1 (April 1943), 3–4. See also Alexander Joseph Young, Jr., *Joe Louis, Symbol 1933–1949* (Ph. D. diss., University of Maryland, 1968), 132. Ivan (Cy) Peterman, "Schmeling's Biggest Round," *Saturday Evening Post*, 218 (29 September 1945), 6.

18. August Schmittner to *Ring* 20 (February 1941), 30; Eddie Dullea to *Ring* 20 (June 1941), 31; John Bruen to *Ring*, as cited in A. O. Edmonds, *Joe Louis*, 85; Pvt. Irish Johnny McGrath to *Ring* 22 (April 1943), 32–33.

19. Buchwald quote from *Durham Morning Herald*, 20 April 1981, 4A, as cited in Sammons, *Beyond the Ring*, 117. For how blacks saw Louis as the greatest champion, see Wendell Smith, "Bomber's Record Establishes Him Greatest of All Champions," *PC*, 13 April 1940, 17. Louis quoted about Conn in Dick McCann, "Conn's Slurs Stir Louis for 2nd Time in Career," *New York Daily News*, 17 June 1941, JLS, vol. 88. Nat Fleischer, "Louis Named *The Fighter of the Year*," *Ring* 21 (February 1942), 3–5. For a good description of the Conn battle, see Sammons, *Beyond the Ring*, 121–22.

20. "Joe Louis Comes Out for Willkie," *Saint Louis Daily Globe-Democrat*, 27 October 1940, JLS, vol. 79, and "10,000 Cheer Louis in Brooklyn Plea for Willkie," *Daily Mirror*, 1 November 1940, JLS, vol. 79. For criticism of Louis for espousing any political views, see "Jack Dempsey Gives Joe Louis a Verbal Punch," *NY Herald Tribune*, 2 November 1940, JLS, vol. 79; "Julian Black Not Responsible for Champ's Campaign Speeches," *PC*, 9 November 1940, JLS, vol. 79; Bill Dooley, "Louis Tried to Help Pal," 12 November 1940, JLS, vol. 79.

21. I have relied on Sammons, *Beyond the Ring*, 123, for this paragraph. Greene quoted in *NYT*, 23 July 1942, 24.

22. Gary Gerstle, *American Crucible, Race and Nation in the Twentieth Century* (Princeton, N.J., 2001), 128–237 especially.

23. Walter White telegram to *Pittsburgh Courier*, 15 November 1941, Box 365, NAACP Papers. Memo to Mrs. Bowman, 19 January 1942, Box 365, NAACP.

24. Louis's remarks are in "Our Joe," unidentified press clipping, n.d., Box 549, NAACP. For more on the subject, see Dominic J. Capeci, Jr., and Martha Wilkerson, "Multifarious Hero: Joe Louis, American Society and Race Relations during World Crisis, 1935–1945," *Journal of Sport History*, 10 (winter 1983), 16. For Jacobs's remarks, see "Poll Favors Louis's Navy Fight," *PC*, 29 November 1941, 15. For the importance of the bout, see Lauren Sklaroff, "Constructing G.I. Joe Louis: Cultural Solutions to the 'Negro Problem' during World War II," *Journal of American History* 89 (December 2002), 958–59. See also Dick Cox, "Terror Thrill for Joe," *Ring* 20 (August 1941), 4–6, 8–9. Hype Igoe, "Conn's Big Gamble," *Ring* 20 (September 1941), 5–6, 45.

25. Dan Parker, "Louis Stops Baer in First," *Daily Mirror*, approx. 10 January 1941, 18, JLS, Miscellaneous Oversize, 1941–1944. The remarks by Nat Fleischer and *Ring* are from Fleischer, "Louis, Back at Peak, Gives Savage Display," *Ring* 21 (February 1942), 6.

26. Parker, "Louis Stops Baer in First," 18, JLS, Miscellaneous Oversize, 1941–1944. Fleischer, "Louis, Back at Peak, Gives Savage Display," *Ring* 21 (February 1942), 6. John Dower, "Race, Language, and War in Two Cultures: World War II in Asia," *The War in American Culture: Society and Consciousness during World War II*, eds. Lewis A. Erenberg and Susan E. Hirsch (Chicago, 1996), 169–201, shows how the racial war in the Pacific differed from the more ideological war in Europe. For a full-blown discussion of his thesis, see John Dower, *War without Mercy: Race in the Pacific War* (New York, 1986). For some of the adulation given Louis, see James Edmund Boyack, "Louis Hailed at Writers' Banquet," *PC*, January 1942, 17.

27. Joe Louis and Edna and Art Rust, Jr., *Joe Louis: My Life* (New York: 1978), 169–72.

28. For the white South, see *Birmingham News*, 8 January 1942, 20, as in Sammons, *Beyond the Ring*, 124. Memo from Wilkins to White, 3 October 1941, Box 365, NAACP. White to Louis, Roxborough, and Black, 3 October 1941, Box 365, NAACP. See also Sklaroff, "Constructing G.I. Joe Louis," 972, and Capeci and Wilkerson, "Multifarious Hero," 17, for Louis's managers wishing him to avoid conscription as long as possible, and the pressures on him to enlist.

29. Paul Gallico, "Citizen Barrow," *Reader's Digest* 40 (June 1942), 21–25. Jimmy Powers and Burris Jenkins cited in Chris Mead, *Champion—Joe Louis: Black Hero in White America* (New York, 1985), 209–10.

30. Gallico, "Citizen Barrow," 21–25. Louis and Rusts, *Joe Louis*, 169.

31. "Joe Louis Hopes Biased Naval Policies Will End," *PC*, 17 January 1942, 4.

32. For the Treasury Bond campaigns, see Lawrence R. Samuel, *Pledging Allegiance: American Identity and the Bond Drive of World War II* (Washington, D.C., 1999), 88–89, 161–62. See also Sklaroff, "Constructing G.I. Joe Louis."

33. *The Real Joe Louis*, U.S. Army Film, 1946, in possession of MacDonald and Associates, Chicago, Illinois. Newsreel is in Mead, *Champion*, 215–16. "Joe Louis Pleads for Justice at N.Y. Fete," *PC*, 23 May 1942, 1, 4. Lary May, "Making the American Consensus: The Narrative of Conversion and Subversion in World War II Films," *The War in American Culture*, eds. Erenberg and Hirsch, 71–102, and Erenberg, "Swing Goes to War: Glenn Miller and the Popular Music of World War II," 144–65, ibid, discuss the fusion of the state and popular entertainment during the war.

34. For Louis's version of the events, see Louis and Rusts, *Joe Louis*, 173. For Willkie's remarks, see "Joe Louis Fighting for Great Causes," *Daily Mirror*, 23 March 1942, 17.

35. For the radio announcer, see James Edmund Boyack, "It Took Joe Louis to Give the War a Name with a 'Punch,'" *Pittsburgh Courier*, 16 May 1942, 17. Capeci and Wilkerson, "Multifarious Hero," 18, is the source for "Keep Your Powder Dry."

36. Carl Byoir, "Joe Louis Named the War," *Collier's* 109 (16 May 1942), 14.

37. George Roeder, *The Censored War, American Visual Experience during World War Two* (New Haven, 1993), 46–47.

38. *This Is the Army* (Warner Brothers, 1943), songs and music by Irving Berlin, dir. Michael Curtiz. For the growing intersections of popular entertainment and the federal government during the war effort, see Lewis A. Erenberg, *Swingin' the Dream: Big Band Jazz and the Rebirth of American Culture* (Chicago, 1998), and Lary May, *The Big Tomorrow* (Chicago, 2000). Daniel M. Daniel, "Joe Louis Stars in 'This Is the Army,'" *Ring* 22 (September 1943), 8–10, 39. Allan Woll, *The American Musical Goes to War* (Chicago, 1983), 121–30, discusses the segregated segment. For "multi-ethnic platoon," see Richard Slotkin, *Gunfighter Nation* (New York, 1992), 318–26.

39. Lauren Sklaroff, "Constructing G.I. Joe Louis," 958–83, and Capeci and Wilkerson, "Multifarious Hero," 5–25.

40. *The Negro Soldier*, dir. Stuart Heisler (Signal Corps, 1944), held by MacDonald and Associates.

41. I am indebted to Sklaroff, "Constructing G.I. Joe Louis," *JAH*, 980–81, for this paragraph. Thomas Webster to Dowdal Davis, 18 April 1944, box 244, entry 91, Civilian Aide to the Secretary of War Records; *CD*, 26 February 1944, 8, both cited in Sklaroff, 981.

42. Chandler Owens, "Negroes and the War," is cited in Mead, *Champion*, 221–22.

43. *Sahara* was another film that associated the victory by an African soldier over a Nazi with the Louis-Schmeling bout. See Roeder, *The Censored War*, 45–46; Thomas Cripps, *Making Movies Black: The Hollywood Message Movie from World War I to the Civil Rights Era* (New York, 1993), 73–78; and Gerstle, *American Crucible*, 412, n. 51. Cripps, *Making Movies Black*, 118, and Roeder, *The Censored War*, 52, discuss the sex hygiene film.

44. Samuel, *Pledging Allegiance*, xiii–ix, 88–89, 127–51, 161–62. For Louis as a bond salesman in Detroit, see *Michigan Chronicle*, 6 June 1942, 1. For the Tam O'Shanter event, see *Detroit News*, 20 July 1943, 19, and 31 July 1943, 14, as cited in Capeci and Wilkerson, "Multifarious Hero," 19. For Louis in Kansas City, see Samuel, *Pledging Allegiance*, 203–4.

45. Louis quoted, in Samuel, *Pledging Allegiance*, 183. For his bond activities, see 182–85, 203–4.

46. Victor G. Reuther to John Gallo, 11 March 1942, Box 31, UAW War Policy Collection, Archives of Labor and Urban Affairs, Detroit, Michigan; MacLean to Marvin H. McIntryre, 20 November 1942, Box 7, Of 93, FDRP; White to Charles Polenti, 30 April 1943, Box 248, NAACP, all cited in Capeci and Wilkerson, "Multifarious Hero," 19–20. "4th Annual American Negro Music Festival," *Chicago Defender*, 24 July 1943, n. p. Thanks to Sam Floyd for the reference.

47. Capeci and Wilkerson, "Multifarious Hero," 19–20.

48. *NYT*, 11 October 1944, 25, as cited in Capeci and Wilkerson, "Multifarious Hero," 20.

49. "Louis on Tour," *Life* 15 (13 September 1943), 34–35. Bethune to Osborn, 1 June 1943, Box 249, entry 196A, Headquarters of Army Service Forces Records, as in Sklaroff, "Constructing G.I. Joe Louis," 972. See 974 for Edwin Henderson to Hastie and Campbell Johnson, 23 December 1941, Box 248, entry 188, Civilian Aide to the Secretary of War Records.

50. F. K. Winant to Louis Lautier, Box 182, entry 188, Civilian Aide to the Secretary of War Records, as in Sklaroff, "Constructing G.I. Joe Louis," 977. Pvt. Tom Ephrem, "Wounded GI Risks Sight to Get Glimpse of Joe Louis," *Ring* 23 (October 1944), 7.

51. Carroll Fitzgerald to Director, Special Service Division, 27 September 1943, Box 182, entry 188, Civilian Aide to the Secretary of War Records; Harrie W. Pearson to Frederick H. Weston, 28 December 1943, Box 248, entry 196A, Headquarters of Army Service Forces Records; S. Robert Lough to Theodore Bank, 4 October, ibid., as cited in Sklaroff, "Constructing G.I. Joe Louis," 975.

52. Louis and Rusts, *Joe Louis*, 175. The remark to Rowe is in Joe Louis Barrow, Jr., and Barbara Munder, *Joe Louis, Fifty Years an American Hero* (New York, 1998), 135.

53. Nat Fleischer, "The Philadelphia Comet," *Ring* 21 (July 1942), 34, for Louis's quote about Blackburn. Louis and Rusts, *Joe Louis*, 177–78.

54. Louis and Rusts, *Joe Louis*, 179. On the segregated seating, see Barrow and Munder, *Joe Louis*, 141–42.

55. Louis and Rusts, *Joe Louis*, 178.

56. Truman Gibson interview with Chris Mead, as reported in Mead, *Champion*, 230–32. Louis and Rusts, *Joe Louis*, 184–85. Barrow and Munder, *Joe Louis*, 142–44.

57. Sugar Ray Robinson with Dave Anderson, *Sugar Ray* (New York, 1970), 122–23. *Richmond Afro-American*, 9 September 1944. Barrow and Munder, *Joe Louis*, 142–44. Thomas R. Hietala, *The Fight of the Century, Jack Johnson, Joe Louis, and the*

Struggle for Racial Equality (Armonk, N.Y., 2002), 287–94, has a good discussion of Louis during WWII.

58. Louis and Rusts, *Joe Louis*, 187–88.
59. Barrow and Munder, *Joe Louis*, 144–45.
60. Quotes in this paragraph are from "Joe Louis Honored as Model Soldier," *NYT*, 24 September 1945, 32.
61. Schmeling, *Autobiography*, 185–86. Kluge, *Max Schmeling*, 352–62.

CHAPTER 7

1. Margery Miller, *Joe Louis: American* (New York, 1945), 163, 180–81. Eleanor Roosevelt, "Joe Louis as Citizen," *New York World-Telegram*, 21 September 1945, in Papers of the NAACP, Reel 11, Part 18: Special Subjects, 1940–1955, Series C: General Office Files, Justice Department—White Supremacy. Frank Sinatra, cited in Neil Scott, *Joe Louis, a Picture Story of His Life* (New York, 1947), Foreword. For the contrasting positions of the United States and Germany after WWII, see Thomas Englehardt, *The End of Victory Culture* (New York, 1994). Wolfgang Schivelbusch, *The Culture of Defeat, on National Trauma, Mourning, and Recovery*, trans. by Jefferson Chase (New York, 2003; original 2001). Daniel M. Daniel, "Louis-Schmeling Bouts Studies in Contrasts," *Ring* 25 (May 1946), 22.
2. Nat Fleischer, "How Much Has Long Layoff Hurt Joe Louis?" *Ring* 25 (April 1946), 3–4. For confident predictions of a postwar boxing boom, see Daniel M. Daniel, "Louis and Conn Out, Return Match Set," *Ring* 24 (December 1945), 3, 34.
3. "The Ring" Editor, "How Joe Shapes Up," *Ring* 23 (January 1945), 3, 35, discusses the condition of both Louis and Conn. Most of those who followed the fight at home did it via radio.
4. Nat Fleischer, "Louis Again Kayoes Conn," *Ring* 25 (August 1946), 3, provides a wrap-up of the fight.
5. Joe Louis and Edna and Art Rust, Jr., *Joe Louis: My Life* (New York, 1978), 196–97, for the speech at the Woodard benefit.
6. Louis's words are in *PC*, 28 December 1946, as in Thomas R. Hietala, *The Fight of the Century, Jack Johnson, Joe Louis, and the Struggle for Racial Equality* (Armonk, N.Y., 2002), 299–300. For his recollection of who was there and what he thought of prejudice, see Joe Louis, "My Toughest Fight," *Salute* 2 (December 1947), 11–16.
7. For the second Conn fight, the Mauriello bout, and the Walcott matches, see Louis and Rusts, *Joe Louis*, 191–207. On his retirement, see Nat Fleischer, "Louis vs. Gus," *Ring* 27 (September 1948), 3–5; Jersey Jones, "Louis' Retirement Leaves a Sad Mess," *Ring* 27 (September 1948), 6–7; Al Buck, "The End of an Era," *Ring* 27 (October 1948), 12–13, 34, and Daniel M. Daniel, "Joe Louis Retires; Glitter Era Ends," *Ring* 27 (October 1948), 3–4, 34.
8. Louis's problems with business investments are detailed in Gerald Astor, . . . *And a Credit to His Race: The Hard Life and Times of Joe Louis Barrow, a. k. a. Joe Louis* (New York, 1974), 239–42. Apparently, at his meeting with Ford executives, Louis bad-mouthed the recent Ford he had bought. For the problems at the Rhumboogie, see Dempsey J. Travis, *An Autobiography of Black Jazz* (Chicago, 1983), 246–47.
9. Joe Louis, "Why I Won't Marry Again," *Ebony* (November 1952), 36.

10. Marva Louis, "Why I Quit Joe," *Ebony* (December 1949), 61–62, 64–70 gives her reasons for divorce. For Louis's womanizing, see Hietala, *The Fight of the Century*, 304–11, and Dan Burley, "The Love Life of Joe Louis," *Ebony* (July 1951), 22–26, 28–31, 34. See also the interviews with Leonard Reed and Sunnie Wilson in Joe Louis Barrow, Jr., and Barbara Munder, *Joe Louis: Fifty Years an American Hero* (New York, 1988), 201–2, 205. On his affairs during the war, see Sugar Ray Robinson with Dave Anderson, *Sugar Ray* (New York, 1970), 117.

11. Donald McRae, *Heroes without a Country, America's Betrayal of Joe Louis and Jesse Owens* (New York: Ecco, 2002), 241. See also Hietala, *The Fight of the Century*, 315–17.

12. Louis and Rusts, *Joe Louis*, 191–92. Marshall Miles and the Mauriello fight is recounted in Astor, *And a Credit to His Race*, 239–40.

13. For the fixed fight offer, see Louis and Rusts, *Joe Louis*, 197–98. McRae, *Heroes without a Country*, 243–45, covers the postwar period. Business with the IBC is in Barney Nagler, *James Norris and the Decline of Boxing* (Indianapolis, 1964).

14. The re-running of film of the Louis-Schmeling bout is from Chris Mead, *Champion—Joe Louis, Black Hero in White America* (New York, 1985), 259. The crying is from A. J. Liebling, *The Sweet Science* (Westport, Ct., 1973; originally 1956), 47. Arthur Daley, "Sports of the Times," *NYT*, 28 October 1951, 138.

15. Louis quoted in Louis and Rusts, *Joe Louis*, 200.

16. Jimmy Cannon quoted in Mead, *Champion*, 271; Jackie Robinson quoted at 273–74. For the integration of baseball, see Jules Tygiel, *Baseball's Great Experiment, Jackie Robinson and His Legacy* (New York, 1983). For the communist influence, see Irwin Silber, *Press Box Red, the Story of Lester Rodney, the Communist Who Helped Break the Color Line in American Sports* (Philadelphia, 2003).

17. Arthur Daley, "Sports of the Times," *NYT*, 19 June 1949, S2. Nunn, cited in Mead, *Champion*, 274–75.

18. *Chicago Defender*, in Mead, *Champion*, 274–75.

19. The marriage to Rose Morgan and the wrestling episode are in Astor, *A Credit to His Race*, 261–64.

20. His mental illness is covered in Mead, *Champion*, 282–87.

21. All quotes are from Astor, *A Credit to His Race*, 268–73.

22. Max Schmeling, *An Autobiography*, trans. George B. von der Lippe (Chicago, 1998), 185.

23. Schmeling, *Autobiography*, 185–86. Volker Kluge, *Max Schmeling, Eine Biographie in 15 Runden* (Berlin, 2004), 362–65.

24. "Schwere Anklagen gegen Schmeling," *Frankfurter Allgemeine Zeitung*, 8 October 1945, as cited in Kluge, *Max Schmeling*, 365.

25. Schmeling, *Autobiography*, 187–88.

26. Kluge, *Schmeling*, 369–74, provides the details of the de-Nazification hearings and the *Vorwärts* charge. See *Vorwärts*, 21 November 1946, in Kluge, 373 n. 271.

27. Kluge, *Max Schmeling*, 374–75. See "Schmeling Declared Non-Nazi," *NYT*, 25 November 1946, 22, for the ruling.

28. "Schmeling in Comeback," *NYT*, 28 November 1946, 48. His announcement is in "Schmeling Beaten, Says He Will Not Fight Again," *NYT*, 1 November 1948, 34.

29. For minks and burghers, see Omer Anderson, "Max's Moxie with Venders," *Vend* (March 1959), 54. Kluge, *Max Schmeling*, 398–401.

30. "Schmeling Faces Inquiry over Visa," *NYT*, 24 March 1948, 33. For the changed view of consular officials in the mid-1950s, see "Schmeling Wins Mink-Lined Crown," *NYT*, 13 March 1955, S6. For more on hostility toward Schmeling in Germany, see "Row over Schmeling Car," *NYT*, 28 April 1948, 38.

31. Schmeling, *Autobiography*, 193–94. For an excellent article on the history of Coca-Cola in Germany, see Jeff R. Schutts, "Born Again in the Gospel of Refreshment? Coca-Colonization and the Re-Making of Postwar German Identity," in *Consuming Germany in the Cold War*, ed. David Crew (Oxford, 2003), 121–50. For a more in-depth examination, see Jeff R. Schutts, "Coca-Colonization, 'Refreshing' Americanization, or Nazi *Volksgetränk*? The History of Coca-Cola in Germany, 1929–1961," (Ph.D. diss., Georgetown University, 2004). Ralph Willett, *The Americanization of Germany, 1945–1949* (New York, 1989), 99–106, touches on the soft drink's role after the war. For Austria, see Reinhold Wagnleitner, *Coca-Colonization and the Cold War: The Cultural Mission of the United States in Austria after the Second World War* (Chapel Hill, 1994).

32. Schutts, "Born Again in the Gospel of Refreshment?" 127–137, discusses how Germans interpreted Coca-Cola. While he does not discuss Schmeling, the article provides the basis for understanding his role with the company. Schmeling was so well known for pitching Coke on television and at sporting events that the radio program "Listen Up" had upbraided him for the practice. He promised to desist. See "Max Schmeling," *Der Spiegel*, 23 September 1959, n.p., for the story. As to appearing at sports events, see "Ehrungen," *Der Spiegel*, 9 September 1959, n.p.

33. See Schutts, "Born Again in the Gospel of Refreshment?" 135–37.

34. Anderson, "Max's Moxie," *Vend* (March 1959), 54–55.

35. Schutts, "Born Again in the Gospel of Refreshment?" 135–36. Schmeling, *Autobiography*, 196.

36. "Bewegungen, Freiheit e. V.," *Der Spiegel*, 4 February 1959, 15–16. Kluge, *Max Schmeling*, 412–13, discusses his early autobiography. The poll denoting Schmeling as an Athlete of the Century is discussed in Hans Joachim Teichler, "Max Schmeling—Der Sportler des Jahrhunderts im Dritten Reich," *Sportzeit* (2001), 7–8. For more on the subject, and the quote, see Hartmut Scherzer, "Max Schmeling, Ein Idol staunt über Seine Bewunderer," *Der Tagesspiegel*, 24 December 1999, *http://ww2.tagesspiegel.de/archiv/* 23 December 1999. The quote from Walter Scheel is from Siegfried Gehrmann, "Symbol of National Resurrection: Max Schmeling, German Sports Idol," *The International Journal of the History of Sport* 13 (1996), 101–13.

37. Kluge, *Max Schmeling*, 405–6, discusses the meeting with Damski and details of the visit to Jacobs's grave.

38. Schmeling and Louis's conversation is from Schmeling, *Autobiography*, 191–92.

39. "Louis and Schmeling Meet Again," *NYT*, 7 September 1966, 57. "The Years Turn Bitter Enemies to Honored Friends," *NYT*, 26 June 1967, 43. "No Hard Feelings," *NYT*, 13 May 1971, 60. See Robert Weisbord and Norbert Hedderich, "Max Schmeling, Righteous Ring Warrior?" *History Today*, 43 (January 1993), 41, discusses the latter photo.

40. For the thirty-fifth anniversary and the quotes, see Gerald Eskenazi, "An Epilogue: Joe Louis and Max Schmeling Meet Again," *NYT*, 9 August 1973, 40. See also "People in Sports," *NYT*, 3 August 1973, 65, and Gerald Eskenazi, "An Encore for Louis, Schmeling," *NYT*, 10 August 1973, 15, 17.

EPILOGUE

1. For Sinatra's words and the Las Vegas memorial, see Mike Littwin, "Joe Louis Eulogized: A Peerless Champion," *Los Angeles Times*, 18 April 1981, 1, 7.

2. Jackson quoted in Littwin, "Joe Louis Eulogized," *Los Angeles Times*, 18 April 1981, 1, 7.

3. Jackson in Littwin, "Joe Louis Eulogized," *Los Angeles Times*, 18 April 1981, 1, 7.

4. For the Arlington burial and the remarks of fans, see Francis X. Clines, "Hundreds Present for Joe Louis Rites at Arlington," *NYT*, 22 April 1981, A1, B5.

5. "German Boxing Legend Max Schmeling Dies at 99," *NYT*, 4 February 2005, *www.nytimes.com/aponline/sportsAP-Box-Obit-Schmeling*. His dream to live to a hundred is mentioned in "Box-Legende Max Schmeling ist tot," *Der Spiegel*, 4 February 2005, *www.spiegel.de/sport/sonst*.

6. "Box-Legende Max Schmeling ist tot," and "German Boxing Legend Max Schmeling Dies at 99." Michael Hirsley, "Max Schmeling 1905–2005: 'A good fighter and a great man' Cast as 'evil' vs. U.S. hero Louis in famous bout," *Chicago Tribune*, 5 February 2005, 1.

7. Hirsley, "Max Schmeling 1905–2005," 1. Schmeling quoted about being happy he lost, in "German Boxing Legend Max Schmeling Dies at 99."

8. Letter to editor, *Ha'aretz*, 17 February 2005, n. p. Thanks to Esther Cohen for alerting me to this source, and to Elliot Lefkovitz for having it translated.

9. Eric Silver, "Outside the Ring," *The Jerusalem Report* (7 March 2005), 10. Thanks to Elliot Lefkovitz for this source.

10. This paragraph relies on Siegfried Gehrmann, "Symbol of National Resurrection: Max Schmeling, German Sports Idol," *The International Journal of the History of Sport* 13 (1996), 112–13. For atonement and the Fair Play Prize, see *Kicker Sportmagazin* (1 October 1979), n. p., in Miscellaneous Schmeling Clipping file, Sporthochschule, Köln.

11. J. C. Alexander and R. N. Jacobs, "Mass Communication, Ritual, and Civil Society," in Tamar Liebes, James Curran, and Elihu Katz, eds., *Media, Ritual and Identity* (London, 1998), 23–41. Thanks to Loyola graduate student Brendan Cunningham for bringing this article to my attention. See Susan J. Douglas, *Listening In, Radio and the American Imagination* (New York, 1999), 199–209, and Benedict Anderson, *Imagined Communities: Reflections on the Origins and Spread of Nationalism* (London, 1983) for the idea of nationalism spread through mass communications.

INDEX

Affairs, Louis having, 88–89
African Americans. *See also*
 Black community; Negroes
 American inheritance for, 209
 better days coming for, 69–
  70
 color line drawn for, 33–34
 direction for, 25–26
 equal rights encouraged for,
  196
 exultant celebrations from,
  125
 fighter as symbol for, 153
 film's racial images of, 188
 inclusive treatment for, 187–
  88
 Louis defeat devastating for,
  98–100, 229
 Louis victory celebrated by,
  151
 oppressed defiance from,
  152–53
 positive aspects for, 196
 race heroes for, *85*
 as sports heroes, 207
 victory poems from, 152
 wartime unity by, 190
Albers, Hans, 17
Alger, Horatio, 51
Ali, Muhammad, 210, 223
Ali-Foreman fight, 228–29
American anti-fascist coalition, 111
American culture, 64
American Jews, 111
American Olympic Com-
  mittee, 57, 75

Americans
 democracy imperiled for, 138
 equal rights for, 196
 identity issues of, 121
 Louis defending, 138, 146
 Louis national hero for, *146*,
  155–56, 175, 183
 Louis support for, 179
 national identity for, 155,
  161–62, 178
 national representative for,
  160
 Nazi claims about, 74
 racial pluralism and, 159
Anderson, Marian, 189
Angelou, Maya, 99
Anti-Nazi League, 139
Anti-Semitism, 159
Armed forces segregation,
  191, 197
Armstrong, Henry, 27, 54, 64,
  81, 128
Armstrong, Louis, 101
Army, 177, 180, 181
 boxing exhibitions for, 190
 Louis causing changes in,
  195–96, 209–10
 Louis discharged from, 200
 Louis enlisting in, 180–81
 Louis's efforts appreciated
  by, 192
Army camp tour, 191–92
Aryan superman, 3–4
Aryan supremacy
 athletics and, 59
 Louis's victory blow to,
  157–58, 225–27, 229–30

Owens destroying, 108
Schmeling hero of, 2, 5
Astor, Gerald, 28
Athletes, 26

Baer, Buddy, 179–80
Baer, Max, 31, 32, 41, 62
 Braddock upsetting, 67
 Schmeling outclassed by, 22
Baker, Russell, 154
Balogh, Harry, 41, 142
Barbour, Warren, 163
Barrow, Joseph Louis. *See*
  Louis, Joe
Barrow, Lillie Reese, 22, 51
Barrow, Munrow, 22
Basie, Count, 81
Basquiat, Jean Michel, 225
Belling, Rudolf, 17
Berger, Meyer, 78
Bergman, Gretel, 61
Berkie, Hans, 38
Berlin, Germany, 16
Berlin, Irving, 186
Bethune, Mary McLeod, 152,
  192
Black boxers
 discrimination experienced
  by, 65
 dying sport revived by, 54
 race inferiority for, 78
 things easing up for, 129
Black champion(s)
 as American democracy ex-
  emplars, 129
 boxing with, 128–29
 Harlem celebrating, 125–26

Black champion(s) (*continued*)
  little hostility toward, 79
  Louis posing as, *135*
Black community
  achievements influencing,
    52–53
  communal outpourings
    from, 87
  cultural pride for, 153
  Louis household name in,
    83–84
  Louis identifying with, 100–
    101
  Louis liberating, 81–82
  Louis's victory triumph for,
    155
  racial sentiment from, 125
  Roxborough advancing, 29
  U.S. war effort needing,
    182–83
  white power challenged by,
    126, 153–54
Black Dynamite: The Story of
  the Negro in Boxing
  (Fleischer), 65
Black folk hero, 81, 86
Black, Julian, 30, 45, 160, 193,
  205
Black masculinity, 87
Black men
  jungle imagery for, 42–43
  poster glorifying, 186
Black menace, 42
Black press
  athlete pride from, 82
  Louis depictions in, 83
Black pride, 80, 127
Black, Timuel, 127
Black youth, 9
Blackburn, Jack, 47, 156
  death of, 193
  heavyweight division doubt-
    ful from, 33
  Louis fight plan by, 141
  as Louis's knowledgeable
    trainer, 31
  manslaughter conviction for,
    45
  training camp closed by, 107
Blacks. *See* African Americans
Bohnen, Michael, 17, 168
Bonaglia, Michele, 13
Bottoms, Bill, 30–31
Boxers. *See also* Black boxers
  erotic appeal of, 16
  as freedoms symbol, 17
  intelligence factor for, 14
  military entered by, 177
  as role models, 59
Boxing. *See also* Black boxers;
  Fight films; Heavyweight
  champion; Prizefighting;
  Sports
  better days coming for, 70
  black champions in, 79, 125–
    26, 128–29, *135*
  changes underway for, 36
  color line broken by, 4, 65,
    124, 210, 225–26

comeback for, 63–64
cultural influence of, 17
depression influencing, 21,
  31
economic opportunities of,
  24
epic battles from, 12
excitement generated by, 9
fraud charged in, 31, 32
Germans rise in, 13
golden gloves saving, 25
Hitler supporting, 60
hotbed for, 11
international politicalization
  of, 3
Louis most valuable in, 168–
  69
Louis respected for, 26
Louis reviving, 37–38
Louis taking lessons for, 25
Louis's first bout in, 31
as mass spectator sport, 35
mixed-race fight for, 40–41
national socialist regime
  showcasing, 37–38
Nazis promoting, 56, 59
northern cities supporting,
  24–25
political dimensions of, 3,
  39–40, 230
political intensification influencing, 106–7
racial issues in, 62
reputation reversed for, 13
revitalization of, 41–42
Schmeling reviving, 56
as trade (craft), 14
Boycott
  American Olympic Commit-
    tee and, 57, 75
  Anti-Nazi League announc-
    ing, 139
  Braddock-Schmeling match
    and, 112
  Schmeling helped avoid, 76
  Schmeling upset by, 112–13
Braddock, James J., 31, 62,
  104
  arthritic hands of, 78
  background of, 122–23
  Baer upset by, 67
  Louis fight preferred for,
    113–14
  Louis knocking out, 125
  Louis overshadowing, 107
  Louis title fight against, 1,
    121, 123–25, *124*
  New York State Athletic
    Commission prohibiting,
    110
  phantom fight with, 118
  as qualifying match, 71
Braddock-Louis exhibition,
  109–10
Braddock-Schmeling match,
  112
Brain trust, 48
Brescia, Jorge, 109
Brier, Royce, 160

Brisbane, Arthur, 40
British troops, 172–74, *197*,
  212
Brooks, Lillie Reese, 210
Brooks, Pat, 26
Brooks-Barrow family
  economics improving for,
    51–52
  impoverishment for, 24
  North not promised land
    for, 23
Broun, Heywood, 1, 158
Brown bomber. *See* Louis, Joe
Brown, Natie, 113
Brown, Prentiss M., 180
Bruen, John, 175
Brundage, Avery, 57, 75
Buchwald, Art, 175
Bülow, Arthur, 12, 19, 73
Burns, Tommy, 33, 34
Byoir, Carl, 184

Cahn, Sammy, 184
Cannon, Jimmy, 141, 209
Capone, Al, 30, 51
Carnera, Primo, 31, 37, 107
  as carnival strongman, 32
  Louis beating, 41
Carnera-Sharkey fight, 32
Carpentier, Georges, 3, 35,
  169
Carroll, Ted, 129
"Carrying the males," 8
Carter, Jimmy, 160
Cartoons, 155–57
  bouts international implica-
    tions from, *157*
  Louis depicted in, 78–80
Casey, Doc, 142
Catholic Youth Organization
  (CYO), 25
Cellar, Emmanuel, 163
Charles, Ezzard, 206
Civic groups, 190
Civil rights
  Louis assisting, 202
  Louis demonstrating for,
    177
  slowed pace of, 230–31
Clarens, George, 42
Clay, Cassius, 220
Coca-Cola, 216–19, 231
Color line
  African Americans and, 33–
    34
  boxing breaking, 4, 65, 124,
    210, 225–26
  brain trust and, 48
  decline of, 163–64
  Ring magazine promoting
    end of, 64
Congress
  federal ban ended by, 162–
    63
  fight films banned by, 34
Conn, Billy, 175, 189, 200,
  201
Cooper, Gary, 136
Copeland, Jack, 54

Corbett, Jim, 34, 164
Corri, Pietro, 20
Corum, Bill, 137, 158
Cosby, Billy, 223
Cowans, Russell, 46
Crib, Tom, 33
Cribbs, Tom, 164
Crime, 28
Cross, Jimmy, 84, 186
Cultural institutions, 75
Culture of defeat, 10
Cummings, Homer, 136
Czapp, Johann, 11

Daley, Arthur, 207
Damski, Paul, 60, 75, 220
Daniel, Daniel M., 149
Dannick, Frederick L., 113
Davis, Benjamin Jr., 196
Davis, Frank Marshall, 112, 152
Davis, Sammy Jr., 223
Delarge, Fernand, 13, 18
Democracy
  army camp tour promoting, 192
  black champions exemplars for, 129
  fascism fought by, 154
  Louis defending American, 146, 150-51, 155-56
  Nazis v., 139-40, 150
  world representative of, 162
Democratic values, 192
Dempsey, Jack, 3, 19, 136
  Louis as best heavyweight felt by, 161
  Louis's toughness questioned by, 78
  millions earned by, 11, 27
  restaurant of, 220
  Schmeling ranked by, 20
  Tunney fight with, 35
De-nazification committee, 214
Depression
  black youth suffering in, 9
  boxing attendance declining from, 21, 31
  Detroit suffering in, 24
  Fascism created by, 9-10
  Madison Square Garden influenced by, 65-66
Detroit (Michigan), 24
Deutsch, Ernst, 17
Diekmann, Max, 13
Diener, Fritz, 13
Dietrich, Marlene, 139
Dimaggio, Joe, 175
Discrimination
  black boxers experiencing, 65
  Louis experiencing, 210
  Louis fighting, 179, 201-2, 226
Ditgens, Heinz, 168, 213
Doakes, Joe, 181
Domgörgen, Hein, 15
Donegan, Dorothy, 190

Donovan, Arthur, 143, 221
Dorsey, Thomas A., 190
Double V campaign, 183
Dovzinsky, Benjamin, 227
Dudas, Steve, 141
Duffy, William, 32

Early, Gerald, 43
Edwards, Harry Stillwell, 79
Ellington, Duke, 81, 84, 183, 189
Ephrem, Tom, 192
Esser, Herman, 116
Ettore, Al, 109
Every, Ed Van, 79

Farley, James, 136, 217
Farnsworth, Bill, 66
Farr, Tommy, 131
Farrell, James T., 90, 91
Fascism
  democracies fighting, 154
  depression creating, 9-10
  domestic supremacy and, 158
Fight films
  congress banning, 34
  enthusiastic crowds watching, 94
  federal ban ended for, 162-63
  Senate focus for, 163
  symbolic German depicted in, 95
"Fight of the Century," 143-45
Fiori, Ernesto de, 17
Firpo, Luis, 3, 35
Fitzsimmons, Bob, 38
Flannery, Harry, 173
Fleischer, Nat, 38, 90, 123
  as boxing expert, 64-65
  Hitler comment by, 174-75
  Louis's postive comments by, 43
  as *Ring* magazine editor, 13
  Schmeling's positive reception from, 19
Foord, Ben, 141
Ford, Henry, 16
Frayne, Ed, 66, 69
Friedman, Walter, 32
Fritsch, Willy, 17

Gable, Clark, 136
Galento, Tony, 142, 170, 175
Gallico, Paul, 42, 181
Garvey, Marcus, 155
Gehrig, Lou, 51
Gehrmann, Siegfried, 16, 18
German athletics, 60-61
German hero, 120
German honor, 73
German Jews
  Hitler's policies against, 135-36
  Nuremburg laws and, 75
  outrages against, 193
  Schmeling assisting, 168, 228

Schmeling conspired against by, 120
Schmeling working with, 76
situation dangerous for, 168
German media
  Goebbels restricting, 73
  national prestige not lost from, 149-50
  patriotic celebrations from, 95-96
  Schmeling's name struck from, 173
Germans
  American conspiracy by, 118
  American racial miscegenation from, 97
  boxing disdained by, 14
  fight films resurrecting, 95
  inferior race stunning, 147
  kidney punch controversial to, 148-49
  Louis boxing instinctual from, 96-97
  Louis savage fighter to, 148
  Louis's title illegitimate for, 130-31
  Negro people and, 97
  racial victory for, 91-92
  Schmeling admired by, 118
  sport strengthening, 58-59
  unfair machinations charged by, 149
Germany. *See also* Weimar culture
  athletes achievement and, 94
  as divided country, 216
  economic miracle for, 219
  fight footage viewing denied in, 149
  Goebbels transforming fight for, 229
  racial definitions for, 62
  redemption sought by, 218-19
  Schmeling defeat embarrassing for, 167
  Schmeling national hero for, 103
  Schmeling's fate in, 165
  Schmeling's loss defeat for, 150-51
  territorial aggression from, 137-38
Gerstle, Gary, 178
Gibson, Truman, 194, 195
Gilford, Jack, 196
Gillespie, Dizzy, 84
Godfrey, George, 36, 108
Goebbels, Josef, 91, 168, 172
  German media restricted by, 73
  German national victory by, 229
  Jewish mistreatment temporarily halted by, 104
  as Minister of Enlightenment and Propaganda, 56
Golden Gloves, 25
Goodman, Benny, 127
Goodwin, Ruby Berkley, 53

Göring, Hermann, 108
Goth, Rolf von, 168, 213
Gould, Joe, 106, 112, 124
Government regulation, 32
"Greatest fight of our generation," 136
Greene, Abe, 163
Grosskopf, Friedrich, 213
Grosz, Georg, 17

Haberman, Joshua O., 225
Hamas, Steve, 55, 71
Hamburg, 150, 198
Hampton, Lionel, 127
Harlan, Veit, 213
Harlem
  black champion celebrated in, 125–26
  Hamburg newspaper view of, 150
  Louis celebrated by, *40, 132, 151*
Harrington, L.E., 80
Harris, Monk, 79
Harten, Thomas, 102
Hayes, B. Weldon, 70
Haynes, LeRoy, 154
Hearst, William Randolph, 66
Heavyweight champion
  Schmeling as, *19*
  white men reserving, 42
Heavyweight division
  Blackburn skeptical about, 33
  Louis best of, 69
  as segregated, 34
Heenan, John C., 3
Heeney, Tom, 3
Helldorf, Graf, 213
Hellmis, Arno, 94, 147
Henie, Sonja, 50
Henry, John, 81
Hero. *See* National hero
Heuser, Adolf, 169
Hitler, Adolf, 116
  anti-semitic policies of, 135–36
  athletic success validation for, 115
  boxing supported by, 60
  European champion plans by, 131
  fight angering, 73
  fight disappointing, 147
  Fleischer commenting on, 174–75
  Louis-Schmeling rematch and, 169–70
  physical training promoted by, 59
  Schmeling solicited by, 58
  Schmeling telegraphed by, 91, 141
  Schmeling's reception by, *93*
  sport reorganization by, 60
  sports politicized by, 117, 134–35, 151
  territorial aggression from, 137–38
  virile fascist man for, 59–60

Hoffman, Heinrich, 168
Holiday, Billie, 196
Hollywood films, 188
Hoover, J. Edgar, 136
Horne, Lena, 50, 99
Hughes, Ed, 156
Hughes, Langston, 188
Humphreys, Joe, 68

Igoe, Hype, 78, 114
Industrialized countries, 9
Internal Revenue Service (IRS), 205
International sport, 2–4
International tensions, 102
Iron Cross, 172

Jackson, Jesse Louis, 223–24
Jackson, Peter, 33
Jacobs, Cashwell, 220
Jacobs, Joe, 19, *61*, 76, 98, 142
Jacobs, Mike, 46, 65, 67, 83, 114
  bout scheduled by, 201
  as Louis's promoter, *66*
  Schmeling rematch sought by, 131
Jahr, John, 212
James, C.L.R., 2, 54
Jefferson, Martha, 211
Jeffries, Jim, 34, 162
Jenkins, Burris Jr., 7, *8*, 9, 94, 159, 181
Jennings, Emil, 17
Jews. *See* American Jews; German Jews
Joe Lewis: Man and Super-Fighter (Van Every), 79
Johnson, Hugh, 161
Johnson, Jack, 27, 34, 78
  heavyweight title held by, 33
  white supremacy challenged by, 42
Johnson, Lil, 86
Johnston, Jimmy, 56, 65
Jones, Jimmy, 51
Julian Black, 30
Jungle imagery, 42–43

Kelley, Edward J., 160
Kells, Clarence H., 197
Kellum, David, 126
Ketchell, Steve, 113
Kid Chocolate, 27
Kidney punch, 148–49
Kieran, John, 106
King, Alan, 223
King, Martin Luther Jr, 202
Kluge, Volker, 214
Kortner, Fritz, 15
Kracken, Jack, 31
Krupa, Gene, 127
Ku Klux Klan, 23
Kuhn, Fritz, 137

LaGuardia, Fiorello, 111
Langford, Sam, 38
Lasky, Art, 123
Lazek, Heinz, 213

Lee, Rocky, 211
Leiper, Henry Smith, 110
Lenny, Harry, 122
Leo, Claudius, 154
Leonard, Sugar Ray, 223
Levine, Lawrence, 81, 153
Levinsky, Kingfish, 41, 80
Lewald, Theodore von, 75
Lewin, Daniel, 168, 228
Lewin, Henri, 168, 228
Lewis, John Henry, 54, 81, 123, 128, 164, 175
Lewis, Theophilus, 70
Lily, William E., 153
Lindsey, Hosea, 225
Lough, Robert, 192
Loughran, Tommy, 122
Louis, Joe. *See also* Brooks-Barrow family; Louis-Schmeling fight; Management, of Louis
  African Americans devastated by loss of, 98–100, 229
  amateur to professional transition for, 28
  America defended by, 138, 146
  America support from, 179
  army boxing exhibitions by, 190
  army changes caused by, 195–96, 209–10
  army discharge for, 200
  army enlistment for, 180–81
  Aryan supremacy influenced by, 157–58, 225–27, 229–30
  avenging loss for, 130
  Baer demolished by, 179–80
  big-time boxing revived by, 37–38
  black community identifying with, 100–101
  black community liberated by, 81–82
  black community victory by, 155
  black equality improved by, 126, 226
  as black folk hero, 81, 86
  Black, Julian, financing, 30
  black press depicting, 83
  black press linking fans with, 82
  black pride galvanized by, 80, 127
  Blackburn planning for, 141
  boxing earned respect for, 26
  boxing industry benefiting from, 63–64
  boxing lessons for, 25
  Braddock fighting, 1, 113–14, 121, 123–25
  Braddock knocked out by, 125
  Braddock overshadowed by, 107

Braddock slugging it out
  with, *124*
brain trust of, *30*
as brown bomber, 8
career pinnacle for, 164–65
career starting for, 22
Carnera beat by, 41
cartoons depicting, 78–80
childhood of, 22–23
civic groups demanding, 190
civil rights assisted by, 177,
  202
civilian life for, 199
clean living for, 46, 49, 54
crime blamed on, 28
death of, 223–25
debt for, 206
democracy defended by,
  146, 150–51, 155–56
Dempsey commenting on,
  78, 161
discreet affairs by, 88–89
discrimination experienced
  by, 210
fair play embodied by, 182
as fighting champion, 163–
  64
financial problems for, 203–6
first professional bout for, 31
Fleischer commenting on, 43
formal burial rites for, 224–25
Harlem crowd celebrating,
  40, *132*, *151*
higher gate attracted by, 114
IRS problem of, 205
Jacob's promoting, *66*
Jefferson third wife of, 211
Ku Klux Klan threatening
  family of, 23
last fight for, *208*
Legion of Merit Medal for,
  197
management crafting image
  for, 47
management teams role in,
  45
Marciano ending career of,
  207
marriage of, 47, 68, 210, 211
Marva and, *204*
Morgan marrying, 210, 211
most valuable boxer award
  for, 168–69
musical tributes to, 85–86
as national hero, *146*, 153,
  175, 183
as national unity symbol,
  183
Nazis supremacy killed by,
  158, 225
Negro people represented
  by, 54
no excuses by, 100
opponents examined by, 200
overconfidence by, 89
overwhelming power by, *144*
paranoia of, 211
political arena entered by,
  175–77

as political symbol, 5
as posing champion, *135*
poster of, *185*
professional wrestling for,
  210–11
propaganda with, 186
public speaking by, 183–84
qualifying match for, 71
as race ambassador, *53*
race mission for, 52
racial discrimination fought
  by, 179, 201–2, 226
racial issues and, 163
racial segregation obstacle
  for, 32–33
racial sentiment about, 125
racism apparent to, 193–94
retiring, 203
right hand defense by, 141
as role model, *44*, *84*, 209
Roxborough developing, 29–
  30
as run-of-mill fighter, 39
Schmeling defeated by, 145
Schmeling defeating, 1, *90*,
  91
Schmeling funeral donation
  for, 223
Schmeling loss revenge for,
  130
Schmeling offered bout
  with, 108
Schmeling poses with, *221*
Schmeling rematch negoti-
  ated for, 131, 133
Schmeling reunion with,
  220–22
Schmeling weigh in for, 72,
  142
segregated army for, *191*
segregated audiences refused
  by, 194–95
self-esteem, decorum of, 48
sense of humor of, 49
Sharkey knocked out by,
  107–8
show business ties for, 84–85
spending problem for, 49
sportswriters shamed by,
  101–2
sportswriters writing about,
  43
title bout training by, 121–
  22, 140
title picture again for, 109
training burden for, 202–3
Trotter married to, 47
as unanimous favorite, 180
undying admiration sought
  by, 181
war effort important to,
  177–78
war named by, 184
weakness for, 88
well planned fight by, 164
well wishers greeted by, *50*
white hope ended by, 162,
  226
white press depiction of, 78–
  79

white supremacy celebrating
  defeat of, 101
Willkie campaigned for by,
  176
women drawn to, 50
as working class hero, 51,
  129–30
as worlds best fighter, 69,
  147
Louis-Baer fight
  as career's best, 68–69
  million-dollar gate for, 67,
    68
Louis-Braddock fight, 1, 113–
  14, *123–24*
  American identity issues
    from, 121
  exultant celebrations from,
    125
Louis-Conn fight, *178*, 201
Louis-Farr fight, 132–33
Louis-Schmeling fight
  account of, 89–90
  American national strength
    from, 140
  cartoons depicting, *157*
  celebrations of, *151*, 152–53
  dramatic tension of, 89
  as exciting sports drama, 8–9
  fighters entering ring for,
    142–43
  as international media event,
    136–37
  international tensions and,
    102
  Louis attacks in, 143–45
  nationalistic views and, 4,
    178
  political drama of, 152, 229
  racial ideologies and, 3
  rematch not approved for,
    169–70
  Schmeling on ropes in, *144*
  weigh in for, 72, 142
  as WWII metaphor, 231
"Low blow champion," 21
Lunceford, Jimmie, 81, 84
Lyons, Alexander, 102

Machon, Max, 119, 212
  camp run by, 12
  fighter rescued by, 145
MacLean, Malcolm S., 190
Madden, Owney, 32, 46, 109
Madison Square Garden, 65–
  66
Mahoney, Jeremiah T., 111
Malcolm X, 125
Management, of Louis
  army induction stalled by,
    181
  business skill of, 46
  gamble by, 67
  image crafted by, 47
  Louis guided by, 45
Marciano, Rocky, 207
Martin, Carl, 86
Massaquoi, Hans, 62, 96
Massara, Charlie, 38

Mathison, Charles F., 20
Mauriello, Tami, 203
May, Karl, 16
McCarthy, Clem, 136
McCoy, Memphis Minnie, 86
McDowell, John, 216
McElvaine, Robert, 52
McGrath, Johnny Irish, 175
McKinney, Thurston, 25
Meisl, Willy, 14
Metcalfe, Ralph, 80, 188
Metzner, Franz, 131, 141
Mildenberger, Karl, 220
Military, 177
Miller, Margery, 199
Millinder, Lucky, 180
Milton, Leonard, 222
Mitchell, Jonathan, 51
Molineaux, Tom, 33
Monroe, Al, 100
Morgan, Rose, 210, 211, 220
Morgenthau, Henry, 138
Morris, Earl J., 127
Moss, Carlton, 187
Mostel, Zero, 196
Murphy, Frank, 160
Musical tributes, 85–86
Musicians, black, 85–86
Mussolini, Benito, 13

Nagel, Conrad, 184
Nagler, Barney, 67
National hero
  Louis as, *146*, 153, 175, 183
  Schmeling as, 2, 5, 91, 92,
    95, 103, 130–31, 219
National socialist regime
  Aryan superman for, 3–4
  boxing revival for, 56
  boxing showcase for, 37–38
  racial anxieties and, 105
  ruling disturbing to, 73
  Schemling's dissatisfaction
    with, 74
Nazis. *See also* Aryan su-
    premacy; Germans; Hitler,
    Adolf; National socialist
    regime
  American Jewish activities
    against, 111
  Americans supporting white
    boxer from, 74
  athletic political revolution
    for, 54
  boxing promoted by, 56, 59
  cultural institutions con-
    trolled by, 75
  democracy imperiled by, 138
  democracy v., 139–40, 150
  Louis killing supremacy idea
    for, 158, 225
  Olympics expressing ideals
    of, 104–5
  Olympics testing theories of,
    105
  party rally by, 55
  power legitimized for, 57
  racial ideologies and, 193,
    231

racial pride in, 160
racial superiority threatened
  for, 73
Schmeling hero for, 91, 92
Schmeling honored by, 57,
  119
Schmeling pressured by, 77
Schmeling refusing award
  from, 115–16
Schmeling relationship
  strained with, 166–67
Schmeling symbol of, 135–
  36, 228
Schmeling used by, 58
sports politicalization by,
  110, 229
as true sportsmen, 149
Negroes
  German attitudes toward, 97
  Louis representative for, 54
  savagery of, 150
Nelson, Carl, 49
Neusel, Walter, 55, 60, 71,
  131, 170, 173, 215
New York State Athletic
  Commission
  Braddock exhibition prohib-
    ited by, 110
  government regulation
    mockery by, 32
Nicholson, George, 114, 190
Noack, Paul, 213
Northern cities, 24–25
Nova, Lou, 170
Nunn, William G., 100, 108,
  125, 127, 153, 209
Nuremburg laws, 75

Office of War Information
  (OWI), 182, 188
Officer Candidate School
  (OCS), 194
Olympics
  boycott of, 57, 75
  Nazi ideals symbolized in,
    104–5
  Nazi theories tested in, 105
Ondra, Anny, 15, *16*, 75
Osten, Hans von Tschammer
  und, 60, 76, 91, 170
Ottley, Roi, 37, 52
Owens, Chandler, 188
Owens, Jesse, 52, 80, 108, 115

Parker, Dan, 155, 179
Pastor, Bob, 113, 127
Patriotism, 160–61
Patterson, Floyd, 223
Patterson, William L., 158
Peacock, Eulace, 80
Peck, Gregory, 136
Perkins, Francis, 138
Perroni, Patsy, 38
Phantom fight, 118
Pickens, William, 189
Political theater, 2
Politics
  boxing with, 3, 39–40, 230
  international sport and, 2–3

Louis entering, 175–77
Louis-Schmeling fight and,
  152, 229
sports victories and, 97
Povich, Shirley, 69
Powell, Adam Clayton, 99
Prejudice, 64
Press, Daniel, 61
Press. *See* White press
Prizefighting
  dramatic arena of, 15
  Schmeling resuming, 213
Propaganda
  black contributions for, 187
  Louis's role in, 186
  political messages of, 188
Public speaking, 183–84

Race ambassadors, *53*
Race riots, 34
Racial hierarchy, 4
Racial identity, 44
Racial ideologies, 3, 193, 231
Racial issues
  black contenders with, 35
  blacks, Jews facing, 159–60
  boxing, 62
  Louis not upsetting tran-
    quility for, 163
  WWII with, 193
Racial segregation, 32–33
Racial victory
  Germans winning, 91–92
  Louis winning, 147
Racism
  Americans struggle with,
    159
  athletic supremacy and, 105,
    230
  Louis not sheltered from,
    193–94
  national socialist regime
    with, 105
  whites not displaying, 128
Ramage, Lee, 38
Randolph, Philip, 182
Reagan, Ronald, 224
Reception, *93*
Repressed people, 152
Resnick, Ash, 211
Retzlaff, Charley, 88
Rice, Grantland, 42, 101, 106,
  164
Richmond, Al, 126
Rickard, Tex, 35, 65, 130
Rickey, Branch, 207
Riefenstahl, Leni, 105
Ring magazine
  color barrier and, 64
  Fleischer editor of, 13
  Schmeling Merit award
    from, 115
Risko, Johnny, 15, 20
Robeson, Paul, 190
Robinson, Bill "Bojangles," 84
Robinson, Donald, 194
Robinson, Jackie, 194, 207
Robinson, Sugar Ray, 190
Rodney, Lester, 112

Role model, *44*, *84*, 209
Roosevelt, Eleanor, 80, 160, 199
Roosevelt, Franklin D., 136, 183
Root, Waverly, 212
Roper, Jack, 175
Rosenbloom, Maxie, 39
Ross, Barney, 64
Rotholtz, Shabbatai, 227
Rowe, Billy, 50, 83, 179, 193
Roxborough, John, 45, 109, 193, 200
  as bail bondsmen, 28–29
  black community advanced by, 29
  phony fight film accused by, 149
"Rumble in the jungle, 228
Runyon, Damon, 66, 122

Sammons, Jeffrey, 31–32, 63, 162
Sayers, Tom, 3
Scheel, Walter, 219
Schindler, Kurt, 75
Schmeling, Max. *See also* Louis-Schmeling fight
  Baer outclassing, 22
  boxing revival by, *56*
  boycott avoided because of, 76
  boycott upsetting to, 112–13
  Braddock no-show for, 118
  British concerned about, 212
  British troops detaining, *197*
  career adventures for, 12
  championship match and, 116
  as Coca-Cola executive, 6, 231
  Coca-Cola license received by, 216–17
  comeback brief for, *215*
  confidence of, 87–88
  controversial punch to, 145
  death of, 226
  Dempsey ranking, 20
  economic uncertainty for, 11
  fate in Germany for, 165
  fighting returned to, 214–15
  Fleischer's positive reception for, 19
  German defeat in defeat of, 150–51
  German media ignoring, 173
  German people admiring, *118*
  Germany embarrassed by, 167
  as Germany's hero, 91, 92, 95, 103, 130–31, 219
  government isolation for, 167–68
  Hamburg fleeing to by, 198
  as heavyweight champion, *19*
  Hitler telegraphing, 91, 141

Hitler's reception for, *93*
Iron Cross received by, 172
Jacobs, Joe, greeting, *61*
Jews assisted by, 168, 228
Jews conspiring against, 120
key members lost for, 142
Louis avenging loss from, 130
Louis defeating, 145
Louis funeral donation by, 223
Louis knocked out by, 1, *90*, 91
Louis offering rematch to, 108
Louis poses with, 221
Louis rematch negotiated for, 131, 133
Louis rematch sought by, 169
Louis reunion with, 220–22
Louis weigh in for, *72*, 142
as low blow champion, 21
mass reception for, *93*
movies starring, 15–16
as national hero, 92, 95
Nazi award refused by, 115–16
Nazi party using, 58
Nazi relationship strained for, 166–67
Nazi relationship with, 74
Nazis honoring, 57, 119
Nazis pressuring, 77
as Nazis symbol, 135–36, 228
Ondra with, *16*
as paratrooper, *171*
paratrooper corps drafting, 170–71
plan formulated by, 88
as political symbol, 1–2, 5
powerful right punches from, 90
prizefighting resumed for, 213
public opinion shocking to, 138–39
qualifying match for, 71
race superiority won by, 92
ranks ascended by, 12–13
reception for, 92–93
redemption for, 227
reputation damaged for, 20, 21
resurgence of, 54
retiring, 173–74
reversal of fortunes for, 10
Ring magazine Merit award for, 115
on the ropes for, *144*
rumors about, 212–13
Sharkey v., 20, 21–22
survival struggle for, 200
title bout training by, 140–41
title contention for, 55
title fight sought by, 117–18
as transatlantic athlete, 18

troubles for, 97–98
U.S. image of, 174
U.S. return for, 216
vending machines introduced by, 217
as wealthy man, 15, 215–18
white press fond of, 79–80
white supremacy embodied by, 151–52
Schultz, Dutch, 32
Schutts, Jeff, 218
Schuyler, George, 86
Schwarzmann, Alfred, 170
Seelig, Erich, 61
Segregation. *See also* Color line; Discrimination
  armed forces, *191*, 197
  German athletics practicing, 60–61
  governments commitment to, 190
  heavyweight division with, 34
  Louis improving, 209–10, 226
  Louis refusing, 194–95
  Louis's army service having, *191*, 197
  racial, 32–33
Sekyra, Joe, 20
Senate, 163
Sharkey, Jack, 14, 15, 32, 77, 226
  Louis knocking out, 108
  Louis's next bout against, 107
  Schmeling v., 20, 21–22
Sharkey-Schmeling fight, 20, 21–22
Shaver, Bud, 161
Show business, 84–85
Siki, Battling, 36
Simms, Eddie, 109
Simon, Abe, 180
Sinatra, Frank, 199, 200, 223
Sintenis, Renee, 17
Smith, Gerald L., 138
Southern press, 64
Spandau, George, 91, 97
Sports
  Germans strengthened by, 58–59
  healthy racial body, Nazis and, 59
  Hitler politicizing, 117, 134–35, 151
  Hitler reorganizing, 60
  Jews commercializing, 18
  Jews conspiring in, 120
  Nazis politicizing, 110, 229
Sports drama, 8–9, 228–29
Sportswriters
  bout downplayed by, 140
  Louis defeat shaming, 101–2
  Louis's strengths reported by, 43
Springer, Axel, 212, 219
Steel workers, *178*
Sternberg, Josef von, 17

Stewart, Walter, 101
Stimson, Henry, 200
Strauss, Sol, 131
Streicher, Julius, 73
Streseman, Gustav, 16
Stribling, Young, 21, 32
Styne, Jule, 184
Sullivan, John L., 33

Taylor, Robert, 136
The Negro Soldier, 187
This is the Army (Berlin), 186
Thomas, Harry, 141
Thomas, Tommy, 123
Thorak, Josef, 17, 98, 104
Title fight
  Louis training for, 121–22,
    140
  Louis-Braddock, 1, 113–14,
    121, 123–25
  Schmeling seeking, 117–18
  Schmeling training for, 140–
    41
Tolan, Eddie, 80
Training, 59, 121–22, 140–41,
  202–3
Transatlantic athlete, 18
Treasury Bond campaigns,
  189
Treaty of Versailles, 10
Trollman, Johann "Rukelie,"
  61
Trotter, Marva
  Louis and, *204*
  marriage of, 47, 68
  well wishers greeted by, *50*
Tschechowa, Olga, 17
Tunney, Gene, 3, 136
  Dempsey fight with, 35
  as Louis spy, 148
  retirement of, 19, 36
Tunney, John, 122
Turner, Lana, 50
Twentieth Century Sporting
  Club

bout promoted by, 7
unprecedented signing by,
  66

United States (U.S.). *See also*
  Americans
  black support needed for,
    182–83
  commercial appeal impor-
    tant for, 62
  racial ideologies and, 193
  Schmeling returning to, 216
  Schmeling's image in, 174
Untermyer, Samuel, 110
Uzcudun, Paolino, 20, 54, 72,
  88

Vending machines, 217
Victories, 97
Vidmer, Richards, 42
Vogt, Riedel, 215

Walcott, Jersey Joe, 203, 207
Wallace, Henry, 202
Walsh, Davis J., 42, 51, 101
Ward, Arch, 28
Washington, Chez, 54
Webb, Chick, 81
Webster, Thomas, 188
Weigand, Myrtle, 140
Weimar culture
  boxing's role in, 14
  excitement of, 16–17
White hope, 162
White men
  black champion accepted by,
    129–30
  diverse national identity for,
    161
  heavyweight crown reserved
    for, 34, 42
  racial animosity not dis-
    played by, 128
White power, 126, 153–54,
  226, 230

White press
  Louis's depiction in, 78–79
  Louis's depiction trans-
    formed by, 156
  patriotism stressed by, 160–61
  Schmeling admired by, 79–80
White supremacy
  black menace threatening,
    42
  Louis defeat celebrated for,
    101
  Schmeling embodiment of,
    151–52
White, Walter, 190
White women, 46
Wiggins, William H., 85, 156
Wilkins, Roy, 52
Williams, Holman, 26
Williams, Joe, 134, 140
Williard, Jess, 35
Willkie, Wendell, 175, *176*,
  184
Wills, Harry, 36, 42, 64, 108
Wilson, Freddie, 49
Wilson, George J. (Jackie),
  190
Wilson, Teddy, 127, 196
Winant, F.K., 192
Wood, Wilbur, 10, 31
Woodard, Isaac, 201
Working class hero, 51, 129–
  30
World War II
  deep racial conflicts and, 193
  Louis-Schmeling fight meta-
    phor for, 231
  positive aspects of, 196
  posters for, 184–85
Wright, Richard, 87, 112, 152,
  158

Young, Faye, 126

Ziff, Sid, 150